SOUTHERN BIOGRAPHY SERIES

William J. Cooper, Jr., Editor

ZACHARY TAYLOR

Zachary Taylor, a daguerreotype *circa* 1850.
Courtesy Chicago Historical Society.

Zachary Taylor

SOLDIER, PLANTER, STATESMAN

OF THE OLD SOUTHWEST

K. JACK BAUER

LOUISIANA STATE UNIVERSITY PRESS

BATON ROUGE

Copyright © 1985 by Louisiana State University Press
All rights reserved
Manufactured in the United States of America
Designer: Barbara Werden
Typeface: Linotron Sabon
Typesetter: G & S Typesetters, Inc.

LIBRARY OF CONGRESS CATALOGING IN PUBLICATION DATA

Bauer, K. Jack (Karl Jack), 1926–
   Zachary Taylor: soldier, planter, statesman of the old Southwest.

   (Southern biography series)
   Bibliography: p.
   Includes index.
     1. Taylor, Zachary, 1784–1850. 2. Presidents—United
States—Biography. 3. Generals—United States—
Biography. 4. United States. Army—Biography.
5. United States—History—War with Mexico, 1845–1848—
Campaigns. I. Title. II. Series.
E422.B26 1985   973.6′3′0924[B]   85-11028
ISBN 0-8071-1237-2 (cloth)
ISBN 0-8071-1851-6 (paper)

Louisiana Paperback Edition, 1993
02 01 00 99   5 4 3

FOR

DODIE AND ANNE

WITHOUT WHOM

THIS WOULD NEVER HAVE BEEN

CONTENTS

MAPS

ILLUSTRATIONS

ACKNOWLEDGMENTS

JUST AS any historical account is to a large part a product of all the writers who preceded, so it is also the result of efforts by a large number of people, some known and a greater number anonymous, who provide the infrastructure of research: the archivists, librarians, technicians, and clerks who so efficiently and helpfully assist the researcher. In particular I want to thank the following: Mary Anne Hickey of the Buffalo and Erie County Historical Society; James H. Bentley of the Filson Club; Barbara E. Benson of the Historical Society of Delaware; Eric Pumroy of the Indiana Historical Society; Harriet McLoone of the Huntington Library; James C. Klotter and Linda Anderson of the Kentucky Historical Society; William J. Marshall and Clare McCann of the University of Kentucky Library; Paul Heffron, C. F. W. Coker, Marianne Roos, Charles Kelly, and John McDonough of the Library of Congress; Gisela J. Lozada of the Louisiana State University Library; Richard Sommers and Valarie Metzler of the Military History Institute; Steven Eric Nielsen and Bonnie Wilson of the Minnesota Historical Society; William Hanna of the Mississippi Department of Archives and History; Beverly D. Bishop and Janice L. Fox of the Missouri Historical Society; Richard A. Shrader of the Southern Historical Collection, University of North Carolina; Amy L. Hardin of the Historical Society of Pennsylvania; Barbara Taylor of the Princeton University Library; Karl Kebelac of the University of Rochester Library; Robert Seager II of the Henry Clay Papers; and Lynda L. Crist of the Papers of Jefferson Davis.

In addition, the largely anonymous staffs of the libraries who made their collections available to me earn praise and thanks which I could not deliver in person: Center of Military History, National Archives, Naval Historical Center, New York State Library, Rensselaer Polytechnic Institute, Russell Sage College, State University of New York at Albany, Troy Public Library, Union College, United States Military Academy, Williams

College, and Yale University. Special thanks are due Jean E. Houghtaling, the interlibrary loan specialist of Rensselaer's Folsom Library, who searched out and borrowed the elusive items which only a historian would want at an engineering school.

Very special and personal thanks are due Francis Krauskopf, Linda McCurdy, Roderick Brumbaugh, and E. B. Meader for quite different forms of assistance at critical moments in the research and writing of the book. Drs. John K. Mahon, T. R. Young II, and Ernest M. Lander, Jr., took time from their excessively busy schedules to read parts of the manuscript. Each pointed out shortcomings and offered suggestions which immeasurably improved the book. They proved once again that they are in the truest sense of the word professionals. The manuscript benefited greatly from its reading by William J. Cooper, Jr., the general editor of the Southern Biography Series. This was one of the advantages of writing in an area of expertise of your editor. Finally, but most important, the manuscript has been read, reread, listened to, and lived with by my wife Dorothy Sargent Bauer, who possesses some of the best eyes for grammatical disasters and ears for maladroit flights of rhetoric. Unfortunately, all of them together cannot completely excise poor writing or errors of fact or interpretation. Those are my contributions.

The maps are the work of J. R. Elliott, who brought his own special brand of perspicacity and artistic flare to their drafting. Marion T. Quiroga typed the manuscript, along with her assistants Mary Jo Donnelly and Mary Hoglund, and cast her critical editorial eye over the manuscript. To all of them, and others whom I have not named, go my deep thanks.

ABBREVIATIONS

AAAG	Acting Assistant Adjutant General
A&IG	Adjutant & Inspector General
A&IGLR	Office of the Adjutant & Inspector General, Letters Received, 1805-1821 (NA, RG 94, M566)
AG	Adjutant General
AGLR	Office of the Adjutant General, Letters Received, Main Series (NA, RG 94, M567)
AGLS	Office of the Adjutant General, Letters Sent (NA, RG 94, M565)
AGRL	Office of the Adjutant General, Register of Letters Received, Main Series (NA, RG 94, M6)
AHR	*American Historical Review*
Ann. Rpt. 1847	Annual Report of the Secretary of War, 1847 (*Senate Executive Documents*, 30th Cong., 1st Sess., No. 1)
AO	Army of Occupation
AOGO	Army of Occupation, General Orders (NA, RG 94, M29)
AOLB	Army of Occupation, Letter Books (NA, RG 94)
AOLR	Army of Occupation, Letters Received (NA, RG 94)
AOSO	Army of Occupation, Special Orders (NA, RG 94, M29)
ASP:IA	*American State Papers: Indian Affairs*
ASP:MA	*American State Papers: Military Affairs*
Calif. & N. Mex.	*California & New Mexico* (*House Executive Documents*, 31st Cong., 1st Sess., No. 17)
HQLS	Headquarters of the Army, Letter Books (NA, RG 108)
HQUL	Headquarters of the Army, Letters Received, Unregistered Series (NA, RG 108)

HSPa	Historical Society of Pennsylvania
IHS	William Henry Smith Library, Indiana Historical Society
JMSIUS	*Journal of the Military Service Institution of the United States*
JSH	*Journal of Southern History*
KHS	Kentucky Historical Society
LC	Library of Congress
LEA	Office of the Secretary of the Navy, Letters to the President and Executive Agencies (NA, RG 45, M473)
M/	National Archives Microcopy/roll number
Mex. War Corres.	*Mexican War Correspondence* (*House Executive Documents*, 30th Cong., 1st Sess., No. 60)
MHI	U.S. Army, Military History Institute
MinnHS	Minnesota Historical Society
MoHS	Missouri Historical Society
MVHR	*Missouri Valley Historical Review*
NA	National Archives
NASP:NA	*New American State Papers: Naval Affairs*
NYHS	New York Historical Society
NYPL	New York Public Library
NYSL	New York State Library
OIA:LR	Office of Indian Affairs, Letters Received (NA, RG 75, M234)
r	Roll
RG	Record Group
2MD:LR	2d Military District, Letters Received (NA, RG 393)
ser	Series
6MD:OB	6th Military District, Orders Book (NA, RG 393)
Smith:TLA	Justin H. Smith Papers, Latin American Collection, University of Texas, Austin
SWHQ	*Southwestern Historical Quarterly*
SWLR	Office of the Secretary of War, Letters Received, Registered Series (NA, RG 107, M221)
SWMA	Office of the Secretary of War, Letters Sent, Military Affairs (NA, RG 107, M6)
SWML	Office of the Secretary of War, Miscellaneous Letters Sent (NA, RG 107, M370)

SWRR	Office of the Secretary of War, Register of Letters Received, Main Series (NA, RG 107, M22)
SWUR	Office of the Secretary of War, Letters Received, Unregistered Series (NA, RG 107, M222)
Taylor, Scott Corres.	*Correspondence Between the Secretary of War and Generals Scott and Taylor and Between General Scott and Mr. Trist* (*House Executive Documents*, 30th Cong., 1st Sess., No. 56)
UKL	University of Kentucky Library
UM:C	William L. Clements Library, University of Michigan
USMA	United States Military Academy Library
UTA	University of Texas, Austin, Archives
WDLB	Western Division, Letter Books (NA, RG 393)
WDLR	Western Division, Letters Received (NA, RG 393)
WSHSC	*Wisconsin State Historical Society Collections*
Yale:M&A	Yale University Library, Manuscripts & Archives Division
Yale:WA	Yale University, Beinecke Rare Book and Manuscript Library, Western Americana Collection
ZT	Zachary Taylor
ZT(KHS)	Zachary Taylor Papers, Kentucky Historical Society
ZT(LC)	Zachary Taylor Papers, Library of Congress
ZT(LSU)	Zachary Taylor Papers, Louisiana State University Library
ZT(Minn)	Zachary Taylor Papers, Minnesota Historical Society
ZT(UKL)	Zachary Taylor Papers, University of Kentucky Library

PREFACE

MOST OBSERVERS who described Zachary Taylor in middle and later life agreed that he looked like a prosperous farmer. His countenance, as it appears in the few surviving photographs, is weathered and lined. He looks, as one would expect, like a man who has spent most of his adult years in command of troops in the field or those manning frontier posts. The eyes are sharp, the mouth firm, and the features lean. Few contemporaries who penetrated that façade left us a sketch of the personality that lay behind it. Zachary Taylor was truly an individual who reserved the understanding of his personality for a limited few; most of them did not, or could not, record it on paper.

When faced with an indistinct figure the biographer can often deduce the shape of a character by becoming immersed in the correspondence of the individual. Unfortunately, too little of Taylor's personal correspondence survived the years of frontier service and the sacking of Richard Taylor's plantation in 1862 to offer guidance. Moreover, what information we possess about the soldier-turned-politician is conflicting. Two men who knew him well, Jefferson Davis and Ethan Allen Hitchcock, describe figures so dissimilar as to cause the biographer to wonder if they knew the same man. To the politician Jefferson Davis, his sometime aide, son-in-law, and later confidant, Taylor was a self-educated, selfless public servant. To the often arrogantly critical Hitchcock, he was an untutored, unread, unimaginative, self-centered petty schemer. While it is possible that both men were correct, it is more likely that each saw what he wished to find and that Taylor was unlike the individual described by either.

The character of Zachary Taylor, insofar as we can determine it, reflected the traditions amongst which he grew to manhood and the impact of forty years of national service, most of it in posts on or adjacent to the frontier. Taylor's long, self-acknowledged attachment to the soil as the chief source of wealth reflected his Virginia heritage and Kentucky upbringing. His investments were those to be expected of a land-oriented individual: land, banks, buildings, and more land. Nevertheless, Taylor, despite his initial inclinations and later appearances, was not a Jacksonian land speculator. He belonged to the next generation of plantation owners who could no longer count on cheap lands and high cotton prices. In his last years he willingly allowed his agents to lead him away from the purchase of land. The shift of investments clearly placed Taylor among the new group of southern capitalists, like his friend Maunsel White, who began to move their capital out of land into commerce and industry as the price of cotton fell in the 1840s.

Taylor's instinctive and slowly developing distaste for cotton revealed itself in his efforts to diversify his crops and his refusal to invest the proceeds from the sale of Cypress Grove in a new plantation. His ambivalence at the shift is reflected in his willingness to stake his son to one. Taylor's seemingly unconscious economic decision that cotton planting had ceased to be the way to wealth may well offer an explanation for his disinclination as president to support any extension of slavery while accepting it where it already existed. That Taylor sensed the difficulties that cotton planting would during the 1850s does not mean that he was a protoindustrialist or even saw merit in a shift of investments to commerce. Such a claim would have to rest on the argument that he possessed clearer economic insight than he demonstrated in practice or that he understood the forces at work about him. There is no evidence that he did.

One of the anomalies of Taylor's southern birth and attachment was his championing of antisouthern issues while president. His opposition to the extension of slavery into the new territory acquired from Mexico, his resistance to the exercise of dominion over Santa Fe by southerners in Austin, and the threat to resort to force if necessary to preserve the Union all appear counter to his southern birthright, as does his mid-administration embrace of protectionism. Actually his support of the issues is logical if one views Taylor's motivations as nationalistic, a scarcely difficult explanation when one considers his long army service. Taylor, like Andrew Jackson in somewhat similar circumstances, found his nationalism much stronger than his sectionalism. It is therefore ironic that until his death he opposed the compromise which brought a peaceful solution to the Crisis of 1850 and won a decade of peace and unity. Taylor looked to an immediate showdown over sectionalism as desirable, firmly believing that the threat of force would bring southern hotheads to their senses.

Much of this book, like most of Taylor's life, must deal with the antebellum army. Taylor's career, mirroring that of most of his fellow officers and their men, was not only unexciting, but mundane and boring. He saw little combat in the War of 1812, and all of that in the backwater of

ZACHARY TAYLOR

CHAPTER I

Young Zachary

THE FIRST DECADE of independence for the new United States was a time of uncertainty, of economic discouragement, of political instability, and of social upheaval. It wrought great changes in American life as new groups rose to dominance in the nation. Moreover, few except the most optimistic could look forward with assurance to the survival of the uniquely American social system and government which emerged from the practical experience of self-government. In Virginia the realities of a depreciated currency, declining productivity of the old tobacco lands, and the bestowal of government into the hands of the land-hungry plantation radicals like George Washington and Thomas Jefferson ensured a free and open access to the presumably highly fertile lands to the west.

Nevertheless, in the Old Dominion more than in most northern states, an extremism permeated the prevailing mood. It notably affected the demobilized young officers whose wartime service had given them a sense of their own strength and competence. For them also waited large tracts of western land as recompense for the salary which the state could not pay in cash during wartime. To many, only in western lands was there enough speculative value to be worth the gamble. The younger sons of Virginia's landowners found the trek westward especially attractive since they usually had sufficient capital to acquire western lands as well as the tradition and experience to develop their acres.

One such was Richard Taylor. He belonged to a family which in its 150 years in Virginia had acquired both wealth and standing. A graduate of William and Mary, he fought with various Virginia Continental units during the Revolution, rising from first lieutenant to lieutenant colonel;

served in the Virginia Assembly; and acquired the Hare Forest estate in Orange County. At the age of thirty-five, in 1779, he married Sarah Dabney Strother, the daughter of an old and established Virginia family. Two years later their first child, Hancock, was born. In 1782 a second son, William Dabney Strother, followed. Since the Hare Forest property produced insufficient income to support the small family, the young veteran elected to accept the 8,166 acres of western lands which Virginia offered him as a bonus for his wartime service.[1]

Taylor sold his property and prepared to follow his eldest brother to the outpost village of Louisville. In October 1783 Richard received an initial land grant of 1,000 acres.[2] Since Mrs. Taylor's third pregnancy complicated the move, her husband arranged for her to complete her confinement at Montebello, a plantation about twelve miles from Hare Forest owned by his cousin Valentine Johnson. There, either in the main house or in one of the log cabins which served as guest houses, Zachary Taylor was born on November 24, 1784.[3]

The 400 rolling acres Richard Taylor selected for his home farm fronted on the Muddy Fork of the Beargrass Creek, about five miles east of the Louisville settlement at the falls of the Ohio. Taylor called his quickly erected log house Springfield. It lay near the Locust Grove estate of Colonel William Croghan, brother-in-law of the Revolutionary War hero George Rogers Clark, and the imposing stone "Soldier's Retreat" of Colonel Richard Clough Anderson. As a result, young Zachary grew up in close proximity, if not friendship, to two boys destined for distinguished careers in the army. Colonel Croghan's son George, seven years younger than Zachary, joined the army at the outbreak of the War of 1812. He earned a reputation as the heroic defender of Fort Stephenson in 1813 and from 1825 until 1849 served as an inspector general. Colonel Ander-

1. Holman Hamilton, *Zachary Taylor* (2 vols.; Indianapolis, 1941, 1951), I, *xv*; John H. Gwathmey, *Historical Register of Virginians in the Revolution, 1775–1783* (Baltimore, 1979), 761; Francis B. Heitman, *Historical Register of the Continental Army During the War of the Revolution* (Baltimore, 1967), 534. Sarah Strother's sister Elizabeth was the mother of Brigadier General Edmund Pendleton Gaines. James W. Silver, *Edmund Pendleton Gaines* (Baton Rouge, 1949), 5.

2. Willard Rouse Jillson, *The Kentucky Land Grants* (Louisville, 1925), 125.

3. Hamilton, *Taylor*, I, 21, 25, 260; Brainerd Dyer, *Zachary Taylor* (Baton Rouge, 1946), 3, 5; ZT Autobiography, 1, in ZT(LC), ser 1, r 1. The baby was named for his Taylor grandfather. Various army and other records call him Zachariah but Taylor preferred Zachary in later life. He customarily signed his name Z. Taylor. Six babies followed Zachary: a boy probably born in 1786 who died in infancy; George (1790–1829), Elizabeth Lee (1792–1845), Joseph Pannill (1796–1864), Sarah Bailey (1799–1851), and Emily Richard (1801–1841).

son's son Robert also entered the army. He graduated from West Point in
1824 and earned subsequent fame in 1861 as the defender of Fort Sumter.[4]

Once his wife and infant son were ready to travel, Taylor returned to
Virginia to fetch them. The family traveled overland to Redstone Creek in
Pennsylvania, where they embarked on a flatboat for the trip down the
Monongahela and along that stream to Pittsburgh. From there they
drifted down the Ohio to their new home. The family settled in its new
home by the late summer of 1785.[5]

Life in Louisville differed little from that in most frontier communi-
ties. Until "Mad Anthony" Wayne's successful Fallen Timbers campaign
against the Indians north of the Ohio in 1794, the inhabitants lived in
fear of attack. Richard Taylor may have served in some of the campaigns
to pacify the local redmen, but details have not survived beyond a report
that he was wounded in a skirmish at Greenville in western Kentucky in
1795. The Indian threat as well as the village's remoteness limited Louisville's growth. In 1800 the census credited it with a mere 359 inhabitants,
although visitors estimated the number as closer to 800. The latter must
have been an overestimation, since the 1810 census counted just over
1,000 people living there. No matter what its size, Louisville was a wealthy
community. As the settlement at the falls of the Ohio it had a commercial
importance. Goods moving upriver had to be landed there to bypass the
rapids, as did most cargoes floating downstream. The latter commonly
sought refuge in the harbor at the mouth of Beargrass Creek close by the
Taylor farm. From its earliest days Louisville attracted merchants, land
speculators, and successful farmers as well as aspiring politicians. The
citizens of Louisville were men of substance who supported a society
which rivaled that in longer-established urban centers. During the years
of Zachary Taylor's youth Louisville changed from a frontier to a sophisticated settlement which drew its wealth from its trade, its surrounding
tobacco fields, and its whiskey distilleries. By the early years of the new
century some of its finer homes compared favorably with those in Philadelphia or New York.[6] Visitors, while complaining of the town's sanitary
conditions, often noted the frequency of parties and the high styles worn

4. Dyer, *Taylor*, 6; Hamilton, *Taylor*, I, 25; Holman Hamilton, "Zachary Taylor: Resident or Fighter in Fifteen States," *American Heritage*, IV (Summer 1953), 10–11.

5. ZT Autobiography, 1; Hamilton, *Taylor*, I, 25, dates the arrival as sometime before
August 2.

6. Dyer, *Taylor*, 7–8; Richard C. Wade, *The Urban Frontier* (Chicago, 1976), 14–17,
110, 198; Oliver Otis Howard, *General Taylor* (New York, 1892), 21, engaged in nineteenth-
century romanticism when he reported: "small encounters between the white men and sav-
ages were almost daily occurrences."

at them. Silk stockings and parasols commonly graced the city's mansions by the turn of the century. Growing up in such a maturing city left a mark on Taylor which he never eradicated, nor wished to remove.

The Taylors prospered along with the town. Richard Taylor proved to be a strongly motivated, intelligent land speculator. By 1797 he owned 1,650 acres in Jefferson County alone, 400 of them being the productive acres of the Springfield farm, where the family now inhabited a large brick house. The senior Taylor possessed another 10,000 acres elsewhere in the state. While this did not make the colonel a major landholder, it clearly stamped him as a land speculator. His tax returns showed that his slaves expanded from seven in 1790 to twenty-six in 1800. Ten years later their numbers had risen to thirty-seven, which made him one of the larger slave owners in the region. Taylor also served in a number of civil posts. He was a justice of the peace, a county magistrate, a delegate to the state conventions in 1785 and 1788, as well as a state legislator. President George Washington appointed him collector of the Port of Louisville. In 1812, 1816, 1820, and 1824 Taylor served as a presidential elector supporting Madison, Monroe, and Clay.[7]

Richard Taylor appears to have concerned himself about his children's education, but very little concrete information survives. Young Zachary attended a school taught in Louisville by Elisha Ayer, an itinerant Connecticut schoolmaster, as well as one operated by Kean O'Hara. O'Hara, who later became a significant figure in Kentucky educational history, was an Irish-born classical scholar enticed away from the Danville Academy by Governor Isaac Shelby. Nevertheless, Zachary's formal education was limited, and his earliest surviving writing suffers from poor spelling and unusually bad grammar, while his hand was that of a near illiterate. His penmanship would improve in later life, but at best it was never easy to read. At some time in his life Zachary Taylor developed a great regard for education. One of his marks as a post commander was the great attention he paid to the schools maintained for the children of those stationed there. At least three of his children attended eastern schools, and his son Richard studied in Edinburgh and Paris, before graduating from Yale.[8]

It is uncertain when young Zachary first demonstrated any interest in military affairs. The aura of the military life, in at least its romantic aspects, was never far away as he grew up. His father's distinguished Revolutionary War service and the atmosphere of the frontier could scarcely

7. Jefferson County Tax Lists, 1790–1810, in KHS; Dyer, *Taylor*, 9–10; Hamilton, *Taylor*, I, 30–31. The Filson Club's Miscellaneous Papers contain a receipt signed by him in 1787 for the impressment of a pack saddle used in that year's expedition against the Wabash Indians.

8. Hamilton, *Taylor*, I, 28–29; Dyer, *Taylor*, 11.

have been ignored by a boy growing into adolescence. It does not appear that he performed any military service in his youth, although it is possible that he spent a few days in some hastily organized but now forgotten unit. The tradition, for instance, that he joined a militia company during the Burr Conspiracy excitement in 1806 cannot be substantiated.[9] Undoubtedly the acceptance of a second lieutant's commission in the Regiment of Artillerists by his eldest brother William in February 1807 stirred his interest.[10] Precisely what efforts were exerted by the family to secure the appointment do not show on the surviving record. However, Richard Taylor's position in Kentucky, his Revolutionary War service, and his political connections were more than adequate to gain the appointment. It is probable that Richard's cousin James Taylor in Newport, Kentucky, contributed substantially to the selection because of his political prominence and his close connection with the War Department.

During the spring of 1808 Congress reponded to the *Chesapeake* affair of the previous June and the dangers inherent in the stepped-up diplomatic activities of the Jefferson administration by nearly tripling the size of the army, adding eight regiments to serve for five years. Their officer billets were filled almost exclusively from civilian life. Among the new officers were Winfield Scott, Abram Eustis, Talbot Chambers, James Bankhead, and Zachary Taylor. On April 16, 1808, Congressman Buckner Thurston and the Kentucky congressional delegation responded to a request from Secretary of War Henry Dearborn by submitting a list of twenty-six names of men recommended for commissions.[11] As in the case with William's commission the previous year, we do not know what behind-the-scenes activities, if any, preceded the selection. The tradition that James Madison, a distant relative, played a significant role seems doubtful.[12]

Taylor's commission, dated May 3, 1808, appointed him a first lieutenant in the 7th Infantry, a regiment largely recruited in Kentucky. His pay of thirty dollars per month and two rations per day was respectable enough for a frontier farmer but the uniform must have had as much appeal. It fairly sparkled: a knee-length, single-breasted blue coat with cuffs and standing collar trimmed in gold topped blue pantaloons and a white belt. On his head the lieutenant wore a blue chapeau bras or cap. The

9. Howard, *Taylor*, 22; Charles J. Peterson, *The Military Heroes of the War with Mexico* (Philadelphia, 1856), 140; Hamilton, *Taylor*, I, 262.

10. Francis B. Heitman, *Historical Register and Dictionary of the United States Army* (2 vols.; Washington, 1903), I, 949; Dyer, *Taylor*, 14.

11. C. Joseph Bernardo and Eugene H. Bacon, *American Military Policy* (Harrisburg, 1955), 105–107; James Ripley Jacobs, *The Beginnings of the U.S. Army, 1783–1812* (Princeton, 1947), 269–70; Dearborn to Thurston, April 16, 1808, in SWML, III, 223 (M370/3); Thurston to Dearborn, April 16, 1808, in SWRR, IV (M22/4).

12. Howard, *Taylor*, 24.

senior officers of the new regiment were experienced men. Colonel William Russell was a Kentuckian who had served as a lieutenant during the Revolution and as a lieutenant colonel of the volunteers raised during the 1793 and 1794 Indian scares. The lieutenant colonel, the Pennsylvanian Robert Purdy, had served in the regular army from 1792 to 1803. The third senior officer was Major Elijah Strong of Connecticut, a regular officer who had entered the service in 1793 as an ensign.[13]

Taylor accepted his appointment on June 6, but when he actually entered active service is unknown.[14] Colonel Russell immediately assigned him to recruiting. His initial post was as assistant to Captain Edward Hord at Washington, Kentucky. Upon reporting, he found Hord both sick and unsuccessful. Taylor shortly moved his recruiting efforts to Limestone but found few men interested in joining the army. He complained to his father: "The people appear to be more averse to a military life in this part of the country than at Louisville or any other place I have ever yet been at." Taylor subsequently shifted his activities to Maysville, where he encountered better success and remained until March 1809.[15]

In late April Taylor and his recruits departed Newport, Kentucky, by boat for New Orleans. They joined other detachments to form a force of about 2,000 men collected by Brigadier General James Wilkinson to turn back a rumored British attack on the Crescent City. Most of the officers, like Taylor, were freshly appointed from civilian life and few of the men had previously tasted military discipline. The result was chaos.

New Orleans was scarcely a healthy location for the newly raised force. It was built on low ground which so often flooded that the houses stood on wooden stilts or elevated terraces. They commonly sported iron-grilled balconies in order to take advantage of the gentle summer breezes. The city lacked a sewage system, so garbage was thrown into the streets where it remained emitting noxious odors until a rainstorm swept it away. Yet Wilkinson, who had been trained as a physician, took little notice of the climate, a neglect which reflected more the state of medical knowledge than derelictions on the part of the army's commander. When the general reached New Orleans in April he found 1,733 sick and demoralized men on the rolls. They had succumbed to the blandishments of the local prostitutes, whiskey dealers, and gamblers, and suffered the agonies

13. Heitman, *Historical Register*, I, 94, 809, 854, 932, 949; *ASP:MA*, I, 433–34; Dyer, *Taylor*, 15.

14. ZT to Dearborn, June 6, 1808, in SWLR, 1808 (M221/32).

15. ZT to Richard Taylor, November 24, 1808, in Alice Elizabeth Trabue Papers, Filson Club, Louisville, Ky., folder 50; ZT to James Morrison, December 8, 1808, in Henry Clay Papers, LC, r 10; Hamilton, *Taylor*, I, 34, 163.

of poor camp sanitation. Only two surgeons, desperately short of medicines, were present to treat the 550 most ailing soldiers housed in a barracks temporarily converted to a hospital.[16]

Despite the orders of the new secretary of war, Dr. William Eustis, Wilkinson kept his force within an easy march of New Orleans by shifting his camp in June to Terre aux Boeufs on the English Turn, about twelve miles south of the city. Here the army spent the summer months camped on a swampy plain three feet below the level of the river. The men lived in leaking tents which lacked mosquito netting and they sloshed through a quagmire after every rain. They ate wormy bread and rancid pork and slapped at insects. Nor could they flee to the doubtful sanctuary of summertime New Orleans because they too often lacked uniforms and seldom received their pay on time.[17] By the time Wilkinson moved his command in September to healthier locations on the high ground at Fort Adams and Natchez, the army was in wretched condition. Nearly half died from ailments contracted at Terre aux Boeufs, or on the boats carrying them northward.[18]

How much of the horror of the Terre aux Boeufs camp Taylor actually experienced is unknown. In May and June of 1809 he temporarily commanded Fort Pickering on the Chickasaw Bluffs near modern Memphis, Tennessee. The fort was a small stockade mounting a few light cannon, but it commanded both the Mississippi River and the immediate surrounding country. The assignment must have been an emotional one, for it was here that his elder brother had been killed by Indians the previous year. It is from here also that we have the earliest word portrait of Zachary Taylor. A visitor describes climbing 120 blood-stained squared log steps to reach the post where he was received by Taylor "with civility not unmixed with a small degree of pompous stiffness of office." [19]

16. ZT to James Taylor, April 24, 1809, in ZT(KHS); Dearborn to Wilkinson, December 2, 1808, in *ASP:MA*, I, 272; Hamilton, *Taylor*, I, 35; James Ripley Jacobs, *Tarnished Warrior: Major General James Wilkinson* (New York, 1938), 247, and *Beginnings of the Army*, 344–45; Rembert W. Patrick, *Aristocrat in Uniform: General Duncan L. Clinch* (Gainesville, 1963), 16–17; Francis Paul Prucha, *The Sword of the Republic* (New York, 1969), 97–98; Mary C. Gillett, *The Army Medical Department, 1775–1818* (Washington, 1981), 140.

17. The difficulties of the Terre aux Boeufs camps are described in detail in *ASP: MA*, I, 268–95; Gillett, *Medical Department*, 141–42; Jacobs, *Beginnings*, 346–50; Jacobs, *Tarnished Warrior*, 251–52.

18. Jacobs, *Tarnished Warrior*, 252–60; Prucha, *Sword of the Republic*, 98.

19. Hamilton, *Taylor*, I, 35–35. Hamilton concludes that W. D. S. Taylor was killed about June 3, 1808 (p. 264). The official record is silent. The description is from Fortescue Cuming, "Sketches of a Tour in the Western Country," in Reuben Gold Thwaites (ed.), *Early Western Travels, 1748–1846* (32 vols.; Cleveland, 1904–1907), IV, 295.

Whether Taylor remained at Fort Pickering or returned to New Orleans is not certain, although there is a tradition that he served as Wilkinson's aide until he contracted yellow fever and was invalided to Louisville to recover. He was in Louisville in September and October of 1809. The following month the adjutant and inspector general in Washington directed the young lieutenant to report to Washington, Mississippi Territory. It is not clear when Taylor left Louisville. Tradition holds that he remained until March 1810 and sailed a flatboat loaded with cargo to New Orleans before reporting. What we do know is that Brigadier General Wade Hampton on April 27, 1810, ordered him back to Kentucky because his company had been broken up to provide filler for other units. Taylor reached home by May 20.[20]

The return to Louisville permitted Taylor and Margaret Mackall Smith to be married June 21. "Peggy," as her husband called her, was a native of Calvert County, Maryland, aged twenty-one years. Her father Walter was a planter who educated his daughter at home. She was without intellectual pretentions but like her husband had an intense dedication to the education of her children. The view of her that has come down to us is that of a very competent, unpretentious woman who was thoroughly capable of handling the difficulties of raising a family in the often spartan quarters of frontier posts or of surviving extended periods of separation from her husband. A very religious individual and a devout Episcopalian, who never succeeded in getting her husband to join the church, she was a lady who shunned the petty social posturing that occupied the lives of many army wives. During her later years she was plagued by ill health. She could not stand the physical rigors of official duties and delegated the exhausting demands of the receiving line and hostessing official functions to her daughter Betty during the White House years. Yet even then she maintained an active personal social calendar and outlived her husband. It was a successful marriage. The couple remained devoted to each other throughout their lives.

Taylor had met his bride in the autumn of 1809, while she visited her sister Mrs. Samuel Chew. If, as appears probable, Taylor delayed his return south as long as possible it was to court the slender, stately, young Marylander. Shortly after his return from Mississippi the young couple settled upon a June wedding. They took out a marriage license on June 18 and were married three days later in a double-log cabin on what came to

20. Howard, *Taylor*, 26; Hamilton, *Taylor*, I, 264; ZT, Subsistence Account, May 1–August 31, 1809, in ZT(KHS); A&IG to ZT, November 29, 1809, in AGLS, I, 58 (M565/3); Hampton, Endorsement on Cantonment Washington Order, April 27, 1810, and ZT to Eustace [sic], May 20, 1810, both in SWLR 1810, T-50 (M221/40).

be known as Wolf Pen Road, not far from his father's estate. We know none of the details of the wedding nor of the honeymoon.[21]

As a wedding present they received 324 acres of farmland at the mouth of Beargrass Creek from Colonel Taylor. Although then rated only as second-class land on the Jefferson County tax rolls, it is today in downtown Louisville. It was the first land acquired by Zachary Taylor and started his career as a landowner. He subsequently sold the farm for a handsome profit. At about this time Taylor, who had earlier learned surveying, undertook to delineate lands that his brother Hancock owned in Woodford County, south of Frankfort. In payment he received a small parcel of thirty-eight acres, which he sold in December 1810.[22] It is the only recorded instance of Taylor's acting as a surveyor, but the knowledge would have been relatively easy for him to acquire in Louisville. Indeed, it was common for bright young men on the frontier to act as part-time surveyors. They had merely to know enough mathematics, as Taylor did, to make the necessary calculations.

The army contributed its share of happiness to the couple in November. On the thirtieth Taylor became a captain. While the increased pay of forty dollars per month and three rations a day eased his finances, the continued appointment in the 7th Infantry must have disturbed him. It resulted from an inherent weakness in the army's promotion system. Promotions were normally governed by openings within one's own regiment. Only on rare occasions, and then only because of special circumstances, was an officer promoted into another regiment. In 1810 promotion was further complicated by the division of the army into its permanent or "Peace Establishment" force of 2,765 officers and men and the "Additional Military Force" authorized in 1808, to which Taylor belonged. The latter numbered 4,189 officers and men but had been raised for five years only and could be dissolved at any time by an economy-minded Congress, which had already halted further recruiting. Obviously no Peace Establishment officer sought the uncertainty of a promotion into one of the 1808 regiments. This ensured that promotions came relatively rapidly for officers like Taylor who remained in service in the "Additional Military Force," even though they had seen only limited service.[23]

The additional salary and the income from the Beargrass Creek prop-

21. Hamilton, *Taylor*, I, 27; ZT Autobiography, 1.

22. Jefferson County Tax List, 1810, in KHS; ZT, deed to J. G. Finne, Jr., December 1810, in ZT(KHS); Hamilton, *Taylor*, I, 37, II, 24, 34.

23. Heitman, *Historical Register*, I, 949; Dyer, *Taylor*, 27. Taylor did not receive the actual commission until 1811. ZT to Major A. Y. Nicoll, June 10, 1811, in Andre De Coppet Collection, Princeton University Library.

erty eased the financial worries for the new family, which grew to three on April 9, 1811, with the birth of Ann Mackall Taylor. She was born in or near Louisville, probably on the Beargrass Creek property, and received the name of her maternal grandmother.[24] For the months between the summer of 1810 and late spring of 1811 Taylor's duties are uncertain. He appears to have been physically present in Louisville much of the time, probably on recruiting duty, since in March 1811 he complained that he had not been paid for seven months.[25] This was a common complaint among officers stationed at distances from paymasters, since the latter alone dispensed wages. In this instance Taylor would have been paid by the regimental paymaster, on whose books he was carried, but that officer infrequently visited recruiting offices, preferring instead to wait for the officers on that duty to return to the regimental headquarters. Despite the uncertainty of his paydays, Taylor now had a sufficient income to permit him to purchase bank stock. In 1812 or 1813 he also purchased a female house slave, his first, but complained that she had proven to be a "hard bargain." In December 1813 he asked his brother Hancock to buy him a likely looking seventeen- or eighteen-year-old boy for work around the house.[26] The years before and during the War of 1812 were evidently kind to Taylor's finances.

Shortly after Ann's birth Taylor received unorthodox orders. They were the result of an unusual situation at Fort Knox, Vincennes, Indiana Territory. The post had long been racked by a personal feud between its commander, Captain Thornton Posey, and Lieutenant Jesse Jennings. On June 24, 1811, Posey shot and killed Jennings during an altercation. Major George Rogers Clark Floyd, as the senior officer in the area, ordered Taylor to assume command of the fort, since he was the only regimental officer available in whom Floyd had any confidence. Taylor took command on July 10. He promptly put the garrison to work repairing both the dilapidated post and their slack discipline. By early August, he had restored both.[27]

Taylor remained at Vincennes until August, when he traveled to Frederick, Maryland, as a potential defense witness in the court martial of General Wilkinson. The trial involved Wilkinson's complex relationship with the Spanish authorities in Louisiana, his connection to the Burr Conspiracy, and the Terre aux Boeufs disaster. Although we know today that the

---

24. Hamilton, *Taylor*, I, 37; William H. Samson (ed.), *Letters of Zachary Taylor from the Battle-Fields of the Mexican War* (Rochester, 1908), x.

25. ZT to James Taylor, March 9, 1811, in ZT(UKL).

26. ZT to Hancock Taylor, December 22, 1813, in Trabue Papers, folder 50.

27. ZT to Eustis, July 16, 1811, in SWLR 1811, T-167 (M221/40); Hamilton, *Taylor*, I, 37–38.

charges were valid, Wilkinson was found not guilty and resumed his military career. Taylor never testified but the absence from Indiana caused him to miss William Henry Harrison's Tippecanoe campaign. Had he been present, Taylor undoubtedly would have accompanied the army, since Harrison had placed the young captain in command of the eighty light troops who were the pick of his rough-hewn army.[28]

After the Wilkinson trial, Taylor resumed recruiting duty in Louisville. Regulations were now explicit as to the men to be enlisted: citizens of suitable size, sound constitution, and bodily ability. If minors appeared at his rendezvous Captain Taylor had to secure the written consent of their parents and attach the document to the enlistment papers. As the clouds of war with Britain gathered during the winter and spring of 1812, Taylor stepped up his efforts. In January he came under the control of his regimental commander, Colonel William Russell, who assumed charge of recruiting in Kentucky and Ohio.[29] This was the first time Taylor had come into close contact with the officer who would play a major role in his career during the next three years.

As part of the preparations for operations against the British in the Northwest, Secretary of War Eustis on March 6, 1812, directed Taylor to form a company, even if understrength, from his Louisville recruits and hasten to Fort Harrison, Indiana.[30] Captain Taylor received the order in April and reached the post about May 3, having spent fifty-nine dollars of his own money to move his men. The necessity for Taylor to rely on his own funds to move the detachment is a good example of the logistic problems facing the army on the northwestern frontier. Neither government transportation nor supply stocks existed in adequate quantities for the forthcoming operations. Taylor relieved Captain Josiah Snelling of the 4th Infantry, who with his company rejoined his parent organization in Brigadier General William Hull's army of militia and regulars assigned the task of defending Detroit and invading western Canada should war develop.[31]

Fort Harrison was a small stockaded post constructed on a bluff overlooking the Wabash River about sixty miles north of Vincennes, near the

28. A&IG to ZT, July 22, 1811, in AGLS, I 1/2, 126 (M565/3); Hamilton, *Taylor*, I, 38.

29. A&IG to ZT, December 6, 1811, January 4, 18, March 6, 1812, in AGLS, I 1/2, 238, 258, 313 (M565/3).

30. A&IG to Russell, to ZT, March 6, 1812, in AGLS, I 1/2, 312–14; Eustis to Harrison, March 7, 1812, in Clarence Carter and John Porter Bloom (eds.), *The Territorial Papers of the United States* (28 vols.; Washington, 1934–75), VIII, 170.

31. ZT to J. T. Eubank, July 25, 1812, in Alfred W. Van Sinderen Collection, Box I, folder 12, Yale:M&A; ZT Autobiography, 2; Alec R. Gilpin, *The War of 1812 in the Old Northwest* (Lansing, 1958), 38–39; Hamilton, *Taylor*, I, 39.

present-day city of Terre Haute, Indiana. Its black walnut pickets, implanted in October 1811 by Governor William Henry Harrison's troops advancing toward their victorious Tippecanoe fight, enclosed approximately one acre. Three wooden blockhouses stood at the corners.[32] Although the local Indians initially appeared peaceful, Taylor drove his men to strengthen the fort while he kept an alert eye on happenings upstream at Prophetstown near the Tippecanoe battlefield. There the most hostile of the Indians could be expected to collect. By early August the Indians' activities convinced Taylor that they planned to attack either Fort Harrison or Vincennes. Despite the efforts to strengthen it, one visitor described Taylor's post as "feeble" and noted that thirteen of the fifty-five-man garrison were sick. The sick list grew daily, he noted.[33]

Taylor's concern for the safety of his command increased as travelers and newspapers brought reports of the steady drift toward war with Britain. The garrison at Fort Harrison apparently received little hard news from the East, although rumors of developments and occasional directives from General Hull's headquarters did make their way to the Wabash. It is also clear from the surviving correspondence that Taylor was in frequent contact with the territorial capital at Vincennes. If hostilities developed, Taylor could hope that his little band would not be caught unawares.

32. Gilpin, *War of 1812 in the Old Northwest*, 13; A. C. Duddleston, "Fort Harrison in History," *Magazine of American History*, XXVIII (1892), 21; George Pence, "General Joseph Bartholomew," *Indiana Magazine of History*, XIV (1918), 291; ZT to R. M. Thompson, May 10, 1850, in IHS.

33. Harrison to Eustis, May 27, June 3, ZT to Harrison, August 9, 1812, in Logan Esarey (ed.), *Messages and Letters to William Henry Harrison* (2 vols.; Indianapolis, 1922), II, 56–59, 82–83; ZT to Eubank, July 25, 1812, in Van Sindren Collection; T. R. Richardson to Gibson, August 12, 1812, in William Henry Harrison Papers, LC, ser 1, r 1.

CHAPTER II

Taste of Battle

EVENTS IN the West moved rapidly following the June 18, 1812, declaration of war against Great Britain. One post after another fell. On July 17 the isolated Mackinac post at the confluence of Lakes Huron and Michigan surrendered. Its seizure ensured British command of the route west and the water highway to the upper Mississippi River. Upon learning of the loss of the northern fort, Major General William Hull, the governor of Michigan Territory and commander of the Army of the Northwest, directed the evacuation of Fort Dearborn at what is today Chicago. Its garrison was massacred August 15 as it attempted to retreat to Detroit. The following day Hull surrendered his army and Detroit to an inferior British force. The capitulation left the frontier nearly denuded of regular troops but caused the settlers in Kentucky to volunteer in large numbers for what they anticipated would be a relatively easy counteroffensive.

Tecumseh, the great architect of Indian resistance to American settlement in the Northwest, seized the moment to strike at the frontier defenses. Two days after the fall of Detroit he left Malden, Ontario, to activate his offensive, which he scheduled for the September full moon. Pigeon Roost in southern Indiana received the initial attack on September 3. About twenty settlers lost their lives and a number of houses burned before the raiders departed. Hostilities began at Fort Harrison the following day. From September 5 to 9 a large band of Winnebagos unsuccessfully attacked the northernmost post on the Mississippi, Fort Madison in present-day Iowa, while a lighter attack struck Fort Wayne on the sixth.[1]

1. Alec R. Gilpin, *The War of 1812 in the Old Northwest* (Lansing, 1958), 137; John K.

The strongest blow fell on weakly garrisoned Fort Harrison. Taylor had only sixteen healthy men and he himself was recuperating from an attack of bilious fever. The remaining thirty-four men were under the care of Surgeon's Mate Lemuel B. Clarke. Although there had been warning of the impending attack, no signs of Indian hostility disturbed the routine of the post until September.[2] That afternoon the sentries at the fort heard Indians exchanging turkey-call signals in the woods nearby and alerted the garrison. A pair of civilians rashly volunteered to investigate. They never returned, although four shots were subsequently heard. The garrison and its feverish commander passed an uneasy night and in the morning a patrol found the scalped bodies of the two men. That evening a delegation of Delawares, Potawatomis, Kickapoos, and Miami under Chief Lenar, all followers of Tecumseh's brother, "the Prophet," appeared with a white flag and announced that a representative of the Indians would visit the fort the following day to request food for their starving brethren. Taylor recognized the request as a sham and ordered the garrison, including the convalescents, all of whom volunteered for duty, to prepare to receive an attack.

Taylor kept his sentries especially alert during the night. About 11:00 P.M. a sentinel fired on some Indians stealing toward the fort. The Indians, later estimated at 450 braves, responded with heavy musketry to cover a handful who crept up to the fort and reached in through small holes in one of the blockhouses to start fires. Unfortunately the blockhouse held the contractor's supplies including some whiskey, which caused a spectacular blaze that spread to the adjoining barracks. "Most of the men immediately gave themselves up for lost," Taylor reported, "and I had the greatest difficulty in getting my orders executed—from the raging of the fire—the yelling and howling of several hundred Indians—and cries of nine women and children." At that point two of his strongest men jumped over the wall and fled. Yet, somehow, Taylor organized a defense. While most of the men held off the Indians, a handful, including Dr. Clarke, climbed onto the roof of the barracks. Despite the musket balls whooshing past them, they pulled off shingles to prevent the fire from spreading. One of the exposed men on the roof was killed and two others were injured. The women, after their initial fright, joined in the defense by carrying water to the men fighting to extinguish the blazing timbers of the blockhouse. The destruction of the blockhouse left a twenty-foot gap

---

Mahon, *The War of 1812* (Gainesville, 1972), 67; Bruce E. Mahan, *Old Fort Crawford and the Frontier* (Iowa City, 1926), 44–46; ZT to Harrison, August 9, 1812, in IHS.

2. ZT to Harrison, August 9, 1812, in IHS; Gibson to Eustace [*sic*], September 2, 1812, in Clarence Carter and John Porter Bloom (eds.), *The Territorial Papers of the United States* (28 vols.; Washington, 1934–75), VIII, 198.

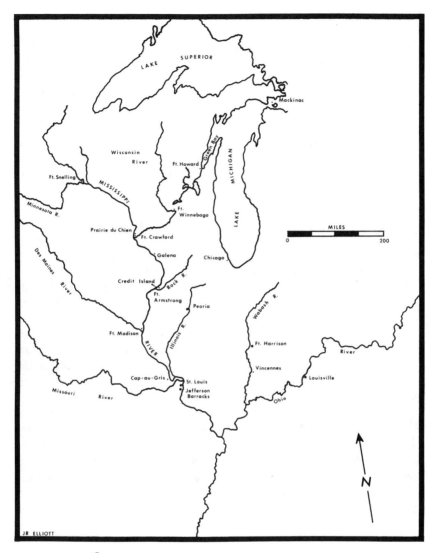

Lake Superior

Mackinac

Wisconsin River

Ft. Howard

Green Bay

LAKE MICHIGAN

Ft. Snelling

MISSISSIPPI

Minnesota R.

Ft. Winnebago

Prairie du Chien

Ft. Crawford

Des Moines River

Galena

Chicago

Credit Island

Rock R.

Ft. Armstrong

Peoria

Wabash R.

Ft. Madison

RIVER

Illinois R.

Ft. Harrison

River

Vincennes

Louisville

Cap-au-Gris

St. Louis

Jefferson Barracks

Missouri River

Ohio

MILES

0   200

N

JR ELLIOTT

WAR OF 1812 AND NORTHERN FRONTIER

in the defenses but the garrison successfully plugged it with makeshift breastwork. As the light from the dying fires faded so did the attack. By 6:00 A.M. it was over. Fort Harrison had been saved at a cost of two soldiers killed and two wounded. When daylight returned on the fifth the weary garrison replaced the emergency breastwork with a more substantial one and prepared to beat off an attack which never came. The Indians, having found the garrison capable of holding its defenses, did not renew the assault but contented themselves with slaughtering the hogs and horses grazing outside the walls. The redmen drove off all the cattle they found but fortunately did not destroy the corn standing in the nearby fields.

Even though they did not renew their attack, the Indians kept a close blockade on the fort. It forced the garrison to subsist on green corn, their other supplies having been lost. The closeness of the ring around them became clear to the Americans when two messengers sent to Vincennes on the tenth had to return because their canoe could not pass the Indians' watch fires along the Wabash. Three days later Taylor sent two other men overland. They reached Vincennes on the sixteenth.[3]

Taylor handled his defense with courage, firmness, and sense. It earned him strong commendation from Harrison and a brevet as major, the first honorary promotion awarded during the war. Congress had created the brevet commissions on July 6 in an effort to reward meritorious conduct. Such a commission conferred rank and title but no additional pay, except in the occasional instance in which an officer exercised command according to his brevet rank. Although conceived as a wartime measure to reward heroism in an army which eschewed medals, brevets proved to be more harmful than helpful. In 1818 Congress added a provision permitting the award of brevets to officers who had served ten years in grade. This resulted in indiscriminate awards which complicated the command structure and led to complaints by Taylor and others of favoritism in the conferring of brevets.[4]

3. The account of the defense of Fort Harrison is derived from: ZT to Harrison, September 10, 13, 1812, in *Niles' Weekly Register*, III (1812–13), 90–91; A. C. Duddleston, "Fort Harrison in History," *Magazine of American History*, XXVIII (1892), 22–24; Gilpin, *War in the Old Northwest*, 137–38; Mahon, *War of 1812*, 67; H. M. Brackenridge, *History of the Late War Between the United States and Great Britain* (Philadelphia, 1844), 64–65; Robert D. McAfee, *History of the Late War in the Western Country* (1816; rpr. n.p., 1966), 153–54; Benson J. Lossing, *The Pictorial Field Book of the War of 1812* (1869; rpr. Somersworth, N.H., 1976), 317–18; T. H. Palmer, *Historical Register of the United States* (4 vols.; Philadelphia, 1814–16), II, 38.

4. Francis B. Heitman, *Historical Register and Dictionary of the United States Army* (2 vols.; Washington, 1903), I, 949; Henry L. Scott, *Military Dictionary* (1862; rpr. New York, 1968), 111; William Addleman Ganoe, *The History of the United States Army* (Ashton,

Meanwhile, Kentucky volunteers, responding to the threat of the Indians, gathered in mid-August at Louisville and elsewhere along the Ohio.[5] As soon as he was aware that Fort Harrison had been attacked, Acting Governor John Gibson at Vincennes also appealed for help. The first Kentuckians, 241 men from Henderson County, reached the Indiana capital on September 15.[6] Meanwhile, on the fifth Gibson had sent a mounted party to reopen communications with Taylor but they were turned back by the Indians halfway to their objective. The following day the acting governor dispatched a second party. They returned to report that they believed the fort had not fallen, although they could get only to within nine miles of it. On the tenth Colonel William Russell arrived to relieve the harried politician of the military responsibility. He collected about 1,000 rangers and 2,000 militia. They relieved Fort Harrison without incident on September 16, although a separate wagon train with supplies was cut to pieces. A second supply column was more successful. Russell left a small detachment to garrison the post and brought the remainder of his force back to Vincennes.[7]

Following the surrender of General Hull at Detroit, William Henry Harrison assumed charge of the defenses in the Old Northwest.[8] He immediately adopted a strategy to prevent a recurrence of the raids. It involved sending fast-striking columns to destroy the villages from which the hostile Indians had come. One force from Fort Wayne destroyed the Potawatomi villages along the Elkhart River near present-day Ligonier, Indiana; a second struck the Miami villages at the fork of the Wabash River near Peru. The third column combined 2,000 Kentucky mounted militia and the handful of regulars at Vincennes under the Revolutionary

---

Md., 1964), 121; *Annals of Twelfth Congress*, 1583. Although dated September 5, Taylor's brevet was issued on October 29. Eustis to ZT, October 29, 1812, in SWMA, VI, 215 (M6/6). Harrison attempted unsuccessfully to get Dr. Clarke a line commission. Harrison to Eustis, n.d., in Richard C. Knopf, *William Henry Harrison and the War of 1812* (Columbus, Ohio, 1951), 55.

5. Harrison to Eustis, August 18, 1812, in Logan Esarey (ed.), *Messages and Letters of William Henry Harrison* (2 vols.; Indianapolis, 1922), II, 88; McAfee, *War in Western Country*, 157.

6. Gibson to Brigadier General J. Winlock, to Hopkins, both September 9, 1812, in "Some Letters of John Gibson," *Indiana Magazine of History*, I (1905), 128–30.

7. Gibson to Harrison, September 12, 1812, in William Henry Harrison Papers, LC, ser 1, r 1; Gibson to Russell, September 16, 1812, in "Some Letters of Gibson," 130; Gilpin, *War in the Old Northwest*, 138; McAfee, *War in the Western Country*, 155–56.

8. Harrison received an emergency appointment as major general of Kentucky militia on August 20. Two days later he was commissioned a federal brigadier general. President Madison appointed him to command of the Northwestern Army on September 17. Gibson to Colonel William Hargrove, August 20, Eustis to Harrison, August 22, September 17, 1812, in Esarey (ed.), *Messages & Letters*, II, 91–92, 136–37.

War veteran, congressman, and Kentucky militia major general Samuel Hopkins. Governor Isaac Shelby of Kentucky in a flight of self-delusion called the militia men the best he had seen "in the western country, or anywhere else."[9]

Hopkins planned to destroy the Indian settlements along the Wabash before swinging west to eliminate those in Illinois. If successful, his expedition would remove most of the threat to the western Indiana and Illinois borders. Rain delayed the force's departure from Vincennes with the result that the green men arrived at the staging point of Fort Harrison, on October 10 with their ardor much tarnished. Many refused to continue further and returned home. They left behind a weary, saddle sore, sullen, and disheartened collection of frontiersmen.[10] Not even Hopkins, as accomplished a politician as he was, could rouse much fighting spirit. Five days later, after replenishing their supplies, the rump force departed. It crossed the Wabash about eighty miles from the Kickapoo villages, which were its initial objectives. That day the prairie caught fire. The Americans saved their camp only by starting a backfire. Whether the conflagration was started by careless whites or set by Indians is not clear, but the skittish Kentuckians concluded that redmen skulking about in the tall grass had been the incendiaries. Moreover, the grass along the route was so poor that the horses soon began to fail, while the guides could not agree on the best route to the Kickapoo villages. By the nineteenth the army had marched as far as it wished to go, even though it had yet to see an Indian. Hopkins called a council of his officers to find out what their commands wished to do. He hoped to entice about 500 men to continue but could not, even after having Taylor, who served as his aide, address the troops. The congressman-general had no choice but to accept the recommendation of the council that the expedition be abandoned. It was a very disheartened Samuel Hopkins who led his men back to Fort Harrison and on to Kentucky for discharge.[11]

9. Shelby to Hopkins, September 12, to Harrison, September 26, 1812, in Esarey (ed.), *Messages & Letters*, II, 131–32, 154; Gilpin, *War in the Old Northwest*, 139; Mahon, *War of 1812*, 68; Harry L. Coles, *The War of 1812* (Chicago, 1965), 57.

10. The Kentuckians had not been federalized because Governor Shelby had no authorization to call out the force and could not await its arrival from Washington. Neither did the men's thirty-day service count against their militia obligation. John Wallace Hammack, Jr., *Kentucky and the Second American Revolution: The War of 1812* (Lexington, 1976), 44. By September 12, two to three hundred men had returned home. Robert Hamilton, "The Expeditions of Major-General Samuel Hopkins up the Wabash, 1812," *Indiana Magazine of History*, XLIII (1947), 396.

11. Hammack, *Kentucky & Second Revolution*, 45; Brackenridge, *History of the Late War*, 62–63; Gilpin, *War in Old Northwest*, 147–50; Holman Hamilton, *Zachary Taylor* (2 vols.; Indianapolis, 1941, 1951), I, 45; McAfee, *War in the Western Country*, 158–60;

The expedition gave Taylor his earliest experience with raw volunteers. The bitter taste never left him. Throughout his career he was leery of citizen-soldiers and employed them as infrequently as possible. The relationship was reciprocal. Very few volunteer or militia units ever performed well as part of a Taylor-commanded force. Indeed, his only battle in which non-regulars performed well was Buena Vista, where most of the volunteers either had seen earlier action or were products of John Wool's harsh training.

Hopkins' plan for the Illinois sweep also included an expedition by Colonel Russell and Governor Ninian Edwards with 400 rangers and Illinois militia up the Illinois River to the Kickapoo settlements around Peoria. Russell with the rangers departed Vincennes the day after Hopkins, made contact with Edwards, and reached his objective a week later. The Americans found few Indians, destroyed some houses and canoes, and returned southward, having been only slightly more successful than Hopkins' men.[12]

Not disconcerted by the failure of his initial expedition, Hopkins decided upon a second. He gathered three regiments of Kentucky militiamen, Taylor's company of regulars, a company of rangers, and some scouts, about 1,200 men in all, at Fort Harrison. High water delayed their departure until November 11. The men marched up Harrison's road alongside the eastern bank of the swollen river while seven boats in the stream ferried supplies. On the nineteenth the force reached Prophetstown, near the Tippecanoe battlefield. They burned its 40 houses. About 300 men pressed on to the Winnebago towns on Ponce Passu Creek but found them abandoned. The men returned after burning 160 houses and destroying the corn standing in nearby fields. Although 700 Miamis, Winnebagos, Kickapoos, and Potawatomis were encamped nearby, they remained out of contact until the twenty-first. That day they attacked a patrol, killing one man. The following morning about 60 mounted men returned to reclaim the body. They suffered eighteen casualties in a well-executed ambush. Inexplicitly, the Indians abandoned their strong position nearby and none of Hopkins' scouts could locate them. Since ice had started to form along the banks of the Wabash, Hopkins ordered a withdrawal. The Kentuckians began their trek homeward on the twenty-fifth. They reached the relative comfort of Fort Harrison after five miserable days spent marching through cold and snow.[13]

Niles' Weekly Register, III (1812–13), 170, 204–205; Hamilton, "Expeditions of Hopkins," 393–96.

12. Hamilton, "Expeditions of Hopkins," 399–400; Lossing, *Field Book*, 336; Gilpin, *War in the Old Northwest*, 147–49.

13. Mahon, *War of 1812*, 69–70; Brackenridge, *History of the Late War*, 63; Hamilton,

Following the return of Hopkins' force to Vincennes, Taylor received sick leave in Louisville to recover from the arduous campaign. Although he hoped to join the forces in the East once his health had been restored, the orders never arrived. Taylor, therefore, returned to Fort Knox in Vincennes to superintend recruiting in Indiana and Illinois. In June he marched his recruits to join Colonel Russell at Fort Vallonia, about fifty miles north of Louisville. On July 1, 1813, Russell led his command of 573 men, mostly rangers and volunteers, in a five-column sweep through central Indiana to the Mississinewa villages. From there they marched along the Wabash to Fort Harrison. Taylor commanded the central column on the five-hundred-mile, four-week march. Again the Americans saw no Indians and had to content themselves with burning empty villages. Apparently the Indians had followed Tecumseh into Canada. In any event there was no further Indian trouble in Indiana that year.[14]

Taylor returned to Vincennes, where he assumed command of the 140-man post as well as continuing his recruiting duties. Convinced that he was stuck there for the duration of the war, he brought his family from Louisville. Here his second daughter, Sarah Knox, was born. Her first name came from her paternal grandmother and her middle one honored her father's command.[15]

While Taylor fretted over his inactivity at Vincennes, events were taking place along the Mississippi River which would return him to action. Following the 1812 attack on Fort Madison the War Department had ordered the post abandoned. Nevertheless, the garrison did not depart until forced out by a second Indian assault in September 1813. Their departure further reduced the American influence on the upper Mississippi, already limited by the dominating presence of British traders. The senior Ameri-

---

Taylor, I, 46; Hamilton, "Expeditions of Hopkins," 394–402; Sara Jane Line, "The Indians of the Mississinewa," *Indiana Magazine of History*, IX (1913), 188–89; Hopkins to Shelby, November 27, 1812, in John Brannan, *Official Letters of the Military and Naval Officers of the United States During the War with Great Britain in the Years 1812, 13, 14, & 15* (Washington, 1823), 95–97; McAfee, *War in Western Country*, 160–62; Gilpin, *War in the Old Northwest*, 149–50.

14. ZT to T. H. Cushing, February 2, 1813, in IHS; Gilpin, *War in the Old Northwest*, 197; George Pence, "General Joseph Bartholomew," *Indiana Magazine of History*, XIV (1918), 295; George Pence, "Indian History of Bartholomew County," *Indiana Magazine of History*, XXIII (1927), 226; Hamilton, *Taylor*, I, 47; Brainerd Dyer, *Zachary Taylor* (Baton Rouge, 1946), 26; ZT Autobiography, 3.

15. ZT to J. C. Breckenridge, December 22, 1813, in Breckenridge Family Papers, XXXIII, LC; Hamilton, *Taylor*, I, 48, 57; Return of Garrison, Fort Knox, March 1814, in ZT(LC), ser 2, r 1. It is uncertain whether Knox was born on March 6 of 1814 or 1815. See the discussion in Haskell Monroe, *et al.* (eds.), *The Papers of Jefferson Davis* (4 vols.; 1971–   ), I, 524.

cans in the West recognized the problem, but the demands of the war farther east deafened the Washington authorities to their cries for assistance. A good example was the abandonment of the plan to reestablish
Fort Madison because the troops involved were ordered to the Niagara
frontier. As a result the northernmost posts along the river were a series
of small blockhouses shielding the St. Charles settlement on the Missouri
River.[16]

The most active and able British agent on the upper Mississippi was
the trader Robert Dickson. He held the loyalty of most of the northern
tribes for Britain. In 1812 he had led a band, which included Black Hawk,
in the capture of Mackinac and at Detroit. After the failure of Tecumseh's
attacks during that summer and fall, Dickson secured approval to bring
the western tribes into the war. As a result, in January 1813 he became
superintendent of Indian affairs west of Lake Michigan. In April 1814 he
recruited 300 Menominees, Winnebagos, and Sioux at Prairie du Chien
and led them to Green Bay to join in operations against Detroit.[17]

Rumors of Dickson's recruiting at Prairie du Chien reached St. Louis in
January 1814 and touched off fears of a British-Indian attack. Governor
William Clark of Missouri Territory, the fabled co-leader of the Lewis and
Clark expedition, who commanded there in the absence of a regular militia officer, prepared to respond. He asked for authority to recruit volunteers to man keel boats for an expedition upriver. Secretary of War John
Armstrong referred the proposal to brigadier general and former governor Benjamin Howard, who now held overall responsibility for western
defense.

Howard responded by raising three companies of rangers in Illinois
and ordering Taylor with the troops from Vincennes to the threatened
area.[18] We do not know when Taylor reached the Mississippi, although he
was there on April 29, when as the senior officer he directed Lieutenant
Joseph Perkins of the 24th Infantry to take command of the Fort Knox
detachment and accompany Clark on an expedition to Prairie du Chien.[19]
Clark had decided to seize that post in order to prevent Dickson and

16. Mahan, Fort Crawford, 46–49, 53; Robert W. Frazer, Forts of the West (Norman,
1965), 70.

17. Statement of Dickson, December 3, Dickson to George Prevost, December 23, 1812,
in Esarey (ed.), Messages & Letters, II, 235–36, 251–52; Mahan, Fort Crawford, 49–51;
Reginald Horsman, The Frontier in the Formative Years, 1783–1815 (Albuquerque,
1975), 173.

18. Howard to Secretary of War, May 15, 1814, in Carter, Territorial Papers, XVI, 423;
ZT Autobiography, 3; William T. Hagan, The Sac and Fox Indians (Norman, 1958),
60–61; William E. Foley, A History of Missouri (3 vols.; Columbia, Mo., 1971), I, 156.

19. ZT to Perkins, April 29, 1814, in AGLR 1814 (M566/35). It is filed with other com-

other British agents from permanently winning allegiance of the Indians who traded there and thus crippling settlement in northern Illinois and Missouri. On May 1 Clark departed Cap-au-Gris on the Mississippi about twelve miles above the mouth of the Cuiure with 60 men of the 7th Infantry and 140 Illinois and Missouri rangers. The five keel boats moved upriver with little difficulty until at the mouth of the Rock River they had a skirmish with some Sac. When the expedition reached Prairie du Chien the small garrison of local militiamen offered no resistance. Clark landed Perkins' command June 2 with orders to construct and garrison a fort. It was named Fort Shelby in honor of the governor of Kentucky. Clark then returned to St. Louis, followed by one of the ranger companies, arriving June 30. Howard, who had reached the Missouri settlement on May 8, ordered Lieutenant John Campbell of the 1st Infantry to Fort Shelby with a reinforcement of forty-five regulars and sixty-five rangers. Their boats were accompanied by two additional boats freighting contractor's and sutler's stores. The force sailed July 4 and reached Rock Island on the eighteenth. The following day Campbell's flotilla became separated in a gale and when he sought shelter at what is now known as Campbell's Island he was attacked by the Indians. The American expedition was shattered by the assault and forced to retreat to St. Louis. One of the ironies of the defeat was that some of the survivors were rescued by the gunboat *Governor Clark* fleeing from Prairie du Chien. Campbell lost sixteen men killed and over twenty wounded, along with one of his boats.[20]

When Dickson and Lieutenant Colonel Robert McDouall at Mackinac learned of the seizure of Prairie du Chien they prepared to reclaim the key post. Dickson assigned half of his Indians to the task while McDouall contributed a local militia force, the Michigan Fencibles, and two companies of Canadian voyageurs. The expedition was placed under the former trader Lieutenant Colonel William McKay. Since the Indians wanted a piece of artillery, McDouall assigned Sergeant James Keating of the Royal Artillery and a three-pounder to the force. McKay's men left Mackinac on June 28 for Green Bay. There another volunteer company and some additional Indians joined. When the force reached Prairie du Chien

plaints from Colonel W. P. Anderson of the 24th Infantry over the assignment of elements of the regiment to Mississippi River operations without his knowledge.

20. William A. Meese, "Credit Island," *Journal of the Illinois State Historical Society*, VII (1914–15), 352; Donald Jackson (ed.), *Ma-Ka-Tai-Me-She-Kiakiak—Black Hawk: An Autobiography* (Cambridge, 1955), 88–90; McAfee, *War in Western Country*, 439–40, 443–44; Mahan, *Fort Crawford*, 52–53, 47–59. Where Taylor spent the period is not certain. Howard in his May 15 letter states he was ascending the Mississippi, but Taylor in his autobiography does not mention accompanying Clark. He may have been at Fort Lookout near Portage des Sioux.

it included 120 whites and about 500 Sioux, Winnebago, Menominee, and Chippewa, roughly a third of the number of Indians Dickson had expected.

Perkins' men, assisted by volunteers from the crew of the *Governor Clark* which remained in support, built a standard small frontier fort: a rectangular stockade with blockhouses at opposite corners. In addition to the muskets of its garrison it mounted six small guns. McKay laid siege to the post for two days using his one artillery piece to neutralize the gunboat. On July 19, when McKay had only six rounds left for his cannon, Perkins surrendered. McKay, who had problems restraining his Indians, hastily paroled the Americans and sent them to St. Louis.[21]

The fall of Fort Shelby and the defeat of Campbell's expedition confronted Howard with a difficult problem. He had only 120 regulars, ten companies of rangers, and a handful of local militia units to protect the Indiana, Illinois, and Missouri frontiers. The pressures under which he worked brought on a fever from which he subsequently died. On August 22 Howard directed Taylor to lead a force of rangers and militia upstream as far as the Sac villages at the mouth of the Rock River, if possible destroy them and the nearby cornfields, and then return to the mouth of the Des Moines. There the force would build a fort.[22]

The expedition sailed from Fort Independence at Cap-au-Gris in a fair wind at noon on August 22. On board the eight keel boats were 430 men. Good fortune did not accompany them for long. Two days into the trip measles appeared and before the epidemic subsided one man had died. The boats worked their way through narrows between river islands, under sail whenever possible, but their crews frequently rowed against the current during calms. On September 4 the small convoy reached the mouth of the Rock River. Since many Indians were visible on shore, Taylor had a white flag hoisted on his boat in hopes of enticing the natives to a council. The natives showed no such disposition. Indeed, unknown to Taylor, Captain Thomas G. Anderson, McKay's successor at Prairie du Chien, had sent Lieutenant Duncan Graham with thirty soldiers, a three-

21. McDouall, Address, June 5, 1814, in Esarey (ed.), *Messages & Letters*, II, 652–55; Meese, "Credit Island," 353-54; Milo M. Quaife, "A Forgotten Hero of Rock Island," *Journal of the Illinois State Historical Society*, XXVIII (1930–31), 656–58; Mahan, *Fort Crawford*, 54–57; J. Mackay Hitsman, *The Incredible War of 1812* (Toronto, 1965), 204; McDouall to Lieutenant General Gordon Drummond, July 16, McKay to McDouall, July 27, 1814, in William Wood (ed.), *Select British Documents of the Canadian War of 1812* (4 vols.; Toronto, 1920–26), IV, 253–55, 257–59.

22. Fort Independence, GO, August 22, 1814, in ZT Autobiography, 5–10. Howard died September 18 but Colonel Russell did not arrive to assume command until October. Gilpin, *War in the Old Northwest*, 251.

pounder, and two swivels to assist the Sac in halting the American expedition.

The Indians unsuccessfully attempted to lure the Americans ashore by driving a herd of horses onto Credit Island just above the mouth of the Rock River and onto the west bank opposite it. By 4:00 P.M. the wind rose to nearly hurricane strength. Since the anchors were too weak to hold the vessels in such a blow and he was afraid that they might be blown on some nearby sandbars, Taylor had his squadron run ashore on a small six-to-eight-acre willow-covered island about sixty yards above Credit Island. There they spent an uneasy night.

Shortly before daylight some Indians on the island fired upon the boat bearing Captain Samuel Whiteside's company, mortally wounding one man. The Americans returned the fire. When daylight permitted him to survey the situation, Taylor ordered Whiteside to land his company and clear the island. "All of you who are not cowards, follow me," shouted the ranger. His men quickly drove the Indians back to Credit Island. While Whiteside's men kept up a spirited fire, Captain Nelson Rector's company took their boat downstream to rake the island with their swivel guns and destroy some canoes beached there. Meanwhile, Lieutenant Graham had arrived from Rock Island with the British artillery. He emplaced the gun on the western shore about 350 yards from the American boats. Sergeant Keating's first shot hit the bow of one of them.

The Americans were surprised by the unexpected shelling and the strong resistance encountered from the Indians, but they quickly recovered their wits and worked their boats out into the stream. Whiteside dropped his craft down to rescue Rector's boat, which had gone aground. While this was going on Rector's men drove off a large number of Indians in a fifteen-minute battle. Paul Harpole, one of the men in the stranded boat, succeeded in getting a towing cable to Whiteside's keel boat. He then stood in the water calmly shooting at the Indians until hit. Since his force was clearly outgunned and outnumbered, Taylor ordered a retreat. He had lost fourteen men wounded, of whom three later died. Once away from the half-heartedly pursuing Indians, Taylor held a council of war which concurred in his decision to withdraw to the Des Moines and carry out the second portion of his orders.[23]

On reaching the Des Moines River, Taylor selected a high bluff on the

23. ZT to Howard, September 6, 1814, in *Niles' Weekly Register*, VII (1814 Supplement), 137–38; "Journal of trip, leaving August 22, 1814 from Cap au Gris," in Maher Collections, MoHS; Jackson, *Ma-Ka-Tai-Me-She-Kiakiak*, 90–91; Dyer, *Taylor*, 27–30; Hagan, *Sac and Fox*, 69–72; Hamilton, *Taylor*, I, 49–53; John T. Kingston, "Early Western Days," *WSHSC*, VII (1876), 311–12; Meese, "Credit Island," 359–66; Gilpin, *War in Old Northwest*, 250–51; Mahan, *Fort Crawford*, 60–61; Mahon, *War of 1812*, 288–89;

east bank of the Mississippi (present-day Warsaw, Illinois) as the site for the new fort. Fort Johnson, as it was named, was a twelve-foot-high oak palisade fifty yards square. The location had the strong drawback that it was commanded by a small hill about 750 yards to the north. On October 1, before the post was completed, Taylor returned to St. Louis to assume temporary command of the troops in Missouri following the death of General Howard. About three weeks later the Fort Johnson garrison also reached St. Louis. When expected supplies did not appear Captain James Callaway of the rangers had evacuated and burned the post. It was not rebuilt.[24]

In November Colonel Russell arrived from Vincennes to assume the Missouri command. Almost immediately Russell and Taylor hastened up the Missouri River some two to three hundred miles to succor the settlers around Boone's Lick who reported an infestation of Indians. The expedition encountered no evidence of a serious threat. The following month Taylor returned to command at Vincennes. There he remained until the end of the war.[25]

During the fall of 1814 the absence of any promotion began to nag Taylor. Other officers commissioned after him and claiming no more distinguished careers had been promoted over him, or so it seemed to the Kentuckian. Taylor seldom exhibited strong ambition and normally refrained from promoting his own interests. Yet, his patience had a limit and when that was reached he could become extremely active. The same pattern applied to his relations with others. He was slow to anger and to find fault but once he concluded that an individual had treated him unfairly Taylor would respond viciously.

Taylor undoubtedly had valid grounds for his complaint. Of the seventy-eight majors whose commission dates were between September 1812 and May 1814 (the date of Taylor's belated promotion) thirty-eight had dates of rank as captain which were later than his. Only one of those commissioned between June 1814 and the end of the war was senior to him. It appears that Taylor's problem was one inherent in the army's system of promotion within regiments rather than by seniority among all officers holding a rank. Of the five captains in the 7th Infantry who ranked Taylor all except one (Enos Cutler, who left the line to become an assistant inspector general) were promoted in sequence. On the other hand, only one

Quaife, "Forgotten Hero," 660–61; John Shaw, "Shaw's Narrative," *WSHSC*, II (1856), 220–21.

24. Meese, "Credit Island," 367; Dyer, *Taylor*, 31–32; Hamilton, *Taylor*, I, 53–54; ZT Autobiography, 12; Kate L. Gregg, "The War of 1812 on the Missouri Frontier," *Missouri Historical Review*, XXXIII (1938/39), 337.

25. ZT Autobiography, 13–14; Foley, *History of Missouri*, I, 159.

of the four majors appointed in the regiment during the war was drawn from its ranks.[26]

Taylor enlisted the assistance of Colonel Russell, who wrote to the secretary that the hero of Fort Harrison was "a most valuable officer" from a very respectable family who was concerned about the promotion of officers his junior. Whether, as Taylor seems to have believed, his promotion had been delayed by complaints from Colonel William P. Anderson of the 24th Infantry is not evident. Anderson, an argumentative Tennessean who was a cross that a number of officers had to bear, had complained about the use of some of his command by Taylor on the Mississippi.[27] Taylor himself solicited letters of support from Indiana delegate Jonathan Jennings, Colonel Richard M. Johnson, General Hopkins, Louisville's Representative Stephen Ormsby, and Alexander Stuart. Taylor also wrote to Adjutant and Inspector General Daniel Parker on November 29 inquiring of the specific nature of the complaints against him which had prevented his being promoted. Parker replied January 2, 1815, that "No complaints have been made against you for any questions" and that he had never been superseded in promotion. Parker concluded his letter by informing Taylor that he had been promoted to major in the 26th Infantry. He was to join his regiment at Plattsburgh, New York.[28]

The commission was formally issued on February 1 but carried a date of May 15, 1814. That was three days after the 26th Infantry had been formed out of the 48th Infantry. Isaac Clark of Vermont, the longtime commander of defenses at the head of Lake Champlain, was the colonel and Taylor the senior major. Another Vermonter, Orsamus C. Merrill, who transferred from the 11th Infantry as a major on June 7, received the lieutenant colonelcy. The second majority went to Isaac Finch, a New Yorker who had been a first lieutenant in the 16th Infantry.[29] Despite its creation in the spring of 1814 the regiment appears not to have been organized until late in the year and did not complete recruiting before the end of hostilities.

Taylor never joined his new unit because of the arrival of peace and congressional action on March 3, 1815, which reduced the army from a wartime high of approximately 60,000 men to 10,000 men. This involved demobilizing 177 (82 percent) of the field and 1,605 (78 percent) of the

26. Heitman, *Historical Register*, I, *passim*.

27. Dyer, *Taylor*, 33–34; Hamilton, *Taylor*, I, 55–55, 57; Anderson to Monroe, October 27, 1814, in AGLR, 1814 (Anderson), with enclosures.

28. Hamilton, *Taylor*, I, 56–57; Parker to ZT, January 2, 1815, AGLS, III 1/2, 282 (M565/5); ZT Autobiography, 14.

29. Heitman, *Historical Register*, I, 125; William A. Gordon, *A Compilation of Registers of the Army of the United States from 1815 to 1837* (Washington, 1837), 11, 32.

company officers. To implement the law and to select the officers to be retained, Acting Secretary of War Alexander J. Dallas convened a board composed of Generals Jacob Brown, Andrew Jackson, Winfield Scott, Edmund P. Gaines, Alexander Macomb, and Eleazer W. Ripley. They proposed a set of geographical military divisions and districts for the administration of the army, apportioned the peacetime units among them, and selected the officers to be retained either in their wartime rank or at a reduced one.

Under the new organization the 26th Infantry, along with the 15th, 30th, 31st, and 45th infantries, was integrated into the Regiment of Light Artillery. Of the twelve majors in the six regiments, only three, including Taylor, were retained in service. The senior artilleryman, Abram Eustis, received the sole majority allotted to the new unit. Taylor and James Dorman of the 34th Infantry were offered captaincies with brevet ranks of major. Five of the majors demobilized were senior to Taylor and several had long and distinguished careers.[30]

Taylor visited Washington in an attempt to upset the decision. He joined Colonel Thomas D. Owings of the 28th Infantry and Major William Bradford of the 21st in a protest to President Madison. The president wrote Dallas supporting Taylor's retention as a major, pointing out that the fact that he had not been promoted faster during the war was due to oversight. When an opening occurred shortly afterwards, the president suggested that this would allow Taylor to retain his majority. Dallas refused to act, however, because the board had already reported and he could not change the printed army register. Despite Madison's efforts on his behalf, Taylor long harbored intense resentment against both men. In 1821 he described Madison as "a man perfectly callous & unacquainted with the noble feelings of a soldier" and Dallas as "a lawyer grown grey in iniquity & chicanery, whose profession was to prevent right, a man better calculated for the associate of Robespierre than the minister of a free, enlightened & great republic."[31]

On May 5 Taylor was ordered home to await orders. By that time he knew that his new assignment was to the 7th Infantry, in which he would be the third-ranking captain.[32] Taylor had been better treated than he be-

30. Heitman, *Historical Register*, I, 52, 110, 125, 130, 132–33; Gordon, *Compilation of Registers*, 57–71; *Niles' Weekly Register*, VIII (1815), 222–30; Dyer, *Taylor*, 35.

31. Dyer, *Taylor*, 26; Madison to Dallas, May 10, 19, Dallas to Madison, May 21, 1815, in George Mifflin Dallas (ed.), *The Life and Writings of Alexander James Dallas* (Philadelphia, 1871), 412, 421–23; ZT to Jesup, June 18, 1821, ZT(LC), ser 2, r 1.

32. Parker to ZT, May 5, 1815, in AGLS, III 1/2, 368 (M565/5). John Machesney and Richard Whartenby, the two senior officers, had earlier dates of rank than Taylor both as captains and majors.

lieved. His wartime service had been respectable but not distinguished. He had spent the time in essentially administrative commands along a quiet sector. As a result he had done little to draw attention of the War Department officials or of the service's senior officers. Yet, despite his weak record, Taylor was offered a continuation in the service. It was a recognition of his potential, not of his wartime service. Taylor viewed matters differently. To him a reduced commission was a "razeed" appointment which damned the officer who accepted it.[33] It was a degradation which his sense of pride would not permit him to accept. On June 9, 1815, Taylor formally refused the pro-offered commission without waiting to find out how many officers would reconcile themselves to their new commissions. Secretary Dallas accepted his resignation on the fifteenth. Taylor returned to Louisville sometime before June 15 to start his new life as a farmer.[34]

CHAPTER III

A Career Resumed

HAVING PUT ASIDE his hat, epaulets, and sword, Zachary Taylor returned to Louisville and to his new role of farmer. Although he had fought hard to retain his rank and clearly felt rancor over his failure to do so, Taylor looked happily toward his new profession. One of the consistent threads in his character was a strong attachment to the soil. It caused him to write to one of his relatives, "I can assure [you] I do not regreat [*sic*] the change of calling or the course I have pursued."[1] The euphoria died quickly. Within a year he looked back at the experience and snorted, "[It] affords nothing sufficiently interesting to trouble my friends by communicating with them on the subject."[2] Taylor's love, it quickly became clear, was *of* the soil, not working it.

As matters developed, Taylor's resignation from the army was premature. The army's officer corps divided into two substantial blocks. The line, composed of officers of the infantry, rifles, and artillery, could command mixed bodies of troops in the field or hold administrative posts involving command of divisions or districts. The second group served in the staff corps; such officers as the quartermasters, paymasters, adjutants general, and inspectors general were considered specialists and their commissions conferred no command authority outside of their own corps. The two groups were mutually exclusive in that an officer belonged to either staff or to the line. While line officers occasionally switched to staff positions, the reverse seldom occurred and then only to a roar of disapproval by line officers who saw the opportunity for advancement reduced.

1. ZT to W. B. Taylor, April 25, 1816, in Presidents Papers, MoHS.
2. ZT to J. C. Breckenridge, April 12, 1817, in Breckenridge Family Papers, LC.

Two vacancies soon developed among the infantry majors. Both were created by removing staff officers from the line regiments: John Wool of the 6th Infantry became one of the inspectors general with the rank of colonel while Charles K. Gardner of the 3d Infantry resumed his wartime role in the adjutant general's office. The vacancy in the 3d Infantry was offered to Taylor. Why he was chosen from among the large group of wartime majors who refused reduction is not known. Probably it reflected the earlier abortive effort of President James Madison to keep him on the rolls. Taylor did not seek the reinstatement, nor did his brother Joseph, who received reappointment as a 2d lieutenant of Artillery at the same time. It is possible that both their father and James Taylor wrote President Madison soliciting his support. In any event, the two Taylors were among the large number of officers announced May 17, 1816, to fill vacancies created by transfers and the rejection of commissions earlier offered. Zachary's commission did not reach Louisville until August, giving him time to put his affairs in order.

As a major Taylor received a salary of fifty dollars per month plus allowances. The latter included four rations, worth twenty cents apiece, ten dollars per month forage for his horses, and quarters of one room and a kitchen. He could employ two servants and expect the army to transport five hundred pounds of his personal baggage. The commander of the 3d Infantry, Colonel John Miller, was a Buckeye who had commanded both the 17th and 19th infantries during the war in the operations around Detroit. Since Lieutenant Colonel Matthew Arbuckle was in Georgia commanding the 7th Military Department, Taylor became the second-ranking officer with the regiment.[3]

He notified Brigadier General Alexander Macomb, head of the 5th Military Department at Detroit, that "as soon as I can arrange my private business, which will be in a very short time, I shall report myself in person."[4] What he did not inform Macomb of was that his wife was pregnant again. The day of the dispatch of the letter, August 15, a third daughter, Octavia Pannill, was born.[5]

Taylor probably reported to Detroit in late September. He received orders to Fort Howard at Green Bay on Lake Michigan, where in the spring he would assume command. The route west carried him first to Macki-

3. *Ibid.*; William A. Gordon, *A Compilation of Registers of the Army of the United States from 1815 to 1837* (Washington, 1837), 90–91; Brainerd Dyer, *Zachary Taylor* (Baton Rouge, 1946), 38–39; Holman Hamilton, *Zachary Taylor* (2 vols.; Indianapolis, 1941, 1951), I, 60; Thomas M. Exley, *A Compendium of Pay of the Army from 1788 to 1888* (Washington, 1888), 90.

4. ZT to Macomb, August 15, 1816, in A&IGLR 1816 (M566/93); *ASP:MA*, I, 800–802.

5. Hamilton, *Taylor*, I, 296.

nac, the headquarters of the regiment. In November Taylor departed for Green Bay in company with Robert Dickson, now returned to his normal role as an Indian trader, and two officers who were to join the garrison. They traveled in an open boat, but because the lake had started to freeze, the usual ten-to-twelve-day trip took thirty. En route they rescued six castaway mariners from an island. Soon after they reached the Wisconsin shore the bad weather forced the group to abandon their boat and proceed overland.[6] After that introduction to a late fall in Wisconsin, Taylor found the winter much less trying than he had anticipated.[7]

The Green Bay post had been established the previous summer by Colonel Miller. Its placement was part of a conscious effort to overawe the local Indians, who reputedly continued to be strongly pro-British. Miller and his engineer, Major Charles Gratiot, selected a site at the mouth of the Fox River. The fort, built by its 300-man garrison under Lieutenant Colonel Talbot Chambers of the Rifle Regiment, commanded the eastern end of the most widely used track from the lakes to the Mississippi. The nearly all-water route along the Fox and Wisconsin rivers was the same employed so successfully by Dickson and McKay during the war. Green Bay village squatted near the fort in shaggy squalor. It contained about forty families, nearly all headed by French-Canadian trappers, universally described by visitors as the uneducated and unappealing fathers of large flocks of halfbreeds. Most worked for the large Indian trading houses and all were strongly influenced by British agents like Dickson.[8]

When Chambers and his command trudged westward through the spring slush to repeat their construction assignment at Prairie du Chien, Taylor remained behind with two companies to complete Fort Howard. Although two more companies were en route, he did not consider the force adequate to defend the post. The garrison, he argued, should be maintained at 300 men or the fort should be abandoned. With more than usual insight, he recognized the importance of the command of the lakes, noting in a letter to a friend that the post could not be held without it.[9]

The white painted post stood on a sandy ridge on the north bank of

6. ZT to Breckenridge, April 12, 1817, in Breckenridge Family Papers; Dickson to Lawe, November 25, 1816, in "Lawe and Grignon Papers, 1794–1821," *WSHSC*, X (1888), 134; Hamilton, *Taylor*, I, 60–61. In 1849 one of the party applied for a patronage job on the basis of his assistance during the trip. Taylor turned him down on the basis that he had been paid already. ZT to J. W. Webb, July 27, 1849, in James Watson Webb Papers, Yale:M&A.

7. ZT to Taliaferro, March 14, 1817, in Laurence Taliaferro Papers, r 1, MinnHS.

8. James H. Lockwood, "Early Times and Events in Wisconsin," *WSHSC*, II (1856), 103–104; Francis Paul Prucha, *Sword of the Republic* (New York, 1969), 127–28; ZT to Breckenridge, April 14, 1817, in Breckenridge Family Papers; Dyer, *Taylor*, 40; Hamilton, *Taylor*, I, 60.

9. ZT to Breckenridge, April 14, 1817, in Breckenridge Family Papers.

the Fox River near its mouth. It consisted of log barracks which delineated three sides of a square parade ground within a thirty-foot-high stockade strengthened by blockhouses at each corner. Taylor considered the location poor because of the swampy ground nearby, the lack of an easily reached woodlot, and the proximity of commanding high ground across the river.[10]

His most pressing problem on assuming command was completion of the post. He did so with an eye to the comfort of those stationed there. His own quarters were outfitted in a manner which belied their presence at an isolated frontier post. Travelers who visited the post and the local inhabitants whom he entertained noted the mahogany furniture, especially a huge sideboard, and good china which Taylor had brought in with the supplies. These reflected a side of the Kentucky gentleman which would surface frequently during the next thirty years; he believed that whenever possible his home should be as comfortable as it would have been in Louisville or in later life at Baton Rouge. Yet, when in the field he lived a rough, frugal life little different from that of his men and often less comfortable than some of his officers. Whether Mrs. Taylor actually made the trip to Green Bay or whether the preparations for her comfort were in vain, we do not know. Local lore insists she lived in Green Bay, but there is no independent evidence.[11]

The early months of Taylor's command at Green Bay gave further indication of his temper. He suffered from what modern sociologists sometimes call the thirty-year-old syndrome. At the age of thirty-three he had considerable experience and clearly believed that he was better equipped to solve the problems of a peacetime army than his superiors, whom he viewed as being bogged down in bureaucratic pettyfogging. In time he would mellow and gain maturity of outlook but it did not occur during the Green Bay years.

Taylor grew very impatient with the problems of serving under General Macomb. When Colonel Miller left the area during the spring, Taylor became the senior officer of the 3d Infantry on the lakes. The regulations issued by General Macomb effectively denied him authority over the regiment by placing the commander of Fort Howard under the commander at Mackinac. This was especially galling for Taylor since this subordinated

10. Henry R. Schoolcraft, *Narrative Journal of Travels Through the Northwestern Region of the United States* (Albany, N.Y., 1821), 369; Edgar Bruce Wesley, *Guarding the Frontier* (Westport, Conn., 1970), 125; ZT to Colonel J. L. Smith, September 28, 1819, in UM:C.

11. Louise Phelps Kellogg, "Old Fort Howard," *Wisconsin Magazine of History*, XVIII (1934–35), 128; Hamilton, *Taylor*, I, 62; ZT to Hancock Taylor, October 13, 1817, in ZT(UKL).

him to Lieutenant Colonel John McNeil of the 1st Infantry. At their first meeting, McNeil had expressed his distaste for Taylor in such "vulgar and backguard epithets" that the latter attempted to have a court of inquiry convened and considered issuing a challenge to a duel. He was dissuaded from pressing his demand by Lieutenant Colonel Thomas S. Jesup, who was soon to become quartermaster general and was Taylor's chief political friend and mentor within the service. When Taylor learned that McNeil might join the 3d Infantry he vehemently protested. Luckily the transfer did not occur until after Taylor had left the regiment, so a further confrontation was avoided.

In July, when McNeil left Mackinac, the command devolved upon Captain Benjamin K. Pierce of the Corps of Artillery. Taylor rebelled at submitting his reports through a junior officer, until he was explicitly directed to do so. Even then he did so with ill grace. In responding to the directive from the assistant adjutant general at Detroit, Taylor complained that he could not furnish some of the information "until this post is furnished with blank forms or paper." That nearly insubordinate response received the appropriate indictment of "frivolous complaints." Nevertheless, some forms were still missing a year later. Taylor's prickliness undoubtedly stemmed in part from his fear that Congress would soon further reduce the size of the army, thereby once again turning him into an unwilling civilian.[12]

Despite Jesup's counsel to be more amenable in his relations with the staff in Detroit, Taylor continued his ill-tempered correspondence. In October 1817 he refused to bring recruits destined for his command to Green Bay because of supply shortages which he considered to be the fault of Macomb's staff. In mid-January 1818 he complained that "unless considerable exertions are made to forward a supply of provisions early in the Spring, the Troops here must suffer very much."[13] The supply problems which Taylor encountered at Fort Howard were symptomatic of a broader problem which the army faced with the use of contractors to provide rations at its posts. The failure of the system led to the enactment of the April 14, 1818, law which transferred responsibility for food and liquor to the Subsistence Department and other supplies to the quartermaster general.[14]

Taylor considered "differences among gentlemen of the Army unpleas-

12. ZT to Hancock Taylor, July 6, to Jesup, October 15, 1817, and [1818], in ZT(LC), ser 2, r 1; ZT to AAG Detroit, August 14, 1817, to Major Perrin Willis, May 18, 1818, in A&IGLR 1817, 1818 (M566/101, 113); Dyer, *Taylor*, 42–43; Hamilton, *Taylor*, I, 63, 270.

13. ZT to Willis, January 17, 1818, in A&IGLR 1818 (M566/113).

14. James A. Huston, *The Sinews of War: Army Logistics, 1775–1953* (Washington, 1966), 112.

ant & disagreeable at any place," but especially unfortunate at isolated frontier posts where "bikering [sic] among themselves . . . makes their situation truly deplorable."[15] Yet, his relations with some of his junior officers rapidly deteriorated during the long cold Wisconsin winter. On February 4 he learned that no whiskey remained for issue to the troops. Half of what was needed to carry the garrison until a new supply arrived was available locally, but the contractor's agent, who held it, wanted $2.00 per gallon, or 72 cents above the contract price. After consulting his company commanders, Taylor rejected the offer and ordered issuance of liquor halted. That seemed to satisfy everyone, but not for long. By February 22 Lieutenant Collin McLeod, an old warhorse retained from the prewar army, was so vocal in his disapproval that Taylor was forced to take cognizance. McLeod became so abusive that Taylor had him arrested. McLeod and Lieutenant Turbey F. Thomas responded with counter-charges. A subsequent court martial sentenced McLeod to be cashiered. The verdict was overturned on a technicality by Secretary of War John C. Calhoun despite the opinion of Adjutant and Inspector General Daniel Parker that the trial had been fair and McLeod blameworthy. Both Mc-Leod and Thomas were permitted to resign later in the year.[16]

Whatever his concern about his relations with the Detroit staff or his troublesome lieutenants, Taylor was gratified by the visit in early summer by Inspector General Colonel John E. Wool. Wool appeared pleased with the state of the garrison and Taylor in turn was "much pleased with him, as a Gentleman, & think him an honor to his profession."[17] At about the same time Taylor received word that Jesup had secured him a furlough, and at the completion of the McLeod court martial Taylor left September 1 for Louisville.[18]

The first weeks in Louisville he spent on furlough, but on October 27, 1818, he formally reported as superintendent of recruiting for the 3d Infantry. At the same time he asked for permission to visit Washington once he had his recruiting stations established. It was not granted. What Taylor had in mind is not clear, although it probably related to his desire to trade billets with an officer attached to one of the regiments stationed in the

15. ZT to Taliaferro, March 14, 1817, in Taliaferro Papers.

16. ZT to Willis, May 18, 24, Fort Howard Regimental O, February 5, 1818, in A&IGLR 1818 (M566/113); Calhoun to President, September 3, Parker to Calhoun, October 16, 1818, in Robert L. Meriwether, et al. (eds.), The Papers of John C. Calhoun (14 vols.; Columbia, S.C., 1959–   ), III, 98, 211.

17. ZT to Jesup, [June 1818], in ZT(LC), ser 2, r 1. Taylor would have been even more pleased with Wool had he known that he too had had a run-in with Macomb over the latter's language. Wool to Macomb, May 15, 1817, in John E. Wool Papers, Box 1, NYSL.

18. ZT to Jesup, [June 1818], in ZT(LC), ser 2, r 1; Smith to Major R. M. Kirby, June 16, 1818, in A&IGLR 1818 (M566/113).

south. The exchange was not forthcoming, in any event. For the next year Taylor remained in Louisville administering recruiting stations and thinking about ways to improve the search for new soldiers. The latter led him to complain about quality of clothing furnished his recruits and the distances his recruiters had to go in search of men. His suggestion was that young officers be sent to the regiment rather than to recruiting so that they could explain the realities of service to potential recruits.[19] Taylor apparently believed that such information would prevent the misunderstandings which led to unhappy recruits and the high rate of desertions among newly enlisted troops.

In late June 1819 Taylor joined President James Monroe and Major General Andrew Jackson at a breakfast in Frankfort and accompanied the president as he paid a visit to the self-proclaimed slayer of Tecumseh, Colonel Richard M. Johnson.[20] The invitation again demonstrated the esteem enjoyed by Taylor and his family among the leaders of his state. The twentieth of April, 1819, brought Taylor promotion to lieutenant colonel of the 4th Infantry, then stationed in Florida. Taylor finally had secured his coveted southern appointment. As events transpired, Taylor never joined his new regiment because George M. Brooke of the 8th Infantry offered to exchange with him. The exchange officially took place August 13, 1819, although the revised commission was not dispatched until the first of September.[21]

The promotion brought a welcome ten dollars per month increase in Taylor's salary to sixty dollars. With the new rank came also an additional ration and one dollar per month in added payment for forage. The promotion also coincided with the birth of a fourth daughter. Margaret Smith arrived on July 27, 1819.[22]

The 8th Infantry, commanded by Colonel Duncan L. Clinch, "an officer of pride & correct deportment, but of moderate talents," was in Alabama chiefly involved in road building. In 1816 President Monroe had ordered the army to build military roads, nominally to ease troop and supply movements, but also to assist the progress of settlement and to contribute to the discipline and health of the soldiers. That year Congress appropriated money to build "Jackson's Military Road" from Columbia,

19. ZT to Parker, October 27, December 10, 14, 1818, January 18, April 14, 1819, in A&IGLR 1818, 1819 (M566/113, 128); ZT to Callender Irvine, December 11, 1818, in Dreer Collection, HSPa.

20. Hamilton, *Taylor*, I, 65; Dyer, *Taylor*, 45.

21. Francis B. Heitman, *Historical Register and Dictionary of the United States Army* (2 vols.; Washington, 1903), I, 88–89, 949; Dyer, *Taylor*, 46; Hamilton, *Taylor*, I, 65; A&IG to ZT, September 1, 1819, in AGLS, V, 285 (M565/6). The commission is in ZT(LC), ser 4, r 2.

22. Exley, *Compendium of Pay*, 49; Hamilton, *Taylor*, I, 270.

Tennessee, to Madisonville, Louisiana. It was completed in 1820. As a part of the project the 8th Infantry constructed an offshoot which ran from the Pearl River to Bay St. Louis on the Gulf of Mexico.[23]

Taylor did not immediately join the road builders. He asked Colonel Robert Butler, Jackson's adjutant, for a postponement in reporting until the ice left the river and he could travel by steamer. Although initially granted, the request was revoked on December 11 and the Kentuckian directed to proceed without delay.[24] Even so, Taylor did not leave Louisville until February. He convoyed his family as far as Bayou Sara, Louisiana, on the Mississippi near St. Francisville, before continuing on to New Orleans and Madisonville.

During his New Orleans stay Taylor became embroiled in a "singular occurrence," as he reported to Jesup. The latter and Colonel Daniel Bissell were in contention to fill the vacancy caused by the resignation of Brigadier General Eleazer W. Ripley. A friend of Bissell accused Taylor of hostility to the colonel and demanded to know if Taylor opposed his promotion. Taylor affirmed his support for Jesup but insisted he cared not who received the appointment if his friend did not. Taylor informed the emissary that if that did not satisfy Bissell "the Genl might select the grounds on which we meet." The duel did not occur. Bissell allowed that he was satisfied, which Taylor snorted was "only from the teeth outwards."[25] Taylor's antipathy toward Bissell was long-standing and grew out of the colonel's dissoluteness. Taylor later described him as having "lost his energies as a soldier," and charged that "his morals are so bad that he ought not to have been suffered to remain in command of young officers." However, he charitably added that Bissell "has sunk so low, that he is rather an object of pity than contempt."[26]

In March Taylor joined the 8th Infantry about 120 miles northeast of Madisonville near the boundary of the Choctaw lands. The reality of his command was disheartening. The 420 men under Captain Willis Foulk were nearly all recruits "without organization, subordination or discipline, and without harmony among the officers." They had accomplished

23. Colonel A. P. Hayne, "Confidential Report of the Southern Division of the Army, 1817," in Inspector General Reports 1814–1823, Records of the Inspector General's Office (NA, RG 159), I, 112 (M624/1); Harold L. Nelson, "Military Roads for War and Peace—1791–1836," *Military Affairs*, XIX (Spring 1955), 5–7.

24. ZT to Butler, November 12, 1819, in Andrew Jackson Papers, ser 1, LV, r 28, LC.

25. ZT to Jesup, April 20, 1820, ZT(LC), ser 2, r 1.

26. ZT to W. B. Taylor, April 25, 1816, in ZT(LC), ser 2, r 1. As early as 1817 Colonel Hayne complained of Bissell's "disposition & dissipated habits." Two years later he described him as "a dissipated inefficient officer." Hayne, Confidential Report 1817, p. 53; Confidential Report 1819, p. 102, both in IG Reports (M624/1).

little, for which Taylor blamed Colonel Clinch. Since Clinch was one of the more competent regimental commanders of the period, it seems unlikely that he was at fault. The project lacked systematic planning or organization. The men were on the verge of starvation, having been on half rations for six weeks. Supplies from New Orleans had to be freighted up the Pearl River and came infrequently; only beef of poor quality could be secured locally. The quartermaster could hire neither horses nor oxen since the planting season had started. However, that probably was less of a loss than Taylor believed since the spring rains had turned the road into a ribbon of mud.

Taylor organized what resources he had and built a storehouse at the Choctaw Six Towns to house officers' baggage and free the regiment's wagons to haul provisions and supplies. He directed his quartermaster to purchase whatever flour and meat he could, despite the high price, arguing that it was still cheaper than bringing it from New Orleans. Having solved his supply problems for the moment, Taylor pushed his men to complete their public-works activities. He expected to finish the road all the way to the Gulf by May 20, which anticipated an average construction of three miles per day.[27]

In keeping with his interest in land, Taylor wrote Jesup that he would "look about me" when the road construction was finished and report upon the potential of the area as a permanent home.[28] In part Taylor's concern arose from the renewed threat of discharge since congressional retrenchment had forced restructuring of the army. In the complex series of shifts which resulted, Taylor retained his rank and command. He credited this to Jesup while complaining that his cousin President Madison had done nothing to support him. So distraught was Taylor over the recurring threat of dismissal that he considered resigning. "Disbandment," he wrote Jesup, "has no terror," but his private affairs were not in good enough condition for him to depart voluntarily.[29] His disenchantment arose from his belief that "the axe, pick, saw & trowel, has become more the implement of the American soldier than the cannon, musket or sword." After noting that some of the recent graduates of West Point "would do honor to any army," he worried that "a military education will be but of little service for unless practice can be blended with theory, the latter will be of but little service, better to have a practical, than a theoretical soldier, if they are to possess but one qualification, but when a soldier can combine both, it gives him every advantage. . . . Such unfortunately

27. ZT to Jesup, April 20, 1820, in ZT(LC), ser 2, r 1.
28. *Ibid.*
29. ZT to Jesup, June 18, 1820, in ZT(LC), ser 2, r 1.

is the passion in our country for making roads, fortifications, and building barracks. . . with soldiers. . . that a man who would make a good overseer, or negro driver, is better qualified for our services, than one who received a first rate military education." [30]

Taylor's life lapsed into the routine of post activities after the road was completed to Bay St. Louis. The command busied itself building barracks and improving the cantonment while its commander found time for thought. If Ethan Allen Hitchcock is to be believed, which is sometimes difficult, Taylor read little in this period, although he liked to discuss what he did read (Hume's *History of England*) in detail. He also thought about the changes necessary to strengthen the army. This led him to suggest an enlarged peacetime officer corps similar to Secretary John C. Calhoun's expandable army concept so as "to organize and put in operation a respectable army in the event of war." He proposed to reduce the number of senior officers and surgeons; to streamline the purchasing procedures; to foster the commissary department; and to establish an invalid corps of aged or infirm officers. The latter was a concept to which Taylor would return in later years. [31]

The stay of Mrs. Taylor and the children at Bayou Sara with her sister Mrs. Samuel Chew proved tragic. During the early fall of 1820 the whole family contracted a "bilious fever" which killed the two youngest girls. [32] When Taylor learned of the illnesses on September 18, he hastened to the bedside of the stricken ones. He did not expect his wife to recover since "at best her constitution is remarkably delicate." She survived but the experience left Taylor with a dread of the miasmas and mists of the delta country. [33] It caused him to abandon thoughts of purchasing a plantation since, as he wrote Jesup, he had decided against retiring there. He would prefer, he said, to return to Kentucky. [34]

Taylor's difficulties with Colonel Bissell continued. No sooner had the troops completed their barracks at Cantonment Bay St. Louis and prepared to take a well-deserved respite, than Bissell as departmental commander ordered two companies to construct a post at Baton Rouge. Moreover, he habitually detached from the regiment groups of enlisted

30. ZT to Jesup, September 18, 1820, in ZT(LC), ser 2, r 1.

31. ZT to Jesup, December 15, 1820, in ZT(LC), ser 2, r 1; Hitchcock, "Memoirs," 10, in W. A. Croffut Papers, IV, LC; Ethan Allen Hitchcock, *Fifty Years in Camp and Field*, ed. W. A. Croffut (New York, 1906), 46–47.

32. Octavia died July 8 and Margaret on October 22. ZT to Jesup, September 18, 1820, in ZT(LC), ser 2, r 1; Hamilton, *Taylor*, I, 69.

33. Hamilton, *Taylor*, I, 65; Hudson Strode, *Jefferson Davis, American Patriot* (New York, 1955), 94; ZT to Jesup, September 18, 1820, in ZT(LC), ser 2, r 1.

34. ZT to Jesup, December 15, 1820, ZT(LC), ser 2, r 1; Hamilton, *Taylor*, I, 69.

men without their officers. This so angered Taylor that he hoped Bissell would be ordered in to effective retirement in St. Louis.[35]

On December 12, 1820, Secretary Calhoun sent the House of Representatives his long awaited plan to reduce the army to 6,000 men. In it he argued for a skeleton peacetime force capable of wartime expansion. The concept of maintaining a disproportionately large number of officers, which was the kernel of the secretary's plan, did not excite members of Congress.[36] The Congress wrote its own plan, which called for a force of 6,183 men, the reduction to be accomplished by the elimination of two regiments, including the 8th Infantry, the geographical divisions and numbered administrative departments, and a reduction in the number of staff and general officers. The single major generalcy went to Jacob Brown and the two brigadier general billets were filled by Winfield Scott and Edmund P. Gaines. Once again Taylor was in an exposed position, the seventh-ranking of the nine infantry lieutenant colonels. The revised organization called for only seven regiments. However, when the Board to Reduce the Military Peace Establishment (Generals Brown, Scott, and Gaines) met, it had not only to reduce the number of senior infantry field officers but find places for Brigadier General Henry Atkinson, Andrew Jackson's adjutant Colonel Robert Butler, and artillery Lieutenant Colonel William Lindsey. By shifting Inspector General John Wool once again to a purely staff appointment, dropping three colonels and two lieutenant colonels, and shuttling the remainder about in a game of musical chairs, the board saved the rank of all the surviving officers except Atkinson. When the final assignments were announced on June 1, 1821, Taylor was posted to the 1st Infantry.

Almost immediately the carefully crafted arrangement threatened to collapse. General Atkinson refused his appointment as an adjutant general and requested command of an infantry regiment. That had the effect of dropping Butler to lieutenant colonel and Taylor to major. When Taylor learned of the probability of his demotion he was mortified and announced he would join the "disbanded officers" if he could not retain his rank. Luckily Lieutenant Colonel George E. Mitchell of the 3d Artillery resigned, allowing Lindsey to return to his original arm and opening a vacancy in the 7th Infantry for Taylor.[37]

35. ZT to Jesup, September 18, 1820, ZT(LC), ser 2, r 1.

36. *ASP:MA*, II, 188–93.

37. ZT to Jesup, June 15, 18, 1821, in ZT(LC), ser 2, r 1; Lieutenant Colonel Henry Leavenworth to Calhoun, June 29, Jackson to Calhoun, July 29, Calhoun to Monroe, October 14, 1821, in Meriwether (ed.), *Papers of Calhoun*, VI, 227, 294–96, 436; Brown to Secretary of War, May 14, 1821, in *ASP:MA*, V, 118; Hitchcock, "Memoirs," 10–11; Heitman, *Historical Register*, I, 81–96, 142; Chester L. Kieffer, *Maligned General: The*

While the maneuvering over ranks and retention continued in Washington, Taylor remained at Bay St. Louis with the remains of the moribund 8th Infantry. Most of the men were integrated into the 7th Infantry, which was ordered from the Georgia-Florida border to the southwest as a result of the Adams-Onis Treaty. On August 16 Taylor formally joined the regiment as its second-in-command. The regimental commander was Matthew Arbuckle, with whom Taylor had earlier served in the 3d Infantry.[38] In October and November Taylor, with the troops at Bay St. Louis, joined the rest of the command in a trek by water to its new posts along the southwestern frontier. Taylor and four companies took post at Natchitoches on the Red River.[39]

The division of the regiment reflected the magnitude of the task assigned it. Arbuckle's men had the dual responsibility of protecting western Louisiana and Arkansas from incursions by adventurers and Indian raiders from Texas and of keeping order among the redmen. Of particular concern were the Osages in Kansas, who reacted violently to the entry onto their traditional lands of tribes retreating westward under the pressure of white settlements like the Delaware, Sac, Fox, Shawnee, Iowa, and Kansas. The Osages also harassed the Cherokee and Choctaw settlers transferred from the southeast into their new lands in the Indian Territory.[40]

Taylor and his command reached Natchitoches on November 19. He chose a point on the crest of a high bluff above Bayou Pierre, about twelve miles from Natchitoches, for a temporary post. It carried the elegant title of Fort Selden.[41] Shortly after the turn of the year Taylor received an order from General Gaines at New Orleans directing him to search out a more permanent site which would be healthy and combine defensive strength with ease of access to the frontier. The site should also be near a navigable stream so as to simplify logistics. Taylor, after scouting possible sites, settled upon Shields's Spring, about twenty-two miles southwest of Natchitoches and east of the present town of Many, Louisiana. It stood atop the ridge in the San Antonio Trace which divided the watersheds of the Red and Sabine rivers.[42]

Biography of Thomas Sidney Jesup (San Rafael, Calif., 1979), 94. Taylor credited Jesup with his retention but the evidence is ambiguous.

38. 1st Infantry Returns, June–September 1821, in Office of the Adjutant General (NA, RG 94), Regimental Returns (M665/1).

39. Edwin C. Bearss and Arrell M. Gibson, *Fort Smith, Little Gibraltar on the Arkansas* (Norman, 1979), 50; Arbuckle to Captain T. E. Hunt, July 26, 1821, in A&IGLR 1821 (M566/144).

40. Hamilton, *Taylor*, I, 70.

41. 7th Infantry Return, November 1821 (M665/65); Robert W. Frazer, *Forts of the West* (Norman, 1965), 63–64.

42. Frazer, *Forts of the West*, 60–62; Gaines to ZT, January 4, 1822, WDLB; Henry Putney Beers, *The Western Military Frontier, 1815–1846* (Philadelphia, 1935), 68.

Gaines visited Fort Selden in March 1822. He reported the post in good order and the men well drilled. On the twenty-eighth he agreed to Taylor's choice for the site of the new post. It was named Cantonment Jesup in honor of the quartermaster general. Although it was a healthy post noted for its large and productive gardens, its location was questioned by some officers who felt it was too distant from the sensitive portions of the Indian frontiers.[43] The post returns for May and June show Taylor at Fort Jesup with four companies totaling 135 men. During July to September he was absent at Fort Smith but returned in October. Meanwhile, in July Taylor had been transferred back to the 1st Infantry, although for unrecorded reasons the shift was backdated to the first of the year.[44]

While at Fort Jesup Taylor became embroiled in one of those unsightly internecine feuds which racked the antebellum army. He had a very low opinion of Colonel Arbuckle, which he apparently made no effort to hide. This antagonism increased during his stay at Fort Smith, normally Arbuckle's post, where he found the officers split into pro- and anti-Arbuckle factions. Among the latter Taylor found an active ally in Surgeon Thomas Lawson. In August Taylor notified Arbuckle that he was planning to submit to General Gaines charges brought by Lawson against Lieutenant Richard J. Walsh, one of the strongest of Arbuckle's partisans. The latter responded by ordering three crucial witnesses away on detached duty, thereby destroying the case. In December Gaines investigated and brought Arbuckle to trial for neglect of duty, but the charge could not be sustained.[45]

In November Taylor reported to the 1st Infantry's main installation, Cantonment Robertson at Baton Rouge. Although medical officers complained of the poor health of the garrison, Taylor's new post was the best he had yet drawn. It sat among a collection of prosperous plantations which grew sugar, cotton, and cattle on highly cultivated fields and pastures. It occupied the first patch of high ground as one proceeded up the river from New Orleans. The permanent brick barracks, started by the 8th Infantry in 1820, were progressing satisfactorily. The 1823 inspector general's report considered their condition to be "tolerable." The design called for two ranges of officers' quarters and two barracks. Each bar-

43. Hamilton, *Taylor*, I, 71; Colonel George Croghan, Report of a Tour. . . 1827, in IG Reports, II, 153, 160 (M624/2).

44. Fort Jesup Post Returns, May–November 1822, Office of the Adjutant General (NA, RG 94), Returns of Posts (M617/554); Heitman, *Historical Register*, I, 82, 949. The 1st Infantry Returns for July and August carry Taylor as transferred from the 7th Infantry; in October and November it carried him "not joined" (M665/1).

45. Bearss and Gibson, *Fort Smith*, 70–74; See also ZT to Lawson, October 12, 1824, in Miscellaneous Papers, NYHS.

racks was 180 feet by 36 feet, two stories high with "a piazza" on one side. When completed the post was adequate for eight companies. As Taylor would later complain, the lack of a wall around the installations permitted the soldiers to mingle with the local inhabitants to the detriment of health and morals. The post also contained a three-story arsenal building measuring 90 feet by 36 feet, as well as a 55-by-30-foot brick powder magazine and workshops which allowed it to serve as the ordnance storage point for the forces assigned to the defense of the Gulf coast.[46]

The move to Baton Rouge could not have come at a more propitious time for Taylor:

> As to myself [he wrote Jesup] I have at present nothing in view, my days of castle building are passed, my private affairs have gone so rapidly from bad to worse in Kentucky that I have even given up the most distant hope of acquiring a moderate share of wealth. I shall however always hold myself in readiness to quit the Army & return to private life at any moment.[47]

Except for leave during March and April of 1823 Taylor continued in command at Baton Rouge until March 1824.[48] The demands on his time were not great and he turned once again to consideration of the conditions of service. In January 1824 he wrote an eight-page letter to Congressman John Floyd concerning the "military establishment." Taylor attacked the number of regulations governing the army and proposed the revision be made by Congress, not a board of officers. He feared the latter would be too self-serving. Taylor wanted pay set by law, by which he apparently meant the abolition of the practice of awarding special allowances to officers at the discretion of the secretary of war. He wished the award of brevet promotions strictly controlled because of what he perceived as the perversion of the system through widespread assignment of officers to duty in their brevet rank. Noting that the repeal of corporal punishment frequently forced officers to award overly severe punishments, he argued for a military criminal code. Since the punishments tended not to be uniform, they helped increase the flow of deserters. Taylor suggested the elimination of the posts of the major general, the two inspectors gen-

46. Cantonment Robertson Post Return, December 1822 (M617/84); Gaines, Report on Condition of Troops & Posts, 1823, pp. 6, 8, 208, in I. G. Reports, I (M624/1); ZT to Jesup, January 20, 1824, in ZT(LC), ser 2, r 1; Eastwick Evans, "A Pedestrious Tour. . . ," in Reuben Gold Thwaites (ed.), *Early Western Travels, 1748–1846* (32 vols.; Cleveland, 1904–1907), VIII, 379; Jesup to Secretary of War James Barbour, March 24, Colonel George Bomford to Barbour, March 28, 1828, in *House Documents*, 20th Cong., 1st Sess., No. 230, pp. 5–6, 8.

47. ZT to Jesup, [December, 1822], in ZT(LC), ser 2, r 1.

48. 1st Infantry Returns, March 1823–March 1824 (M665/1).

eral, and the surgeon general as unnecessary in peacetime.[49] Although the arguments were sometimes convoluted and not always clear, the main deficiency of Taylor's letters was their length. He seems never to have realized that the politicians to whom they were addressed had neither the time nor the inclination to plow through the multi-leaved communications he occasionally sent them.

Despite his later disclaimers of concern with politics, Taylor had an interest in the events of the day. He wrote Jesup in 1824 commenting extensively on the Monroe Doctrine, with which he agreed, and prophesied that "the nation will be prepared to go any lengths in preventing European potentates from interfering with the affairs of [the former Spanish colonies] so far, as . . . compeling them to submit to the mother country." He praised the decision to avoid interference in European affairs, especially the Greek war for independence, pointing out that Greece to the Europeans was like South America to us.[50] Four years later he expressed the hope that the days of John Quincy Adams in the White House would be numbered, although his reasons were not clearly expressed. They may have been a reaction to the appointment of General Macomb as general-in-chief of the army in 1828. Macomb was admittedly a compromise choice since the naming of either of the leading contenders, Winfield Scott or Edmund Pendleton Gaines, would have cleaved the army into two irreconcilable factions, so great was the animosity between the two men and their supporters. Taylor avoided taking sides, although he made no effort to hide his preference for either of the others to Macomb.[51] That, however, merely reflected his continued antagonism growing out of their confrontation ten years earlier. Unlike Winfield Scott, Zachary Taylor harbored grudges and forgave his enemies slowly. Moreover, Taylor, like many of the officers who served their entire careers on frontier duty, harbored a prejudice against those officers whose assignments kept them close to salt water and the politics of the nation's capital. To them Macomb and the long-tenured chiefs of the staff bureaus personified the pettifogging and unrealistic negativism, which verged on jobbery, into which the army's command had lapsed.

In January 1824 Scott passed through Baton Rouge on an inspection tour. He brought the news that Taylor had been ordered back to Louisville as superintendent of recruiting service in the Western Department. The assignment surprised Taylor, who had not sought a change and considered it "very much at variance with my interest & consequently with

49. ZT to Floyd, January 15, 1824, in George F. Holmes Papers, I, 4–7, LC.
50. ZT to Jesup, January 20, 1824, in ZT(LC), ser 2, r 1.
51. ZT to Larson, August 28, 1828, in ZT(LC), ser 2, r 1.

my inclinations." He worried in particular about his ability to settle satisfactorily his affairs. Nevertheless, Taylor cleared his responsibilities and left Baton Rouge on February 24. He remained on recruiting duty until December 1826.[52]

As superintendent of recruiting Taylor had responsibility for subordinates at Cincinnati, St. Louis, and Natchez, and authority to transfer the latter office to Louisville. The next thirty-four months were uneventful as Taylor administered his department, and he seems not to have ventured far from Louisville except for an occasional trip to Cincinnati. Undoubtedly more important to him was the opportunity to look after his investments in Kentucky, although nothing concerning them has survived. During the Louisville years two babies joined the family: Mary Elizabeth, the captivating Betty of later years, on April 20, 1824, and the long-sought son, Richard, on January 27, 1826.[53]

In November 1825 Adjutant General Roger Jones asked Taylor for his views on the recruiting service. Taylor responded on New Year's Eve. He argued that the best points in the west for recruiting were Cincinnati, St. Louis, Natchez, New Orleans, and Louisville. Nashville and Lexington, he reported, were the most successful points. Pittsburgh was a potentially good source of men also but it lay in the Eastern Department. He suggested sending newly recruited men to their regiments soon after signing as a step to reduce desertion. Recruiting officers should be rotated annually, one in the spring and one in the fall, but successful ones should be extended, he believed. Taylor strongly recommended that "none but officers of experience, industry, inteligence [sic], & the most exemplary morals" be sent on recruiting duty, since they must "conciliate the good feelings of the citizens among whom they are located, instead of geting [sic] into difficulties with the civil authorities."[54]

Although formally relieved of his recruiting duties on February 21, 1826, Taylor made an inspection trip to Natchez and New Orleans during the early spring. Before he could rejoin his regiment he received orders to sit on the court martial of Engineer Major Samuel Babcock at Cantonment Morgan in Cincinnati. The case grew out of Babcock's disputed payments for the removal of snags on the Ohio River. The court found him guilty but recommended clemency. President John Quincy Adams concurred and the engineer served until 1830.[55]

52. ZT to Jesup, January 20, 1824, in ZT(LC), ser 2, r 1; 1st Infantry Returns, February 1824–December 1826 (M665/1); Baton Rouge Post Return, February 1824 (M617/84).

53. AG to ZT, March 17, 1824, in AGLS, VI, 463–64 (M565/6); Hamilton, *Taylor*, I, 75; ZT to Jesup, June 17, 1824, in ZT(LC), ser 2, r 1.

54. Jones to ZT, November 25, 1825, in AGLS, VII, 186 (M565/7); ZT to Jones, December 31, 1825, in AGLR 1825, T-94 (M567/17).

55. AG to ZT, February 21, 1826, in AGLS, VII, 242 (M565/7); ZT to AG, February 22,

Later orders in June directed Taylor to remain at Western Department Headquarters in Cincinnati. The directive must have been welcome since it kept him from a direct confrontation with his longtime enemy John McNeil. The latter had transferred from the 3d Infantry to assume command of the 1st Regiment following the removal of Colonel Chambers. As galling as McNeil's assignment must have been, Taylor could not complain of being passed over for promotion. As the fifth-ranking lieutenant colonel he was still too junior for consideration as a regimental commander.[56]

During the autumn of 1826 Taylor joined General Scott, Lieutenant Colonels Enos Cutler (3d Infantry) and Abram Eustis (4th Artillery), Captain Charles J. Nourse, Major General Thomas Cadwalader of the Pennsylvania Militia, and Adjutants General William H. Sumner of Massachusetts and Beverly Daniel of North Carolina as a board to consider improvements in the organization of the militia. Taylor reached Washington on October 3 and took a room at Basil Williamson's Mansion House on the northeast corner of 14th Street and Pennsylvania Avenue. It was the first time he had visited the capital in eleven years. Neither President John Quincy Adams nor Vice-president John C. Calhoun was in residence, but Taylor's cousin, Secretary of War James Barbour, and Postmaster General John McLean were present. Whether Taylor made other than courtesy calls on the officials is not clear. Indeed, we know nothing of his social activities.[57]

The board resulted from a congressional directive for the formulation of "a complete system of tactics and exercise for the cavalry and artillery of the militia." Very few states had adopted manuals for their cavalry and artillery and none was in general use. The board circulated a series of questions to the states but did not receive responses from six. The twenty-seven governors or adjutants general who did reply argued that volunteers were a more efficient way to raise men during wartime than calling out the militia. Almost to a man they considered the ninety-day limit on the duration of militia service to be too short to produce any benefit. Moreover, the traditional militia musters produced more men than the country needed in any foreseeable war. The board recommended limiting liability for militia service to men between 22 and 36 or 40 years of age, since it would produce the 400,000 men that their estimates required as an optimum. They proposed an adjutant general of militia to supervise the state forces and a militia adjutant general and quartermaster general in each state to handle its continuing responsibilities. The board recom-

1826, in Presidential Papers, Filson Club, Louisville; Leland R. Johnson, *The Falls City Engineers* (Washington, 1974), 54.

56. AG to ZT, June 13, 1826, in AGLS, VII, 300 (M567/7); *ASP:MA* III, 567.

57. Hamilton, *Taylor*, I, 75–76.

mended that the following standard organization be used in all states: companies not to include more than one hundred men; two brigades to a division and not more than one brigade per congressional district. In addition the board recommended that camps of instruction be established for militia officers in order to instill a common doctrine. Taylor, like Scott, seems to have resisted efforts to enhance the peacetime training of the militia in an attempt to make it more regular in character. Their War of 1812 experience caused both to fear that a blurring of the distinctions between the regulars and the militia or volunteers would weaken their regulars' claim to retention if the army passed through another massive growth and sharp retrenchment. They need not have worried. Although the plan received the approval of both Secretary Barbour and President Adams, it died a quick death in Congress.[58]

Taylor left Washington on January 22, 1827. After traveling two nights and most of a third he reached Wheeling on the Ohio. There he hastily boarded a steamer bound for Louisville. The voyage was a difficult one lasting seven days because of the low water level in the river. Moreover, the weather was the coldest in the region in thirty years. Fearful that the river might freeze, Taylor promptly set out on a downriver trip and reached Baton Rouge by the middle of February. He went immediately to New Orleans to take command of the post on February 20.[59] Taylor and his 116-man garrison occupied an old barracks which Inspector General George Croghan reported as in a "high & airy situation." The men demonstrated "exact" discipline and were "likely to remain so, under the uniform and steady direction of Lieut. Col. Taylor." The training, Croghan reported, was more advanced than in any other command he had visited that year. Their duty, General Gaines explained, was to "cooperate with the revenue officers and other civil authorities, to prevent violations and evasions of the law; and to suppress any disorders which may grow out of the recent or future disturbance in Texas, or in the present contest between Mexico and the Spanish West India islands."[60]

Despite his instructions to Taylor, General Gaines disliked stationing a garrison in New Orleans, especially during the fever season. He denounced Fort St. Philip, which guarded the downriver approach to the

---

58. Report of Board of Officers Relative to the Militia, November 26, 1826, in *ASP:MA*, III, 388–488; John K. Mahon, "A Board of Officers Considers the Condition of the Militia in 1826," *Military Affairs*, XV (Summer 1951), 85–94.

59. ZT to Jesup, January 29, 1827, in ZT(LC), ser 2, r 1; Hamilton, *Taylor*, I, 77; Baton Rouge and New Orleans Post Returns, February 1827 (M617/84, 843).

60. Croghan, Report of a Tour of Inspection During the Spring, Summer, & Fall of 1827, pp. 138–41, in I. G. Reports, II (M624/2); Gaines to ZT, March 1, 1827, in WDLB, IV, 57.

city, as the most objectionable in the United States because of the climate, mud, mosquitoes, alligators, and lack of local timber. Under no circumstances, he cautioned the authorities in Washington, should northerners or new recruits be sent there. Gaines directed Taylor to have the garrison shift to Pass Christian, Mississippi, during the bad months and authorized the construction there of temporary barracks. Despite Gaines's directive and Colonel Croghan's contention that the New Orleans barracks were "high & airy," Taylor on July 1 shifted his command from the city to Baton Rouge for the summer.[61]

Since his orders were only temporary, in late November Taylor brought his men back to the Crescent City despite the fact that the barracks had been sold during the summer. Major George Bender, the local quartermaster officer, had to rent the old Spanish barracks for $5,000 per year to house the men. He thought it a waste of money, as he complained to Jesup, since no threat of a slave uprising existed at New Orleans, and Baton Rouge was just as useful as a base in case of troubles at the upriver plantations. Taylor remained at New Orleans until May 1, 1828. In the interim the 1st Infantry had been shifted north to the upper Mississippi because of the growing Indian unrest in the region. So swift was Taylor's departure that he had to leave without settling his private affairs.[62]

With his departure for the northern Mississippi, Taylor brought to a close a long and successful series of tours in Louisiana. He had little opportunity to distinguish himself but had largely avoided the petty conflicts that marred the officer corps of the period. In the long run, perhaps more important was the acquisition of the first of his Louisiana plantations, for throughout the rest of his life he would consider Baton Rouge his home. Moreover, the success of his cotton plantation led him ever deeper into speculation in the rich farmlands in northern Louisiana and Mississippi. As he drew closer to the downriver planters in outlook he became less attached to that of his Kentucky roots.

61. Gaines to ZT, and to AG, both June 8, 1827, in WDLB, IV, 98; Croghan, Report of a Tour. . . 1827, I. G. Reports, II, 139 (M624/2); James W. Silver, *Edmund Pendleton Gaines* (Baton Rouge, 1949), 99.

62. Bender to Jesup, December 19, 1827, in *House Documents*, 20th Cong., 1st Sess., No. 230, p. 7; Lieutenant E. G. W. Butler to ZT, October 29, 1827, Lieutenant P. H. Galt to ZT, April 3, 1828, in WDLB, IV, 178, 226; New Orleans Post Return, May 1828 (M617/843); ZT to Lawson, August 28, 1828, in ZT(LC) ser 2, r 1.

CHAPTER IV

Years on the
Northern Mississippi

IMMEDIATELY UPON transferring command at New Orleans to Major William S. Foster, Taylor boarded a steamer for St. Louis en route to his new command at Fort Snelling in Minnesota. Mrs. Taylor and presumably some of the children accompanied him. During the latter stages of the trip Mrs. Taylor was confined to her cabin with an attack of chills and a fever. The Taylors arrived at the isolated northern post on May 23, 1828.[1]

There were few more imposing stations in the United States than Fort Snelling. A massive bastion thrust up from the steep western bank of the Mississippi River immediately north of the mouth of the Minnesota River. The fort stood atop the bluff where it stretched north and west of the tower to form a large quadrangle. It was well built but too extensive for its normal two- or three-company garrison. The commandant's quarters which the Taylors occupied faced the parade ground. It contained four rooms on the main floor, with kitchens and pantries filling the basement. When over her illness, Mrs. Taylor quickly immersed herself in the domestic duties which she so enjoyed.[2]

The bustle of the 130-to-140-man garrison, the constant flow of young

1. New Orleans & Fort Snelling Post Returns, May 1828 (M617/843, 1193); ZT to Lawson, August 28, 1828, in *Minnesota History*, XXVIII (March 1947), 15–19.

2. Gaines, Report of Inspection . . . 1827, in *ASP:MA*, IV, 122; Marcus L. Hansen, *Old Fort Snelling* (Minneapolis, 1958), 75; ZT to Maunsel White, August 6, 1829, in ZT(LSU).

officers, and the thrill of the garrison's parades must have brightened greatly the lives of the elder Taylor girls, who were now reaching young womanhood. Seventeen-year-old Ann was the belle of the post. Her three younger sisters also attracted the attention of the young gentlemen of the post, who reveled in the presence of four attractive, intelligent, and respectable young ladies. In Ann's case her swain was Assistant Surgeon Robert C. Wood, a Rhode Islander who had joined the army's medical service in 1825. They were married September 20, 1829, when Taylor commanded at Fort Crawford.[3]

The 1st Infantry had been rushed northward in the spring of 1828 because of a fear that the arrival of warm weather would kindle an Indian war. Conditions were ripe. The Winnebagos were agitated by encroachments on their lands south of Prairie du Chien by lead miners and other perceived injustices. Prompt action by Governor Lewis Cass of Michigan Territory and the local military commanders, notably Brevet Brigadier General Henry Atkinson, temporarily quieted matters.[4] Although the hostilities threatened to involve the Fort Snelling garrison, Taylor received no instructions regarding Indians from his supervisors in Washington or Jefferson Barracks during the fourteen months he commanded. Nor, as he complained during the summer of 1828, was the garrison large enough to carry out its normal housekeeping duties, let alone contend with hostile Indians.[5]

In April 1829 Colonel Henry Leavenworth, the acting departmental commander, ordered a company sent to Fort Crawford at Prairie du Chien. The shift was part of the preparations for a great council with one to two thousand Winnebagos, Potawatomis, Ottawas, Chippewas, Sioux, Sacs, Foxes, and Menominees to be held there in July. Taylor followed soon afterwards, transferring command of Fort Snelling to Captain John H. Gale on July 12. He reached Prairie du Chien five days later in the midst of the council but seems to have played only a small role, if any at all. He was present, however, when Brevet Brigadier General John McNeil, Indian Superintendent Caleb Atwater, and Agent Peter Menard signed treaties with the Chippewa, Ottawa, and Potawatomi which transferred eight million acres of land to the United States.[6]

3. Hansen, *Old Fort Snelling*, 59; Evan Jones, *The Citadel in the Wilderness* (New York, 1966), 122; Royce Gordon Shingleton, *John Taylor Wood* (Athens, Ga., 1979), 2,4; Holman Hamilton, *Zachary Taylor* (2 vols.; Indianapolis, 1941, 1951), I, 273; Holman Hamilton, "Zachary Taylor and Minnesota," *Minnesota History*, XXX (June 1949), 97–110.

4. Henry Putney Beers, *The Western Military Frontier, 1815–1846* (Philadelphia, 1935), 73–79; Francis Paul Prucha, *Sword of the Republic* (New York, 1969), 163–67.

5. Lieutenant Osborn Cross to AG, April 1, 1829, in AGLR 1829, T-47 (M567/48); ZT to AG, July 1, 1828, in Allyn K. Ford Collection, r 5, MinnHS.

6. Captain P. H. Galt to ZT, April 29, 1829, in WDLB, IV, 350–51; Caleb Atwater,

Taylor found four companies comprising 183 officers and men on duty when he reached Fort Crawford. He assumed command on July 18, two days after his predecessor Major Stephen W. Kearny departed.[7] When the last of the Indians left on August 10, Taylor put his men to work building a new fort. The original fortification at Prairie du Chien had been built in the flood plain and over the years it had been badly damaged. Prior to Taylor's arrival Major Kearny had selected a new site on a bluff about fifty or sixty feet above the eastern shore of the river and approximately a mile from the old post. In Taylor's eyes the site had several drawbacks, the chief one being that it was a quarter of a mile from the nearest river landing. He worried, in addition, about the availability of water at the site and complained that the fort was located on the edge of the village, "where every other house at least is a whiskey shop." Their inhabitants he viewed as "individuals of the most dissolute habits and character, whose object and business is to debauch the Soldiers, and to which in great measure may be attributed the desertions which are constantly occurring as well as the large number of those who are annually discharged on Surgeon's certificate of disability." Taylor preferred a location on the west bank of the Mississippi, but by the time of his arrival it was too late to shift the site.[8]

When completed the new post was an imposing structure. It was a rectangle whose north and south sides were formed by a stockade of one-foot-square pine logs, sixteen feet high. A pair of single-story stone barracks with elevated basements, each 175 feet long and 35 feet deep and separated by a 26-foot-wide sally port, formed the east and west walls. The structures were expensive to build but in the 1830s were considered the best barracks existing at any post. Inside the quadrangle were the officers' quarters and the storehouses. The latter, 250 feet long and 35 feet deep, marked the northern and southern limits of the parade ground. Each building had a gabled, shingled roof which extended ten feet inside the fort to form the covering for a paved porch. The flagstaff stood in the southeast corner near the powder magazine. A sixty-foot-deep well was opened in the northeast corner. A stone hospital building was erected south of the fort and the commandant's quarters stood north of the post.[9]

Remarks Made on a Tour to Prairie du Chien (Columbus, Ohio, 1831), 69; Bruce E. Mahan, *Old Fort Crawford and the Frontier* (Iowa City, 1926), 145–51.

7. Fort Crawford Post Return, July 1829 (M617/264). Kearny's biographer believes that the two officers were on poor terms. Dwight L. Clarke, *Stephen Watts Kearny: Soldier of the Old West* (Norman, 1961), 41. This appears doubtful, at least from Taylor's side.

8. ZT to Jesup, December 15, 1829, in ZT(LC), ser 2, r 1; to Atkinson, July 3, 1836, in AGLR 1836, T-172 (M567/132).

9. John H. Fonda, "Early Wisconsin," *WSHSC*, V (1868), 242–45; Mahan, *Fort Crawford*, 134, 138–39; Croghan to Macomb, December 9, 1833, in I. G. Reports, IIIa, 130–31 (M625/3).

The stay at Fort Crawford appears to have been especially social for the Taylors. They lived in the first frame house in the village, which had been built in 1826 for Judge James H. Lockwood. It had two stories and was thirty by twenty-five feet with a cellar kitchen and a wing sixteen by twenty-six feet. The ground floor was divided by a hall into a sitting room or parlor and a back bedroom. As he did at other posts, Taylor put down a "hospitable cellar" to fete his visitors. Taylor seldom, if ever, joined them since he did not usually drink any beverage stronger than iced milk. Mrs. Taylor kept busy with her household chores and supervised the two house slaves, Will and Sally. The Taylors frequently entertained Major John Garland, the quartermaster responsible for the actual construction of the post, and his wife as well as Post Surgeon and Mrs. William Beaumont. Beaumont was already involved in his noted experiments with Alexis St. Martin's digestive tract but there is no evidence that they made any impression on Taylor. At least three other socially acceptable women lived in the village, the wives of the American Fur Company's representative Joseph Rolette, Winnebago Indian Agent Joseph M. Street, and Judge Lockwood. Taylor often insisted that visitors to Prairie du Chien or officers joining the post stay at his quarters until their accommodations were ready. In one case, at least, he lent the visitor a horse for the duration of his stay.[10]

Nor was the social or intellectual life of the fort confined to dinner parties. Caleb Atwater describes the post library as containing works on history, geography, mathematics, chemistry, and science along with files of the *National Intelligencer* and the *National Gazette*. Nathan S. Jarvis, who arrived in 1833 as post surgeon, noted that the library subscribed to New York, Philadelphia, Washington, and Boston newspapers.[11] Even if the library was good by frontier post standards, there is some question about how widely it was used. Captain Ethan Allen Hitchcock, whose intellectual arrogance was legendary, denounced the officers of the garrison as knowing little of books and of being careless and uninformed in discussions.[12]

Elizabeth Baird, the wife of a Green Bay lawyer, described a ball held

10. James H. Lockwood, "Early Times and Events in Wisconsin," *WSHSC*, II (1856), 156–57; Atwater, *Remarks Made on a Tour*, 178–79; Jones, *Citadel in the Wilderness*, 124–25; Hamilton, *Taylor*, I, 110, 117, 119; Mahan, *Fort Crawford*, 250; Ella C. Brunson, "Alfred Brunson, Pioneer of Wisconsin Methodism," *Wisconsin Magazine of History*, II (1918–19), 137; [Thomas B. Thorpe], "General Taylor's Residence at Baton Rouge," *Harper's New Monthly Magazine*, IX (1854), 764.

11. Atwater, *Remarks Made on a Tour*, 178–79; Nathan S. Jarvis, "An Army Surgeon's Notes of Frontier Service," *JMSIUS*, XXXIX (1906), 133.

12. Ethan Allen Hitchcock, *Fifty Years in Camp and Field*, ed. W. A. Croffut (New York, 1909), 71.

in her honor at the unfinished fort. Windows, doors, and roof were missing but the floor, she reported, was smooth and a good surface for dancing. "The party," wrote the guest of honor, "was a delightful one." Another visitor recounted the recurring "Gumbo Balls," harlequinades at which the voyageurs, hunters, and the half-breeds of the settlement were included.

Sure to leave a memory on visitors were the theatrical efforts. One traveler described a performance which included the English comedy *Who Wants a Guinea* and Fielding's afterpiece for *Don Quixote in England*, along with the songs and recitations. Another visitor reported attending a performance of *The Poor Gentlemen* in a room of the fort. The scenery had been painted by the soldiers, who fashioned lights by placing lanterns on bayonets. The seats were arranged so that they rose like the pit of an orchestra. The theater was divided into three parts. The first contained officers and their families; the second held soldiers; and the third was left for Indians, Negro servants, and "gumboes."[13]

For sportsmen attached to the garrison the hunting opportunities were plentiful, especially during the duck season. "More are kill'd," wrote one officer, "than are count'd. Ducks are finest I have ever eaten." Grouse, snipe, elk, bear, and wolves in great numbers also awaited hunters.[14]

Taylor's interest in education has been noted earlier. In about 1834 he hired Joseph T. Mills to tutor his children. Mills also taught the other children of the garrison and upon his departure Post Chaplain Richard F. Cadle became the teacher. In 1835 or 1836 Taylor sent his two younger children away to school. Betty journeyed to a Philadelphia boarding school, probably Miss Lyman's, while Dick returned to Kentucky. He later studied in Edinburgh and Paris before returning home to graduate from Yale in 1845.[15] Taylor also strongly supported the efforts of Indian Agent Street to build the school for the Winnebagos which was promised in the Treaty of 1832. Street received authorization to establish a school in the tribal lands west of the Mississippi, but the directive was countermanded in 1833 as a result of pressure from the American Fur Company, which wished to keep the Winnebagos concentrated east of the river. Street per-

13. Mahan, *Fort Crawford*, 245, 247–50, 253; Elizabeth T. Baird, "Reminiscences of Life in Territorial Wisconsin," *WSHSC*, XV (1900), 232–33.

14. Jarvis, "Surgeon's Notes," 132; Mahan, *Fort Crawford*, 250.

15. Clarence Carter and John Porter Bloom (eds.), *The Territorial Papers of the United States* (28 vols.; Washington, 1934–75), XXVII, 696n; Brainerd Dyer, *Zachary Taylor* (Baton Rouge, 1946), 93; Hamilton, *Taylor*, I, 114; Anson Phelps Stokes, *Memorials of Eminent Yale Men* (2 vols.; New Haven, 1914), II, 343; Catherine Clinton, "Equally Their Due: The Education of the Planter Daughter in the Early Republic," *Journal of the Early Republic*, II (1982), 49.

sisted and ultimately built a stone schoolhouse on the Yellow River in Iowa. It taught young Indians reading, writing, arithmetic, gardening, agriculture, spinning, weaving, sewing, and other "useful" subjects.[16]

The proximity of Prairie du Chien was a vexing one for Taylor. Legally the village was an island in the midst of Indian territory which prevented the army from halting liquor sales to either soldiers or Indians. Taylor constantly complained of the drunkenness of the garrison. He wrote Jesup that had the post been placed across the river it would have required "a road up a bluff some 2 or 3 hundred feet high, which I am confident could have been done in less than 12 months, by the labour of one half the men who will be lying in the guard house to sober."[17]

The problems with the garrison loom large in Taylor's correspondence during his early years at Fort Crawford, yet they seem only slightly worse than those faced by most commanders in the era. The quality of recruits attracted to the army prior to the Panic of 1837 was not high. Many were foreign immigrants who had failed to find employment in the civilian economy. The low pay and mediocre food and clothing provided enlisted men, as well as the relatively harsh conditions of service, attracted few native-born Americans, who had greater opportunities either in factories or as farmers in the west. It is not surprising that the desertion rate from the army during the 1820s and 1830s consistently ran high and that recruits were scarce. Few companies, let alone whole regiments, ever reported their authorized strength present at one time.[18] Taylor concluded that the companies even at full strength were too small for service on the frontier. Moreover, he criticized company commanders for employing soldiers as personal servants in their homes or as groundsmen or stockmen. That obviously reduced the number of the available men in each of the regiments. Another very necessary diversion of manpower was farming. In an effort to improve the diet of the men stationed at the isolated forts, the War Department after 1818 required the cultivation of post gardens and encouraged hunting and fishing by the garrisons. In addition, whenever possible, the garrisons were expected to raise their own beef and pork plus the forage for the horses and mules provided the post.[19]

The influx of foreigners often created unforeseen results. Taylor found

16. Mahan, *Fort Crawford*, 201–202.

17. ZT to Jesup, December 15, 1829, in ZT(LC), ser 2, r 1; Francis Paul Prucha, *American Indian Policy in the Formative Years* (Cambridge, 1962), 117–18.

18. See Russell F. Weigley, *History of the United States Army* (New York, 1967), 167–69; C. Joseph Bernardo and Eugene H. Bacon, *American Military Policy* (Harrisburg, 1955), 163–65.

19. ZT to Jesup, December 4, 1832, in Thomas Sidney Jesup Papers, LC; Erna Risch, *Quartermaster Support of the Army* (Washington, 1962), 203–204.

himself in one of those situations at Fort Crawford. He mustered the garrison for a dress parade and on inspection spotted a large, stout German recruit out of line. The German was a willing soldier but understood little English. When ordered to dress the line he did not do so, which Taylor took as a willful disobedience of orders. He stopped in front of the German and applied a normal Taylor punishment, "wooling," in which he grabbed the man by the ears and shook him. The German, who was not used to such treatment, responded by felling his assailant with one blow. Technically, that was mutiny and the officers rushed with drawn swords to seize the man. Taylor got up, brushed off the dust, and ordered, "Let that man alone, he will make a good soldier." He did.[20]

During the spring of 1830, work on the unfinished Fort Crawford was interrupted by the renewed threat of Indian hostilities. In April Taylor learned that a party of Sioux and Menominee had attacked a group of Fox south of Prairie du Chien. He soon received reports that large bodies of Sioux, Winnebagos, and Menominees were preparing further attacks on the Fox. Taylor and Indian Agent Street warned the Indians against hostilities. Moreover, Taylor worried that he had but 150 men available for service, far too few if it became necessary to intervene. Luckily, Street temporarily settled the difficulties, which flared up again later in the summer. A second gathering at Prairie du Chien in July arranged for a forty-mile-wide neutral zone between the tribes in Iowa which reduced the danger.[21]

Concurrent with the unrest among the Indian tribes, there arose a new problem of lead miners transgressing on the Fox lands around Dubuque. The Indian subagent at Galena requested troops from Fort Crawford. Taylor refused because he wanted to husband his command for work on the post and he suspected General Atkinson would dispatch troops from Jefferson Barracks. Colonel Willoughby Morgan, who assumed command of the 1st Infantry on April 23, and Major Kearny from Jefferson Barracks successfully removed the miners without drawing upon Taylor's garrison.[22]

As matters developed Taylor could not have participated in the summer

20. Fonda, "Early Wisconsin," 241.

21. Macomb to ZT, April 4, 1830, HQLS, 2/1, p. 250 (M857/1); ZT to Taliaferro, May 14, 1830, in Laurence Taliaferro Papers, r 5, MinnHS; to Gaines, May 14, 1830, in AGLR 1830, T-76 (M567/56); Mahan, Fort Crawford, 152–54.

22. ZT to Atkinson, June 17, Atkinson, Proclamation, June 21, Atkinson to Morgan, June 22, 1830, all in WDLR, Box 1; Francis B. Heitman, Historical Register and Dictionary of the United States Army (2 vols.; Washington, 1903), I, 726; Prucha, American Indian Policy, 181.

efforts to remove the miners. During the spring he had requested a seven-months furlough, but its approval was delayed by a shift of Western Department commanders. Taylor intended that the furlough start in November to permit him to attend to his personal financial problems in Louisiana. But Mrs. Taylor, who was in Louisville, fell ill. Colonel Morgan promptly granted Taylor a sixty-day leave with permission to apply for a furlough at its expiration. Taylor departed Fort Crawford on July 3, and the furlough was approved by Winfield Scott when he took command of the department.[23]

Taylor, who had served for ten years as a lieutenant colonel, waited impatiently for the award of a brevet commission as colonel, as provided for in army regulations. He vented his frustration in letters to a pair of senators and the adjutant general. He muttered to General Jones that he ought to "throw aside his brevet commission as not worth having." To the senators he complained of the delay of two years in the Senate's action on brevet commissions and noted that every line colonel except the recently appointed Willoughby Morgan was a brevet brigadier general. Moreover, James B. Many, whose date of rank was subsequent to his, had already received his brevet colonelcy. Taylor appears to have been particularly irked by the granting of a brevet to Colonel Charles Gratiot for meritorious service after less than a year as chief of engineers. Taylor argued that the provision of the 1818 law which permitted officers on duty in their brevet rank to draw the pay and emoluments of that rank had been manipulated through favoritism and intrigue to the detriment of those serving in their lineal rank. He suggested that brevet promotions for ten years in grade be halted once they had been granted to all officers currently entitled to them.[24]

Taylor's leave expired March 3, 1831, but General Gaines ordered him to head a court martial sitting at Baton Rouge later in the month. When that duty was finished Taylor returned to Louisville to prepare to return to the upper Mississippi, only to receive orders on July 11 to return to Louisiana. Why he was sent there is not clear; Taylor insisted that he did not seek the assignment. On August 8 he assumed command of the post at

23. Lieutenant E. G. W. Butler to ZT, June 8, 1830, in WDLB, V, 88; ZT to AAAG Western Department, July 7, 1830, in ZT(LC), ser 2, r 1; Fort Crawford Post Return, August 1830 (M617/264); Winfield Scott, Memoirs of Lieut.-General Scott, LL.D. (2 vols., 1864; rpr. Freeport, N.Y., 1970), II, 391.

24. ZT to AG, September 6, 1830, in AGRL, VI, 414 (M711/7); to Senator George Poindexter, December 26, 1829, ZT(LC), ser 2, r 1; to Senator J. S. Johnston, December 24, 1831, Johnston Collection, HSPa; Dyer, Taylor, 73–74; Hamilton, Taylor, I, 82. The Poindexter letter is misdated; he was not appointed senator until 1830. Taylor's brevet commission as colonel was dated April 29, 1829, but apparently was not issued until 1836.

New Orleans. Shortly afterwards he requested a temporary exchange of stations with Lieutenant Colonel David E. Twiggs of the 4th Infantry. That was an obvious effort to prolong the stay in Louisiana at a difficult personal moment. Nevertheless, the War Department responded negatively and Adjutant General Jones ordered him back to Fort Crawford.[25]

Taylor interpreted the directive to return north as a censure and complained to Jones. The adjutant general denied any such intent and pointed out that Fort Snelling, still Taylor's nominal post, was the second most important station for his regiment. Scarcely mollified, if at all, by the sophistry of the War Department, Taylor did not hasten to comply. He continued to exercise command in New Orleans until October 25 and did not even acknowledge the orders to return to Fort Snelling until November 9. Moreover, he informed the Washington bureaucrats he could not proceed there until the ice left the river in the spring. Meanwhile, he asked General Gaines for a furlough.[26]

During Taylor's absence Indian troubles continued to brew along the northern Mississippi River. During the spring of 1831 Black Hawk, an old Sac warrior who refused to recognize the tribe's sale of its lands in Illinois, led about three hundred others of the disaffected "British band" back to the alienated lands. In June General Gaines, with troops from Jefferson Barracks, Fort Crawford, and Fort Winnebago plus 1,600 militia, forced Black Hawk to agree to stay west of the Mississippi.[27]

In anticipation of further trouble in 1832, General Atkinson shifted part of the 6th Infantry from Fort Leavenworth to Jefferson Barracks. He held them there rather than sending them north. Taylor later criticized the decision, arguing that: "Had the garrison of Fort Armstrong [Rock Island] been re-inforced as [it] could, & ought to have been, with three or four companies from Jefferson Barracks the moment the Mississippi was clear of ice, which was the last of March, there would have been no indian war."[28]

Stirred by fears of intertribal hostilities growing out of the murder of some Menominees by the Sac and the Fox, the Washington authorities

25. Western Department Order 2, 45, January 16, July 11, 1831, in General Henry Atkinson, Order Book 1830–32, Army Continental Commands (NA, RG 393); New Orleans Post Returns, August 1831 (M617/843); ZT to Jesup, July 4, December 4, 1831, in ZT(LC), ser 2, r 1; Jones to ZT, October 5, 19, 1831, in AGLS, IX, 331, 336 (M565/8); Dyer, *Taylor*, 74–75.

26. AG to ZT, November 19, 1831, in AGLS, IX, 355; ZT to AG, November 9, 1831, in AGRL, VII, T-108, (M711/7); Lieutenant G. A. McCall to ZT, November 27, 1831, in WDLB, VI, 10.

27. James W. Silver, *Edmund Pendleton Gaines* (Baton Rouge, 1949), 142–45; Mahan, *Fort Crawford*, 158–9; *House Documents*, 22nd Cong., 1st Sess., No. 2, pp. 180–89.

28. ZT to Jesup, December 4, 1832, in ZT(LC), ser 2, r 1.

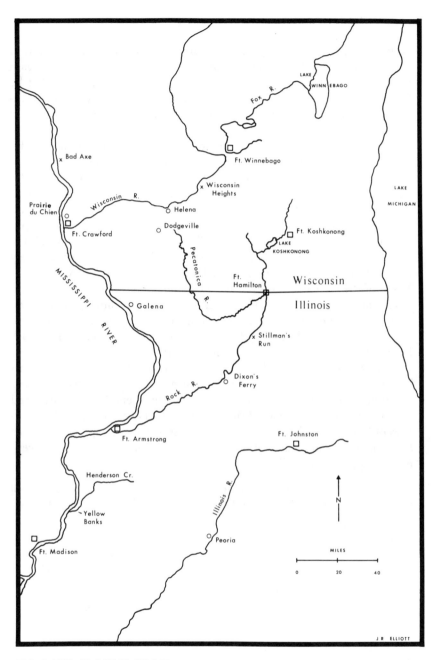

BLACK HAWK WAR

authorized the use of troops, if necessary, to maintain peace.[29] Atkinson responded in April by leading six companies of the 6th Infantry upstream to the trouble spot. On reaching Fort Armstrong he discovered that he faced an even greater problem. Black Hawk, with about four hundred Indians, mostly women and children but including the murderers, had again crossed the Mississippi.[30]

On the thirteenth Atkinson warned Governor John Reynolds but did not ask for assistance. Reynolds, nevertheless, directed the 1,700 militia from the northwestern part of the state to assemble at Beardstown under Brigadier General Samuel Whiteside. He had been one of Taylor's lieutenants at Credit Island. While the militia assembled, Black Hawk's band peacefully moved up the Rock River Valley toward the Winnebago Prophet's village (modern Prophetstown, Illinois). The whites, however, were not certain what would follow. Atkinson thought hostilities were unlikely unless efforts were made to force the Indians back across the Mississippi. Many of the civilians, however, were convinced that Black Hawk's band would attack the frontier once their women and children were safe. Therefore, to be ready for any development, Atkinson requested 3,000 mounted Illinois militia join the regulars at Dixon's Ferry on the Rock River. He later shifted the rendezvous to Fort Atkinson.[31]

Atkinson made a last-ditch effort to convince the Indians to return home. It failed, and Black Hawk's emissary reported: "His heart is bad and if you send your officers to him, he will fight them." Taylor disagreed with the strategy. He believed that Atkinson had overestimated the numbers of Black Hawk's warriors and underestimated the capabilities of his own forces. An immediate pursuit, Taylor concluded, would have "very much crippled" the Indians.[32]

29. Macomb to Atkinson, March 17, 1832, in HQLS, 4/2, pp. 49–51. See also McCall to commanders of Forts Snelling, Crawford, and Armstrong, March 14, 1832, in WDLB, VI, 80.

30. William T. Hagan, "General Henry Atkinson and the Militia," *Military Affairs*, XXIII (1959/60), 194, and *The Sac and Fox Indians* (Norman, 1958), 142–44; Michael Paul Rogin, *Fathers and Children* (New York, 1975), 235; Henry Smith, "Indian Campaign of 1832," *WSHSC*, X (1888), 153–54; Hamilton, *Taylor*, I, 84; Roger L. Nichols (ed.), "The Black Hawk War: Another View," *Annals of Iowa*, XXXVI (1961–63), 527–30; Frank E. Stevens, *The Black Hawk War* (Chicago, 1903), 110–11.

31. Atkinson to Macomb, April 18, May 25, 1832, in AGLR 1832, A-64, 82 (M567/66); R. Carlyle Buley, *The Old Northwest* (2 vols.; Bloomington, Ind., 1962), II, 67–68; Hagan, *Sac and Fox*, 148; Hagan, "Atkinson & Militia," 194; Stevens, *Black Hawk War*, 113.

32. Atkinson to Black Hawk, et al., April 24, Gratiot to Atkinson, April 27, 1832, in AGLR 1832, A-82 (M567/66); Hagan, *Sac and Fox*, 153–56; Roger L. Nichols, *General Henry Atkinson* (Norman, 1965), 160–61; Gratiot's Journal in Milo M. Quaife (ed.), "Journals and Reports of the Black Hawk War," *MVHR*, XII (1925), 398; Buley, *Old Northwest*, II, 68; ZT to Jesup, December 4, 1832, in ZT(LC), ser 2, r 1; Stevens, *Black*

The cause of Black Hawk's return to the east side of the Mississippi so soon after his agreement with Gaines is not entirely clear. On a broad perspective it was in part a refusal to accept the devouring of traditional Indian lands by the insatiable land hunger of the whites. As such Black Hawk's reaction was in direct variance to that of the great Sac chief Keokuk and most of the tribe. In 1832 Black Hawk was 65 years old. He had long been pro-British. During the War of 1812 as one of Dickson's recruits he had participated in the Battle of the Thames as well as the Campbell's Island clash. In 1832 he was misled by his advisors into believing that other tribes were ready to join in a drive against the whites and that the British would send aid.[33] Ma-Ka-Tai-She-Kia-Kiak, or Black Hawk as history normally calls him, was a striking figure with his Roman nose, full mouth, sharp chin, and piercing eyes. Although only 5 feet 4 or 5 feet 5 inches tall, his spare frame and his presence made him appear to stand much taller, as did his practice of wearing only a small tuft of gray hair at the crown of his head.[34]

Taylor, who had become the colonel of the 1st Infantry on April 4 following the death of Colonel Morgan, learned of the situation on his arrival at Galena, Illinois, during his belated return to the northern frontier. He left his family there and hastened northward to assume command of the regiment. He formally did so at Fort Armstrong on May 7, 1832. His new rank brought Taylor an increase in pay to seventy-five dollars per month and allowances which included six rations, two servants for whom he was allowed five dollars per month, and twelve dollars per month for forage. It represented a 25 percent increase in salary and a slight addition to the allowances which he drew as a lieutenant colonel.[35]

On May 8 Atkinson organized his army for the coming campaign, giving command of the regular troops, six companies of the 6th Infantry and four of the 1st Infantry, to Taylor. On the ninth Atkinson directed Whiteside to lead his three regiments of militia to Black Hawk's encampment by way of the Winnebago Prophet's village. "Should Genl. Whiteside," read the order, "however on reaching the Prophets village be of the opinion that it would be prudent to come up with the enemy with as little delay as

Hawk War, 114–15; Donald Jackson (ed.), Ma-Ka-Tai-Ma-She-Kiakiak—Black Hawk: An Autobiography (Urbana, 1955), 138–39.

33. Rogan, Fathers and Children, 234–35; Stevens, Black Hawk War, 17; Mahan, Fort Crawford, 162–65.

34. Reuben Gold Thwaites, "The Story of the Black Hawk War," WSHSC, XII (1892), 220–21; Niles' Weekly Register, LXIII (1832–33), 79.

35. Heitman, Historical Register, I, 81, 949; 1st Infantry Return, May 1832 (M665/1); ZT to Lawson, August 16, 1832, Miscellaneous Papers, NYHS; Thomas M. Exley, A Compendium of the Pay of the Army from 1785 to 1888 (Washington, 1888), 49.

possible he will move upon him, and make him surrender at discretion or coerce him to submission." Governor Reynolds accompanied the militia. Meanwhile Taylor's regulars would move upstream in boats and meet the militia at Dixon's Ferry. Atkinson accompanied the waterborne party; this was a mistake, since it deprived him of effective control of the militia.[36]

While Whiteside and his 1,300 undisciplined horsemen rode up the south bank of the Rock River, Taylor with about 300 regulars, 400 Illinois footsoldiers, and the supplies embarked in a keelboat and five or six Mackinaw boats. En route Whiteside and Reynolds encountered Majors Isaiah Stillman and David Bailey with a mounted battalion of 341 men, which was not included in the contingent mustered into federal service. Reynolds, over Whiteside's objections, directed Stillman to "coerce" Black Hawk's band, then at the mouth of Old Man's Creek, to surrender. The combined Illinois forces marched into Dixon's Ferry on the twelfth. The following day Stillman's force departed on its mission.[37]

By now Black Hawk had concluded that he had been deceived and that few Indians would rally to his cause. Moreover, the overwhelming strength of the white troops in the field made the safety of his little band, encumbered with large numbers of women and children, doubtful. He decided to surrender if the opportunity appeared. On May 14, while the Indians were camped on Sycamore Creek, the approach of Stillman's horsemen offered that chance. Black Hawk dispatched three braves with a white flag to the American camp to discuss arrangements for the band's return to Iowa. The Indians had great difficulties making themselves understood; the Illinoisans had no Sac interpreters and the presence of the redmen within their camp excited the militia. Then the five Indian observers, placed in the nearby hills by Black Hawk to watch over the treatment of the emissaries, were spotted by some of the sharper-eyed militia. Groups of Americans rushed the Indians and killed two. In the confusion within the militia camp one of the flag bearers was also killed.

Most of the surviving Indians fled back to Black Hawk's camp and forty or fifty of them hastily prepared an ambush. When the undisciplined and disorganized militia entered the trap, possibly one man fell to Indian fire and the remainder fled. Another eleven men died in futile efforts to cover the flight. The militia fled through their camp and onto Dixon's Ferry, twenty-five miles away. Some continued their flight all the

36. Right Wing, Western Department, Order 8, 9, 12, & 13, May 8–9, 1832, in 6MD:OB, I, 7–9; Atkinson to Reynolds, Reynolds to Atkinson, May 8, 1832, in AGLR 1832, A-82 (M567/66); Stevens, Black Hawk War, 126.

37. Smith, "Indian Campaign," 156; Right Wing, Western Department, Order 12, 13, May 9, 1832, in 6MD:OB, I, 9; Nichols, Atkinson, 162; Atkinson to Macomb, May 19, 1832, in AGLR 1832, A-82 (M567/66); Mahan, Fort Crawford, 169.

way home. Nearly all reported, on reaching the safety of Dixon's that they were the sole survivor of the force which had been attacked by as many as 800 Indians. Not surprisingly, the clash has gone down in history as "Stillman's Run." Taylor, upon learning the details, pronounced the flight "the most shameful . . . that ever troops were known to do."[38]

Governor Reynolds responded to the disaster by calling out an additional 2,000 mounted volunteers. More significant, however, was the arrival at Dixon's on May 17 of the waterborne force. Two days later Atkinson led Whiteside's men and the regulars up the Rock River after the Indians. Black Hawk, meanwhile, moved along the Kishwaukee River in hopes of reaching the Mississippi in southern Wisconsin. Atkinson's pursuit failed to locate the fleeing band, so on May 26 he released the militia.[39]

Taylor's reaction to the march of the militia was exceedingly negative. "The more I see of the militia," he wrote Atkinson, "the less confidence I have in their effecting anything of importance; and therefore tremble not only for the safety of the frontiers, but for the reputations of those who command them."[40] It is another indication of the intense distrust of the militia which would characterize his relations with them throughout his career.

Atkinson joined the 300 men whom Reynolds had induced to continue in service at Fort Johnston (Ottawa) on May 29. He ordered Taylor to erect a post at Dixon's Ferry which would be used as a rendezvous for the volunteers and regulars who would patrol the threatened region. While Taylor and the regulars at Dixon's pushed construction of the fort and

38. Stevens, *Black Hawk War*, 132–38; Thwaites, "Black Hawk War," 236–38; Nichols, *Atkinson*, 163; Buley, *Old Northwest*, II, 69–70; Perry A. Armstrong, *The Saulks and the Black Hawk War* (Springfield, Ill., 1887), 330; Hagan, *Sac and Fox*, 158–60; Mahan, *Fort Crawford*, 169–70; Jackson (ed.), *Ma-Ka-Tai-Me-She-Kiakiak*, 141–45. The quotation is from ZT to Lawson, August 16, 1832, in Miscellaneous Papers, NYHS.

39. Atkinson to Macomb, May 19, 25, ZT to Atkinson, May 26, Reynolds to Atkinson, May 26, 1832, in AGLR 1832, A-82, 83 (M567/66); Right Wing, Western Department, Order 17, Special Order 11, May 18, 22, 1832, in 6MD:OB, I, 10, 13–14; Buley, *Old Northwest*, II, 71–72; Hagan, "Atkinson & Militia," 195; Nichols, *Atkinson*, 164–65; Stevens, *Black Hawk War*, 161. Taylor served temporarily as inspector general of the militia force in the vain hope that he could instill some discipline.

40. ZT to Atkinson, June 2, 1832, in AGLR 1832, A-104 (M567/66). There is a tradition of a confrontation at an undefined point in the campaign in which Taylor told recalcitrant militiamen that many of them might become congressmen "and thus arbiters of the fortunes of humble servants of the republic like myself." If so, "I expect to obey you" as I now "obey those who are in present authority." They had ordered him to follow Black Hawk and to "take you with me as soldiers." He pointed to flatboats drawn up on the bank and the regulars on the prairie behind the civilian soldiers. They embarked. Charles J. Peterson, *The Military Heroes of the War with Mexico* (Philadelphia, 1856), 144.

continued the fruitless search for the elusive Black Hawk, Atkinson organized a new army. He formed the militia into three brigades and sent them to Dixon's in late June. The lead element, a spy battalion under Major John Dement, arrived on the twenty-second. They were exhausted from a tiring march and rebelled when Taylor immediately ordered them to Galena in order to prevent a threatened siege. Taylor exploded: "You are citizen-soldiers and some of you may fill high offices, or even be president some day, but never unless you do your duty. Forward! March!" Dement, who better understood his men, responded: "Sir, your allusions are . . . entirely uncalled for from a man who . . . would entrench himself behind walls and send to the front men who have never seen service." Then, turning to his men, the militiaman said, "You need not obey his orders. Obey mine and follow me." They did and performed exemplarily in keeping the road to Galena open. Although Taylor's reaction is not recorded, he seems to have kept his temper in check.[41]

Atkinson and the main body of troops reached Dixon's during the morning of June 25. After ordering Brigadier General Milton K. Armstrong's brigade to the Plum River in order to prevent the Indians from crossing the Mississippi, Atkinson led the regulars and Brigadier General James P. Henry's brigade up the Rock River. On June 30 Atkinson's force crossed the Wisconsin River near present-day Beloit, Wisconsin, and by July 2 had reached the Koshkonong region where Black Hawk had been camping. There the Americans awaited the return of Alexander's brigade from its fruitless trip up the Mississippi.

The Illinois militiamen, like so many of their predecessors, found campaigning distasteful. No longer was it an afternoon's frolic but a succession of tiring marches, often through mosquito and black fly infested swamps while eating inadequate, scarcely digestible, and poorly prepared food. They began to drift home and by mid-July only about half of them remained to answer the roll call. Even the depleted force was more than Atkinson needed. "I have," he wrote Winfield Scott, "too many militia in the field to get along without great difficulty." His concern was primarily over the quantity of supplies consumed by such a large force. The logistic problems soon forced Atkinson to send two of his brigades to Fort Winnebago for supplies.[42]

On July 19 General Henry's brigade and a detachment of Michigan

41. Hamilton, *Taylor*, I, 91–93; Atkinson to Reynolds, May 29, to ZT, June 7, 11, 1832, in AGLR 1821, A-104 (M567/66); Buley, *Old Northwest*, II, 72; Stevens, *Black Hawk War*, 197–98.

42. Atkinson to ZT, June 22, to Scott, July 15, 1832, in AGLR 1832, A-104 (M567/66); Hamilton, *Taylor*, I, 94; Right Wing, Western Department, Order 28, 44, June 26, July 5, 1832, in 6MD:OB, I, 27, 29; Buley, *Old Northwest*, II, 72–73.

mounted men under Colonel Henry Dodge struck out toward the Wisconsin River. Luck visited them and on the nineteenth day they hit Black Hawk's trail. Two days later they found the Indians along the banks of the Wisconsin. The resulting Battle of Wisconsin Heights was a brilliantly conducted rear guard stand by about fifty braves. During the night following the battle Black Hawk's lieutenant Neapope made an impassioned call for quarter, but unfortunately he delivered it in Winnebago, which none of the whites understood. The Americans thought he was haranguing the Sacs to resume the fight![43]

On July 26 Atkinson ordered Taylor's regulars, along with 950 Illinois mounted men and Dodge's horsemen, to follow the retreating Indians. The 1,300-man force crossed the "Ouisconsin" during July 27–28. Black Hawk, meanwhile, retreated westward across the Kickapoo Hills in a desperate effort to reach the Mississippi River. On Wednesday, August 1, his bedraggled and travel-worn band arrived on the banks of the great river near the mouth of a small stream called the Bad Axe, about forty miles upstream from Fort Crawford. The Indians did not have enough canoes to take the whole party across so they built a raft. It capsized and many of the passengers drowned. Before another effort could be made to cross the broad expanse of water, the smoke of an oncoming steamer appeared. She was the hundred-ton side-wheeler *Warrior* under charter to the army.

When the steamer came within hailing distance, Black Hawk hoisted a white flag and asked to surrender. The steamer's captain, John Throckmorton, thought it was an ambush and demanded that Black Hawk come on board. Lacking a canoe, the Indian could not. Whereupon Throckmorton had the troops on board open fire from their six-pounder field gun. It roared three times, that being all the canister shells on hand, but the effect was devastating. Twenty-three Indians lay dead. Throckmorton kept his vessel just off the Indian crossing as long as his fuel supply lasted, and the soldiers on board released a drumfire of musketry. When the stock of fire wood dropped below the safe margin, the steamer headed downstream to Prairie du Chien to resupply.

When Atkinson and the American column approached during the following morning Black Hawk attempted to decoy them into an attack on the empty Indian encampment while the bulk of his men escaped. It nearly worked. Atkinson was deceived and led the regulars and two-thirds of the volunteers in an attack on the camp. General Henry, left to protect the American baggage with his brigade, once again proved his

43. Buley, *Old Northwest*, II, 74–75; Hagan, *Sac and Fox*, 177–80; Jackson (ed.), *Ma-Ka-Tai-Me-She-Kiakiak*, 155–56; Stevens, *Black Hawk War*, 217–20; Mahan, *Fort Crawford*, 173.

luck. His scouts detected the main group and he led 300 men in an attack which drove the Indians into the river. It was a difficult fight. The braves fought desperately, but they were weak from the long flight and outnumbered. After three hours it turned into a massacre.

Taylor reached the scene very late in the fight and played only a minor role. The *Warrior* arrived at the Bad Axe just in time to ferry Taylor and a detachment of regulars to some islands in the Mississippi to which some of the Indians had fled. Taylor's force cleared the islands and returned to the Wisconsin side. In all, about 150 Indians died in the Battle of the Bad Axe; 300 escaped, and an additional 50 surrendered to Atkinson's men. The whites lost 24 men killed and wounded.[44]

The Americans did not tarry at the battlefield any longer than necessary. They collected their dead and wounded and disposed of the bodies of the Indians before boarding the *Warrior* for the short trip to Fort Crawford. Taylor disembarked there on August 4 to find his wife and daughter Knox impatiently awaiting him. In part their warm welcome reflected the less than cordial one they had received from the post quartermaster, who had refused to allow them to occupy the post commander's quarters since Taylor had not yet announced his resumption of command. He did so on the following day and life gradually settled back into the routine of a somnolent frontier post. During the remainder of the summer Taylor employed his troops in pushing the construction of the post. By fall the troops and supplies could be moved there and the old post abandoned.[45]

Various administrative details had to be settled before the Black Hawk War could be declared at an end. On August 6 Atkinson ordered the discharge of the volunteers, thanking them with more than a touch of irony for their "subordinate and general good conduct." Three days later Winfield Scott arrived to assume command but left for Fort Armstrong on the tenth in company with Atkinson and the bulk of the regulars.[46]

Black Hawk was seized on August 25 by a pair of Winnebagos who delivered him to Indian Agent Street. When he learned of the capture,

44. 1st Army Corps Orders, July 26, August 5, 1832, in 6MD:OB, I, 38–40; Hamilton, *Taylor*, I, 96–97; Thwaites, "Black Hawk War," 257–60; Hagan, *Sac and Fox*, 187–91; Fonda, "Early Wisconsin," 261–63; Smith, "Indian Campaign," 163–64; Charles Bracken, "Further Strictures on Ford's Black Hawk War," *WSHSC*, II (1856), 414; Stevens, *Black Hawk War*, 221–24; Jackson (ed.), *Ma-Ka-Tai-Me-She-Kiakiak*, 158–62.

45. Hamilton, *Taylor*, I, 110; Mahan, *Fort Crawford*, 136; Fort Crawford Post Return, August 1832 (M617/264).

46. 1st Army Corps Order 69, August 6, 1832, in 6MD:OB, I, 42–43; Hamilton, *Taylor*, I, 97–98; Dyer, *Taylor*, 83; Scott had been sent from the east with about 1,000 troops but had been delayed at Chicago by a cholera epidemic which nearly wiped out his force.

Scott sent Lieutenant Robert Anderson to fetch the Sac and other Indian prisoners at Fort Crawford. During the trip upstream on the *Warrior* from Fort Armstrong, cholera broke out among the guards and Anderson himself was so weakened by illness that Taylor assigned his adjutant, Lieutenant Jefferson Davis, to accompany the party. It was an interesting convergence of the man whose defense of Fort Sumter would spark the Civil War and the leader of those trying to divide the nation. The two young lieutenants and their handful of guards shepherded Black Hawk, his two sons, the Winnebago Prophet, and thirty others on board the steamer *Winnebago* on September 3. Because of cholera at Fort Armstrong, Scott ordered the prisoners taken to Jefferson Barracks.[47]

The Sac and Fox had until June 1, 1833, to leave the mineral lands around Dubuque, but squatters began to drift over from Galena in September 1832. The Indian agent at Rock Island got most of the miners to return east of the Mississippi, but a group soon returned. The agent appealed for help and on September 3 Atkinson ordered Taylor to provide assistance. He waited until the river froze and in early February 1833 dispatched Lieutenant John R. B. Gardenier to warn the miners to leave. Lieutenant George Wilson followed with a small detachment. When it became apparent that the force was inadequate, Taylor ordered Lieutenant John J. Abercrombie and Jefferson Davis there with an additional thirty men. Davis, who knew many of the miners from his service around Galena during the Black Hawk War, talked them into departing. Nevertheless, Taylor kept troops in the region until the Indians vanished.[48] The following year Taylor was not so prompt. He used the appearance of cholera among the garrison and the limited number of men available as an excuse to ignore orders to interpose a force between the Sioux and Chippewa in northern Wisconsin.[49]

47. Davis and Anderson, Receipt, September 3, 1832, and Anderson, Muster Roll Book, in Haskell Monroe, *et al.* (eds.), *The Papers of Jefferson Davis* (4 vols.; Baton Rouge, 1971–), I, 252, 254–55; Robert Anderson, "Reminiscences of the Black Hawk War," *WSHSC*, X (1888), 172; Anderson to E. B. Washburne, May 10, 1870, in Armstrong, *Saulks and Black Hawk War*, 372–76; Street to F. P. Blair, September 3, 1832, in *Niles' Weekly Register*, XLIII (1832–33), 78–79; Buley, *Old Northwest*, II, 78; Prucha, *Sword of the Republic*, 230; Hudson Strode, *Jefferson Davis* (New York, 1955), 74–75.

48. ZT to AAAG Right Wing, Western Department, March 25, 1833, in AGLR 1833, A-60 (M567/78); Mahan, *Fort Crawford*, 198–200; Nichols, *Atkinson*, 177; Milo M. Quaife, "The Northwestern Career of Jefferson Davis," *Journal of the Illinois State Historical Society*, XVI (1923/24), 10. The removals involved Taylor in a lawsuit over his authority to remove the trespassers. ZT to Jesup, July 15, 1834, in UM:C.

49. Atkinson to ZT, May 30, June 9, July 7, ZT to Lieutenant A. S. Johnston, June 27, 1833, in AGLR 1833, A-119, 125 (M567/78); ZT to Johnston, June 23, 1833, in War Department Papers, MinnHS; Dyer, *Taylor*, 84.

The protection of Indian lands was not the only topic riling Taylor's mind. Captain Hitchcock reported that Taylor in 1834 had become violently anti-Jacksonian but did not explain what caused the shift. Although the factors were undoubtedly complex, it is difficult to avoid the supposition that the precipitating factor was Jackson's assault on the Bank of the United States and the danger that it presented to the conservative banking practices which Taylor believed in. During one of their discussions Taylor read Hitchcock a three-page "little note" to a congressman on his perennial concern, brevet rank. Hitchcock condescendingly noted that Taylor did not realize that it was too long and extremely parochial in outlook.[50] The John J. Crittenden Papers at the Library of Congress contain a copy of an undated fifty-two-page letter to Representative Abijah Mann, Jr., supporting efforts to abolish the office of general-in-chief and to equalize pay of army and navy officers. In it Taylor also reiterated his theme of the misuse of brevet ranks.[51] Nor did he remain entirely aloof from the political squabbles within the service, although he ignored them as much as possible. In 1834 he complained about a rumored exchange of posts between the 1st and 7th infantry regiments because it would place Colonel Arbuckle under the command of his junior, Brevet Brigadier General Henry Leavenworth.[52]

Even when he concerned himself with the kinds of intellectual minutiae which delighted Hitchcock and consumed so much time and energy of his contemporaries in the service, Taylor did not forget his prime responsibility to keep his men well trained. After his 1834 visit to Fort Crawford, Inspector General George Croghan reported the garrison to be the best-trained command he had seen that year and described the discipline as "exact."[53]

The issue of traders rights, especially the policing of their importation of alcohol into Indian lands, haunted most frontier commanders. Nearly all fur traders included alcohol among their trade goods although its sale to Indians was prohibited. The American Fur Company, and most of its American competitors, insisted that alcohol was a necessary trade item for them since the British traders with whom they competed offered it.[54]

Congress on July 9, 1832, explicitly prohibited the entry of liquor into Indian Territory. That month one of Taylor's subordinates, Captain Wil-

50. Ethan Allen Hitchcock, Memoirs, 69–73, in W. A. Croffut Papers, IV, LC; Hitchcock, Fifty Years in Camp and Field.

51. ZT to Mann, [1836?], in John J. Crittenden Papers, V, 872–887, LC.

52. ZT to Jones, May 7, 1834, in ZT(UKL).

53. Croghan to Macomb, November 15, 1834, in I. G. Reports, III (M624/3).

54. The problem of alcohol as trade goods is discussed at length in Hiram M. Chittenden, The American Fur Trade of the Far West (2 vols., 1902; rpr. Stanford, 1954), I, 22–31.

liam R. Jouett at Fort Snelling, instituted tight checks on the boats passing his post. He warned the local agent of the American Fur Company of the new policy and subsequently searched a pair of Mackinaw boats. One belonged to the company, the other to its agent Joseph Renville. The army investigators found sixteen kegs of alcohol and "high wines" on board, which they confiscated.

The company and Renville sued Jouett, who spent much time and $642.37 of his own money defending against the suit. He won but did not receive reimbursement by the government until 1835. During the lengthy correspondence between Jouett and Washington, Taylor complained about the War Department's failure to support its officers in the field when they clashed with local interests. Officers involved in upholding the law, he noted, were harassed by local sheriffs and forced to defend themselves in distant courts. This was one of the liabilities of frontier service which caused many officers, Taylor among them, to consider returning to civilian life. The Indian agent at Prairie du Chien complained: "If something more effectual is not done to protect the officers of the Government against the *cupidity of the Traders*, they will be reduced to the *alternative* of deciding between pecuniary ruin, on one hand, and disobedience of orders on the other."[55] Moreover, the detachment of their subordinates on instructions from the Washington authorities often left the frontier posts so short of officers that none could be sent to enforce the prohibition.[56]

On July 22, 1834, Taylor acquired additional duties as Indian agent for Prairie du Chien when Street was ordered to Rock Island. The shift was probably engineered by the American Fur Company. This made Taylor responsible for the Winnebagos and part of the Sioux. He disliked the job. It added responsibilities to those which he already had as post and regimental commander but brought no additional salary. To add to his frustrations, the Office of Indian Affairs ignored virtually all of his recommendations. As his experience with the office developed, he became increasingly testy in his dealings with the administrators in Washington. During the summer of 1836 he responded with a particularly heated letter to a long request for information on the Indians in his charge. He refused, he wrote, to provide the information or to undertake other tasks which interfered with his military duties.[57]

Taylor was particularly incensed by the activities of the American Fur

55. *Ibid.*, I, 345, 355; Prucha, *Sword of the Republic*, 203–204; Prucha, *American Indian Policy*, 130–32; *ASP:MA*, V, 506–11; Street to Cass, December 5, 1832, in Carter and Bloom (eds.), *Territorial Papers*, VIII, 551. Cass to ZT, November 6, 1834, in *ibid.*, 815, agreed to defend officers against suits growing out of official duties.

56. For example see ZT to AG, May 20, 1834, in AGLR 1834, T-93 (M567/101).

57. Dyer, *Taylor*, 92–94; Commissioner Elbert Herring to ZT, July 22, 1834, in Office

Company and its chief agent in Prairie du Chien, Joseph Rolette. Operating through agents at Prairie du Chien and Fort Snelling, Rolette and the American Fur Company controlled the fur pelt traffic in the upper Mississippi valley during the 1830s and 1840s. Rolette, naturally, feared the agrarian resettlement program which the commissioners of Indian affairs in Washington pushed during that period. This caused him to oppose the establishment of the Winnebago school and all other institutions and regulations which he saw as seducing the natives away from trapping. The difficulties he faced in forcing the company to obey the Indian trade regulations caused Taylor to grumble: "Take the American Fur Company in the aggregate and they are the greatest scoundrels the world ever knew." The army officer believed that Rolette was behind the orders for the transfer of Street and he was concerned that if he acted against the company he would be attacked with little opportunity to defend himself. In July 1835 he wrote that the Winnebagos would live in peace with their neighbors were they not being stirred up by the company.[58]

In September 1836 Taylor complained to the commissioner of Indian affairs of the arduousness of his duties as agent, while at the same time suggesting that the agents at both Rock Island and Fort Snelling could divide his responsibilities between them.[59] Nevertheless, he considered Prairie du Chien to be the best location for an agent on the upper Mississippi. Indians could visit there without passing white settlements and the Winnebagos passed by when going from one portion of their lands to another. It was, in addition, a convenient point for the Sioux to visit.[60]

Taylor had a respite from his duties as commander and agent during the fall of 1834. He took leave from August 12 to December 11. Apparently, he spent the time in Kentucky or Louisiana, although the evidence is unclear. Locating schools for both Betty and Dick absorbed a considerable period of time.[61]

While Taylor was on leave a Sac and Fox band murdered ten Winnebago braves and several women and children near Prairie du Chien. The patrols sent out from Fort Crawford failed to intercept the culprits, but Agent Sweet succeeded in quieting matters. In May 1835 Taylor and Street convinced the Sac and Fox and the Winnebagos and the Menominees to sign a peace treaty and cease harassing each other.[62]

---

of Indian Affairs (NA, RG 75), Letter Book, XIII, 238–40 (M21/13); Mahan, *Fort Crawford*, 208.

58. Mahan, *Fort Crawford*, 62, 73, 191; Hamilton, *Taylor*, I, 115; ZT to Superintendent William Clark, July 2, 1835, in OIA:LR (M234/697).

59. ZT to Harris, September 4, 1836, in OIA:LR (M234/697); Hamilton, *Taylor*, I, 115.

60. Mahan, *Fort Crawford*, 204–205.

61. 1st Infantry Returns, October–December 1834 (M665/2); ZT to Jesup, July 15, 1834, in ZT(LC), ser 2, r 1.

62. Mahan, *Fort Crawford*, 205–206; Dyer, *Taylor*, 90.

More personal matters hung over Taylor during 1835. At the end of the Black Hawk War he had made Lieutenant Jefferson Davis his adjutant, which brought Davis into close contact with the family and especially Sara Knox Taylor. "Knox," as she seems to have been universally called, was a gay and vivacious eighteen year old with a slim figure, her father's hazel eyes, and a mass of wavy brown hair. Among her contemporaries she was noted for exquisite hands and feet. She had a good education, having been tutored by Thomas Elliott in Louisville and attended the Pickett School in Cincinnati. She was attracted to the bright, energetic young lieutenant only four years away from the Plains of West Point, and he to her. The attraction blossomed into love but here the father intervened. Taylor adamantly opposed his daughter's marrying an army officer, although he had no personal objections to Davis. "I know enough of the family life of officers," he said to a friend, "I scarcely know my own children or they me." As the devotion deepened, Taylor apparently also developed personal objections to his adjutant. Tradition, for which there is scant evidence, suggests it grew out of Davis' support of Brevet Major Thomas F. Smith during a dispute over the dress to be worn at a court martial and a particularly boorish performance by Davis at an Indian wedding.[63]

Despite the obstacles raised by Taylor, the courtship continued. The two lovers contrived to meet surreptitiously with the aid of Captain and Mrs. Samuel McRee and Mary Street, the daughter of the Indian agent. Although Taylor sent the lieutenant on several missions which kept him away from the fort for varying stretches of time, Davis did not finally leave Fort Crawford until the spring of 1833 when he was promoted to 1st lieutenant and assigned to the newly formed 1st Dragoons. His first assignment was recruiting in Kentucky, where he was happily received by members of the Taylor clan. After receiving a furlough, he returned to Fort Crawford to resume his pursuit of the fair Knox. She was willing but Davis could not overcome the opposition of Taylor. The lovers nevertheless secretly became engaged before Davis left to rejoin the dragoons at Fort Smith, Arkansas.[64]

Taylor's opposition to Knox's marriage to Jefferson Davis had been one of a number of factors in convincing the latter that he should leave the army. His resignation took effect on June 30, 1835. As soon as he began his terminal leave, Davis hastened to Louisville, where Knox was staying

---

63. Hamilton, *Taylor*, I, 100–103; Strode, *Davis*, 78–79; Hitchcock, Memoirs, 75; Dunbar Rowland (ed.), *Jefferson Davis Constitutionalist* (10 vols.; Jackson, 1923), VIII, 383–84, reprints an 1879 letter from Davis discussing his difficulties with an unnamed colonel at Fort Crawford. Internal evidence suggests it refers to Willoughby Morgan, not Taylor.

64. Strode, *Davis*, 80.

with her aunt Mrs. John G. Taylor. The two lovers decided upon a quick marriage which took place at Mrs. Taylor's home, Beechland, on June 17. The ceremony was performed by the rector of Christ Church, Louisville, but only after Davis and the bride's uncle Hancock had signed a bond certifying that she was of age. That afternoon the bride hastily wrote her mother: "You will be much surprised, no doubt my dear Mother, to hear of my being married so soon." She also thanked her father for money that he sent her.[65] It seems very clear that while Taylor tried to discourage the marriage, at least as long as Davis remained in the army, he accepted it and bore no ill-will toward either his daughter or his son-in-law.

In August Knox wrote a happy letter to her mother from Warrenton, Mississippi. Almost immediately, however, both the bride and groom were stricken with malaria. They continued on to Locust Grove, north of Baton Rouge, in hopes that the healthier climate there would bring remission. Davis survived but Knox died September 15, 1835.[66] The tragedy grieved Taylor deeply and brought back some of the bitterness he felt toward Davis. In later years the two men were reconciled, but the steps involved cannot be reconstructed.

In 1830 Congress had authorized building of a military road from Chicago to Green Bay and from there to the portage between the Fox and Wisconsin Rivers. Reduction in the Green Bay garrison and employment of the men at Fort Winnebago in the construction of their barracks delayed the start on the stretch west of Green Bay. Secretary of War Lewis Cass proposed on January 4, 1832, that the road be continued to Prairie du Chien because of problems with navigation on the Wisconsin. On September 1, 1832, he ordered the laying out of a road from Fort Howard to Fort Crawford. The preliminary survey was not ready until February 1835.[67]

The Fort Crawford garrison received responsibility for the approximately 110-mile section east to Fort Winnebago. The troops had to cut down steep hills, build seven bridges, and construct causeways. During the summer of 1835 Taylor employed the entire Fort Crawford garrison

65. Sara Knox Taylor to Margaret Mackall Smith Taylor, June 17, Bond of Davis and Taylor, June 17, 1835, in Monroe (ed.), *Papers of Davis*, I, 406–407, 409; Strode, *Davis*, 79, 95–96.

66. Knox Davis to mother, August 11, 1835, in Monroe (ed.), *Papers of Davis*, I, 475; Strode, *Davis*, 103–104.

67. Cass to Speaker of the House, January 4, 1832, Jesup to Cass, February 1835, in *ASP:MA*, IV, 815–16, V, 512–13; Cass to Major Henry Whiting, September 1, 1832, in Carter and Bloom (eds.), *Territorial Papers*, VIII, 520–21; Mahan, *Fort Crawford*, 208–209.

except for five officers and ninety-two men on the road. They finished their section by August, although the map and field notes upon which the work depended did not even leave Washington until April. At best the road was a crude track. In timbered country the troops merely cut a path two rods wide but left the stumps, cut low enough to permit wagon axles to pass over them. In swampy stretches the road was made firm by corduroying or placing logs transversely to distribute the weight of the vehicles. Where streams could not be forded, rough bridges were erected. Through the open prairie the road merely consisted of two furrows cut in the ground as a guide to teamsters. The road was really passable only in dry weather or when frozen. Yet, when the section through to Green Bay was completed in late 1837 it became one of the more important immigrant routes to the upper Mississippi valley.[68]

Taylor was nearly drawn into a further road building assignment during 1836. In April Secretary Cass recommended construction of a road paralleling the frontier. He prepared to erect stockaded forts with log blockhouses adequate to withstand any Indian attacks at points along the route, while stressing the obligation to protect the uprooted tribes from the indigenous ones who saw their hunting lands preempted. Such a cordon of posts along the road, if they contained adequate garrisons, would be able to protect the frontier settlements against Indian raiders.[69]

Cass decided that the road should run from some point on the Mississippi between Fort Snelling and the Des Moines River to Forts Leavenworth and Towson before passing west of the Arkansas settlements. The commission of three officers designated to select the route was also directed to determine where the garrison should be stationed. Cass designated Taylor as the senior member. He declined and the assignment went to the recently promoted Colonel Stephen W. Kearny.[70] The general discussion of the need to build a new line of frontier forts of which the building of the road was one aspect led to the submission of a report by Quartermaster Major Trueman Cross. Cross and the chief engineer, Brigadier General Charles Gratiot, proposed a line running from Fort Snelling

68. Jones to ZT, April 15, 1835, in AGLS, XI, 288–89 (M565/9); ZT to AG, August 14, 1835, in AGRL, X, T-198 (M711/9); Dyer, *Taylor*, 91; Mahan, *Fort Crawford*, 209–10; Prucha, *Sword of the Republic*, 191–92.

69. Cass to Jackson, April 7, 1836, in *Senate Documents*, 24th Cong., 1st Sess., No. 293, p. 4.

70. Cass to ZT, W. G. McNeil, and T. F. Smith, July 16, C. A. Harris to ZT, September 9, 1836, in Carter and Bloom (eds.), *Territorial Papers*, XXVII, 621–23, 651n; Atkinson to ZT, August 22, 1836, in 6MD:LB, I, 156; Jones to ZT, July 19, 1836, in AGLS, XII, 482 (M565/9); Right Wing, Western Department, Special Order 10, September 28, 1836, in 6MD:OB, I, 82.

through Fort Crawford, a new, unnamed post on the upper Des Moines River, Council Bluffs, Fort Leavenworth, an unnamed post on the Neosho, Fort Gibson, Fort Smith, Fort Coffee, and Fort Towson to Fort Jesup. Between the posts would be depots and points of refuge. The reserves for that line would be held at Jefferson Barracks and Baton Rouge. Taylor disagreed and argued for a line of temporary posts which could be moved as the frontier changed or as the demands for protection shifted.[71] It was a plan quite close to that ultimately adopted for the policing of the plains after the Mexican War.

The hanging of a Winnebago at the Mineral Point jail during the summer of 1836 caused that year's annual Indian scare. Taylor doubted the possibility of trouble because the Indians lacked sufficient powder or lead. Brigadier General George M. Brooke at Fort Howard, however, feared an extensive uprising and requested Taylor to send three companies to Fort Winnebago. He did in early June and accompanied them but found no indication of trouble and returned with his men in late June.[72]

On orders from Washington, Governor Henry Dodge of Wisconsin Territory called a council with the Winnebagos at Prairie du Chien in late August. His objective was to purchase the remaining Winnebago lands east of the Mississippi. Taylor convinced the chiefs of the bands attached to his agency to attend, although he reported that they had been depleted by a smallpox epidemic. During the council, he provided the military show of force from the Fort Crawford garrison and a pair of companies transferred from Fort Snelling.[73]

No sooner had life at Fort Crawford returned to normal from the Indian negotiations than Taylor received orders to assume temporary command of the right wing of the Western Department at Jefferson Barracks outside of St. Louis. He transferred command of Fort Crawford to Captain William R. Jouett on November 16 and assumed his new responsibilities on the last day of the month.[74] It was Taylor's first major command. He held it for six months while Atkinson was in the east sitting on the court of inquiry which considered the conduct of the Seminole War by Generals Scott and Gaines.[75] The six months passed relatively peacefully.

71. *ASP:MA*, VII, 779–85; Beers, *Western Military Frontier*, 128–29.

72. Lieutenant William Chapman to Brooke, April 3, Brooke to ZT, June 3, to Jones, June 16, 1836, in Carter and Bloom (eds.), *Territorial Papers*, XXVII, 33, 57–58, 60; ZT to Atkinson, May 28, July 3, 1836, in AGLR 1936. A-158, T-172 (M567/116, 132); Atkinson to ZT, June 212, 1836, in 6MD:LB, I, 126–27.

73. ZT to Dodge, August 28, 1836, in OIA:LR (M234/697); Right Wing, Western Department, Special Order 7, September 3, 1836, in 6MD:OB, I, 81.

74. Right Wing, Western Department, General Order 11, 12, October 31, November 30, 1836, in 6MD:OB, I, 83; Fort Crawford Post Return, November 1836 (M617/265).

75. Nichols, *Atkinson*, 197–98.

A flare-up between the Sac and Fox and the Sioux along the Wisconsin border threatened to spread during the early months of 1837. Nothing untoward occurred, however, before Atkinson returned to resume command on May 1.[76] Nevertheless, Taylor, who had authorization for a six-months leave to visit his children at their schools in Kentucky and Philadelphia as well as attend to his private affairs, returned north in case the anticipated Indian problems developed. He left Jefferson Barracks on May 19 and resumed command at Fort Crawford on the thirtieth.[77] Events far to the south, however, interposed to prevent Taylor's taking his leave or implementing an agreement for exchange of commands with Colonel Enos Cutler of the 4th Infantry.[78] In June the regiment was alerted to a move to the southwest frontier and on July 18 Taylor transferred responsibility for Fort Crawford to General Brooke, the commander of the 5th Infantry. That day Taylor, with the Fort Crawford elements of the 1st Infantry, embarked on steamers for the trip south. At Jefferson Barracks on the twenty-second the Fort Snelling garrison joined, so that for one of the few times in its history the entire regiment was together.[79]

Even if the years on the upper Mississippi had kept Taylor away from close supervision of his plantations, those were years of high cotton prices, and he had good managers on his lands. His surviving letters do not complain of his financial problems as stridently as those written in the twenties or in the forties. It therefore seems reasonable to assume that the thirties represented the peak of his benefit from his land speculations. Professionally, the years spent in Wisconsin Territory were productive. They established Taylor as a competent if unexciting officer who could handle difficult assignments with ease; proved once again that he was a successful detachment commander who kept his men trained and ready for field service; and an officer who stayed out of the swirling and debilitating internecine warfare of army politics. The latter centered around the two brigadier generals Winfield Scott and Edmund P. Gaines, who constantly disputed seniority and collected strong partisans around them. The two men and their supporters seldom cooperated except under the

76. Jones to ZT, January 27, 1837, in Carter and Bloom (eds.), *Territorial Papers*, XXVII, 720; ZT to Kearny, February 14, to Jones, February 20, to Dodge, March 5, 1837, in 6MD:LB, I, 183–84, 186–92; Right Wing, Western Department Order 1, 5, 8, March 2, April 25, May 1, 1837, in 6MD:OB, I, 84–85, 87.

77. Fort Crawford Post Return, May 1837 (M617/265); Hamilton, *Taylor*, I, 121; ZT to Jones, March 19, 1837, in 6MD:LB, I, 196; ZT to Jones, May 8, 1837, in AGLR 1837, C-184 (M567/138).

78. Cutler to AG, March 13, ZT to Jones, April 4, 1837, in AGLR 1837, C-184 (M567/138); Jones to ZT, April 24, 1837, in AGLS, XIII, 347 (M565/10).

79. Atkinson to ZT, June 25, 1837, in 6MD:LB, I, 211–12; ZT to Jones, July 24, 1837, in AGLR 1837, T-179 (M567/153); Fort Crawford Post Return, July 1837 (M617/265).

severest of pressures. Promotion and selections for special assignment were often colored by the stance exhibited by an officer in relation to the dispute. Taylor, even if not close to the pro-Scott faction, did not earn their enmity. Nor was he so closely identified with the pro-Gaines western faction as to be excluded from consideration during their periods of exile.

CHAPTER V

Florida

THE INTENDED destination of the 1st Infantry when it left the upper Mississippi was the southwestern frontier in Louisiana. Taylor could look forward to opening his regimental command post at Fort Jesup, which he had established fifteen years earlier. But that was not to be. While the regiment descended the Mississippi en route to its new station, the Washington authorities grew concerned about the failure of Brigadier General Thomas S. Jesup's initial efforts to pacify the Seminoles in Florida. On June 2 Chief Osceola had freed from the collection point near Fort Brooke on Tampa Bay some 700 Indians awaiting movement to new homes in the Indian Territory. Jesup charged Osceola with perfidy and seized him despite a white flag. This renewed the war.

The Seminole War[1] grew out of the desires of the whites to expand settlement deeper into the northern reaches of Florida Territory; the national policy of removal of eastern Indians; the Seminoles' desire to remain independent despite the Jackson administration's wish to subordinate them to the Creeks; and the very difficult problem of the Seminoles' Negroes, many of whom were claimed as runaway slaves by Creek and white owners. In 1835 efforts began to coerce the Seminoles to join the trek westward. Their failures ruined more military and political reputations than all the wars fought by Americans up to that time. No commander could devise a successful means of countering an elusive foe who

---

1. For background discussions of the war see John K. Mahon, *History of the Second Seminole War* (Gainesville, 1967), chaps. 3–5; Michael Paul Rogin, *Fathers and Children* (New York, 1975), 236–38; Edwin C. McReynolds, *The Seminoles* (Norman, 1957), chaps. 9–10.

75

operated from bases in the swampy, nearly impenetrable middle of the peninsula, and no political or military leader could design a settlement which would entice the Indians to agree to an abandonment of their lands.

The Seminoles themselves had an interesting history. They were composed primarily of descendants of individuals who had broken away from the Creeks early in the eighteenth century. They split into two main linguistic divisions, the Muskogee and the Mikasuki. In practice, the Mikasuki were the most strongly anti-removal, apparently because of their long experience with the Americans in Georgia and Alabama. In 1823 the Treaty of Moultrie Creek limited the Seminoles to the area south of the Withlacoochee River and north of Lake Okeechobee except for a few bands left on the Apalachicola River. The arrangement never worked. The Indians insisted the area was too small and began to reoccupy territory they had surrendered. This naturally brought them into conflict with the Floridians. By 1830 the Floridian authorities began to insist that the federal government move the Seminoles into the lands in the west reserved for them. The Seminoles discerned no advantage in a move which would place them in close proximity to their Creek enemies but in 1832 agreed to inspect their western lands. The government secured the agreement of a few Seminole chiefs to immigration in the Treaty of Fort Gibson in 1833, but when the army began enforcing the removal agreement in November 1835 the dissident bands resisted.[2]

The collapse of General Jesup's pacification efforts caused the War Department to shift the 1st Infantry's destination to Florida. On the last day of July 1837, Adjutant General Roger Jones ordered the regiment to prepare for service in Florida with a planned arrival at Tampa Bay between October 10 and 15. The delay permitted Taylor to take a leave starting on August 12.[3]

After visiting Kentucky, Taylor reached New Orleans on November 3. There he took charge of the Louisiana and Missouri volunteers bound for Florida. They arrived at Fort Brooke five days later. The post was a picketed enclosure with a pair of blockhouses, surrounded by a dry eight-foot-deep moat containing pointed stakes. Its residents drank water so heavily flavored with sulphur and iron that local housewives laced it with molasses to cover the smell and taste. Tampa was noted for the incidence of colds and stomach upsets which the inhabitants blamed on the bad water. The sick often taxed the hundred-bed general hospital, which crowned a

2. Alfred Jackson Hanna and Kathryn Abbey Hanna, *Lake Okeechobee* (Indianapolis, 1948), 36–38.

3. War Department General Order 50, July 31, 1837, in *Niles' Weekly Register*, LII (1837), 373; 1st Infantry Return, August 1837 (M665/2). The return states the leave was for six months but Taylor rejoined his regiment in Florida on November 8.

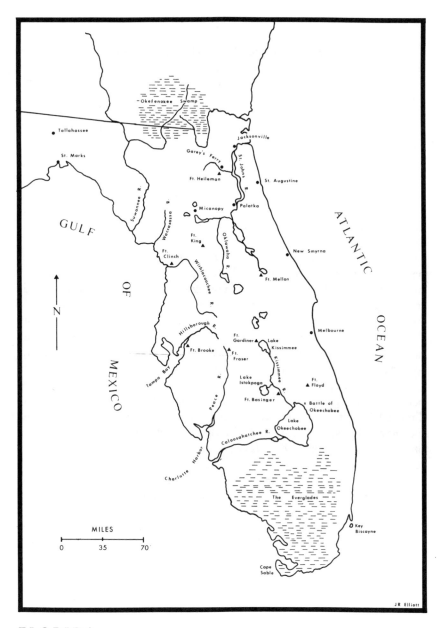

Okefenokee Swamp

Tallahassee

St. Marks

Garey's Ferry
Jacksonville

Ft. Heileman

St. Augustine

Micanopy
Palatka

Ft. King

Ft. Clinch

New Smyrna

Ft. Mellon

GULF

OF

MEXICO

ATLANTIC OCEAN

Suwannee R.

Wacceassa R.

Oklawaha R.

St. Johns R.

Withlacoochee R.

Melbourne

Ft. Gardiner
Lake Kissimmee

Ft. Brooke

Ft. Fraser

Kissimmee R.

Ft. Floyd

Hillsborough R.

Tampa Bay

Lake Istokpoga

Peace R.

Ft. Basinger

Battle of Okeechobee

Lake Okeechobee

Caloosahatchee R.

Charlotte Harbor

The Everglades

Key Biscayne

Cape Sable

N

MILES

0   35   70

JR Elliott

FLORIDA

hill overlooking the Hillsborough River where a grove of live oaks offered shelter from the heat of the Florida sun.

On his arrival Taylor learned that Jesup had assigned to the 1st Infantry responsibility for the area bounded by the Withlacoochee River, Charlotte Harbor, and Pease Creek (the Peace River). Counting the 288 men of his regiment, seven companies of the 4th Infantry, Missouri volunteers under Colonel Richard Gentry, and a group of Delaware and Shawnee Indians, Taylor commanded about 1,400 men.

The strategic problem facing Jesup was intricate. His opponents were scattered. Sam Jones with about 1,500 hostiles was believed to be on the upper St. Johns, while scattered bands were north of Fort Mellon and Tampa Bay. Others operated further south. Jesup's plan called for the establishment of a string of posts from Charlotte Harbor on the Gulf of Mexico to the Suwannee River and thence to St. Augustine. From these base points four columns would drive into the Indian areas. One under Brigadier General Joseph M. Hernandez of the Florida militia would strike from St. Augustine to scour the area between the St. Johns and the Atlantic; a second under Brevet Brigadier General Abram Eustis of the 1st Artillery would operate on the west side of the St. Johns; the third column, a regiment of Louisiana volunteers under Colonel Persifor F. Smith, would move down the Caloosahatchee River and then clear the area south of it as far as Cape Sable. The fourth column under Taylor had orders to penetrate into the heart of Seminole country by opening a road from Tampa Bay to the head of Pease Creek before pressing on to the Kissimmee River. Loosely coordinated with these forces was a waterborne force of sailors and soldiers under Navy Lieutenant Levin N. Powell which was to traverse the Everglades south of Smith's area.[4]

Upon his arrival at Tampa, Taylor ordered 40,000 rations moved to Fort Fraser, a depot on Pease Creek about forty miles to the east, built by the advanced guard under Lieutenant Colonel William S. Foster of the 4th Infantry. The lift took three trips by the eighty available wagons. Taylor with the 1st Infantry followed at the end of November. Calling up Colonel Gentry's regiment, a company of Florida volunteers, and one of Missouri spies, Taylor pushed on to the Kissimmee, which his advance elements reached during the afternoon of December 3. En route the troops

4. Mahon, *Seminole War*, 219–20; Chester L. Kieffer, *Maligned General: The Biography of Thomas Sidney Jesup* (San Rafael, Calif., 1979), 190–91; ZT to Jesup, November 11, 1837, in ZT(LC), ser 2, r 1; *House Documents*, 25th Cong., 2nd Sess., No. 133, p. 6; Jesup to Poinsett, July 6, 1838, in *Senate Documents*, 25th Cong., 2nd Sess., No. 507, pp. 5–7; Rembert W. Patrick, *Aristocrat in Uniform: General Duncan L. Clinch* (Gainesville, 1963), 63; Mary C. Gillett, "The Army Medical Department, 1818–1865" (MS in Center of Military History, Washington, D.C.), III, 16.

bridged several streams and constructed causeways through swamps. In one notable instance, they fashioned a bridge 412 feet long to get the wagons across Buffalo Ford. Once he had bridged the Kissimmee and built Fort Gardiner on the east side, Taylor halted his advance to await word of the success of Jesup's efforts to talk the hostiles into surrendering.[5]

While the main body marked time, scouts spread out from Fort Gardiner to seek Indian trails. On December 4 they found one and prepared to follow it, while Taylor sent a call for talks to Alligator, one of the Seminole leaders believed to be nearby. Late on the fourth the messengers returned with a subchief of Alligator's band. With this promising development, Taylor was encouraged to dispatch his Shawnee scouts to locate other Indians willing to surrender. On the sixth they returned with two, who while willing to submit were in no hurry to do so. That evening Colonel Gentry's mounted Missouri volunteers rode into camp and that more than offset the departure of the Florida volunteers, whose time had expired. By December 17 Abraham, Taylor's go-between, assured him that Alligator would surrender. In return Taylor permitted Abraham to return to his camp for two of his children.[6]

On the seventeenth Taylor decided to lead his 300 mounted men on a search of the country west of the Kissimmee as far as Lake Okeechobee and the Caloosahatchee River. That plan aborted when Jesup's negotiations collapsed and he directed Taylor to move against the hostiles with the least possible delay. Taylor decided to push down the west side of the Kissimmee with his whole force of 1,032 men, three-quarters of whom were regulars, in hopes of intercepting the hostiles known to be camping around Lake Istokpoga or cutting off others attempting to escape Jesup. Finally he believed that a large force would overawe the redmen and hasten their surrender. He further hoped to open communications with Colonel Smith's force.[7]

The advance guard departed on December 19, a day ahead of the main body. During the evening of the twentieth the campaign achieved its first success when sixty-four Indians formally submitted. Taylor sent them back to Tampa under escort of some of the Shawnee. Late on the following night his scouts reported discovery of a camp containing about twenty-two others who wished to surrender. After sunrise on the twenty-second Taylor and a mounted column reached the campsite near the Istokpoga outlet of

5. ZT to Jesup, November 20, 26, December 4, 1837, in AGLR 1837, J-250, 265, 267 (M567/146); ZT to Jesup, November 1837, in ZT(LC), ser 2, r 1.

6. ZT to Jesup, December 7, 1837, in AGLR 1837, J-274 (M567/146); ZT to Jesup, December 17, 1837, ZT(LC), ser 2, r 1.

7. ZT to Jesup, December 17, 19, 1837, in ZT(LC), ser 2, r 1, AGLR 1837, J-286 (M567/146); ZT to Jones, January 4, 1838, in ASP:MA, VII, 986.

Lake Okeechobee. One of the old men in the camp claimed that Alligator wished to avoid Sam Jones and his band of Mikasukis, who were about twenty miles away beyond the Kissimmee preparing to fight. Taylor sent the old man to request that Alligator meet him the following day. After being joined by its infantry the American force marched to the anticipated meeting site. At about eleven o'clock that night the messenger returned with an ambiguous response from Alligator and word that the Mikasukis had not moved.

Taylor sensed that he was close to his hoped-for fight but realized that his force must move rapidly in order to catch the elusive Indians. During the morning of December 23 he had his men erect a depot for his heavy equipment, artillery, and extra supplies near Lake Istokpoga. It was garrisoned by Captain John Munroe with his artillery company, the pioneers, pontoniers, the sick, and most of the Delawares. On the twenty-fourth Taylor and the rest of his force reached Alligator's camp on the edge of a cabbage-tree hammock. That landmark thrust up from a large prairie and bore evidence of a large number of former residents. A few Indians, mostly women and children, remained behind. They reported that Sam Jones was about ten or twelve miles away in a swamp.

Taylor sent the noncombatants back to Munroe and pushed on for the hostiles' camp. As the force crossed a dense cypress swamp it captured an Indian scout who confirmed the information already received. He further reported that a large body of Seminoles under Co-a-coo-chee or Wild Cat were undoubtedly camped with Alligator about five or six miles away, near the Mikasukis. Since it was late, Taylor had his men bed down for the night. The whites reached the Seminole camp at about 11:00 A.M. on Christmas Day. In their hasty evacuation the Indians had abandoned freshly butchered beef and left fires burning. Taylor's men also found a herd of two to three hundred cattle and ponies peacefully grazing on the prairie. A warrior seized nearby, who may have been a plant, pointed to a "dense hammock on our right" about a mile away where he reported the Indians had retreated.

Taylor held a council of war and proposed to make a mass frontal attack on the position. Apparently Colonel Gentry of the Missourians countered with a suggestion for encirclement, but Taylor downplayed the tactic, asking if Gentry was afraid to charge the Indian works. Actually the army had not yet scouted the battlefield, so it was not yet certain that an encirclement was feasible. More important, Taylor, whose tactical ideas were limited at best, had a natural inclination for a direct attack. Nevertheless, the exchange with Gentry would have devastating effect during the battle.

In preparation for his attack, Taylor organized his force into two lines, an arrangement which has long been questioned by commentators. The first line consisted of the Missouri volunteers deployed as skirmishers. They were to enter the hammock, but if they came under attack or heavy pressure they were to fall back and re-form behind the second line, composed of the 4th and 6th Infantry. Taylor held his 1st Infantry, the strongest force on the field, in reserve and sent Captain George W. Allen with two mounted companies of the 4th Infantry to scout the swamp to the right of the Indian position. Taylor never explained his rationale for this formation but it is reminiscent of the classic one used by Daniel Morgan at the Battle of Cowpens. But this had a significant difference; Morgan's men were standing on the defense, not attacking. More likely, the arrangement reflected Taylor's low opinion of the volunteers. In nearly every instance in which he had seen volunteers in action they had shown little discipline or battlefield stamina. It is reasonable to assume that Taylor believed that if he placed the volunteers in the van and they broke under fire the damage would be less than if they were used as the shock troops to deliver the main attack. Moreover, if they did break he could hope to re-form some of them to return to the battle. Thirdly, if the resistance was light, the volunteers would have the dual benefits of a baptism of fire, always difficult for green troops, and the boost in morale which would come from a successful attack. It is also possible that Taylor saw in their tendency to disorganized firing and impulsive advances an advantage in a fight against equally undisciplined defenders.

The Indian position was well chosen. It was on a hammock in a swamp three-quarters of a mile wide covered with five-foot-high saw grass and Palmetto trees growing from a knee-deep ooze of water and mud; it was impenetrable for horses and nearly so for men on foot. The Seminoles had cut corridors through the grass to provide clear fire for their muskets and notched the trees on the hammock from which to steady their guns. Lake Okeechobee glimmered not far beyond. Between 380 and 480 Indians manned the defenses. Sam Jones with about 180 hostiles held the right side of the Seminole line; Alligator with 120 manned the center; another 80 warriors under Wild Cat defended their left flank. The Indian sharpshooters took positions in the trees. The Indians' force was an informal combination of different camps each of whose warriors was independently commanded. No Indian exercised overall command. Nor was the large body of Negro warriors present. The attack began at about 12:30 P.M. on a pleasant day. All men were dismounted. The Missourians advanced cautiously but drew no Indian fire until about twenty yards from their position. Then the warriors began shooting. Their fire was well aimed and deliberate. Some of the Missourians claimed that the 6th Infantry fire also struck them. Gentry, perhaps stung by Taylor's earlier comments, kept his men advancing. A score of Missourians were hit and Gentry dropped. When the skirmishers saw their leader fall they broke and without his commanding presence could not be re-formed behind the regulars as Taylor planned.

The regulars pressed forward. The five companies of the 6th Infantry caught by fire from both Alligator's and Wild Cat's followers in one of the corridors took heavy casualties. They lost nearly every commissioned and noncommissioned officer, including Lieutenant Colonel A. Ramsay Thompson. Only the sergeant major, four sergeants, and sixty men were unscathed. They were forced back but re-formed and resumed their attack. Thompson, who had received two wounds early in the battle, urged his regiment forward, calling, "Keep steady, men, charge the hammock— remember the regiment to which you belong." He was cut down by a third bullet. Meanwhile, Lieutenant Colonel Foster with the 4th Infantry and a pair of 6th Infantry companies as well as some of Gentry's men on the left of Taylor's line encountered little opposition from Sam Jones and his warriors, who fled at the start of the assault. The infantrymen occupied the abandoned positions and chased fleeing defenders to the lake. At roughly the same time that the regulars turned the Indian right flank, Captain Allen and his mounted men worked around the Indian left. Once he was sure that Allen had been successful, Taylor ordered the 1st Infantry to follow. After the infantry loosed a volley which certified its arrival in the fight, the remaining defenders joined in the race through the swamp toward Lake Okeechobee. From there they dispersed in small groups. The fight had taken about two and a half hours.

The Battle of Lake Okeechobee was one of the bloodiest in all the history of nineteenth-century Indian warfare. Indian losses are difficult to determine, but between 11 and 14 are believed to have died. Taylor's troops lost 26 men killed and 112 wounded. The 6th Infantry alone suffered 20 killed and 55 wounded of its 220 men engaged; the Missourians 2 killed (including Gentry) and 25 wounded.[8] The Okeechobee fight was not only the largest clash of the seven-years-long Florida conflict but it was the only time the Indians chose to stand and fight. As events would

8. The battle and its preliminaries are covered in ZT to Jones, January 4, 1838, in *ASP:MA*, VII, 986–99; Brainerd Dyer, *Zachary Taylor* (Baton Rouge, 1946), 107–109; Holman Hamilton, *Zachary Taylor* (2 vols.; Indianapolis, 1941, 1951), 130–33; Mahon, *Seminole War*, 227–28; Francis Paul Prucha, *Sword of the Republic* (New York, 1969), 292; John T. Sprague, *The Origins, Progress, and Conclusion of the Florida War* (New York, 1848), 203–13; McReynolds, *The Seminoles*, 201–203; Virginia Bergman Peters, *The Florida Wars* (Hamden, Conn., 1979), 153–55; George Walton, *Fearless and Free* (Indianapolis, 1975), 175–76; ZT to Jesup, December 26, 1837, in *Niles' Weekly Register*, LIII (1837/38), 337. J. Floyd Monk, "Christmas Day in Florida," *Tequesta*, XXXVIII (1978), 5–38, is a detailed reconstruction of the battle.

demonstrate, the results convinced them of the correctness of their Fabian strategy. The battle brought Taylor his brevet promotion to brigadier. Adjutant General Jones in congratulating Taylor on his success conveyed his "highest commendation" and opined that: "The chivalry displayed by the officers and men under your command in the recent action near Lake Ocha-Chobee, when so many of your brave companions have fallen, has never been surpassed."[9]

The performance of the Missourians became a subject of extended debate. Some observers like James K. Polk saw it as a reflection of a general problem with volunteer services. "Our citizen soldiers behaved as they always do," the future president wrote, "& ran out of danger so soon as the action commenced. Poor Col. Gentry a brave man, fell mortally wounded, & not enough of his men remained to carry him from the field."[10]

In view of the later recriminations which arose in Missouri over the treatment of the volunteers, it is noteworthy that Taylor received a testimonial from a group of eight officers over the treatment that the unit received.[11] Nevertheless, recriminations began as soon as the report of the battle became public. On February 14, 1838, Senator Thomas Hart Benton introduced a resolution requesting a copy of the report from the War Department because he understood that the volunteers "had been mistreated." Senator John J. Crittenden, already a champion of Taylor, defended him as a "brave, skillful, and determined soldier." Secretary of War Joel R. Poinsett penned a conciliatory letter which satisfied Benton if not the local Missouri politicians. During the spring of 1839 the Missouri legislature formulated charges against Taylor which prompted him to request a court of inquiry. Secretary Poinsett refused on the reasonable ground that the necessary officers could not be spared from Florida and that, in any event, no need existed.[12]

The victors made little effort to pursue the departing warriors. It would have been extremely difficult under the best of circumstances but nearly impossible for Taylor's tired men who were hampered by the

9. Jones to ZT, January 31, April 11, 1838, in AGLS, XIV, 185–86, 227–28 (M565/10). It carried a December 25, 1837, date. Taylor later complained of the delay in the conferring of the brevet. ZT to Jesup, April 26, 1838, in ZT(LC), ser 2, r 1.

10. Polk to J. A. Thomas, January 27, 1838, in Herbert Weaver, *et al.* (eds.), *Correspondence of James K. Polk* (5 vols.; Nashville, 1969), IV, 342.

11. Major H. H. Hughes *et al.* to ZT, February 8, 1838, in *Senate Documents*, 25th Cong., 2nd Sess., No. 356, pp. 6–7.

12. *Congressional Globe*, 25th Cong., 2nd Sess., 182–83, 193; Poinsett to ZT, October 8, 1839, in SWMA, XXI, 153–54 (M6/21); Macomb to ZT, May 5, 1839, in HQLS, 5/3, pp. 487–88 (M875/21); Report of Officers of the Missouri Volunteers, n.d., in *Senate Documents*, 25th Cong., 2nd Sess., No. 356, pp. 1–6; Resolution of Missouri Senate and House, February 13, 1839, in AGLR 1840, B-69 (M567/202). The journal of the Missouri legislature's Committee of Investigation is in MoHS.

large number of dead and injured. They spent the remaining hours of Christmas collecting the dead and wounded and building a foot bridge to a dry campsite under the direction of Taylor's brother Joseph. During the twenty-sixth the force buried their dead and sent out scouts who failed to locate any of the fleeing Indians but did return to camp with 100 ponies and 300 cattle. The force broke camp on the twenty-seventh to make a slow and painful trek back to Fort Basinger. The wounded traveled on horse litters, which must have been pure hell for many of them. They reached the temporary depot at about noon on December 28 and Fort Gardiner, on the last day of the year. From there Taylor sent the 4th Infantry to Fort Fraser while the remnants of the 6th convoyed the wounded to Tampa. While the foot soldiers plodded forward, Taylor rested his horses and the 1st Infantry at Fort Gardiner preparatory to returning to the swamps.[13]

In January 1838 Captain Allen with his two mounted companies traversed the region north of Colonel Smith's area of operation without success. Taylor followed this later in the month with a shift of 1st Infantry to Fort Basinger in an effort to open communications via the Kissimmee and Lake Okeechobee with his southern subordinate. Since Smith had a fleet of mackinaw boats, Taylor thought this could simplify his supply problems. At the same time he complained that Brevet Brigadier General Walker K. Armistead had also issued orders to Smith, an apparent transgression of his command authority. It raised the question, said Taylor, of whether Armistead was to supersede him, an event which he claimed did not disturb him since he was "by no means ambitious of a separate command."[14]

On the eighteenth Taylor's men made contact with Jesup's forces about twenty miles east of Fort Floyd. This gave the Americans a line across the middle of the peninsula. Two days later Taylor left Fort Gardiner to pursue the hostiles "in whatever direction I may hear of their being in force." By the end of the month it was evident that the Indians had split up into many small parties. Taylor, with about eight hundred regular infantry, seventy-five Missouri volunteers, fifteen Indians, and the two mounted companies from the 4th Infantry, swept the western shore of Lake Okeechobee in an effort to force the hostiles eastward into the arms of Jesup. The column encountered no Indians before receiving orders on February 4 to pursue a trail into the Everglades.[15] Taylor's eleven-day sweep carried him sixty miles southward of Lake Okeechobee but again his men met no hostiles. The lack of contacts convinced Taylor that the Indians could not

13. ZT to Jones, January 4, 1838, to Jesup, December 26, 31, 1837, in ZT(LC), ser 2, r 1.
14. ZT to Jesup, January 12, 1838, in ZT(LC), ser 2, r 1.
15. ZT to Jesup, January 20, 30, February 1, 2, 5, 1838, in ZT(LC), ser 2, r 1; ZT to Munroe, January 28, 1838, in Miscellaneous Papers, NYHS; Mahon, Seminole Wars, 233.

again be brought to battle. He suggested, therefore, that the army keep the Seminoles and their allies away from the settled areas while Revenue Cutters patrolled the coast to interdict potential supply sources. A prolonged stay in the Everglades, he concluded, would discourage the natives and bring them out to surrender.[16]

Taylor followed that maneuver with a waterborne thrust by two companies under Major Bennet Riley of the 4th Infantry to the southeastern end of Okeechobee, where they constructed a blockhouse in hopes of forcing the Indians deeper into the inhospitable depths of the Everglades. A second force under Major Gustavus Loomis of the 1st Infantry again scoured Lake Okeechobee during mid-March seeking hostiles and destroying canoes. They returned with rumors that Alligator wished to surrender. After Jesup sent three of the Seminole chiefs, including Abraham, to serve as intermediaries, Alligator and 360 of his followers surrendered during late March and early April, to Taylor or elements of Persifor Smith's command.[17]

Following the successes of Jesup, Taylor, and Smith in securing the submission of the bulk of the Indians still at large, the War Department ordered Jesup back to Washington. General Order 7, issued April 10, announced that Jesup anticipated completing active operations by May 1 and assigned Taylor command on the peninsula with a garrison consisting of his regiment, the 6th Infantry, six companies of the 2d Infantry, four of the 2d Dragoons, and such Florida militia as he might need. The artillerymen, 4th Infantry, Marines, and balance of the 2d Dragoons would join General Scott in superintending the removal of the Cherokees. The appointment caught Taylor by surprise, since he had anticipated leaving Florida once the campaign ended. He was so disenchanted with service there that he wrote Jesup: "I . . . will at any moment with great pleasure, yield [command] to anyone who the Department may at any time designate to supercede [sic] me." Taylor viewed his appointment as an interim one and anticipated holding the command only during the summer pending the assignment of a new commander.[18]

By May, Jesup's prediction of an early end to hostilities was already clearly overly optimistic. About 3,000 Indians, 400 to 500 of them warriors, remained outside of American control, but more dangerous was the

16. ZT to Jesup, February 10, 13, 1838, in AGLR 1838, T-38, in ZT(LC), ser 2, r 1.

17. ZT to Jesup, February 15, March 20, 30, April 4, 1838, in ZT(LC), ser 2, r 1; Jesup to Jones, March 11, 1838, in Clarence Carter and John Porter Bloom (eds.), *The Territorial Papers of the United States* (28 vols.; Washington, 1934–75), XXV, 493; Jesup to Poinsett, July 6, 1838, in Sprague, *Florida War*, 195.

18. Headquarters of the Army, General Order 7, April 10, 1838, in *Niles' Weekly Register*, LIV (1938), 97; ZT to Jesup, April 26, to Hancock Taylor, August 14, 1838, in ZT(LC), ser 2, r 1, ser 6.

resumption of attacks by scattered bands. Nevertheless, Jesup formally transferred command to Taylor on May 15. The new head of what was officially called the Army of the South established his headquarters at the 1st Infantry's base camp at Fort Brooke.[19] Taylor's initial plan was to drive the hostile Indians south and east of the line from St. Augustine through Garey's Ferry and Fort King to Tampa Bay. This he believed would keep them away from "every portion of Florida worth protecting." Moreover, this would cut off their supplies and hasten the Indian decision to accept removal. The argument rested on Taylor's conviction that only through starvation could the Indians still at large be brought to surrender. The slow and methodical plan, unfortunately, was politically naïve and irritated Governor Richard Call and the Floridians, who wished a more active campaign to bring the murders and other depredations to an end.[20]

Meanwhile, Taylor collected the 322 Indians who had already surrendered at Tampa. Nearly all of them started their trek west during June, but an additional 400 to 500 remained at large.[21] Complicating the army's problem in handling the Indians was the presence among them of forty to fifty Negroes. They were a mixed group of free men and escaped slaves whose ownership was uncertain. Taylor informed the War Department that he would neither seize Negroes belonging to the Seminoles nor return runaways unless the legal owner could prove his claim. This position placed the army commander in the midst of the long-standing question of the disposition of Negroes captured by the Creeks. The latter had turned down an offer of $8,000 for their claims to the blacks as captured enemy property made by Jesup before he returned north. Shortly afterwards they disposed of those claims to James C. Watson of Georgia for $15,000. Watson sent his brother-in-law Nathaniel F. Collins to secure about seventy then in the custody of the army. When Collins demanded their surrender, the officers involved refused. General Gaines supported his juniors, arguing that the Negroes were prisoners of war and could not be released. Collins' subsequent efforts to entice Marine Lieutenant John G. Reynolds, in charge of the emigrant group, to release them to him failed, as did efforts to enlist the governor of Arkansas and General Matthew Arbuckle. Between 300 and 400 Negroes ultimately accompanied the Seminoles to their new home in the Indian territory.[22]

19. Army of the South Order 119, May 15, 1838, in Army Continental Commands (NA, RG 393), 1st Division, Army of the South, Orders; Dyer, *Taylor*, 114.

20. ZT to Call, May 18, 1838, in AGLR 1838, T-125 (M567/176); Mahon, *Seminole War*, 247; Walton, *Fearless and Free*, 189.

21. Undated memorandum, in Thomas Sidney Jesup Papers, VII, LC.

22. ZT to Jones, June 2, 1838, in AGLR 1838, T-119 (M567/176); Rogin, *Fathers and Children*, 239; McReynolds, *The Seminoles*, 212–13; Mahon, *Seminole War*, 251–52;

Taylor's starvation campaign received a boost in mid-June when the first pair of revenue cutters reported for duty on his patrol line. At the same time Secretary Poinsett gave him control of the army's steamer *Poinsett* and authority to draft up to 1,000 Florida militia, the latter the result of pressure from the Floridians. In July Navy Lieutenant John T. McLaughlin sailed for Florida with further reinforcements for the patrol force.[23] While Taylor spent most of June and July inspecting his command with visits to Fort King, Micanopy, and Fort Heileman and to the Okefenokee Swamp, several patrols skirmished with small bands without accomplishing anything. Taylor asked for, and received, retention of the entire 2d Dragoons in Florida in order to enlarge his mounted force.[24]

The frustration of trying to locate the elusive enemy prompted Taylor to consider unconventional methods. In late July he suggested using tracking dogs and asked for permission to acquire an experimental pack of bloodhounds with their handlers. Recognizing the possible accusations of their misuse, Taylor assured his superiors, "I wish it distinctly understood, that my object in employing dogs, is only to ascertain where the Indians can be found, not to worry them." Poinsett agreed to the use of dogs for tracking only and so informed Taylor on the last day of August.[25] The general must have had second thoughts about employing the bloodhounds, since he did not further pursue their purchase. The Florida legislature, not surprisingly, felt less concern over the human rights of the hostiles and authorized acquisition of the dogs. Their agent in Havana purchased a pack of thirty-three bloodhounds noted as trackers of Negro runaways and hired five experienced handlers. Governor Robert R. Reid offered them to Taylor, but they proved worthless. The dogs, bred and trained to follow Negro scent, could not track that of Indians.[26] While the experiment was a failure and never involved hostile Indians, it provoked

Walton, *Fearless and Free*, 190–92. See also ZT to Colonel James Logan, September 9, 1841, in AGLR 1841, T-273 (M567/239).

23. Lieutenant G. H. Griffin to Captain W. A. Howard, June 15, 1838, in AGLR 1838, T-169 (M567/177); Poinsett to ZT, June 1, 1838, in Carter and Bloom (eds.), *Territorial Papers*, XXV, 512; Jones to ZT, June 14, 26, 1838, in AGLS, XIV, 320, 338 (M565/10); George E. Buker, *Swamp Sailors* (Gainesville, 1975), 71; Walton, *Fearless and Free*, 193.

24. Mahon, *Seminole War*, 248; Hamilton, *Taylor*, I, 135; ZT to Jones, June 16, July 13, 1838, in AGLR 1838, T-137, 173 (M567/177); Jones to ZT, July 16, 1838, in AGLS, XIV, 359 (M565/10).

25. ZT to Jones, July 28, 1838, Poinsett to ZT, January 26, 1840, in *Senate Documents*, 26th Cong., 1st Sess., No. 187, p. 5; Thomas to ZT, August 31, 1838, in AGLS, XIV, 441 (M565/10).

26. Sprague, *Florida War*, 239–40; Walton, *Fearless and Free*, 205–207; *Niles' Weekly Register*, LVIII (1840), 137; Reid to ZT, January 16, 1840, in Army Continental Commands (NA, RG 393), 9th Military District Returns; ZT to Reid, March 23, 1840, AGLR 1840, T-140 (M567/218).

extensive comment in Congress and would be unearthed as anti-Taylor propaganda during the 1848 election.[27]

As the campaign dragged on without any sign of ending, Taylor came to the conclusion that it could be brought to a close only by providing security to the existing settlements and by encouraging additional colonization so that the weight of numbers would prevent further Indian incursions. Governor Call, Reid's predecessor, favored establishing military colonies on the lands cleared by military operations. He too believed that forcing the hostiles into the Everglades where their food would be restricted to the few wild edibles which grew there would be successful.[28] But he overlooked the plentiful fish and birds there. As a result the harassing of the Seminoles had less effect than Taylor or Call expected; few Indians waded out of the swamps to surrender. Further north and west the army's pressure did have effect, especially around the Apalachicola River, where in October Taylor superintended the embarkation of the last 220 Apalache Indians.[29]

Meanwhile, the return of the cooler weather allowed Taylor to lead his forces back into the field. The return of active operations must have been welcomed by many of the troops. Conditions in the base camps were frequently, if not universally, bad. Drunkenness was common and whiskey smugglers rampant. When caught, the latter's punishment was picturesque, if not especially effective. According to one contemporary, three smugglers had a six-foot-long plank with holes for their heads placed on their shoulders; high paper caps set on their heads; large dragging ropes tied to their waists; faces blackened; and empty bottles suspended from the yoke. They were then marched around the camp to the tune of the Rogue's March and expelled.[30] He did not indicate how long they waited before returning. Taylor himself complained that his personal mess had no vegetables and that the flour was both sour and full of weevils. Pork and bacon were "not the best" and the beef poor, but fish, he reported, was plentiful at Tampa, although the heat limited their use. Further complicating life for the troops was a shortage of surgeons to treat the large sick list.[31]

27. *Congressional Globe*, 26th Cong., 1st Sess., 183–84, 198, 201–204, 252; Charles Stearns, *Facts in the Life of General Taylor, the Extensive Slaveholder, and the Hero of the Mexican War* (Boston, 1848).

28. ZT to Jones, August 4, 1838, in AGLR 1838, T-196 (M567/177); Call to ZT, August 21, 1838, in Carter and Bloom (eds.), *Territorial Papers*, XXV, 528–31.

29. ZT to Jones, October 27, 1838, July 20, 1839, in AGLR 1838, T-272 (M565/177); Sprague, *Florida War*, 222.

30. Nathan S. Jarvis, "An Army Surgeon's Notes of Frontier Service," *JMSIUS*, XXXIX (1906), 458.

31. ZT to Hancock Taylor, August 14, to Lawson, September 7, 1838, in ZT(LC), ser 6, AGLR 1838, T-259 (M567/177).

Conditions improved markedly after the arrival during the late fall of Jesup's deputy Colonel Trueman Cross as quartermaster of the Army of the South. He introduced a series of reforms in logistics which improved the performance of the troops in the field but earned him the displeasure of many officers. He required that officers issue stores themselves rather than hiring civilian agents; that soldiers replace clerks and laborers wherever possible; that the number of officers' horses taken into the field be limited; that the use of ambulances be restricted to sick and wounded; and finally that the teamsters be held responsible for the supplies entrusted to them and that they be punished if they molested civilians.[32] Taylor expressed pleasure in his report on the campaign: "Not withstanding our operations have extended over more than fifty thousand square miles no want of transportation or supplies have been experienced, owing to the judicious arrangements of Colonel Cross . . . and his able assistants."[33]

At the end of November Taylor commanded 3,300 regulars and 372 militia. The 1838/39 plan of campaign called for Colonel David E. Twiggs to lead a mixed command from his 2d Dragoons, the 4th Artillery, and two companies of Florida militia into the region between the Atlantic coast and the St. John's River, ranging as far south as New Smyrna. A smaller force under Lieutenant Colonel Alexander C. W. Fanning of the 4th Artillery would cooperate by reestablishing Fort Mellon at the south end of Lake George. Lieutenant Colonel Davenport with elements of the 1st Infantry and 2d Dragoons would patrol between the Withlacoochee and the Suwannee. Lieutenant Colonel John Greene of the 6th Infantry with a detachment of foot soldiers would patrol west of the Suwannee an area from which the Apalaches had just been removed. Major Gustavus Loomis with a mixed unit of infantry and dragoons drew the unenviable assignment of pacifying the Okefenokee Swamp and its surrounding region in conjunction with Georgia volunteers under Brigadier General Charles Floyd. The objective of all these operations was to drive the hostiles south of the line from New Smyrna to Fort Brooke. Once that territory had been pacified, Taylor envisioned constructing a network of roads strengthened every twenty miles by a strongpoint.[34] It was an ambitious scheme but one that recognized the critical element in defeating a guerrilla enemy. To be successful, the defender must separate the guerrilla from his normal supply sources and win the local population's cooperation so that they will provide neither supplies nor shelter to him. To accomplish this the defender must have a strong, mobile force which can

32. Mahon, *Seminole War*, 253.

33. ZT to Jones, July 20, 1839, in AGLR 1839, T-234 (M567/197).

34. ZT to Jones, November 17, 1838, July 10, 1839, in AGLR 1838, T-297, 1839, T-234 (M567/177, 197); Sprague, *Florida War*, 221–27.

strike hard and fast and he must conduct a political campaign which will win the goodwill, if not the support, of local inhabitants.

Taylor left Fort Brooke on November 25 to join Davenport, but their operations produced no contacts. In mid-December the general moved on to Fort Frank Brooke near Deadman's Bay, but thrusts from there into the swamps west of the Suwannee were equally unsuccessful in locating hostiles. Nor did the other field forces he visited have better luck. Taylor, as one of his lieutenants reported, had been "gulled by the treacherous Indians." On January 5, 1839, he was at Fort Fanning on the Suwannee. The inability to bring the Indians to battle or to force them to accept emigration forced him to recast his plans. It was now unlikely, he wrote Adjutant General Jones, that the Indians could operate in force north of the Kissimmee. Therefore, he proposed what came to be known as his "squares" plan. This called for laying out districts measuring twenty miles on a side. A post near the center, manned by an officer and twenty men, half mounted, would provide security. To blanket the region between Georgia and the Gulf of Mexico and west from St. Augustine to the Oklawaha and Waccasassa rivers would require four regiments with sixty men per company, or 2,400 men. He also asked for four or five light vessels to cruise off the coast. Taylor argued that such an arrangement would give sufficient security to permit settlers to return to their homes.[35]

Approval for the squares program came from Washington in late January. General-in-Chief Alexander Macomb forwarded the news on the twenty-third.[36] Taylor promptly set his officers to work establishing the system. As it worked in practice the garrison of each fort or stockade patrolled on alternate days. Each square had a road around its perimeter and where they existed the hummocks were interconnected with trails. To ease the logistical burden, each garrison received a supply of seeds so that it could grow a part of its food. Taylor pushed the program as rapidly as possible and on July 20 claimed that every swamp and hummock between Fort Mellon and Tallahassee had been searched.[37] In the ten months between October 1838 and July 1839 Taylor's soldiers built 53 posts, 848 miles of wagon roads, and 3,643 feet of causeways or bridges. Undoubtedly, Taylor's plan if carried out to its full dimensions would have forced

35. ZT to Jones, December 5, 1838, January 5, July 20, 25, 1839, in AGLR 1838, T-317, 1839, T-13, 234 (M567/177, 195, 197), Andre De Coppet Collection, Princeton University Library; Hamilton, *Taylor*, I, 137; J. H. La Motts to William Beaumont, December 18, 1838, in William Beaumont Papers, MoHS.

36. Jarvis, "Army Surgeon's Notes," 271; Macomb to ZT, January 23, 1839, in HQLS, 5/3, p. 396 (M875/2); ZT to Jones, July 20, 1839, in AGLR 1839, T-234 (M567/197).

37. ZT to Greene, February 18, to Twiggs, February 18, March 15, July 20, 1839, in AGLR 1839, T-72, 85, 234, (M567/197); Hamilton, *Taylor*, I, 138; Mahon, *Seminole War*, 249.

the Indians to surrender or eke out a marginal existence in the Everglades. The rest of the peninsula was either occupied by settlers or patrolled by the army garrisons.

In February Taylor sent Davenport with four companies of infantry and one of dragoons to drive the remaining hostiles east of the Suwannee. The expedition was a good example of the difficulties which the Army of the South faced. It was dispatched to counter a band which Taylor insisted numbered no more than twenty or thirty warriors. "It is unfortunate," he complained to Roger Jones, "for the reputation of the Army in Florida that the enemy do seldom come in collision with any portion of it; although efforts amounting to recklessness have been made unparalleled in the annals of Indian warfare. . . . Their whole object appears to keep out of the way of the Regulars who have increasingly pursued them in large and small bodies penetrating their hiding places in every direction and driving them therefrom." [38]

Such limited actions did not appease the Floridians, who wanted more activity. In February Governor Call suggested that twelve companies of volunteers be raised and offered to the federal government, even if Taylor refused them. His legislative council complied on March 2. Three days later Taylor accepted them but specified that only half be mounted, since such units were of little use in the hummock country where he believed most of the remaining Seminoles to be. [39]

Into Taylor's potentially successful efforts to force the remaining hostiles into submission strode the large boots of his former commander and antagonist, Major General Alexander Macomb. Since lesser-ranking generals had failed to bring the conflict to a close, Secretary Poinsett ordered the general-in-chief to Florida on March 18. Macomb was to "adopt such measures as may seem to you most expedient to secure the protection of the settlers in Middle and East Florida, prosecute the war with vigor, and to bring it to a speedly and successful termination." If it would contribute to that end, the new commander could sign a truce which permitted the Seminoles to live south of 27°30', roughly the northern end of Lake Okeechobee. [40]

Macomb arrived at Garey's Ferry south of Jacksonville during April 5. Taylor and Twiggs greeted him after the 2d Dragoons band played "Hail to the Chief." Taylor, whose disenchantment with service in Florida we have already noted, discovered much to his chagrin that Macomb viewed

38. ZT to Jones, March 8, 1839, in AGLR 1839, T-87, (M567/197).
39. ZT to Davenport, February 28, to Call, March 11, Call to ZT, March 6, 1839, in AGLR 1839, T-72, 99, 111 (M567/197); Mahon, *Seminole War*, 254.
40. Poinsett to Macomb, March 18, 1839, in Carter and Bloom (eds.), *Territorial Papers*, XXV, 597–98.

his mission as purely diplomatic. He declined to take command of the war and insisted on merely conducting negotiations with the Seminoles. Taylor, therefore, left the following day to continue the squares program along the Suwannee. Macomb issued a call for a council with the Indians on May 1 at Fort King.[41] The naïveté of the call must have amused Taylor, since the self-proclaimed truce prevented his employing the regulars to counter several small bands of renegade Creeks who had drifted into Florida. The best he could do was to provide the local authorities with supplies for their forces.[42] Undoubtedly, Macomb's actions reinforced Taylor's clear dislike of the commanding general that extended back to his Green Bay years. Although the direct evidence is scant, it can be inferred from comments in Taylor's few surviving unofficial letters that he considered Macomb an office-bound general who had little understanding or appreciation of the western officers who served extensively along the Indian frontier. To Taylor it appeared that Macomb lacked both an understanding of the Seminoles and the wit to contend with them.[43]

Taylor rejoined Macomb at the end of April for the latter's May 1 council at Fort King. No hostiles appeared. Taylor remained until the morning of May 6, when he left for Tampa to start a campaign to push the Indians south of the twenty-eighth degree (the Melbourne–Tampa Bay–Lake Kissimmee) line. If the hostile bands could be kept south of there, Macomb assured the secretary of war, they would do little damage. Six days later Macomb sent Taylor a long account of his initial meetings with the Indians and approved a line of posts to protect the settled areas. The long-delayed council finally occurred on May 18. Macomb believed the meeting settled the conflict and two days later proclaimed the war at an end. The reality was different, since he had met with only one of four hostile Seminole bands. Moreover, the agreement provided that the Indians withdraw south of Pease Creek, below the twenty-eighth degree line, only by July 15. Taylor and many of the experienced officers in Florida doubted that any cease-fire would hold as long as there were Indians left on the peninsula. Long, frustrating experience convinced them that Macomb's arrangements would merely leave local inhabitants facing armed and hostile natives living in a nearby sanctuary. The prospects, they realized, would not make happy Floridians.[44]

41. Macomb to Secretary of War, April 6, 1839, *ibid.*, 602–603, to ZT, April 13, 1839, in HQLS, 5/3, pp. 477–80 (M875/2); Mahon, *Seminole War*, 255–56.

42. ZT to Call, April 9, 1839, in AGLR 1839, T-126 (M567/197).

43. See Hamilton, *Taylor*, I, 139.

44. Hamilton, *Taylor*, I, 138; Macomb to Poinsett, May 6, 22, 1839, in Carter and Bloom (eds.), *Territorial Papers*, XXV, 608–609, *Niles' Weekly Register*, LVI (1838/39), 249; Macomb to ZT, May 12, 19, 1839, in HQLS, 5/3, pp. 494–502 (M875/2); Mahon, *Seminole War*, 256–58; Walton, *Fearless and Free*, 198–200.

Macomb followed his agreement with reductions in the Florida forces. He directed Taylor to send most of the dragoons north to Georgia, cut the ten infantry companies to six, shift the 3d Artillery to New Orleans and release any unneeded militia.[45] By mid-July Taylor had received intelligence that the Tallahassee would not accept the settlement and asked Captain Isaac Mayo, commanding the navy's force in Florida waters, to interdict possible trade with Cuba and the Bahamas, paying particular attention to the west coast between the Suwannee and St. Marks.[46]

On July 23 the truce collapsed. A group of approximately 160 Indians, who undoubtedly did not feel themselves bound by the truce, attacked and overran a fortified trading post being constructed on the Caloosahatchee River inside the Indian reservation. Eighteen soldiers were killed while $2,000 to $3,000 in trade goods, $1,500 in silver coin, and a substantial number of Colt rifles were lost. The detachment commander, Lieutenant Colonel William S. Harney, and fourteen men escaped. Despite both Harney and Captain Mayo's seizing hostages to prevent a recurrence, for most whites the attack signaled the final Indian violation of the truce.[47]

On October 17 Macomb directed Taylor to occupy the territory north of a line running from Palatka on the St. Johns River to the mouth of the Withlacoochee while retaining the posts south of that line at Tampa and Key Biscayne. This was the area already largely covered by Taylor's squares program. In order to provide the manpower necessary to conduct these operations, the War Department canceled the withdrawal of the 3d Artillery and ordered the remainder of the 2d Dragoons and a levy of new recruits to join the Army of the South. Taylor freed six companies by replacing them on guard duty in east Florida with a regiment of Florida volunteers. By the end of October he was ready to resume active operations in the field once the weather improved. On paper he had 186 officers and 2,815 regulars plus 793 Florida mounted volunteers available at the end of November.[48]

"The past season," Taylor wrote his brother in January, "was one of the most unhealthy ever known in Florida." He himself fell victim to a fever which confined him to bed for nearly two weeks. Under the care of his

45. Macomb to ZT, May 19, 1838, in *Niles' Weekly Register*, LVI (1838/39), 249.

46. ZT to Mayo, July 16, 1839, in Naval Records Collection of the Office of Naval Records & Library (NA, RG 45), Records Relating to the Service of the Navy and Marine Corps on the Coast of Florida, 1835–1843 (hereinafter cited as Seminole War Letters), 113.

47. Mahon, *Seminole War*, 261–63; Mayo to Secretary of the Navy, July 30, 1839, in Seminole War Letters, 114.

48. Macomb to ZT, October 17, 25, 1839, in HQLS, 5/3, pp. 521–22, 524–25 (M857/2); Jones to ZT, October 24, 1839, in AGLS, XVI, 4 (M565/11); ZT to Poinsett, October 27, 1839, in ZT(LC), ser 2, r 1.

son-in-law Dr. Robert C. Wood and nursed by his wife, Taylor gradually improved. Not surprisingly the regimen of calomel and hot drinks left him very weak.[49]

In December the new campaign started. As a result of illness the number of men carried on the company rolls and those actually available had little similarity. For his campaign Taylor could count on only about 10 percent of the numbers appearing on the rolls. But they were numerous enough to permit him to sweep through middle Florida and break up the bands there, even if he could not drive all the warriors beyond the Withlacoochee.[50]

On February 26, 1840, Taylor, worn out and discouraged by his lack of success and ill health, asked for relief from the Florida assignment by May 1. Formal approval came in General Orders No. 22 on April 12, 1840. It directed Brevet Brigadier General Walker K. Armistead to assume the command on May 1. Mail between Washington and Tampa during the spring of 1840 was so poor that Taylor did not receive the orders to turn the command over to Armistead. He temporarily transferred command to Twiggs and departed from Fort Brooke May 1 in company with Mrs. Taylor on board a steamer. Five days later Armistead issued the orders announcing his assumption of command.[51]

Judged in terms of success in pacifying the Florida peninsula, Taylor's two years in command were little more productive than those of Jesup or Scott or Armistead. Yet, for a variety of reasons generally not under his control, Taylor missed most of the opprobrium which Florida service attracted to command there. His victory in the only large battle of the conflict went far in earning him distinction and it shielded him from public notice of his lack of other successes. In retrospect it is evident that the presence of Macomb served as a lightning rod to attract most of the negative attention which could have been focused on the Army of the South during 1839 to 1840. Even more important to Taylor's future image was his acquisition of the nickname of "Old Rough and Ready" which his troops bestowed upon him in recognition of his willingness to share their

49. ZT to J. P. Taylor, January 11, 1840, in ZT(LC), ser 2, r 1; Dyer, *Taylor*, 123; Hamilton, *Taylor*, I, 140.

50. Mahon, *Seminole War*, 265; ZT to Call, December 7, 1839, to R. R. Reid, February 25, 1840, in AGLR 1840, T-16, 105 (M567/217–18).

51. ZT to Jones, February 26, 1840, in Sprague, *Seminole War*, 242–43; Headquarters of Army General Order 22, April 21, Army of Florida Order 1, May 6, 1840, in Army Continental Commands (NA, RG 393), 9th Military District, Orders 1840; ZT to Jones, May 11, 1840, AGLR 1840, T-182 (M567/218). In July when Senator Thomas Hart Benton proposed raising 3,200 volunteers for the war, Taylor recommended one of the senior commands be given to Persifor Smith. ZT to Poinsett, July 18, 1840, in DeCoppet Collection.

privations while in the field.[52] From his long experience on the frontier Taylor had developed an understanding of Indians and the methods of containing their style of guerrilla warfare. His squares program, when viewed against later experience in Mexico, the Philippines, and Vietnam, was a practical solution to the problem of containing an enemy who could not be brought to battle. He enlarged upon his ideas in a long letter to Secretary Poinsett on his departure from Florida. Solving the Indian problem, the ailing general argued, could be accomplished either by covering the peninsula with twenty thousand men or building a cordon of posts stretching from the mouth of the Waccasassa River to Fort King, then across to the Oklawaha River and eastward to Fort Gates at the north end of Lake George. From there Taylor proposed the line run to the Atlantic ocean near New Smyrna. As a former commander, Taylor believed that the Floridians, like many of the frontier settlers he had dealt with farther north, could contribute more to their own defense than they chose to do. He also suggested that regiments sent to Florida be kept up to strength so as to reduce the need to call for local volunteers to fill out the forces available on the peninsula.[53]

52. *General Taylor and His Staff* (Philadelphia, 1848), 81; Dyer, *Taylor*, 126; Silas Bent McKinley and Silas Bent, *Old Rough and Ready* (New York, 1946), 5.
53. ZT to Poinsett, May 11, 1840, in AGLR 1840, T-200 (M567/218).

CHAPTER VI

Return to the Southwest

GENERAL ORDER 22, which relieved Taylor of command in Florida, granted him leave until December 1840. The Taylors proceeded by sea to Pensacola, where they disembarked and traveled overland to New Orleans, arriving on May 21, 1840. They continued north by river steamer to Baton Rouge and Louisville. On July 10 they reached Washington, D.C., where Taylor conferred with officials at the War Department. Since it was mid-summer and few senior bureaucrats remained at their posts in the sweltering heat, the discussions must have been limited. The Taylors' grand tour next took them to Philadelphia, where they visited Lieutenant Colonel and Mrs. William Davenport. There, also, they were reunited with Betty, who was on vacation from her boarding school. She accompanied her parents for the remainder of the trip.

The next step was Boston. That visit also had an educational objective in that it permitted Taylor to meet James Gordon Carter of Lancaster, Massachusetts. Taylor had decided to send Richard, now thirteen, to Carter to be prepared for college, Harvard if possible. "He is a youth," wrote the adoring father, "as far as I can know or can learn [,] of good morals . . . possessing a warm & affectionate disposition, perhaps a little hasty as to temper, but which no doubt can be readily controlled. . . . He does not I apprehend lack the capacity as to the acquiring of a substantial education . . . but may want application." From Boston the family traveled west to Niagara Falls and western Pennsylvania before returning to Louisville in September.[1]

The trip revived Taylor both in spirit and in health. He reported ready for duty in mid-September and requested assignment in Louisiana, preferably at Baton Rouge or New Orleans. If that request could not be honored, he wished that he be placed on waiting orders. Either assignment, he anticipated, would allow him to attend to his Louisiana plantations.

During the early months of 1841 Taylor showed an hitherto unexposed portion of his character. He viewed the newly elected William Henry Harrison administration as the potential savior of a nation wracked by what Taylor considered the corruption of Andrew Jackson and the ineptitude of Martin Van Buren. How much of Taylor's sudden interest resulted from political conviction and how much from the coincidence of his relatively close personal ties to the president and the secretary of war designate, John Bell, is unclear. It is evident, however, that Taylor placed himself politically in the Whig camp, even if he did not parade that fact publicly. In January he sent John J. Crittenden a pair of letters for possible delivery to Harrison and Colonel Charles S. Todd, a fellow Kentuckian who was one of Harrison's closest advisors. The letters apparently have not survived so we cannot be certain of their contents, but evidence of Taylor's interest in the administration is amply proven.[2] In May Taylor recommended that Secretary Bell appoint Major Ethan Allen Hitchcock as commissioner of Indian affairs. Taylor envisioned Hitchcock serving as the advisor to the secretary on the "details of the service," since Bell could not "derive any great aid from the opinions of the heads of the Bureaus at Washington." Most of the latter, Taylor wrote, had been stationed there so long that "they have lost sight of & know almost nothing of the wants of the troops in the field or upon the frontier."[3] Whatever interests Taylor may have had in utilizing his political connections with the administration vanished after the death of Harrison and the resignation of Bell.

Taylor continued in charge at Baton Rouge through May 1841, broken only by a short stay in New Orleans in January. On May 1, however, Adjutant General Jones directed him to relieve Brevet Brigadier General Matthew Arbuckle as commander of the 2d Military Department at Fort Gibson in the Cherokee portion of the Indian Territory. He left June 2 but

1. 1st Infantry Returns, April–December 1840 (M665/2); Holman Hamilton, *Zachary Taylor* (2 vols.; Indianapolis, 1941, 1951), I, 142; Brainerd Dyer, *Zachary Taylor* (Baton Rouge, 1946), 128; Holman Hamilton, "A Youth of Good Morals," *Filson Club History Quarterly*, XXVII (1953), 305–306.

2. ZT to Crittenden, January 29, 1841, in John J. Crittenden Papers, VII, r 4, LC.

3. ZT to Hitchcock, May 19, 1841, in ZT(LC), ser 2, r 1.

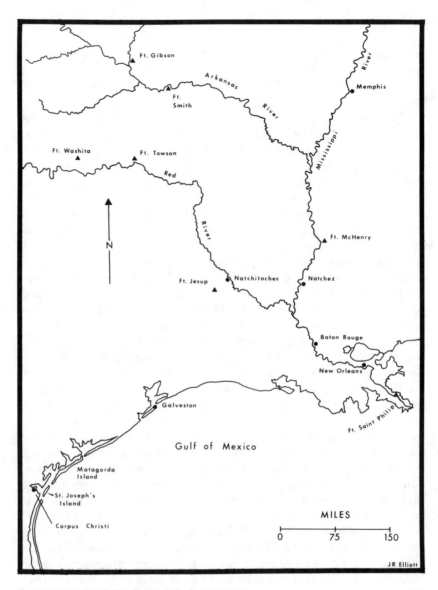

Ft. Gibson

Arkansas River

Memphis

River

Ft.
Smith

Ft. Washita

Ft. Towson

Red

Mississippi

River

N

Ft. McHenry

Ft. Jesup

Natchitoches

Natchez

Baton Rouge

New Orleans

Galveston

Ft. Saint Philip

Gulf of Mexico

Matagorda
Island

St. Joseph's
Island

Corpus Christi

MILES

0   75   150

JR Elliott

SOUTHWESTERN FRONTIER

had a slow journey because of low water in the Arkansas River. Mrs. Taylor and Ann accompanied him. Fort Gibson had been established in 1824 and shifted to its present location five years later. It embraced a rectangle 318 by 348 feet, the shorter, north-south sides formed by barracks and stores; the longer by pickets. Designed to house five companies, it stood about 150 yards from the river. It had the unfortunate reputation, borne out by medical statistics, of being the most unhealthy post in the army. It suffered from its exposure to the miasmas of the river valley, a poor source of water, and an unfortunate climate.

Taylor viewed his new post with profound misgivings. It was difficult to reach from New Orleans since no stage coaches regularly ran to the Mississippi River, and the Arkansas River was too shallow for navigation. Moreover, his quarters were uncomfortable. Taylor shortly shifted his headquarters to Cantonment Belknap near Fort Smith.[4] Indeed, the whole assignment brought forth one of Taylor's strongest outbursts of self-pity, despite the recognition of his brevet rank. He complained to Hitchcock that his private affairs had suffered so badly during his absence in Florida that it would need his presence in Louisiana for eight or nine months to right them. Moreover, he pointedly remarked that Inspector General John Wool had been "stationary at his domicile or private residence for more than twenty years." That circumstance, Taylor claimed, permitted him to amass a large fortune. He also objected to Wool's recent selection as brigadier general since it moved him into the line ahead of several more senior colonels.[5]

Taylor's concern about Fort Gibson coincided with a reevaluation of the Indian Territory posts which had been started by the Van Buren administration before it left office. During the fall of 1839 Chief Engineer Colonel Joseph G. Totten, Lieutenant Colonel Sylvanus Thayer in charge of building the defenses of Boston, Quartermaster Major Trueman Cross, and Chief of Ordnance Lieutenant Colonel George Talcott studied the frontier defense problem in light of the transfer of the eastern tribes beyond the Mississippi. They recommended a new line of posts anchored by two major installations: Fort Towson housing a five-hundred-man gar-

---

4. 1st Infantry Returns, February–May 1841 (M665/2); Jones to ZT, May 1, 1841, in AGLS, XVII (565/12); ZT to Hitchcock, July 28, November 3, 1841, in ZT(LC), ser 2, r 1; Lieutenant S. G. Simmons to ZT, June 1841, in Army Continental Commands (NA, RG 393), 2nd Military District Letter Books, IV, 1122–23; Edwin C. Bearss and Arrell M. Gibson, *Fort Smith, Little Gibraltar on the Arkansas* (Norman, 1979), 168; Grant Foreman, *Advancing the Frontier, 1830–1860* (Norman, 1933), 38–39; Gillett, "Army Medical Department 1818–65," IV, 49.

5. ZT to Hitchcock, November 3, 1841, in ZT(LC), ser 2, r 1. Wool was appointed brigadier general on June 25, 1841, to fill the vacancy caused by Scott's promotion. Taylor expected the opening to be filled by the senior line colonel, Abram Eustis of the 1st Artillery.

rison and Fort Gibson with twice that number. The board suggested establishing two-hundred-man posts at Fort Smith, Fort Wayne, and on the Spring River. Additional smaller, one-hundred-man, installations should be built on the Sabine River at the crossings of the Opelousas and Natchitoches roads. In forwarding the report to the House of Representatives, Secretary Joel R. Poinsett called Fort Gibson "the most important point on that frontier." He pointed out that it was connected to Fort Smith and Little Rock by a road constructed by details of soldiers.[6]

From Taylor's point of view, as well as that of Major Charles Thomas, the quartermaster officer responsible for construction, the scale and cost of Fort Smith were excessive. The location, Taylor complained, was unhealthy and often flooded.[7] But before he could turn his attention to that problem, he was confronted by the more mundane activities of frontier patrol. Captain Isaac P. Simonton at Fort Wayne sent him for trial a Missourian who had shot another Missourian on Seneca land. The captain also forwarded complaints filed by individual Cherokees of their harassment by the Arkansas authorities. Simonton further reported that the Cherokees were upset because some of the soldiers at the post had gone in Maysville, Arkansas, for a Fourth of July "frolic," probably with some of the local Cherokee prostitutes, during which an Indian was apparently murdered and another badly beaten. He requested guidance in case the Indians asked for custody of the accused soldiers since the post was defenseless. Taylor responded by strengthening the garrison, ordering defenses built, and directing the transfer of the accused soldier to local civil authorities.[8] Taylor soon concluded that the post should be abandoned. General Scott in the spring of 1842, therefore, ordered its relocation.[9]

At the same time Captain George W. Allen at Fort Towson reported on the activities of a body of Texans who he feared might trespass on Chickasaw lands. He pointed out the importance of establishing a post on the Washita River to protect the Chickasaws from marauders, either red or white. Taylor supported the proposal, which had earlier been made by Arbuckle.[10] This caused the War Department to exchange six companies

6. Poinsett to R. M. T. Hunter, March 21, 1840, and Report of Board, both in *Senate Documents*, 26th Cong., 1st Sess., No. 379, pp. 1–9.

7. Bearss and Gibson, *Fort Smith*, 168–69; ZT to Hitchcock, November 3, 1841, in ZT(LC), ser 2, r 1.

8. ZT to Jones, July 13, Major R. B. Mason to Simmons, September 29, 1841, in AGLR 1841, T-211, 301 (M567/239).

9. ZT to Jones, July 28, October 15, 1841, in AGLR 1841, T-218, 302 (M567/239); Thomas to ZT, September 11, Jones to ZT, December 1, 1841, in AGLS, XVII, 308–309, 413 (M565/12).

10. Allen to ZT, August 14, AT to Jones, June 21, 1841, in AGLR 1841, T-215 (M657/239).

of Twiggs's 2d Dragoons for six companies of the 4th Infantry needed in Florida. The Washington authorities further directed Taylor to reconnoiter the Washita region for a site for the new post. After clearing the project with the Chickasaw leaders, he approved a site approximately a mile and a half east of the False Washita and some thirty miles above its junction with the Red River. Construction of the post, later named Fort Washita, began in the summer of 1842.[11]

Shortly after his return from the reconnaissance Taylor took sixty days leave in another effort to settle his financial problems in Louisiana.[12] He returned in January 1842 and promptly received a directive to reestablish Fort Wayne. Taylor chose instead to construct a new post, Fort Scott, on the Marmaton River in present-day Kansas about fifty miles north of the department's proposed site. There it protected the Potawatomi and checked incursions by the Osage onto Cherokee lands.[13]

Superseding the rather routine concern about Indian disagreements was the danger growing out of the Mexican resumption of war with Texas. On March 5–7 a Mexican force occupied San Antonio, leading the Texas *chargé* in Washington to request efforts to restrain American Indians who might seize the opportunity to raid the Lone Star Republic. On March 26 Taylor received orders to do so, along with a promise of reinforcements. The latter consisted of the entire 6th Infantry from Jefferson Barracks and five companies of the 2d Dragoons from Fort Leavenworth. The infantry marched to Fort Towson while the dragoons rode to Fort Gibson. Three days later the Louisiana posts were added to Taylor's command so that he could head the entire observation force.[14]

Taylor initially placed a company of dragoons at Fort Washita.[15] He followed that advance into Indian country by attending a grand council of the plains tribes. The meeting, called by the Creeks, was at the junction of the Deep Fork and Candian rivers near present-day Eufaula, Oklahoma.

11. Thomas to ZT, August 14, Jones to ZT, December 3, 1841, in AGLS, XVII, 270, 416 (M565/12); ZT to Jones, October 14, 1841, April 17, 1842, in AGLR 1841, T-300, 1842, T-127 (M567/239, 259); Robert W. Frazer, *Forts of the West* (Norman, 1965), 125–26; ZT to Jones, December 23, 1841, in AGRL, XVII, T-284 (M711/14).

12. ZT to Gaines, August 8, 1841, in AGLR 1841, T-239 (M567/239); Lieutenant J. C. Reid to ZT, August 29, 1841, Thomas to ZT, September 2, 1841, in 2MD:LR, Box 3.

13. Raphael P. Thian, *Notes Illustrating the Military Geography of the United States, 1813–1880* (1881; rpr. Austin, 1979), 37; Jones to ZT, February 10, 1842, in AGLS, XVIII, 7–8, 103 (M565/12); ZT to Jones, February 14, March 27, 1842, in AGRL, XVIII, T-58 (M711/15), AGLR 1842, T-103 (M567/259).

14. Spencer to ZT, March 26, 1842, in *Senate Executive Documents*, 32nd Cong., 3rd Sess., No. 14, p. 75; Jones to ZT, March 26, 1842, in AGLS, XVIII, 83 (M565/12); Henry Putney Beers, *The Western Military Frontier, 1815–1846* (Philadelphia, 1935), 163; Thian, *Military Geography*, 37.

15. ZT to Jones, April 17, 1842, in AGLR 1842, T-127 (M567/254).

It met May 15. Taylor, Major William W. S. Bliss, and Indian Superintendent William Armstrong along with several tribal agents met with representatives from the Creeks, Choctaws, Chickasaws, Seminoles, Shawnees,
Delawares, Piankishaws, Kickapoos, Quapaws, Kichees, Wichitas, Paw-
nees, Osages, Caddos, Tawakoni, Senecas, and a few Cherokees. Unfortunately, the tribes beyond the Cross Timbers sent few representatives. Even
so, the camp measured two miles in circumference. Taylor impressed
upon the Indians the need to stay out of Texas; stressed the importance of
preserving peace; and promised ransom for white children seized by the
Comanches. More immediately important was the Cherokee agreement
that the Seminoles could remain on their land. The American negotiators
also arranged for the Kichee, Kiowa, Tawakoni, and Wichita representatives to visit Fort Gibson to renew their allegiance to the United States.
Taylor found the Indians so friendly that he remained only two days before riding on to Fort Gibson.[16]

From Fort Gibson, the department commander continued his inspection tour to Forts Towson (May 28), Washita (May 23), and Jesup (June
17). He endorsed an earlier local proposal for the addition of a post between the two western Louisiana forts but nothing came of it.[17] Following
his return to Fort Smith in July Taylor forwarded to Washington a detailed
report on the posts. Only Fort Gibson, also the target of a negative report
by General Gaines, and the poorly sited Towson drew unfavorable
comments.[18]

Roughly coincident with Taylor's return, his command was again altered. On July 11 the adjutant general promulgated General Order 40. It
redefined the nine military departments and eliminated the two geographical divisions. The motivation appears to have come from the improvement of communications which permitted even the westernmost departments to enjoy relatively rapid contact with Washington. Military
Department No. 2 retained its designation but shed Louisiana, while Fort
Smith continued as departmental headquarters.[19] If anything, Taylor
must have breathed a sigh of relief, for it removed from his responsibility
the two most distant posts.

In October he requested leave to visit New Orleans during December

16. Hamilton, *Taylor*, I, 151; Foreman, *Advancing the Frontier*, 201–204; ZT to Jones,
May 6, 15, 1842, in AGRL, XVIII, T-140 (M711/15), AGLR 1842, T-158 (M567/259).

17. Rice Garland to Secretary of War Spencer, November 24, 1841, in 2MD:LR, Box 3;
ZT to AG, July 5, 1842, in AGFLR 1842, T-198 (M567/259).

18. Gaines to AG, May 31, ZT to AG, July 30, 1842, enclosing the report of Bliss, all in
HQUL, Box 3.

19. Headquarters of the Army, General Order 40, July 11, 1842, in *House Reports*, 28th
Cong., 1st Sess., No. 341, pp. 19–21.

in order to attend to personal business. Adjutant General Jones "cheer-fully" granted him forty days, but Taylor did not depart from Fort Smith until January 12.[20] We know nothing about Taylor's activities while on leave but it is safe to assume that they centered around the financial de-tails of the Cypress Grove purchase. They may also have involved con-cerns growing out of the return of Richard from abroad and his admis-sion to Yale as a junior. Richard had spent about two years studying in Edinburgh and Paris before returning to the United States. In New Haven he was considered to possess "intellectual ability and social charm" but to be rather lazy. He apparently lived well, for his father complained that his expenses were much greater than they should be.[21]

Taylor returned to his command on February 13. He almost imme-diately had to confront growing unrest among the Cherokee political fac-tions. It surfaced in some small election disturbances during August which were handled by the Indian authorities. In the fall Taylor dis-patched a company of dragoons into Indian Territory to quiet Arkansas settlers who were attempting to stir up trouble, in hopes of luring troops and their payroll into the area.[22] Taylor and Bliss in June visited Tahle-quah to participate in the Second Grand Council with the representatives of eighteen tribes. It was an effort by the Cherokee to achieve peace among the tribes. Since the gathering aimed at quieting the Indian fron-tier, it contributed to the same ends that Taylor sought. He returned to Fort Smith pleased with the meeting, very impressed with the serious de-meanor of the participants.[23]

A second occurrence during the summer brought even greater plea-sure. In July Adjutant General Jones proposed that Taylor and Colonel William Davenport of the 6th Infantry switch commands. This appears to have been an effort to allow Taylor to take a post closer to his Louisiana property. The exchange nominally occurred on July 7 but did not affect Taylor's departmental command.[24] Conditions along the Arkansas fron-

20. ZT to AG, October 5, 1842, January 6, 1843, in AGRL, XVIII, T-401, XIX, T-17 (M711/15, 16); Jones to ZT, November 3, 1842, in AGLS, XVIII, 454 (M565/12); Thian, *Military Geography*, 37.

21. Anson Phelps Stokes, *Memorials of Eminent Yale Men* (2 vols.; New Haven, 1914), II, 343–44; ZT to J. P. Taylor, January 29, 1845, in ZT(LC), ser 3, r 11. The Kingsley Memo-rial Collection, Box 13, Yale:M&A, contains a March 6, 1844, letter from Taylor complain-ing of Richard's neglect in writing to his mother.

22. Thian, *Military Geography*, 37; Jones to ZT, March 3, 1843, in AGLS, XIX, 146–48 (M565/13); ZT to AG, March 28, August 15, 1843, in AGLR 1843, T-96, 223 (M567/277); Hamilton, *Taylor*, I, 153.

23. ZT to AG, June 14, 1843, in AGRL, XIX, T-162 (M711/16); Beers, *Western Mili-tary Frontier*, 142; Foreman, *Advancing the Frontier*, 205–206.

24. Jones to ZT, July 3, August 23, 1843, in AGLS, XIX, 353, 434–35 (M565/13); ZT

tier remained reasonably quiet throughout the rest of the year, permitting Taylor to take leave from January 7 to February 6, 1844. Accompanied by Bliss, he again visited New Orleans to meet with his bankers and agents.[25] On his return, Taylor faced a new situation and a new command.

Taylor's preoccupation with land speculation, which the New Orleans visit signified, was of long standing. At the time he left the army in 1816 he joined his father and most other men of property in Kentucky in buying and selling land. He sold his original farm at a 71 percent profit in August 1816 and reinvested the proceeds in a 1,400-acre plot at the mouth of Goose Creek, upstream from his father's estate. It netted him $16,500 when sold four years later. That was two and a half times his investment. Nor apparently did Taylor forgo special opportunities to acquire smaller tracts. On March 18 and April 12, 1820, the Commonwealth of Kentucky granted fifty-acre parcels on Russell Creek, Adair County, to a Zachariah Taylor.[26]

Taylor's investment philosophy envisioned using the rent and interest due him to pay his few debts and to ensure that Mrs. Taylor had sufficient funds to meet her needs when he was in the field. It did not always work as planned, as he wrote to his brother and agent in Louisville in 1817; "Peggy [Mrs. Taylor] has informed me that she has been threatened to be turned out by her landlord." Taylor counseled his brother to lend out any surplus funds at 12 to 15 percent rather than purchasing bank stock. Hancock Taylor continued to act as his brother's agent for many years but was later replaced by John Allison, who married their sister Emily.[27]

Taylor's service in the south during the early 1820s caused him to be attracted to the newly opened cotton lands along the Mississippi River above Baton Rouge. On January 23, 1823, he purchased a 380-acre plantation in West Feliciana Parish, Louisiana, near the Mississippi border and not far from the Deer Range Plantation of his friend Maunsel White, a New Orleans manufacturer. He paid its owner, Byrd Bufford, $2,000 in

to AG, July 25, 1843, in AGLR 1843, T-208 (M567/277); Francis B. Heitman, *Historical Register of the Continental Army During the War of the Revolution* (Baltimore, 1967), I, 92, 949.

25. ZT to AG, November 4, 1843, January 2, 1844, in AGRL, XIX, T-286 (M711/16), AGLR 1844, T-15 (M567/291); Jones to ZT, November 24, 1843, in AGLS, XX, 59 (M565/13); Thian, *Military Geography*, 37.

26. ZT Deposition, October 1, 1816, in Presidential Papers, Filson Club, Louisville; ZT deed to William Taylor, February 10, 1820, in ZT(KHS); Willard Rouse Jillson, *The Kentucky Land Grants* (Louisville, 1925), 740. The identification of the 1820 land grant with Taylor is tentative since there were at least two persons of that name active in Kentucky at the time.

27. ZT to Hancock Taylor, July 6, 1817, April 10, 1821, in ZT(LC), ser 2, r 1, Alice Elizabeth Trabue Papers, folder 50, Filson Club, Louisville.

cash and notes with equal amounts to be paid in 1824 and 1825. Taylor imported twenty-two slaves from his Kentucky farms and put his cousin Damascus Thornton in charge. Thornton was an honest, hard-working, experienced farmer who operated the plantation to the full satisfaction of his employer until his death in 1831. The first year was not a success, however. A September 14 hurricane so devastated the cotton that the eighteen field hands produced only forty bales of cotton worth about $2,400. But after the deductions of Thornton's pay and other overhead expenses the plantation cleared only about $1,500 or $500 less than the year's payments. Taylor retained the plantation until 1841. Three years later he had to take it back when the purchaser could not continue his payments. The plantation remained in Taylor's possession until he finally sold it in May 1849 for $3,000.[28]

Taylor chronically complained about his ill-luck with his investments. The reaction appears to be the anguish of a man with overblown expectations. Moreover, much of his economic difficulty arose from an act of kindness. He had endorsed a note for a friend who defaulted, leaving Taylor to pay. Winfield Scott later noted: "He resolutely refused to take any relief from the stoplaws of the same demagogues, or to pay in their rag currency, and although a dear lover of money, persistently paid his endorsement in specie." In 1829 Taylor placed the losses suffered by his plantations and his liabilities at $20,000. He had earlier offered his interest in land on Goose Creek, east of Louisville, to his brother-in-law John Gibson Taylor, but the deal apparently died, since the land was still for sale in 1830. Taylor's problem also stemmed from the land speculation boom in Kentucky which began in 1815 and burst in the early 1820s. To fund that explosion the state legislature had chartered forty banks, many without sufficient capital, who flooded the state with paper money. When the bubble of speculation broke, the legislature enacted laws favoring the debtors. In a letter to Jesup, Taylor lamented: "The state of the currency in Ky & the course pursued by the legislature of that State for several years past, in relation to contracts, has embarrassed me beyond measure. It is now only with the greatest prudence & economy I can keep my head above water." In later correspondence he complained: "No Country can be prosperous without an able & independent judiciary, & a sound currency, neither of which has this state been blest with for some time past."[29]

28. ZT to Jesup, January 20, 1824, in ZT(LC), ser 2, r 1; to Elizabeth Lee Taylor, August 4, October 8, 1823, in Trabue Papers, folder 50; Dyer, *Taylor,* 255; Hamilton, *Taylor,* I, 72–73; Clement Eaton, *The Growth of Southern Civilization, 1790–1860* (New York, 1961), 61.

29. ZT to J. G. Taylor, March 2, 1829, in Trabue Papers, folder 50; to Jesup, January 20, 1824, January 29, 1827, to Lawson, August 29, 1838, in ZT(LC), ser 2, r 1; Winfield Scott,

In a lacrimose letter to his cousin William Berry Taylor, he complained that the turn of events had to "a great measure blighted" his hopes "to the acquirement of anything like a fortune." It caused him to abandon any hope of establishing himself in comfort in Kentucky and to shift his attention to his Louisiana plantation. "My great anxiety," he wrote to his New Orleans agent, "is to collect means sufficient to enable me to purchase a small plantation on the bank of the Mississippi within the sugar region on which I can locate myself with the prospect of ease & comfort for the balance of my life." [30]

Following his father's death in January 1829, Taylor received the Charles Farm outside of Louisville. Whether the small provision in his father's will reflected Richard Taylor's reduced circumstances or merely indicated that he considered his son adequately provided for is not clear. In any event, Taylor sold the farm during the summer of 1829 for $2,000. [31]

On March 6, 1831, Taylor took a long step in his shift of interests to the lower Mississippi. Probably using the cash generated by the sale of the Charles Farm, he purchased 137 acres in Wilkinson County, Mississippi, from Hamilton M. Orr. The plantation, adjacent to the West Feliciana property, was called the Sligo Tract. It cost $1,500. Taylor hired James Thornton, the brother of the recently deceased Damascus, as overseer of both plantations. Thornton managed the properties until shortly before the Mexican War, earning a high regard from Taylor, who on at least one occasion trusted him with the power of attorney. [32] Taylor added a third plantation to his holdings in 1838 when he bought 163 acres in West Feliciana Parish for $1,965. [33]

On December 15, 1841, he sold the Sligo Tract to Henry H. Wall for

Memoirs of Lieut.-General Scott, LL.D. (2 vols., 1864; rpr. Freeport, N.Y., 1970), II, 390–91; Dyer, Taylor, 65; Hamilton, Taylor, I, 80–81. Taylor did not pay off his debt until 1842. ZT to Hitchcock, July 28, 1841, in ZT(LC), ser 2, r 1. For a contemporary account of the debtor-creditor struggle see Earl Gregg Swem (ed.), Letters on the Condition of Kentucky in 1825 (New York, 1916).

30. ZT to J. G. Taylor, April 12, 1830, in ZT (Minn); to Maunsel White, August 6, 1829, in ZT(LSU).

31. Richard Taylor Will, December 22, 1828, in Miscellaneous Collection, Filson Club; Katherine G. Healy, "Calendar of Early Jefferson County, Kentucky Wills," Filson Club History Quarterly, VI (1932), 312; ZT to Maunsel White, August 6, 1829, in ZT(LSU); Dyer, Taylor, 72; Hamilton, Taylor, I, 79–80. Taylor, who was trapped by winter at Fort Snelling, could not return to Louisville to serve as executor of his father's will. His mother died soon afterwards, in December 1829.

32. Hamilton, Taylor, I, 81–82, 155, II, 30–31. Taylor sold the property in 1841 for $2,062.50.

33. Ibid., I, 142–43; ZT to Jones, September 19, 1840, in Andre De Coppet Collection, Princeton University Library. He sold the plantation in December 1841 at a loss. ZT to Jesup, November 4, 1840, in ZT(LC), ser 2, r 1.

$2,062.50. The transaction was one of a series in which Taylor sold his three contiguous Louisiana and Mississippi properties. Two days after disposing of the Mississippi property he sold the original West Feliciana Parish property to Wall for $7,710 and the 163 acres purchased in 1838 to John Wicker for $1,653.50. He took promissory notes payable in 1843, 1844, and 1845 in payment. All but the last sale represented substantial profits. Over all, Taylor had made 116 percent profit on an investment of $5,130. With the limited cash and notes developed by the sales, Taylor authorized his agent Maunsel White in New Orleans to purchase the 1,923-acre Cypress Grove Plantation on the Mississippi River near Rodney, Mississippi, north of Natchez from John Hagan, Sr. For this plantation, along with its eighty-one slaves, Taylor paid $60,000 in cash, the bulk of which represented the proceeds of the sale of his cotton crops, and $35,000 in notes. Although the property lay in one of the richest cotton producing regions in the South, the plantation took several years to become profitable. Complicating the soldier's financial difficulties was Wall's default of his 1844 payment, which forced Taylor to repossess the West Feliciana property. It was not finally disposed of until the spring of 1849, and then for only $3,000.[34]

James Thornton served as overseer at Cypress Grove until he resigned in 1845. Thomas W. Ringgold replaced him. The initial actions of Ringgold irritated Taylor since the overseer, contrary to his orders, planted a full crop of cotton. But when the price of cotton in 1845 rose higher than it had been in five years, Taylor concluded that the decision had been wise. The two men developed a strong relationship and Ringgold remained in charge as long as Taylor owned the plantation. At intervals while her husband was in Texas and Mexico, Mrs. Taylor lived at Cypress Grove. One English visitor described the plantation house as an unpretentious wooden building with a large library and a colonnaded veranda.[35]

Even though he was seldom in residence, Taylor kept a close watch on the activities of his plantations. He worried about the conditions of his slaves, or "servants" as he referred to them in the more common antebellum euphemism. If the relatively few comments on his slaves which have survived are correct, Taylor's may well have been as well treated and

34. ZT Deed of Sale, December 15, 1841, ZT to J. P. Taylor, June 17, 1843; Henry W. Wall Deposition, May 3, 1844, in ZT(LC), ser 2, r 1; Dyer, *Taylor*, 255, 261, 263; ZT to Hagan, May 26, 1841, in ZT(LSU); Hamilton, *Taylor*, I, 155; Clement Eaton, *The Mind of the Old South* (Baton Rouge, 1967), 73–75. The boundaries of the plantation were not settled until March 1848, when Taylor complained "Cypress Grove. . . has ruined me." ZT to Hagan, March 29, 1848, in ZT(LSU).

35. Dyer, *Taylor*, 64, 257, 261; Hamilton, *Taylor*, I, 79, II, 34–36; Lady Emmeline Stuart-Wortley, *Travels in the United States, etc. During 1849 and 1850* (New York, 1851), 117–19; Holman Hamilton, *The Three Kentucky Presidents* (Lexington, 1978), 23–24.

their welfare as carefully considered as any in the South. Each slave received fresh milk daily and was issued a pound of meat on an average day. The latter was normally pork, although beef and lamb were occasionally substituted. Insofar as possible, all food came from the plantation but sometimes, as in June 1845, Taylor authorized purchase of additional supplies. The overseers had standing instructions to provide an ample supply of bread and an abundance of vegetables. The latter were an especial concern for Taylor, who continually stressed the importance of growing a plentiful supply for the "servants." The Taylor slaves wore comfortable clothes of flannel or calico, depending on the season, and most of the women possessed woolen shawls for additional warmth. The health of his field hands was a prime concern to Taylor, as it was to most plantation owners who realized that the profitability of their holdings was closely tied to the number of healthy hands. Taylor, whose army experience here undoubtedly proved valuable, insisted that sick hands rest until they were well and strong. It appears to have been a successful policy, since the surviving correspondence gives no hint of extensive illness among the slaves. The reports of visitors to the Taylor plantation describe happy, healthy, and well-cared-for slaves who lived in clean, well-furnished cabins. They also benefited from his policy of distributing cash Christmas gifts to the slaves in amounts of as much as $5.00.

Taylor kept a close watch on activities at his plantations. "The subject of farming," he wrote in 1848, "is one to which I have devoted much of my life, and in which I yet continue to take the deepest interest." He was an advocate of both crop rotation and of soil conservation. He experimented with different crops and various strains of cotton. In 1826, for instance, he attempted to locate ten to twenty bushels of Mexican cotton seeds to test. We do not know if he found the seeds, but he seems not to have repeated the experiment. At various times the plantations raised sheep, cattle, hogs, poultry, potatoes, tobacco, corn, wheat, peas, and hay alongside their normal crops of cotton. Taylor in directing the planting might, as he did in 1845, order one to two hundred acres be kept in pasturage and the next year instruct his overseer to plant six hundred acres in cotton, two hundred in corn, and thirty to forty in oats as well as maintaining a ten-acre vegetable garden. At Cypress Grove he also put his slaves to work logging. This was started as an experiment in 1845 in the hope that it would produce enough income to pay for the rope and bagging needed to bale the cotton. The effort coincided with a shortage of locally grown cypress timber and was so successful that three years later the plantation invested in its own sawmill. Taylor also instructed Ringgold to join with neighboring planters in building a levee along

Black Creek and the Mississippi to control the springtime flooding, which devastated the area in 1844, 1847, and 1849.

Since cotton prices boomed until 1840, Taylor must have reaped considerable profit. Although the price declined drastically thereafter, the output of Taylor's plantations rose after 1845. Nevertheless, Taylor continued his complaints about disasters which assailed his fields. His letters constantly note floods, droughts, cutworms, low prices, and mistaken choice of crops. Yet the disasters were no worse than those faced by most farmers and are not really reflected by the surviving production records. Moreover, both his brother-in-law John S. Allison in Louisville and his friend in New Orleans, Maunsel White, made investments for the absent army officer, especially in bank stocks. As a result Taylor acquired a substantial estate for the times and lived well. Even on the frontier, his openhanded entertainment and his extensive cellar attracted frequent mention by travelers.[36]

Prior to his moving to Washington to assume the presidency, Taylor had an inventory made of his property. It showed he owned slaves probably worth $50,000; real estate in Louisville which rented for $600 per year and was sold by his estate for $13,500; bank and utility stocks worth over $11,000; $20,000 on deposit with Maunsel White & Company; the Sligo Plantation, worth $3,000; army pay and allowances of $5,600 per year; the Cypress Grove plantation which was assessed at $8,000 but would be sold for $20,000; farm machinery, horses, cattle, and mules assessed at over $7,000; and $7,500 owed by Joseph Smith, secured by a mortgage. In all Taylor was worth $135,000 to $140,000, roughly $1.3 million in 1983 dollars, a very substantial sum for a Louisiana plantation owner.[37]

In May 1849 Taylor finally sold the Sligo Plantation for $3,000. Unlike

36. Polk to John Coffee, March 16, 1826, in George W. Polk Papers, Southern Historical Collection, University of North Carolina; ZT to Ringgold, June 18, September 15, December 16, 1845, June 9, October 20, November 10, 1846, and January 27, 1847, in Asher Autograph Collection, LC, Miscellaneous Papers, NYHS, and Stephen Currie (ed.), "Zachary Taylor, Plantation Owner," *Civil War History*, XXX (1984), 144–56; to Davis, July 10, 1848, in Jefferson Davis Papers, LC; to Allison, August 3, 1848, in ZT(LC), ser 2, r 1; [Thomas B. Thorpe], "General Taylor's Residence at Baton Rouge," *Harper's New Monthly Magazine*, IX (1854), 764; John Hebron Moore, *Andrew Brown and Cypress Lumbering in the Old Southwest* (Baton Rouge, 1967), 40–44; Charles Sackett Syndor, *Slavery in Mississippi* (Gloucester, Mass., 1965), 183, 185. See also ZT to Davis, July 27, September 18, 1847, in Haskell M. Monroe, *et al.* (eds.), *The Papers of Jefferson Davis* (4 vols.; Baton Rouge, 1971–), III, 449, 478–89; to Wood, November 17, 1847, in De Coppet Collection; Bliss to Hitchcock, May 18, 1845, in Ethan Allen Hitchcock Papers, Box 2, LC.

37. Hamilton, *Taylor*, II, 33.

his previous plantation sales, he did not reinvest the money in land, a decision which brought a commendation from John Allison, who pointed out that money invested at 8.5 percent brought a better return than it would in either a sugar or cotton plantation. Later in the year Allison forwarded offers for some of the Louisville property, but Taylor apparently rejected the offer. During the spring of 1850 he began investing heavily in bank stocks.[38] It marked a drastic change in his investment philosophy and verified his shift from landowner to capitalist—an often unnoted switch which placed Taylor among the new economic leadership in the south who deserted land as the vehicle for the accumulation of wealth.

38. ZT to [?], May 16, 1849 (unfinished draft), Thomas Henderson and Beale to E. H. McGhee, April 29, 1850, McGhee to ZT, July 16, Allison to ZT, July 18, October 14, November 19, 1849, statements of R. W. Latham & Co., February 4, March 15, 1850, all in ZT(LC), ser 2, r 1.

CHAPTER VII

Texas

DURING THE FALL of 1843 Secretary of State Abel P. Upshur initiated negotiations with the Texas agents in Washington over possible annexation of the Lone Star Republic. By mid-February 1844 the discussions appeared sufficiently promising to elicit a Texan request that a naval force be stationed in the Gulf and an army be ready to intervene in case Mexico resumed the war. In April the War Department responded by ordering the initial elements of a corps of observation to the Texas frontier.[1]

Zachary Taylor drew the assignment to command the force. General-in-Chief Winfield Scott on April 23 directed him to relieve Brevet Brigadier General Matthew Arbuckle as commander of the 1st Military District at Fort Jesup. The command included the forces intended for intervention in Texas should the Mexicans move against the Lone Star Republic. One interesting aspect of the order was the assignment of Major William W. S. Bliss as the acting assistant adjutant general for the new command.[2] Scott never explained his rationale for Taylor's selection. It probably reflected the general-in-chief's conclusion that Taylor was the senior departmental commander physically capable of taking the field. Moreover, he was close to the scene and his switch of commands with Arbuckle would cause

1. George Lockhart Rives, *The United States and Mexico* (2 vols.; New York, 1913), I, 596; Henry Putney Beers, *The Western Military Frontier, 1815–1846* (Philadelphia, 1935), 164; William S. Henry, *Campaign Sketches of the War with Mexico* (New York, 1847), 8. See also Justin H. Smith, *The Annexation of Texas* (New York, 1911), 147–80.

2. Jones to ZT, April 23, 1844, in AGLS, XX, 229 (M565/13). Taylor's view of the directive is in ZT to J. P. Taylor, January 29, 1845, in ZT(LC), ser 2, r 1.

minimal dislocation of the command structure. Scott did subsequently take credit for the assignment of Bliss, whom Scott clearly expected to make up for the limitations of his commander.[3] On April 27 General Roger Jones penned confidential instructions assigning Taylor to command of the Corps of Observation and ordering it to the Sabine River. If Mexico attacked Texas during the period between the signing and the ratification of the treaty of annexation, Taylor, like his naval counterpart Commodore David Conner, was to remonstrate with the Mexican commander and warn him that if the treaty went into effect the incursion could bring war. Taylor was directed to open confidential correspondence with President Sam Houston of Texas but not to inform his nominal superior Brigadier General Edmund P. Gaines, the commander of the newly reestablished Western Division, who was often less than discreet with confidential information. Nor was Taylor as commander of the Corps of Observation under Gaines's command.[4] Although his orders did not reach Fort Smith until May 24, Taylor, who had advance warning, transferred command to Arbuckle the preceding day. Taylor rode south on June 6. He reached Fort Jesup on the seventeenth and immediately assumed command of the department.[5]

Mrs. Taylor, who had joined her husband at Fort Smith, returned to Baton Rouge. Despite the availability of quarters in the trim brick buildings of officers' row, she chose to live in a dilapidated cottage on the river bank. The single-story, four-room wooden structure had been built by Lieutenant Colonel Alexander Dickson of the British army when he commanded at Baton Rouge and was used by the Spanish commandants when they took possession in 1779. Its attraction to Mrs. Taylor was undoubtedly the detached location, shade trees, large garden, and the airy galleries along all four sides. She soon had the house refurbished with the aid of her two house slaves and soldiers from the garrison. She lived there throughout her husband's absence in Texas and Mexico, most of the time with her youngest daughter, Betty.[6]

3. Winfield Scott, *Memoirs of Lieut.-General Scott, LL.D.* (1864; rpr. Freeport, N.Y., 1970), II, 381–82.

4. Jones to ZT, April 27, 1844, and Jones, Memorandum, October 7, 1845, in AGLS, XX, 257, XXI, 1019 (M565/13, 14). The Eastern and Western Divisions, abolished in 1842, were reinstituted on April 20, 1844. Raphael P. Thian, *Notes Illustrating the Military Geography of the United States 1813–1880* (1881; rpr. Austin, 1979), 30.

5. ZT to AG, June 4, 1844, in AGRL, XX, T-133 (M711/17); Fort Jesup Post Return, June 1844 (M617/555).

6. Oliver Otis Howard, *General Taylor* (New York, 1892), 76–77; Holman Hamilton, *Zachary Taylor* (2 vols.; Indianapolis, 1941, 1951), II, 28–29; Benson J. Lossing, *The Pictorial Field Book of the War of 1812* (1869; rpr. Somersworth, N.H., 1976), 319, has a sketch, as does [Thomas B. Thorpe], "General Taylor's Residence at Baton Rouge," *Harper's New Monthly Magazine*, IX (1854), 765. The house was demolished in 1859.

Meanwhile, Taylor's command gathered. Eight companies of the 3d Infantry departed Jefferson Barracks at the end of April, and an equal number from the 4th Infantry followed ten days later.[7] On his arrival at Fort Jesup, Taylor sent word to President Houston that 1,000 men, an inflated number, were collected on the border. The courier, Captain Lloyd J. Beall, was to study the route in case the expected orders to march south arrived. Beall returned July 15, by which time Taylor had new instructions to cease communications with Houston because of the June 8 defeat of the treaty.[8]

Death of the annexation treaty did not ease pressures on the Corps of Observation. On June 19 Mexican General Adrian Woll, commanding the troops along the Rio Grande, notified President Houston that his government had abrogated the armistice then in effect between the two governments. On the heels of that warning came reports from Texan spies that the Mexicans were mustering 600 men to attack San Antonio.[9] Nothing developed from those threats. Meanwhile, the Tyler administration decided to secure annexation through a congressional joint resolution.[10]

Luckily, the demands on Taylor during July and August were light, because during this time he suffered a series of attacks of bilious fever. However, despite its commander's disability, the force at Fort Jesup grew through the summer. In early September it numbered 376 dragoons and 290 infantry; it was a well-trained corps, although short of field artillery. The arms were numerous enough, though, to permit the authorities in Washington to issue preparation instructions on September 17 to restrain the Indians along the border if requested by chargé d'affaires to Texas Andrew Jackson Donelson. Taylor suspected that the orders were merely a pretext for an early movement into Texas. The request never came and in early October Taylor sent the troops into winter quarters.[11]

The onset of winter quieted the Indian threat and permitted Taylor to make another trip to Baton Rouge. He departed two days after Christmas. While still on leave, on February 25, 1845, he accidentally met Jefferson Davis. It was their first encounter since Davis' marriage to Knox

7. Henry, *Campaign Sketches*, 8.

8. ZT to AG, June 18, July 15, 1844, with enclosures, in AGLR 1844, T-148 (M567/291), Yale: WA.

9. Woll to Houston, June 19, Colonel J. C. Hays to G. W. Hill, July 21, 1844, in *Congressional Globe*, 28th Cong., 2nd Sess., A-2.

10. J. C. Calhoun to T. A. Howard, June 18, 1844, in William A. Manning (ed.), *Diplomatic Correspondence of the United States, Inter-American Affairs, 1831–1860* (12 vols.; Washington, 1932–39), XII, 73–74.

11. Thomas to ZT, September 17, 1844, in John Frost, *Life of Major General Zachary Taylor* (New York, 1847), 41; Ethan Allen Hitchcock, *Fifty Years in Camp and Field*, ed. W. A. Croffut (New York, 1909), 187; ZT to AG, October 1, 1844, in Yale: WA; ZT to J. P. Taylor, January 29, 1845, in ZT(LC), ser 2, r 1.

Taylor and her death. They were quickly reconciled, if indeed there was any ill-feeling between them, and Taylor sent Davis on to his marriage to Varina Howell with felicitations and best wishes.[12]

When Congress met in December the administration, reacting to the defeat of the treaty, changed tactics and had a joint resolution introduced offering annexation to Texas. After a prolonged debate it cleared both houses of Congress and was signed by President Tyler on March 1, 1845, just before his leaving office.[13] Between March and July the Texans studied their options. Acceptance of the American proposal was not a foregone conclusion. Among other alternatives was continued independence recognized by Mexico. That plan, promoted by Great Britain and championed by Texas President Anson Jones, foundered on the Mexican refusal to consider loss of former territory. No more successful were efforts by American extremists like Captain Robert F. Stockton and former postmaster general Charles A. Wickliffe to incite Texan imperialists into an attack on Mexico. The new administration of James K. Polk, which took office in March, pursued a strategy of graduated pressure. Polk believed that Mexico's impoverished treasury and large external debts, especially to the United States, would force her sooner or later to sell some of her territory. He hoped to use that weakness to secure for the United States a boundary along the Rio Grande as well as title to part or all of California. All that was necessary to accomplish this, Polk assumed, was to convince the Mexicans that the alternative to negotiations was a war which they had no capacity to conduct. Unfortunately for Polk, that very logical argument carried little weight in Mexico City. There the surrender of even one hectare of sacred national soil was unthinkable. War, even to national suicide, was preferable to ignominious acquiescence in the alienation of Mexican land. Thus Mexico still insisted that her border with the United States was along the Sabine River.[14]

All of this maneuvering in Washington and Mexico City, while of im-

12. ZT to AG, December 26, 1844, in AGLR 1844, T-328 (M567/291); Hudson Strode, *Jefferson Davis, American Patriot* (New York, 1955), 136.

13. *Congressional Globe*, 28th Cong., 2nd Sess., 26, 50, 85–87, 362, 372. For good discussions of the annexation debates see: Eugene Irving McCormac, *James K. Polk* (1922; rpr. New York, 1965), 309–14; Charles Sellers, *James K. Polk, Constitutionalist, 1843–1846* (Princeton, 1966), 208–16; Rives, *U.S. & Mexico*, I, 679–94; Smith, *Annexation of Texas*, 328–48.

14. The background of Taylor's move into Texas is discussed from various points of view in K. Jack Bauer, *The Mexican War, 1846–1848* (New York, 1974), 16–18; Norman A. Graebner, "The Mexican War: A Study in Causation," *Pacific Historical Review*, XLIX (1980), 405–26; Frederick Merk, *Manifest Destiny and Mission in American History* (New York, 1963), 41–46; David Pletcher, *The Diplomacy of Annexation* (Columbia, Mo., 1967), 254–71; Glenn Price, *Origins of the War with Mexico* (Austin, 1967), 111–17; Sellers, *Polk*, 222–27; Smith, *Annexation of Texas*.

portance to Taylor in the effects it had on his planning for future operations, reached him more or less secondhand. The Washington authorities, like most political leaders before and since, shared little of their policy or strategic considerations with their field commanders. This was particularly true of the War Department, which provided Taylor with appreciably less political guidance than Secretary of the Navy George Bancroft forwarded to Commodore Conner. As a result, most of the politico-diplomatic activities swirled past Taylor without his being fully aware of events or policy. Taylor made clear his personal opposition to annexation in discussions with Hitchcock, but we do not know the reasoning which led him there.[15]

Despite efforts by Donelson during the spring of 1845 to induce the Texans to request protection, the War Department realistically assumed Taylor's forces would not be ordered beyond the Sabine before fall. General Scott accordingly granted Taylor leave. He departed Fort Jesup on board the side-wheeler *Julia Chouteau* on May 16. At Cypress Grove he had to straighten out the problems caused by the resignation of James Thornton as his overseer.[16]

Taylor returned to Fort Jesup in late May 1845. Shortly afterwards he received Secretary of War William L. Marcy's May 28 warning of an impending order to shift his forces to Texas. On June 15 Bancroft, as acting secretary of war, issued the formal order. Bancroft envisioned the troops boarding warships commanded by Captain Stockton at the mouth of the Sabine River, but no facilities existed, so Taylor wisely chose New Orleans instead. Bancroft directed that the American force take post at a point "on or near the Rio Grande del Norte" which would be "best adapted to repel invasion." The intention was to protect the Texas congress while it considered the annexation offer and to protect the state once it accepted.[17] The order resulted from fears in Washington that the British, who were attempting to mediate the difficulties between Texas and Mexico, might intervene. Donelson, with whom Taylor was in frequent contact, pressed the Texans to ask for protection. The Texas congress did so on June 26. Both Texas Secretary of War William G. Cooke and Donelson hastened to request that Taylor provide troops.[18]

15. Hitchcock, *Fifty Years in Camp and Field*, 202–203.

16. Jones to ZT, May 6, 1845, in AGLS, XXI, 378 (M5656/14); Pletcher, *Diplomacy of Annexation*, 254.

17. Marcy to ZT, May 28, Bancroft to ZT, June 15, ZT to Jones, June 30, 1845, in *Mex. War Corres.*, 79, 81–82, 801; Secretary of State James Buchanan to Donelson, June 15, 1845, in Manning, *Diplomatic Correspondence*, XII, 94–97. Taylor received Bancroft's orders on June 29. Hitchcock, *Fifty Years in Camp and Field*, 192.

18. ZT to Donelson, June 13, 1845, in Andrew J. Donelson Papers, X, r 5, LC; Texas Congress, Joint Resolution, June 26, 1845, in AOLR, Box 1; Cooke to ZT, June 27, Donelson to ZT, June 28, 1845, in *Mex. War Corres.*, 803–806; McCormac, *Polk*, 362.

The Texas convention on July 4 accepted the terms offered by the Joint Resolution of Annexation. Almost coincidentally Secretary Marcy modified Taylor's orders by directing that all Mexican military posts north and east of the Rio Grande not be disturbed. The modification reflected the administration's intention to avoid any aggressive acts unless the Mexicans attacked first.[19] Taylor and Donelson concurred on stationing the troops along a line from Corpus Christi at the mouth of the Nueces River to San Antonio and Austin. Donelson opposed establishing a post south of the Nueces, since the area was in dispute between Texas and Mexico. Taylor, soon after reaching Texas, concluded that his army was too small to risk in the disputed area and that in any event he should not complicate the negotiations between the two nations.[20] The leading element, eight companies of the 4th Infantry, embarked at Grand Ecore, Louisiana, for the trip to New Orleans on July 2. They arrived at Jackson Barracks in New Orleans two days later. The 3d Infantry departed the Red River port on July 7 and reached the Crescent City on the tenth. Twiggs's dragoons rode overland to San Antonio. Meanwhile, the War Department ordered Lieutenant Braxton Bragg with a four-gun field battery to join the Texas force as its artillery arm.[21]

Taylor reached New Orleans on July 15, having delayed his departure from Fort Jesup in order to oversee the arrangements for the dragoon march. He promptly plunged into preparations for the move, asking Commodore Conner for a vessel to convoy the troopships. Five days after reaching New Orleans he alerted Donelson to the impending advance.[22]

During the twenty-third, Taylor with the leading elements of his force embarked on the steamer *Alabama* from the New Orleans levee near the Cotton Press. She proceeded alone, since Taylor left the navy sloop-of-war *St. Mary's* (Commander John L. Saunders) off the mouth of the Mississippi to escort the rest of the force. Two days later the steamer hove to off St. Joseph's Island, about twenty-five miles from Corpus Christi, since the deep draft vessel could approach no closer. High winds and seas kept the troops confined to their cramped quarters until the following day when they moved ashore to camp on the island.[23]

19. Donelson to ZT, July 17, 1845, in AOLR, Box 1; Marcy to ZT, July 8, 1845, SWMA, XXVI, 36 (M6/26); Sellers, *Polk*, 229; Rives, *U.S. & Mexico*, I, 703–18.

20. Donelson to ZT, July 24, 1845, in Manning, *Diplomatic Correspondence*, XII, 455n–56n; ZT to K. Rayner, October 30, 1848, in Yale: WA.

21. Jones to Bragg, to ZT, June 18, 1845, in AGLS, XXI, 527, 529 (M565/14); ZT to Jones, June 30, 1845, in *Mex. War Corres.*, 801; Henry, *Campaign Sketches*, 9–10.

22. Henry, *Campaign Sketches*, 11–16; ZT to Donelson, July 20, 1845, in Donelson Papers, X, r 5; Conner to ZT, July 19, 1845, in AOLR, Box 1.

23. Hamilton, *Taylor*, I, 161–63; ZT to Jones, July 25, 1845, in *Mex. War Corres.*, 97; Hitchcock, *Fifty Years in Camp and Field*, 193–94.

Leaving his troops to be ferried to the mainland by local fishermen, Taylor examined possible campsites on the shores of Aransas and Nueces bays. He selected one just west of the Nueces River at the small settlement of Corpus Christi. The troops from the *Alabama* completed their movement by the end of the month. Later arrivals had an easier trip once small steamers and steam lighters arrived to shuttle men and supplies across the shallow bay to the Corpus Christi installation. Taylor himself reached Corpus Christi on August 15.[24]

The campsite Taylor selected filled the bay side of a spit thrusting into Nueces Bay in what today is the northeastern portion of the city of Corpus Christi. The 3d Infantry camped to the north of the headquarters and the 4th to its south. Other units as they arrived took posts further south. One of the attractions of the location for Taylor was a large level plain about a quarter of a mile from the camp which permitted drilling of large contingents of troops, a practice which the normal distribution of the army in small garrison detachments prevented. Very few of the field officers had ever commanded as much as a full battalion on the drill field, or in combat, so they needed the experience just as much as the enlisted men and junior officers. George G. Meade complained to his wife that the life consisted of "nothing but drill and parades, and your ears are filled all day with drumming and fifeing." One result was a quite creditable review by the troops in mid-September. Even so, Hitchcock insisted that the brigade commanders could not maneuver their commands and that Taylor knew nothing about moving an army on a battlefield. Both were probably true, but the charge was immaterial since the war which they were likely to fight did not involve the intricate maneuvering of units that had marked the Napoleonic battles so admired by Hitchcock.

Taylor described the scene to his daughter as "quite an imposing one; what with instruction, mounting guards, reviews, etc., with between three and four thousand men and two hundered [*sic*] and fifty officers, with five bands. . . ." Taylor did not insist on extensive drill, or upon other activities, with deleterious effects on the discipline of his troops.

Corpus Christi or, as many contemporaries called it, Kinney's Ranch was a nondescript and disorganized collection of twenty to thirty dwellings whose inhabitants made their living largely from smuggling. They numbered less than a thousand when the troops arrived but by November had reached 1,000, and a month later the settlement could claim twice that number. The influx represented primarily the normal collection of whiskey sellers, gamblers, prostitutes, and other camp followers who

24. ZT to AG, August 15, 1845, in *Mex. War Corres.*, 99–100; Nathan S. Jarvis, "An Army Surgeon's Notes of Frontier Service," *JMSIUS*, XL (1907), 435; Henry, *Campaign Sketches*, 30.

congregate around a military installation. Other officers, and undoubtedly some of the men, found pleasure in the out-of-doors opportunities that the area offered. The bay offered excellent waters for rowing and sailing and the beach excelled the Rockaways for bathing, one New Yorker reported. Sheephead, redfish, and red snapper easily yielded to the bait of happy fishermen. Hunting, both nearby and at a distance, attracted many from the army. Later when the dragoons arrived from Fort Jesup, they received lessons in trick riding from some of the Texans.

Yet life was far from idyllic. "Old Rough and Ready" lived up to his nickname and was slow to recognize that the conditions under which his army found itself were detrimental to health and discipline. He considered the troops relatively healthy and comfortable. So they were during most of the summer, although the water supply was alkaline, the commissary limited, and the camp broken up by clumps of brush and shared with rattlesnakes. As the heat of summer took its toll of the energies of the troops, the drills became less frequent and fatigue details more common. Increasingly many of the men indulged in visits to the grog shops, gambling halls, and makeshift brothels that edged the camp. With the deterioration of control came the inevitable increase in brawling and a rise in diarrhea and dysentery. Even among the officers the slackening of control showed. Few shaved and many hunted; fewer led their men onto the drill field.

The officers of the 3d Infantry had a large thatched-roof building constructed which they used for a common dining hall. Other officers (including Lieutenant Ulysses S. Grant) oversaw the erection of an eight-hundred-seat theater and began productions. On January 8, 1846, a group of professional actors graced the stage, the first of a series of itinerant companies of varying quality who played the camps of the American troops in Texas and Mexico.[25]

25. Accounts of life at Corpus Christi can be found in: ZT to [Ann M. Wood], December 15, 1845, in William K. Bixby Collection, MoHS; Bauer, *Mexican War*, 32–35; Alfred Hoyt Bill, *Rehearsal for Conflict* (New York, 1947), 83; E. Kirby Smith, *To Mexico with Scott*, ed. Emma Jerome Blackwood (Cambridge, 1917), 20; Henry, *Campaign Sketches*, 17–199; Hitchcock, *Fifty Years in Camp and Field*, 215; James Longstreet, *From Manassas to Appomattox* (Philadelphia, 1908), 20; George Gordon Meade, *Life and Letters of George Gordon Meade* (2 vols.; New York, 1913), I, 35; Joseph Dorst Patch, *The Concentration of General Zachary Taylor's Army at Corpus Christi, Texas* (Corpus Christi, 1962), 10–11; Darwin Payne, "Camp Life in the Army of Occupation," *SWHQ*, LXXIII (1969–70), 326–42; Richard F. Pourade (ed.), *The Sign of the Eagle* (San Diego, 1970), 5; George Winston Smith and Charles Judah (eds.), *Chronicles of the Gringos* (Albuquerque, 1968), 25–26; Justin H. Smith, *War with Mexico* (2 vols.; New York, 1919), I, 143–44; Edward S. Wallace, *General William Jenkins Worth* (Dallas, 1953), 66–67; Cadmus Marcellus Wilcox, *History of the Mexican War* (Washington, 1892), 13.

As the army grew, Taylor stationed small detachments elsewhere in Texas including Austin, San Antonio, and San Patricio. In August he also added four companies of the Texas Rangers to help shield the Comanche frontier. On August 6 Taylor changed the title of his force from the inappropriate Army of Observation to the unfortunate Army of Occupation.[26]

The shift of titles recognized the new responsibilities of the force. It came at a point when Washington, at least, assumed that a Mexican attack was likely. On the same day that Taylor retitled his force, Adjutant General Roger Jones reported the start of reinforcements toward Texas. The additional troops, the Washington planners believed, would make Taylor's command "fully equal to meet with certainty of success any crisis which may arise in Texas." Taylor also received authority to levy a call for volunteers upon the governor of Texas and a promise of 10,000 muskets and 1,000 rifles to arm them. Other reinforcements including two companies of horse artillery soon followed.[27]

The Washington activities grew out of intelligence of a possible move by the Mexican forces at San Luis Potosí and along the Rio Grande. The information was false. General Mariano Arista, the Rio Grande commander, had orders to remain on the defensive and avoid any provocation because Mexico lacked the resources for a conflict with the Giant of the North. None of his northern garrisons even had a reliable local food supply. Even so, on August 12 a spy reported that Arista and 1,000 men had left Monterrey for the Rio Grande. Two days later Taylor directed Lieutenant Colonel Ethan Allen Hitchcock, commanding the forces already at Corpus Christi, to lay out defenses, and on August 16 he warned the army of the "probability of a conflict."[28] Unbeknownst to Taylor, General Gaines in New Orleans responded to the rumors by calling upon the governor of Louisiana for volunteers to join Taylor. Gaines lacked authority

26. ZT to Anson Jones, August 16, 1845, in *Mex. War Corres.*, 101–102; Cochran to parents, September 27, 1845, in R. E. Cochran Papers, UTA; AO General Order 1, AOGO, I (M29/1); Beers, *Western Military Frontier*, 168.

27. Jones to Colonel Henry Stanton, August 4, to ZT, August 9, 1845, in AGLS, XXI (M565/14); Jones to ZT, August 6, 1845, in *Mex. War Corres.*, 83–84. Artillery regiments were normally assigned to coastal fortifications. One company of each regiment was armed and trained as a horse-drawn field battery while the remainder of the regiment received limited infantry training to permit them to be used in the defense of a port outside of the fixed defenses. That training also prepared the artillerymen to serve as the army's strategic reserve.

28. Acting Secretary of State John Y. Mason to Donelson, August 7, 1845, in Manning, *Diplomatic Correspondence*, XII, 97–98; Gene M. Brack, *Mexico Views Manifest Destiny, 1821–1846* (Albuquerque, 1975), 155; Henry, *Campaign Sketches*, 28; Bliss to Hitchcock, August 14, 1845, in Ethan Allen Hitchcock Papers, Box 2, LC; AO General Order 2, August 16, 1845, in AOGO, I (M29/1).

to make the request, which was countermanded by Secretary Marcy. Later in August Gaines boasted he could assemble 250 battalions of volunteers on the Rio Grande by mid-November. These, with Taylor's regulars, he claimed could take Mexico City by the end of the month.[29] No one in Washington took Gaines's strutting seriously.

Secretary Marcy in late August relayed a new rumor of Mexican preparations for an invasion and directed that the crossing of the Rio Grande by a large force "be regarded as an invasion of the United States and the commencement of hostilities." He enlarged Taylor's authority to call out volunteers in an emergency to include Louisiana, Alabama, Mississippi, Tennessee, and Kentucky.[30] This flare-up caused the War Department to dispatch further reinforcements, notably a battalion of artillerymen under Brevet Lieutenant Colonel Thomas Childs and the 5th Infantry. They brought the force ordered to Texas to 4,330 men, roughly half of the entire army.[31]

During August 29 President Polk and his cabinet decided that in the event of either a Mexican declaration of war or an invasion of Texas, Taylor should consider any crossing of the Rio Grande to be an act of war and drive the invaders back across the river. Occupation of Matamoros and other points close to the waterway was left to his discretion. In support of these operations the naval force in the Gulf of Mexico under Commodore Conner would blockade the Mexican ports, seizing any which could be taken with the forces at hand.[32]

The war scare also had impact in Texas. On August 24 Corpus Christi was hit by a thunderstorm which Colonel Twiggs at San Patricio mistook for a Mexican bombardment of the main post. He led his men on a forced march to the assistance of their comrades only to encounter Taylor, bound

29. Gaines to Governor Alexander Mouton, August 15, in *Congressional Globe*, 29th Cong., 1st Sess., A654; to Jones, August 23, 1845, in AGLR 1845, G-149 (M567/298); Marcy to Gaines, August 28, 1845, in SWMA, XXVII, 68–69 (M6/25); Henry, *Campaign Sketches*, 34.

30. Marcy to Taylor, August 23, 1845, in *Mex. War Corres.*, 84–85; McCormac, *Polk*, 378–79. The letters to the governors conveying Taylor's authority are in SWMA, XXVI, 64–65, 67 (M6/26).

31. Jones to Wool, Brooke, August 23, to ZT, September 13, 1845, in AGLS, XXI, 820, 823, 946 (M565/14). In September, Taylor organized the force into three brigades: 1st Brigade, 8th Infantry and Artillery Battalion; 2nd Brigade, 5th and 7th Infantry; 3rd Brigade, 3rd and 4th Infantry. Brevet Brigadier General W. J. Worth commanded the 1st Brigade while the other two were led by their frequently changing senior officer. The dragoons and the horse artillery batteries were attached to headquarters. AO Order 14, 15, September 26, 28, 1845, in AOGO, I (M29/1).

32. James K. Polk, *Diary of James K. Polk During His Presidency, 1845–1849*, ed. Milo Milton Quaife (4 vols.; Chicago, 1910), I, 9–10; Marcy to ZT, August 30, 1845, in *Mex. War Corres.*, 88–89.

for San Patricio on an inspection trip. By the first week in September spy reports from the Rio Grande confirmed that the Mexican forces had not started warlike preparations. That was further verified by one of Taylor's correspondents after conversations with Arista.[33]

During the fall Taylor sent his engineers on exploratory trips into the disputed zone. In September Captain Thomas Jefferson Cram and Lieutenant George G. Meade surveyed the Nueces River valley as far as San Patricio. They found much high grass and miserable roads. A second group led by Lieutenant Jacob E. Blake covered an area further inland. In November Captain John Sanders reconnoitered the route toward the Rio Grande, as did Meade and Captain Charles A. May; but the latter two were turned back by high waters.[34]

Meanwhile, Taylor concluded that a settlement with Mexico "will be greatly facilitated and hastened by our taking possession at once of one or two points on or quite near [the Rio Grande]. Our strength and state of preparation should be displayed in a manner not to be mistaken." He did not, however, believe his orders permitted the move, since the Mexicans had committed no overt acts. On October 16 Secretary Marcy sent him specific orders to establish winter quarters as near the Rio Grande as prudence and convenience permitted. Taylor, in part because of information from Commodore Conner that the Mexicans planned no northward shift of forces, chose to remain in Corpus Christi.[35]

As a practical matter, the Army of Occupation was scarcely able to move. It lacked transport. Colonel Trueman Cross, who once again served as Taylor's quartermaster, calculated that the force was 85 wagons short of the 265 it needed to maintain a supply line to the Rio Grande. Draft horses proved so difficult to secure that oxen had to be substituted.[36]

As a further complication, heavy rains hit the camp in mid-October, turning the ground to mud and halting further drills. The weather added to the health problems which had begun to appear. During the later fall and winter an average of 10 percent of the officers and 13 percent of the men were ill with diarrhea and dysentery. Nearly all the problems arose from poor camp sanitation, a problem which seems never to have con-

33. ZT to AG, September 6, 1845, in *Mex. War Corres.*, 105; Jarvis, "Army Surgeon's Notes," 436; J. O. Marks to ZT, September 23, 1845, in AOLR, Box 1.

34. AO Special Order 18, 24, 46, September 17, October 2, November 7, 1845, in AOGO, I (M29/2); Meade, *Life & Letters*, I, 28–29; Jarvis, "Army Surgeon's Notes," 437.

35. ZT to AG, October 4, November 7, March to ZT, October 16, 1845, in *Mex. War Corres.*, 89–90, 107–109, 111; Conner to ZT, October 24, 1845, in *House Executive Documents*, 29th Cong., 1st Sess., No. 196, p. 98.

36. Cross to Stanton, September 10, 1845, in *Mex. War Corres.*, 642–43; Erna Risch, *Quartermaster Support of the Army* (Washington, 1962), 242.

cerned Taylor. He was, however, disturbed by the poor quality of tents issued to the 7th Infantry. They were neither wind nor waterproof. Cross requisitioned enough new ones to house 2,000 men, but they arrived too late to be useful. This complicated life for the men camped on the beach at Corpus Christi, since Taylor decided winter quarters should be tents erected on platforms, as had been done in Florida.[37]

Conditions at the Corpus Christi camp deteriorated when a cold snap hit on November 30, leading to fiercely cold and wet conditions for the first half of December. It was the coldest period in the memory of the natives. Surgeon Nathan Jarvis reported that fish froze in the bay. Some soldiers made barriers of chaparral in an effort to deflect the cutting wind that assailed their muslin tents. Others piled earth around their habitations. There are reports of officers improvising stoves from barrels, kettles, and other containers. Even so, the sick list came to include a fifth of the command, while half of the remainder were ailing to a lesser degree. The lumber needed for tent floors did not arrive until mid-January and by then the worst had passed.[38]

As the weather deteriorated, a substantial faction of the officers in the Army of Occupation, including its commander, dipped their pens in ink to argue the persistent question of the relative standing of officers holding brevet ranks. It was a practical matter for Taylor, who aside from his former opposition to it had several officers claiming precedence by virtue of brevets. Taylor, of course, was serving in his brevet rank of brigadier general, having been formally assigned to the command. In mid-November General Scott, pending a definitive ruling from Secretary Marcy, directed that brevet rank should govern. The arguments culminated in Hitchcock's collecting signatures for a memorial to Congress. The practical impact appeared in early February when both Colonel Childs and Colonel Twiggs claimed brigade commands, one by virtue of brevet, the other by lineal rank. It reached a climax on February 24, when Taylor, contrary to Scott's directive, designated Twiggs as the senior officer to "present the Command" during a review of the Army of Occupation. Colonel William J. Worth, rising to the full stature of his brevet commission as brigadier general, refused to serve under Twiggs. Taylor, caught in a quagmire caused

37. Hamilton, *Taylor*, I, 166–67; AO Orders 35, 40, November 4, 12, 1845, in AOGO, I (M29/1); Hatch to Eliza Hatch, October 10, 1845, in John P. Hatch Papers, LC; Risch, *Quartermaster Support*, 244–45; ZT to AG, November 7, 1845, in *Mex. War Corres.*, 111.

38. ZT to T. W. Ringgold, December 16, 1845, in Stephen Currie (ed.), "Zachary Taylor, Plantation Owner," *Civil War History*, XXX (1984), 148; Jarvis, "Notes of a Military Surgeon," 437; AO Order 8, January 19, 1846, in AOGO, I (M29/1); Henry, *Campaign Sketches*, 45; Edward J. Nichols, *Towards Gettysburg* (State College, Pa., 1958), 20; Smith, *War with Mexico*, I, 144. Taylor claimed that the temperature dropped to minus twenty-three, but he was in error. Temperature below zero has never been recorded in Corpus Christi.

by his own misstep, saw no escape except to cancel the review at the last moment, ostensibly because of the weather. Lieutenant Ulysses S. Grant claimed that it was one of the only two times during his service in the Army of Occupation that he knew of Taylor's wearing his uniform.[39] Whether or not the aborted parade altered Taylor's custom of wearing old, nonuniform clothes in the field, his inconsistency in handling the brevet controversy won him little support from his officers.

More serious, as well as a harbinger of things to come, were "outrages of aggravated character" committed by soldiers against both the persons and property of some of the Mexicans living near the camp. As a result Taylor closed the camp each night after tattoo and increased the provost marshal patrols in the vicinity.[40]

Meanwhile, the administration learned that its diplomatic efforts to secure a settlement of the boundary dispute had fallen prey to Mexican internal politics. President Polk's solution was to increase the pressure on the Mexican government by shifting Taylor's command to the Rio Grande and concentrating the naval squadrons in the Gulf of Mexico and Pacific at Veracruz and Mazatlán.[41] The orders, sent by Marcy on January 13, 1846, instructed Taylor "to advance and occupy . . . positions on or near the east Bank of the Rio del Norte as soon as it can be conveniently done with reference to the Season and the routes by which your movement must be made." The secretary suggested detachments be placed at Point Isabel, opposite Matamoros, facing Mier, and near Loredo but left the actual choices to his field commander. Taylor was not to interfere with shipping on the Rio Grande nor to consider Mexico an enemy. Should the Mexicans initiate hostilities, "you will not act merely on the defensive." In the latter case Taylor received renewed authority to call for Texas militia. The orders reached Corpus Christi on February 3.[42]

39. Jones to ZT, November 14, 1845, in AGLS, XXI, 1150 (M565/14); Childs to Jones, February 2, 1846, in AGLR 1846, C-69 (M567/296); Twiggs to Bliss, February 8, Worth to ZT, February 24, 1846, in AOLR, Box 2; AO After Orders, Order 21, February 24, 25, 1846, AOGO, I (M29/1); Ulysses S. Grant, *Personal Memoirs of U.S. Grant*, ed. E. B. Long (Cleveland, 1952), 47. The Twiggs-Worth controversy arose from the fact that Twiggs ranked Worth as a colonel but did not have a brevet commission as a brigadier general. It was a circumstance which had never before occurred in the American army and was not covered by army regulations. It is discussed at length in Colonel Sylvester Churchill to Scott, March 2, 1846, in SWUR (M222), and Smith, *War with Mexico*, I, 144. President Polk decided in favor of lineal rank, the Twiggs position. Marcy, Regulation, March 12, 1846, in AGLR 1846, M-84 (M567/322).

40. AO Order 1, January 2, 1846, in AOGO, I (M29/1).

41. For the background of the decision see: Bauer, *Mexican War*, 24–27; Pletcher, *Diplomacy of Annexation*, 364; Polk, *Diary*, I, 171; Sellers, *Polk*, 398; and Smith, *War with Mexico*, I, 98–99.

42. Marcy to ZT, January 13, to Governor J. P. Henderson, January 20, 1846, in *Mex. War Corres.*, 90–91; Hitchcock, *Fifty Years in Camp and Field*, 207.

The Army of Occupation immediately began preparations for the move southward. Colonel Cross had 307 wagons, 84 of them oxen-drawn, to carry supplies. They were adequate to carry a minimum set of camp and other equipment for the officers and men plus subsistence for twenty days and a sixteen-days' supply of grain for the animals. The remainder of the supplies and the heavy equipment would move by water.[43] Taylor sent Captain Ebenezer S. Sibley with a dragoon company as escort to reconnoiter the road to Matamoros. Captain William J. Hardee led a second party to Point Isabel, where he warned the Mexican officials of the impending march.[44]

While awaiting the completion of preparations for the forward move, Taylor forwarded a remarkable set of letters from the North Mexican separatist politician General Antonio Canales and his agent Colonel José M. J. Carvajal. They proposed to establish an independent North Mexican republic under the protection of the United States. Carvajal asked for arms, money, and an agreement not to advance further. Taylor refused to halt his march but did agree to pass the matter on to Washington.[45] Nothing developed from Canales' proposal.

On February 24 Taylor issued the warning order for the march south. It limited each company to fifteen hundred pounds of baggage and directed that each infantryman and dragoon carry one hundred "buck and ball" cartridges and the artillery bring one hundred rounds of fixed ammunition for each gun. He had earlier asked Commodore Conner to provide naval protection for the vessels carrying the army's heavy equipment and convalescents.[46] The land force began its move on March 1 when Brevet Major William M. Graham of the 4th Infantry escorted the first supply wagons to the advanced depot on the Santa Gertrudis Creek. They were followed on March 8 by the dragoons. A day behind Twiggs's dragoons and Brevet Major Samuel Ringgold's light battery marched Worth's 1st Brigade with Lieutenant James Duncan's battery. The 2d Brigade under Lieutenant Colonel James S. McIntosh of the 5th Infantry followed while the 3d Brigade commanded by Colonel William Whistler of the 4th Infantry formed the rear guard with Bragg's battery. Taylor and his staff accompanied Whistler.[47]

43. Risch, *Quartermaster Support*, 245; AO Order 13, February 6, 1846, in AOGO, I (M29/1).

44. AO Special Order 18, February 6, 1846, in AOGO, II (M29/2); Jarvis, "An Army Surgeon's Notes," 440; Sibley to ZT, February 23, 1846, in AOLR, Box 2.

45. ZT to AG, February 7, 1846, with enclosures, in AGLR 1846, T-51 (M567/327).

46. AO Order 20, February 24, 1846, in AOGO, I (M29/1); ZT to Conner, February 15, 1846, in Yale: WA.

47. ZT to AG, February 26, March 11, 1846, in *Mex. War Corres.*, 117–18, 120; AO Special Order 29, February 29 [*sic*], Order 26, 27, March 4–5, 1846, in AOGO, II, I

Most of the Americans left without regret. As one of the young officers wrote his fiancée, "fight or no fight evry [sic] one rejoises [sic] at the idea of leaving Corpus Christi." Another reported that after the army had departed the camp "looked like a burnt village with nothing but chimnies [sic] standing."[48]

Before his men trudged off into the flat Texas south, Taylor issued an order reminding them:

> The Army of Occupation of Texas being now about to take a position upon the left bank of the Rio Grande, under the orders of the Executive of the United States, the general-in-chief desires to express the hope that the movement will be advantageous to all concerned; and with the object of attaining this most laudable end, he strictly enjoins all under his command to observe, with the most scrupulous regard for the rights of all persons who may be found in the peaceful pursuit of their respective avocations, residing on both banks of the Rio Grande. No person, under any pretense whatsoever, will interfere in any manner with the civil rights or religious privileges of the people, but will pay the utmost respect to both.

He assured the inhabitants that any goods purchased by the army would be at the "highest market price" and had copies printed in Spanish as well as English.[49] The order, probably drafted by Bliss, was strong and straightforward and appears to have been effective. Its impact deteriorated once the army moved beyond the Rio Grande and acquired numbers of semi-disciplined green volunteers. The problem of control of his forces in Mexico was one that Taylor never conquered.

The march to the Rio Grande proved to be as dull and dreary as any American forces undertook during the Mexican War. The route measured about 196 miles but passed through no settlements and offered little potable water. The arid countryside determined that the locations of water points controlled the length of each day's march. Herds of wild horses frequently grazed nearby and some officers caught mustangs which they broke for their personal use. At other times the columns crossed fields of wild lupine, verbena, marigolds, as well as the seemingly unend-

(M29/2, 1); Henry, *Campaign Sketches*, 52. Taylor wrote a new will before starting the march. ZT Will, March 10, 1846, in ZT(LC), ser 2, r 1.

48. Grant to Julia Dent, March 3, 1846, in John Y. Simon (ed.), *The Papers of Ulysses S. Grant* (10 vols.; Carbondale, 1967–   ), I, 74–75; Hazlitt to Mrs. Ingersoll, March 20, 1846, in Robert Hazlitt Letters, USMA.

49. AO Order 30, March 8, 1846, in *Mex. War Corres.*, 119–20. Taylor repeated these instructions after the army reached the Rio Grande. AO Order 38, April 1, 1846, in AOGO, I (M29/1).

ing stands of chaparral interspersed with occasional clumps of trees. Ducks, geese, rabbits, and deer appeared frequently while centipedes, tarantulas, and rattlesnakes were nearly constant companions. Luckily the sultry weather held fair and neither rain nor excessive heat plagued the columns, although dust and ashes from burnt overlands coated them.[50]

On March 15 Lieutenant Schuyler Hamilton with Twiggs's advance guard encountered Lieutenant Ramon Falcon with a Mexican patrol. Hamilton assured Falcon that the Americans came in peace with orders to occupy the left bank of the Rio Grande. The Mexican replied he would report this to his superiors and return the following afternoon with their reply. He warned that any further American advance would provoke Mexican resistance. Twiggs decided to continue forward to good water rather than comply with Falcon's request to wait.[51] It was just as well that Twiggs did not wait, since Falcon did not reappear. On March 18 General Francisco Mejía, the commander at Matamoros, posted a general call of opposition to the "degenerate sons of Washington" and directed his soldiers to do their duty. Taylor concluded that opposition, if offered, would come at the ford of the Arroyo Colorado near present-day Harlington.[52]

The advance guard of Twiggs's command reached the Arroyo Colorado on March 19. Captain Joseph K. F. Mansfield and Lieutenant Jeremiah M. Scarritt of the engineers reconnoitered the brackish lagoon and chose locations for the artillery batteries which would cover the crossing the next morning. They were warned by Mexican officers on the opposite bank that a crossing would be resisted. The sound of bugles directing the movement of Mexican troops hidden by the chaparral on the opposite bank gave credence to the threat. Actually, however, Mejía's order did not permit him to contest the crossing, and when Taylor ignored the warning, he had no choice but to lead his small detachment south once the Americans started their passage.

At approximately 9:15 on the morning of March 20 the 1st and 2d Brigades deployed on the bank of the Arroyo while the artillerymen set up their pieces to cover the ford. The river at that point was about eighty yards wide and about four feet deep. While the Americans prepared to cross the Arroyo, Captain José Barragan, the Mexican adjutant general,

50. Smith, *War with Mexico*, I, 146–47; Grant, *Memoirs*, 31; Smith, *To Mexico with Scott*, 23–24; Cochran to wife, March 25, to parents, April 6, 1846, in R. E. Cochran Papers, UTA.

51. Twiggs to Bliss, March 15, 1846, in Justin H. Smith Papers, Latin American Collection, University of Texas, Austin; Emilio del Castillo Negrete, *Invasión de los Norteamericanos en México* (Mexico, 1890), 114.

52. AO Order 32, 33, March 16, 19, 1846, in AOGO, I (M29/1); Mejía Proclamation, March 18, 1846, in *Mex. War Corres.*, 125–29; Patch, *Concentration*, 18.

delivered Mejía's proclamation and threat to fight. Taylor responded that he would cross immediately. He ordered the crossing at 9:30. Worth and Captain Charles F. Smith led four companies of red-legged infantry into the water, followed by a squadron of horsemen. Other artillerymen stood by their loaded guns ready to smother any Mexican resistance. None came. As soon as the American intention to advance was clear, the handful of Mexican horsemen and their bugles scampered toward the Rio Grande.[53]

The assault force caught its breath on the opposite bank and did not pursue the Mexicans. It marched about three miles beyond the crossing to a spring where the force would camp while awaiting the arrival of the 3d Brigade. Meanwhile, work parties cut down the banks of the Arroyo to ease the passage of the artillery and the wagon trains. The united army set out at 7:00 A.M. on the 23rd "prepared at all moments to repel an attack." The force moved four columns abreast: from left to right 3d, 2d, 1st Brigades, dragoons.[54] The marching troops encountered no obstacles and the country through which they passed was the most pleasant yet encountered. It contained more and lusher vegetation and large numbers of "jackass rabbits." Large flocks of ducks and plovers sprang from the fresh-water ponds that sprinkled the countryside.

When the army reached a parting of the path, Taylor divided his force. The infantry under General Worth continued southward for an additional eighteen miles to the Rio Grande opposite Matamoros. The dragoons escorted the supply train to Point Isabel. Taylor accompanied the latter. En route he met a deputation from Matamoros who delivered a protest from Jenés Cardenes, the prefect of the northern district of Tamaulipas, denouncing the advance as an invasion of Mexican territory and announcing that hostilities had begun. Almost immediately, the Americans spotted the flames of the houses being burned by the retreating Mexicans at Point Isabel. Taylor hurried his horsemen forward in time to put out the fires. The waterborne force containing the heavy material and Brevet Major John Munroe's guard force arrived off Brazos Santiago, the entrance to the harbor, two hours earlier under navy escort.[55]

Although the transports crossed the shallow bar into the Laguna Madre with some difficulty, they anchored off the port shortly after the

53. Brooks to DeLorme Brooks, March 26, 1846, in William T. H. Brooks Papers, MHI; Wilcox, *History of the Mexican War*, 35; Blackwood, *To Mexico with Scott*, 29–30; Henry, *Campaign Sketches*, 59–60; ZT to AG, March 21, 1846, in AGLR 1846, T-97 (M567/327).

54. AO Order 35, March 22, 1846, in AOGO, I (M29/1).

55. ZT to AG, March 25, Cardenes to ZT, March 23, 1846, in *Mex. War Corres.*, 129–32.

land column arrived. Taylor assigned Munroe to command at Point Isabel with two companies as a garrison. Captain Sanders drew the assignment of supervising the construction of works to defend the depot. Late on March 27 Taylor and the dragoons rejoined the main body about ten miles from Matamoros. They reached the Rio Grande the following day and promptly raised a flagpole and the American flag.[56]

The Americans set up camp in a field about a half mile from Matamoros. While the men set to work establishing the post under the interested gaze of the inhabitants on the opposite bank, Taylor sent Worth with a message to Mejía. It empowered Worth to explain the reasons for the movement and enter into temporary arrangements pending the settlement of the boundary issue. Since the Americans had no boats, Worth had to call for one from the Mexican side. Initially his signals were ignored, but in due course a Mexican officer appeared who reported that Mejía would meet only with Taylor but that Brigadier General Rómulo Díaz de la Vega would meet with Worth. They met under a tree on the Mexican bank of the river.

The interview advanced in fits and starts, as none of the Americans spoke Spanish and none of the Mexicans admitted knowing English. As a result, Worth's words were translated into French by one of the American officers and the French into Spanish by a Mexican. When Worth asked to deliver Taylor's letter, la Vega refused but said he would receive it. Worth refused but had the contents read to the Mexican. They elicited the comment that Mexico considered war to have begun. When Worth followed with a request to see the American consul, it was refused—an act of belligerency in American eyes. He warned against armed Mexicans crossing the river and then returned to the American side of the river to report.[57]

Taylor had carried out his orders to move to the Rio Grande and had successfully established American control of the north bank. The passage of the Arroyo Colorado demonstrated once again Taylor's unswerving doggedness once he had decided upon a course of action. It prevented his waivering when confronted by Mejía's bugles and threats of war and kept him from losing control when events on the battlefield favored his opponents. Whether his characteristic unsophisticated inflexibility would

56. *Niles' Weekly Register*, LXX (1846), 112; AO Special Order 40, March 26, 1846, in AOGO, II (M29/2); Henry, *Campaign Sketches*, 63.
57. ZT to Mejia, March 28, 1846, in *Taylor, Scott Corres.*, 393; Minutes of Worth-LaVega Interview, March 28, 1846, in *Mex. War Corres.*, 133–38. Despite his bombast, Mejía returned two captured dragoons on March 31. Mejía to ZT, March 31, 1846, in *Taylor, Scott Corres.*, 394–95; Ramon Alcaraz (ed.), *The Other Side*, trans. Albert C. Ramsey (New York, 1850), 37–38.

serve him as well as the highly charged diplomatic situation he had been thrust into was less evident. That Taylor, one of the least sensitive senior officers in the army, should be charged with the delicate responsibility for command along the Rio Grande in 1846 is one of the ironies of American history.

The formal portrait of Taylor in the dress uniform of a major general.
Courtesy of the National Archives.

Margaret Mackall Smith Taylor as she appeared in later life. From Lila G. A. Woolfall, *Presiding Ladies of the White House*.
Courtesy of the Library of Congress.

Taylor as a young officer, date uncertain but probably as a lieutenant colonel. Painting by an unknown artist.
Courtesy of the White House Collection.

Fort Crawford as first seen by Taylor. From a painting by Henry Lewis in *Das Illustrirte Mississippithal* (Leipzig, 1854).
Courtesy of the State Historical Society of Wisconsin.

Taylor's early commander during the War of 1812, Major General William Henry Harrison. From an engraving by William R. Jones, after a painting probably by Joseph Wood. *Courtesy of the Library of Congress.*

Fort Snelling as it appeared when Taylor was its commander. From Marcus Hansen, *Old Fort Snelling.*
Courtesy of the Minnesota Historical Society.

The senior officer in the army after 1842, Major General Winfield Scott. Oil painting by Miner K. Kellogg.
Courtesy of the New-York Historical Society, New York City.

Taylor's great friend and protector within the military hierarchy, Quartermaster General Thomas S. Jesup.
Courtesy of the National Archives.

Brigadier General Edmund P. Gaines, the long-time commander of the Southern Division of the army and a friend of Taylor, from a Mathew Brady photograph.
Courtesy of the National Archives.

Major General Alexander Macomb, commander of the 5th Department and subsequently general-in-chief, who was the object of much enmity from Taylor. Lithograph by Thomas Sully.
Courtesy of the Library of Congress.

Brigadier General David E. Twiggs, one of Taylor's chief subordinates in both Florida and Mexico.
Courtesy of the Library of Congress.

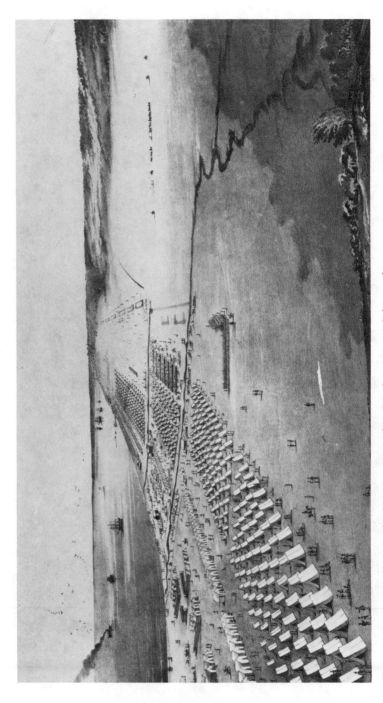

The encampment at Corpus Christi as it appeared in October 1845. A lithograph by Captain D. P. Whiting.
Courtesy of the New-York Historical Society, New York City.

Taylor as he appeared at the start of the war in Mexico. From a sketch by Auguste de Chatillon.
Courtesy of the Library of Congress.

Battle of Palo Alto showing the artillery driving off a party of Mexican lancers.
Official U.S. Navy photograph.

Battle of Palo Alto. The mounted figure in the right foreground is Taylor. From a lithograph by Carl Nebel.
Courtesy of the Library of Congress.

Taylor's second in command in Buena Vista, Brigadier General John E. Wool, in a Mathew Brady photograph.
Courtesy of the National Archives.

Monterrey as viewed from near the Bishop's Palace, in a lithograph by Captain D. P. Whiting.
Courtesy of the Library of Congress.

The hot-headed Brigadier General William J. Worth, who
commanded the crucial western assault on Monterrey.
Courtesy of the National Archives.

Antonio López de Santa Anna.
Courtesy of the Library of Congress.

Taylor in his major general's uniform as painted by Joseph Henry Bush.
Courtesy of the White House Collection.

An idealized representation of Taylor as president painted by Eliphalet Frazer Andrews about 1879, after a contemporary portrait by John Banderlyn. *Courtesy of the White House Collection.*

The combat on the plateau during the later stages of the Battle of Buena Vista. The figure gesturing with his spyglass is Taylor. *Official U.S. Navy photograph.*

Taylor's closest political advisor and the architect of the 1848 presidential campaign, John J. Crittenden, in a daguerreotype taken during the mid-1850s. *Courtesy of the Library of Congress.*

The beautiful "Betty," Mary Elizabeth Taylor Bliss, who served as her father's official hostess at the White House. *Courtesy of the Library of Congress.*

"Dick," Richard Taylor, the president's only son, in a photograph taken after the Civil War.
Courtesy of the Library of Congress.

Vice-president Millard Fillmore as painted by George P. A. Healy.
Courtesy of the White House Collection.

CHAPTER VIII

Fighting Starts

"THE ATTITUDE of the Mexicans is so far decidedly hostile," Zachary Taylor informed his superiors on March 29, 1846. He requested that enough recruits to bring his units up to strength be sent, because the Texas militia lived too far away to increase his army in case of hostilities. That night the American camp slept on its arms because of a report that 600 Mexican horsemen had crossed to the American side of the river. Dragoon patrols checked the security of the supply line to Point Isabel.[1]

The report was unfounded. Brigadier General Francisco Mejía's Army of the North had but 3,000 men and twenty guns, collected at Matamoros. He so feared an American attack that he began construction of a sandbag fort covering the main ferry crossing and lesser works above and below it. A pair of redoubts about 700 or 800 yards from the American camp threatened it with a cross fire. The presence of the Americans, nevertheless, did not prevent Mexican damsels from swimming nude in the river. But when young American officers tried to join them, Mexican guards opened fire. While the engineers rushed the defenses, Brigadier General Pedro de Ampudia hurried his division to join Mejía, covering the 180 miles from Monterrey in four days.[2]

1. ZT to AG, March 29, 1846, in *Mex. War Corres.*, 132–33; Rhoda Van Bibber Tanner Doubleday (ed.), *Journals of the Late Brevet Major Philip Norbourne Barbour . . . and His Wife, Martha Isabella Hopkins Barbour* (New York, 1936), 21–22; Ethan Allen Hitchcock, *Fifty Years in Camp and Field*, ed. W. A. Croffut (New York, 1909), 218.
2. José María Roa Bárcena, *Recuerdos de la invasión norteamericana* (3 vols.; Mexico,

145

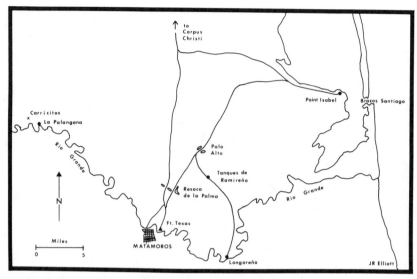

MATAMOROS AND SOUTHERN TEXAS

The Americans too began construction of a work called Fort Texas, whose guns commanded Matamoros. The fort was laid out by Captain Joseph K. F. Mansfield and Lieutenant Jeremiah M. Scarritt, but the concentration of American artillery prevented any enfilading of the Mexican batteries. While work on Fort Texas progressed Taylor strengthened the defenses of Point Isabel with three companies of dragoons. Despite his defensive preparations Taylor doubted that the Mexicans would "attempt any offensive operations."[3]

Desertion was a growing problem. The American army of the 1840s relied heavily for its enlisted men on immigrants and others unable to find regular employment. Since many felt little commitment to the service, such soldiers often left whenever civilian life appeared more attractive,

---

1947), I, 61; Justin H. Smith, *The War with Mexico* (2 vols.; New York, 1919), I, 158; E. Kirby Smith, *To Mexico with Scott*, ed. Emma Jerome Blackwood (Cambridge, 1917), 34; Isaac Ingalls Stevens, *Campaigns of the Rio Grande and of Mexico* (New York, 1851), 18.

3. AO Special Order 41, March 29, 1846, in AOGO, II (M29/2); Doubleday, *Journal of Barbour*, 22; Hitchcock, *Fifty Years in Camp and Field*, 218; ZT to Governor J. P. Henderson, April 3, 1846, in Henderson Family Papers, UTA.

and the presence of a foreign sanctuary across the Rio Grande was an enticement hard for many to ignore. At least two men were shot attempting to swim the river on April 1. The following day General Ampudia issued a call for foreigners in the American force to desert. It had an immediate effect; apparently thirty-six men crossed the following night. The Mexican propaganda made full use of religion, playing on the sympathies of fellow Roman Catholics and on alleged foreign support of Mexico. Nor did the Mexicans overlook the appeal of the gayly dressed señoritas who lined the bank opposite the American positions. On April 20 the Mexican commander added a promise of at least 320 acres of land to each deserter. The Mexican authorities expected as many as 1,500 men including the greater portion of the 7th Infantry to desert. The number of deserters actually crossing into Mexico is not certain but the numbers never reached a magnitude to worry American officers. It is equally clear that very few of them served under the Mexican flag.[4] The Army of Occupation suffered little loss of combat efficiency from the desertions, and it was the view of one of its members that "a better little army than this never took the field."[5]

The attrition among senior officers was high. When President James K. Polk ruled on the long festering dispute over lineal and brevet ranks, he awarded precedence to the former. That caused General William J. Worth, who had very strong feelings on the primacy of the brevet ranks, to resign his commission. He left Texas in April and was in Washington when news of the outbreak of fighting arrived. He promptly withdrew his resignation and returned to the Rio Grande but missed both the battles of Palo Alto and Resaca de la Palma.[6] Other losses of senior officers followed. On April 10 Colonel Trueman Cross, the senior quartermaster officer with the force who had been so successful in straightening out the logistic mess in Florida, was murdered when he rode outside the American camp. He apparently was waylaid by bandits; search parties did not locate his body until the twenty-first.[7] Also on the tenth, Lieutenant Colonel Ethan Allen Hitchcock of the 3d Infantry departed on sick leave.

4. ZT to AG, May 30, 1846, in *Mex. War Corres.*, 302–303; Ampudia Proclamation, April 2, 1846, in John Frost, *Life of Major General Zachary Taylor* (New York, 1847), 48–49; Nathan S. Jarvis, "An Army Surgeon's Notes of Frontier Service," *JMSIUS*, XL (1907), 447; General Mariano Arista, Advise [*sic*] to American Soldiers, April 20, 1846, in AOLR, Box 2; Arista to Ampudia, April 30, Mejía to Arista, May 4, 1846, in Papers Captured with General Arista's Baggage, NYHS; Smith, *War with Mexico*, I, 160–61; K. Jack Bauer, *The Mexican War, 1846–1848* (New York, 1974), 41–42.

5. Hazlitt to [?], April 22, 1846, in Robert Hazlitt Papers, USMA.

6. Worth to AG, April 2, May 9, 1846, in AGLR 1846, W-160, 162 (M567/329); AO Order 42, April 8, 1846, in AOGO, I (M29/1).

7. Smith, *War with Mexico*, I, 176; Ampudia to ZT, April 16, 1846, T-124 (M567/327);

Colonel William Whistler of the 4th Infantry followed on the nineteenth, after being arrested for drunkenness.[8]

While the American command group shook down, events along the frontier moved inexorably toward confrontation. Although the Mexican officials at Matamoros insisted that war existed by American action, they had no authorization to initiate action until April 4. That day the Mexican government directed Major General Mariano Arista, who was en route to Matamoros to assume command, to attack the American invaders.[9] Meanwhile, construction of Fort Texas began on April 6, with each brigade in succession furnishing working parties. Taylor helped to ease the aches of the men working on the fortification by having an extra gill of whiskey issued to them.[10] Need for the post became clearer following the April 11 arrival of Ampudia with the advance element of a reinforcement column of 2,400 men. The Matamoros garrison greeted his arrival with ringing bells and barking cannon.[11]

Ampudia responded with an address to his troops and an order for all Americans in Matamoros to leave within twenty-four hours. The following afternoon he demanded that Taylor withdraw to the Nueces immediately, threatening hostilities if the Americans did not depart. Taylor responded with a mildly worded refusal. He had been orderd to the river by his government and had no authority to withdraw. Since his orders proscribed all hostile acts, the American pointed out that responsibility for any conflict would lie elsewhere. By now Taylor, who knew of the final Mexican refusal to receive John Slidell, believed that fighting would probably start momentarily. He hastened completion of Fort Texas and on the fourteenth ordered a blockade of the Rio Grande.[12] Hostilities

---

Report of Board, April 23, 1846, in AOLR, Box 2; AO Order 50, April 23, 1846, in AOGO, I (M29/1).

8. Hitchcock, *Fifty Years in Camp and Field*, 222; AO Special Order 54, April 19, 1846, in AOGO, II (M29/2).

9. Tornel to Arista, April 4, 1846, XI, 224–25, in Justin H. Smith Papers, Latin American Collection, University of Texas, Austin. The formal declaration of war did not occur until April 23 when President Mariano Paredes y Arriaga declared defensive war. Paredes Manifesto, April 23, 1846, in *Niles' Weekly Register*, LXX (1846), 199. Paredes' odd terminology resulted from the Mexican constitutional provision that only the congress could declare war. The legislature was not in session and Paredes did not wish to bring it together.

10. AO Order 39, Special Order 45, April 6, 1846, in AOGO, I, II (M29/1, 2).

11. Ramon Alcaraz (ed.), *The Other Side*, trans. Albert C. Ramsey (New York, 1850), 39; José C. Valades, *Breve historia de la guerra con los Estados Unidos* (Mexico, 1947), 115; Smith, *War with Mexico*, I, 148; John S. Jenkins, *History of the War Between the United States and Mexico* (Auburn, 1851), 81–82; José Bravo Ugarte, *Historia de México* (3 vols.; Mexico, 1959), III, pt. 2, p. 198. The remainder of Ampudia's force arrived April 14 under Brigadier General Anastasio Torrejón to bring the total force at Matamoros past 4,400 men.

12. ZT to AG, April 15, Ampudia to ZT, ZT to Ampudia, April 12, 1846, in *Mex. War*

drew closer on the eighteenth when Lieutenant Theodoric H. Porter and a small party searching for Cross's murderers were ambushed by Mexican bandits. Porter and one of his men were killed. The deaths shocked the army.[13]

Ampudia planned to begin his offensive on the fifteenth following the arrival of Brigadier General Anastasio Torrejón with the balance of his reinforcements. He canceled the operation on learning that General Arista would supersede him. Arista reached Matamoros on the twenty-fourth. He immediately notified Taylor that hostilities had commenced. The news must have caused great mirth at American headquarters, since it was the fourth time that they had been so notified.[14]

Arista began his long heralded offensive on April 24. He dispatched Torrejón with the sappers, the cavalry, and two companies of light infantry, about 1,600 men, across the river well west of Matamoros. The force would then cut the road between Fort Texas and Point Isabel. At about three o'clock in the afternoon Taylor heard that Mexicans had crossed below his position. It proved false when checked by a dragoon patrol. At 11:00 that night he learned of Torrejón's passage and sent Captain Seth Thornton with two companies of dragoons to investigate.[15]

The following morning Thornton led his command into an ambush at the Rancho de Carricitos, about twenty-eight miles from the American camp. In the effort to break out eleven Americans died and twenty-six, including Thornton, were captured. The first news of the debacle reached Taylor at daybreak on the twenty-sixth when Thornton's guide, who had not been at the ambush, rode into camp. He was followed later in the morning by a dragoon whose wounds could not be treated on the march by Torrejón's surgeon. The two men soon made clear the size of the defeat.[16]

Taylor concluded that "hostilities may now be considered as commenced" and called upon the governors of Texas and Louisiana for four

Corres., 138–40; William S. Henry, *Campaign Sketches of the War with Mexico* (New York, 1847), 74–75, 77.

13. Henry, *Campaign Sketches*, 77–78; George Gordon Meade, *Life and Letters of George Gordon Meade* (2 vols.; New York, 1913), I, 67–68.

14. Alcaraz, *Other Side*, 39–40; Arista to ZT, April 24, 1846, in *Taylor, Scott Corres.*, 395; ZT to Ampudia, April 22, 1846, in *Mex. War Corres.*, 145–47; Smith, *War with Mexico*, I, 149.

15. Alcaraz, *Other Side*, 42; Munroe, Memorandum of Interrogation, April 23, 1846, in AOLR, Box 2; Roa Bárcena, *Recuerdos*, I, 62; Smith, *War with Mexico*, I, 149; Smith, *To Mexico with Scott*, 39.

16. Thornton to Bliss, April 27, Captain W. J. Hardee to ZT, April 26, 1846, in *Mex. War Corres.*, 290–92; Torrejón to ZT, April 25, 1846, in AOLR, Box 2; Torrejón to Arista, April 26, 1846, in Papers Captured with Arista's Baggage; ZT to Crittenden, September 15, 1846, in Mrs. Chapman Coleman (ed.), *The Life of John J. Crittenden* (2 vols.; Philadelphia, 1871), I, 251.

regiments of volunteers each. He hoped that they would be recruited for twelve months, but all were called up under the militia law which limited service to ninety days. They would arrive close on the heels of four companies of the 1st Infantry and 300 regular recruits sent in response to Taylor's earlier requests.[17] After his clash with Thornton, Torrejón led his troops east toward his objective. On the twenty-eighth a second force from Matamoros surprised an encampment of Texas volunteers about seven miles from Fort Texas, killing five men. It caused a near panic at Point Isabel until Major John Munroe could form a 500-man force of artillerymen, Texans, and sailors from the ships in the harbor to defend the base. Torrejón, however, actually planned no assault on the port and concentrated on rejoining Arista as soon as the Mexican main body crossed the Rio Grande. A sweep of the road by an American patrol on April 28–29 encountered no Mexicans.[18]

Captain Samuel H. Walker, the Texas Ranger whose men had been so ignominiously surprised on the twenty-eighth, left Point Isabel on April 29 with a request from Munroe for assistance. He reached Taylor that evening. Taylor, meanwhile, had every man "not detained by other indispensible duty" at work on Fort Texas.[19] The next day Ampudia led the first brigade of Mexicans across the river downstream from Matamoros, followed by Arista with a second brigade. (About 1,400 men remained behind under the Brigadier General Francisco Mejía to protect Matamoros.)[20]

Taylor learned of the crossing about one o'clock on the afternoon of May 1 from a report by Captain Walker. By then it was too late to attempt to throw back the Mexicans. Taylor, being aware of the Mexican reliance on food imported from New Orleans, assumed that the objective of the assault was the supplies at Point Isabel. He hastened to take the bulk of his forces there. He left Major Jacob Brown in command of the still unfinished fort with a garrison of approximately 500 men from the 7th Infantry, the four 18-pounders, and Lieutenant Braxton Bragg's field battery. The rest of the army he organized into two wings under Colonel David Twiggs (3d, 4th, and 5th Infantry, Brevet Major Samuel Ringgold's battery, and three companies of dragoons) and Brevet Lieu-

17. Jones to ZT, April 20, ZT to AG, April 26, 1846, in *Mex. War Corres.*, 96–97, 288.

18. Emilio del Castillo Negrete, *Invasión de los Norteamericanos en México* (Mexico, 1890), 167; Walker to ZT, May 2, Captain G. A. McCall to Bliss, April 30, 1846, in AOLR, Box 2; Jenkins, *History of the War*, 98–99; Charles Spurlin, "Ranger Walker in the Mexican War," *Military History of Texas and the Southwest*, IX (1971), 262.

19. AO Order 53, April 29, 1846, in AOGO, I (M29/1); Jenkins, *History of the War*, 99.

20. Smith, *War with Mexico*, I, 162–63; Roa Bárcena, *Recuerdos*, I, 63.

tenant Colonel William G. Belknap (8th Infantry, Artillery Battalion, Captain James Duncan's battery, and two companies of dragoons). They marched at 3:30 in the afternoon and covered about eighteen miles before bivouacking shortly before midnight without fires on the damp, chilly coastal plain. The Mexicans in Matamoros greeted the departure with rejoicing. They assumed that it signaled an American retreat. Taylor's column reached Point Isabel at noon the next day. He put the men to work strengthening the defenses.[21]

Once he completed ferrying his men across the Rio Grande on May 2, Arista divided his command. Ampudia led the 4th Infantry, the Puebla Battalion, some sappers, and 200 light cavalry to besiege Fort Texas. Their attack on the American fort, coordinated with the Matamoros batteries, started at 5:00 A.M. the next day but inflicted little damage before ceasing again at midnight.[22] Taylor could hear the exchange of fire from Point Isabel. His initial reaction was to lead the field force back, but he soon discarded the idea. Instead he sent Walker with a message of hope and instructions to return with a report on the situation. The Texans were escorted part of the way by a squadron of dragoons under Captain Charles A. May, who had orders to remain until they returned. Walker reached the fort early the next morning, conferred with Brown, and retraced his steps only to discover that May had left. Without May's escort, Walker had to turn back but was able to make the passage safely on the fifth. He reported that the fort had suffered little damage and could hold out until relieved.

During the fourth, the artillery exchange resumed and Mexican light cavalry cut the road from the fort to the coast. The next day Ampudia moved his force into position to start an investment but made little effort to advance his siege lines. The Mexican guns meanwhile kept bombarding. On the sixth a shell mortally wounded Major Brown. That injury preceded Arista's formal summons for the surrender of the fort. The defenders refused.[23]

21. ZT to AG, May 3, in *Mex. War Corres.*, 289–90; AO Order 55, May 1, 1846, in AOGO, I (M29/1); ZT to [Ann Wood], May 13, 1846, in William K. Bixby Collection, MoHS; Smith, *War with Mexico*, I, 163.

22. Ampudia to Mejía, May 2, Arista to Mejía and Ampudia, May 3, 1846, in Papers Captured with Arista's Baggage; Roa Bárcena, *Recuerdos*, I, 63.

23. The siege of Fort Texas is described in Captain E. W. Hawkins to Bliss, May 10, 1846 in *Senate Documents*, 29th Cong., 1st Sess., No. 288, pp. 31–33. See also Arista to Commanding Officer, Hawkins to Arista, May 6, *ibid.*, 35–36; Brown to Bliss, May 4, ZT to AG, May 5, 1846, in *Mex. War Corres.*, 292–94; Bauer, *Mexican War*, 50–52; Robert Selph Henry, *The Story of the Mexican War* (Indianapolis, 1950), 55–56; Jenkins, *History of the War*, 101–106; *Niles' Weekly Register*, LXX (1846), 254; Alcaraz (ed.), *Other Side*, 44; Smith, *War with Mexico*, 176, 464; Spurlin, "Walker in Mexican War," 264.

Taylor had delayed his return to Fort Texas until sufficient reinforcements reached Point Isabel to ensure its safety. On May 6 the expected recruits arrived along with word that part of the 1st Infantry and some Louisiana volunteers were close behind. The next morning, May 7, he ordered the main body to march at three o'clock that afternoon. "The Commanding General has every confidence," he exhorted his troops, "in his officers and men. If his orders and instructions are carried out, he has no doubt of the result, let the enemy meet him in what numbers he may." Taylor, who shared the prejudice of many of the older officers and those used to frontier activity, foresaw little use of the artillery and reminded his army that "their main dependence must be in the bayonet."[24]

The reports of May and Walker placed the main Mexican force astride the Matamoros road about twenty miles from Point Isabel. Most commanders would have limited their column to combat units in order to ensure the greatest flexibility when confronting the enemy, realizing that a victory anywhere along the path to Fort Texas would free the route for the supply train. But Taylor, apparently obsessed with a fear of shortages at the well-stocked Rio Grande position, insisted on burdening the column with two hundred supply wagons. He further inhibited his mobility by including a pair of 18-pounders, each drawn by six yoke of oxen. Taylor, dressed as usual in what one observer called "a simple farmer's apparel," rode on a light wagon driven by one of his slaves. His slow moving force marched only about seven miles before bivouacking.[25]

When he learned that Taylor had left Point Isabel, Arista moved his force from Tanques del Ramireño along a path which intersected the Matamoros–Point Isabel road at Palo Alto. In anticipation of a battle he recalled Ampudia's force from Fort Texas. The two forces reached the vicinity of Palo Alto at about noon on May 8—the Americans after a march of eleven miles, the Mexicans, less than half that. The Mexicans were already in place along the south side of the open plain when the American advance guard with Captain Walker as their guide swung into sight. Mexican cannon greeted them with a few random shots.

The plain of Palo Alto drew its name from the band of tall timber which began there and, interspersed with chaparral and patches of open ground, stretched southward toward the river. The plain itself, about a mile and a half wide and somewhat larger, was flat but pocked by shallow marshy depressions filled with runoff water and a boundary ridge extend-

24. ZT to AG, AO Order 58, both May 7, 1846, in *Mex. War Corres.*, 294–95, 487.

25. Holman Hamilton, *Zachary Taylor* (2 vols.; Indianapolis, 1941, 1951), I, 177; Smith, *War with Mexico*, I, 163–64; Fayette Copeland, *Kendall of the Picayune* (Norman, 1943), 157; *The Rough and Ready Annual* (New York, 1848), 18.

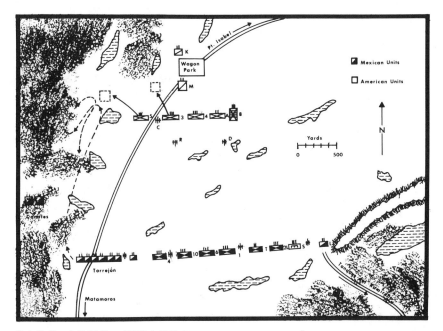

PALO ALTO, PHASE I

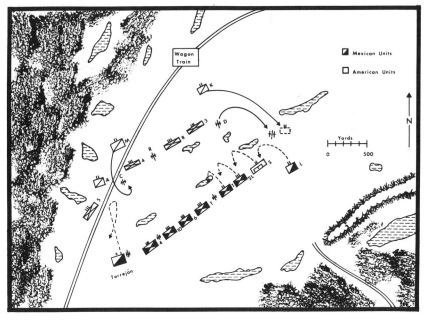

PALO ALTO, PHASE 2

ing northeastward from the Tanques del Ramireño road. Stiff, shoulder-high, sharp-pointed grass inhibited movement by foot soldiers. Chaparral and several of the small marshy depressions fringed the west side of the clearing.

Taylor halted his column about two miles from Arista's line to permit the wagon train to close. The column moved forward again until about three-quarters of a mile separated the two armies. Taylor halted his advance while his men filled their canteens from the nearby Palo Alto water hole and the wagon train moved into a defensive position under the watchful eye of a squadron of dragoons under Captain Croghan Ker. As the Americans returned to their posts they could see the sun glancing off the Mexican bayonets and lances glistening in the bright sunlight and sense penons and flags rustling in the breeze.

While Taylor's men completed their preparations and formed in line of battle, Engineer Lieutenant Jacob E. Blake reconnoitered the field. At about two o'clock Taylor ordered his men forward again, forming them into columns of divisions with the 18-pounders following the road. Apparently, Taylor's plan was to concentrate his strength on his right, adjacent to the road, and open a passage with a bayonet charge. The battle as fought, however, took an entirely different form than what he expected.

Ampudia arrived as the Americans formed. His men took their position on the left of Arista's line. The irregular cavalry who had previously held that part of the position moved west into the chaparral, where they played no role in the battle. The Mexicans formed a thin line, running roughly northeast-southwest for a mile from the road. Torrejón's thousand horsemen drawn from the Presidiales, 7th and 8th Cavalry, and the Light Cavalry stood quietly and slightly advanced on the left. Then came a pair of small cannon, the 4th, 10th, 6th, and 1st Infantry regiments, a company of sappers, and a battery of seven guns. To their right the Mexican line consisted of the Tampico Corps, 2d Light Infantry, a detachment of sappers, a single 4-pounder, and 150 cavalry under General Luis Noriega. All told, Arista commanded about 3,270 men, mixed in quality. Some units were well equipped and led by professionals but others were little more than half-trained collections of Indian conscripts. Arista's formation was well conceived to trap any infantry force launching an attack down the road or across the plain. In either case the cavalry could envelop the attackers.

When the Mexican batteries opened fire, Taylor halted his columns, deployed his troops, and ordered his artillery to return the complement. In keeping with his plan of a thrust down the road, Taylor placed Twiggs astride it with the 5th Infantry (Lieutenant Colonel James S. McIntosh), on the extreme right followed by Ringgold's battery. Then came the

3d Infantry (Captain Lewis N. Morris) and the pair of oxen-drawn 18-pounders on the road under Lieutenant William H. Churchill. The 4th Infantry (Major George W. Allen) was Twiggs's easternmost unit. He held in reserve Ker's and May's dragoon squadrons. Lieutenant Colonel Belknap's 1st Brigade held the left wing of the American force. It deployed from right to left the regimental-sized Artillery Battalion (Brevet Lieutenant Colonel Thomas Childs), Duncan's battery, and the 8th Infantry (Captain William A. Montgomery). The last was slightly refused in order to prevent Mexican cavalry from turning the flank.

At three o'clock the American line was within a half-mile of the Mexicans. Twiggs threw forward Ringgold's battery with May's squadron in support to within about 700 yards of the Mexican position. Belknap sent Duncan's guns about 200 yards ahead of his line. The accurate fire of the two field batteries and of Churchill's heavy 18-pounders forced Arista to abandon any thought of an infantry attack. Instead he ordered Torrejón with his horsemen and a pair of light guns to turn the American right. The cavalryman reluctantly accepted the assignment, fearing the difficulties created by the chaparral through which his men had to pass. He was correct. His horsemen became bogged down in one of the soft patches that dotted the battlefield and gave the Americans time to form defenses. When Lieutenant Leslie Chase reported the movement to Taylor he found the general sitting unconcernably on Old Whitey with one leg hooked over the pommel of his saddle. After hearing Chase's news, he replied, "Keep a bright lookout for them," and returned to his contemplations. Twiggs reacted more positively. He sent his flank regiment, the 5th Infantry, about a quarter of a mile to its right and rear. There the Americans formed a square. Torrejón made his attack in column rather than line and was twice driven off by volleys from the infantrymen at a range of fifty yards. The Mexicans attempted to slide past the 5th Infantry toward the wagon park only to be discouraged by the sight of the 3d Infantry forming its square and by the arrival of Lieutenant Randolph Ridgely's section of guns from Ringgold's battery.

A withering blanket of fire from Duncan's guns smothered Arista's second attack, an assault by the infantry and cavalry on his right, before it could start. The Mexican guns concentrated on the American artillery but accomplished little. The heavy Mexican cannonballs, usually cast of brass, seldom reached the American lines on the fly, probably because of faulty powder, but ricocheted along the ground. They came at such slow speed that American troops normally could dodge them.

About four o'clock a wad from one of Duncan's guns set the grass on fire. The clouds of thick, acrid smoke were propelled toward the Mexican lines by the breezes from the Gulf. The smoke so obscured targets that the American gun had to cease firing for nearly an hour. While the artillerymen enjoyed their respite and replenished their ammunition, both armies changed their positions. Taylor took advantage of a withdrawal by the Mexican left to send Twiggs's wing forward about a thousand yards. Its effect was a thirty-five-degree counterclockwise revolution of the American line. At the same time Arista pivoted his force about the same amount so that the relative position of the two lines remained nearly unchanged.

When the artillery resumed thundering at about five o'clock, Taylor ordered May's squadron supported by the 4th Infantry to turn the Mexican left. May shied from pressing his attack against superior numbers of Mexican horsemen, so the maneuver accomplished little beyond spilling some American blood. Meanwhile, the 4th Infantry received "a most galling fire" from the Mexican artillery across the blackened plain and fell back. The Artillery Battalion then moved up to support the guns and held its ground between the heavy battery and the 5th Infantry under heavy Mexican fire for an hour and a half.

Torrejón's cavalry again approached the American line but fell back under the combined weight of canister fired by the 18-pounders and the musketry of the Artillery Battalion's square. Because of the damage being wrought by Ringgold's and Churchill's guns, Mexican artillery concentrated on them. The counter-battery fire drove Ringgold's battery back and one round mortally wounded its commander.

The Mexican units on the right flank began to waiver under the effective shelling. Their commanders demanded the men either be ordered to attack or be withdrawn outside artillery range. Arista chose the former, adding a cavalry force under Colonel Cayetano Montero to the assault. Duncan, whose targets had been obscured by the smoke of the battle, had just harnessed up his battery to go to Ringgold's assistance when he spotted the Mexican horsemen and realized that if left unchecked they could reach the supply train. He quickly shifted his guns to shield the wagon park. One section went into action ahead of the Mexican column and the other smashed its flank with canister. The artillerymen were quickly joined by Ker's squadron and the 8th Infantry but it was the fire of Duncan's battery which forced the Mexicans to break off their attack. When the Mexicans fell back Duncan again took advantage of the smoke to move his guns unobserved to within 300 yards of the Mexican right flank. From there he opened an enfilading fire which rolled back the Mexican line. Noriega's cavalry increased the panic among the infantry by riding through them, but Arista with some of his officers halted the flight of the weary troops. In a desperate attempt to prevent retreat from again turning into a rout Arista ordered a second attack supported by

Colonel Cauetano Montero's Light Cavalry. The already disheartened men responded weakly and were easily turned back by the Americans.

It was now seven o'clock, and since the Mexican artillery had run out of available ammunition,[26] Arista ordered his men to withdraw on the chaparral-covered high ground behind the right wing. There they bivouacked. Taylor made no effort to pursue, apparently out of fear for the safety of the wagon train and the encroaching darkness. The Americans slept on the battlefield, unsure whether the morning would bring a renewed conflict or a Mexican flight. Taylor's army had won the battle; it held the battlefield. But it had not destroyed the Mexican force nor driven it south of the river. The victory had been won by the artillery, but the infantry proved steady in the face of Mexican shelling although few had directly faced the enemy. The battle had scarcely been fought as Taylor had envisioned. Indeed, he was content to allow his army to fight on the defensive all afternoon, eschewing the bayonet upon which he had planned to rely. This was Taylor's first large battle and the only time he had seen cavalry in action. Their flexibility and speed could not have failed to impress a general whose force was hobbled by a large and vulnerable wagon train. That danger and the realization that clearing the road would not end the threat to his communications as well as the success of the field batteries seems to have led to Taylor's decision not to attack. Nor could he be sure that the lancers could be kept from attacking the flank of any assault force. Casualties in the battle reflected the deadliness of the artillery. Some 92 Mexicans died, 116 were wounded, and 26 more were missing; about 7 percent of the force. The American losses numbered only 9 killed, 44 wounded, and 2 missing, or 2.5 percent of the 2,288 men engaged.[27]

26. Arista had brought only 650 artillery rounds to the battlefield.

27. The description of the Battle of Palo Alto is drawn from ZT to AG, May 16, 1846, with enclosures, in *Senate Documents*, 29th Cong., 1st Sess., No. 383, pp. 2–30; Arista to Ministro de Guerra y Marina, May 8, 1846, in Nathan Covington Brooks, *A Complete History of the Mexican War* (1849; rpr. Chicago, 1965), 135–36; Pedro de Ampudia, *El Ciudadano General Pedro de Ampudia ante el tribunal respectable de la opinión pública* (San Luis Potosí, 1846), 17–23; Belknap to ZT, May 14, 1846, in W. W. Belknap Papers, Princeton University Library; Captain L. B. Webster to sister, May [10], 1846, in Smith-Kirby-Webster-Black-Danner Family Papers, Box 1, MHI; Brooks, *Complete History*, 125–33; Henry B. Dawson, *Battles of the United States by Sea and Land* (2 vols.; New York, 1858), II, 447–50; Lester R. Dillon, Jr., *American Artillery in the Mexican War, 1846–1847* (Austin, 1975), 25; Abner Doubleday, "From the Mexican War to the Rebellion," MS in NYHS; R. Doubleday, *Journal of Barbour*, 54–55; Ulysses S. Grant, *Personal Memoirs of U. S. Grant*, ed. E. B. Long (Cleveland, 1952), 43–45; Henry, *Campaign Sketches*, 90–94; Louis C. Duncan, "A Medical History of General Zachary Taylor's Army of Occupation in Texas and Mexico, 1845–1847," *Military Surgeon*, XXXVIII (1921), 86–88; Jenkins, *History of the War*, 108–12; Oficial de Infantría, *Compaña contra los*

During the night Arista recalled the remaining troops besieging Fort Texas.[28] He decided against renewing the battle at Palo Alto. Instead, he ordered his forces to retire behind the Resaca de Guerrero, or as the Americans called it Resaca de la Palma, a strong defensive position about five miles from Palo Alto.

The troops at Point Isabel spent a worried day. They could hear the thunder of artillery which connoted a battle but they received no news. Luckily for Munroe's peace of mind, Commodore David Conner with four ships of the Home Squadron hove into sight off Brazos Santiago during the late morning. Conner had concluded from the information available in Veracruz that Arista would attack and hastened north. He promptly landed a 500-man party of sailors and marines which stayed ashore until May 13.[29]

When the morning mists lifted from the Palo Alto battlefield at about seven o'clock on May 9, American eyes glimpsed the rear guard of Arista's army riding southward. They followed the rest of the force into the strong defensive position at Resaca de la Palma. Taylor called a council of his senior officers after Twiggs reported that most wished to halt until reinforced. The preponderant opinion at the council agreed but Taylor, supported by McIntosh, Morris, and Duncan, ordered a forward movement[30] telling his subordinates, "I shall go to Fort Texas or stay in my shoes," the western equivalent of "or die in the attempt." Taylor took two immediate steps. He dispatched a dragoon patrol to verify that the Mexicans had departed and directed 220 light troops under Captain George A. McCall of the 4th Infantry to keep contact with the retiring column. He then employed the bulk of his other men in burying the dead, collecting the wounded, and erecting a breastwork containing the two 18-pounders and a pair of 12-pounders to defend the wagon park. Unlike the preceding day, he did not want to be encumbered by the vulnerable train.

Americanos del norte (Mexico, 1848), 8–14; Alcaraz, *Other Side*, 45–50; Roswell Sabine Ripley, *War with Mexico* (2 vols.; New York, 1849), I, 116–24; George Lockhart Rives, *The United States and Mexico, 1821–1848* (2 vols.; New York, 1913), II, 146; John Sedgwick, *Correspondence* (2 vols.; n.p., 1903), I, 15–16; Justin H. Smith, "Official Military Reports," *AHR*, XXI (1915), 97–98; Smith, *War with Mexico*, I, 164–69; George Winston Smith and Charles Judah, *Chronicles of the Gringos* (Albuquerque, 1968), 65–67; Cadmus Marcellus Wilcox, *History of the Mexican War* (Washington, 1892), 51–58; *Niles' Weekly Register*, LXX (1846), 265.

28. Arista to Morlet, May 8, 1846, in Papers Captured with Arista's Baggage.

29. Conner to Bancroft, May 3, in *Niles' Weekly Register*, LXX (1846), 198; Munroe to Conner, May 8, in David Conner Papers, NYPL; Munroe to Bliss, May 9, 1846, in AOLR, Box 2; K. Jack Bauer, *Surfboats and Horse Marines* (Annapolis, 1969), 15–17.

30. Stevens, *Campaigns of the Rio Grande*, 20; Jefferson Davis, "Sketch of Zachary Taylor," MS in Bixby Collection, MoHS; Sedgwick, *Correspondence*, I, 16, assigns the council to the night of the ninth.

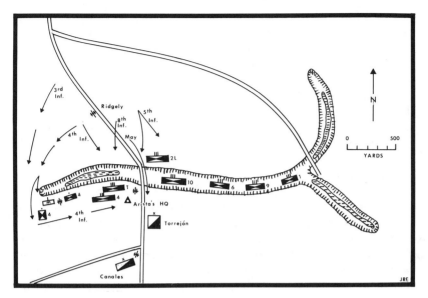

RESACA DE LA PALMA

The Resaca de la Palma, to which Arista's army withdrew, was a bow-shaped, shallow, brush-covered ravine which had once been a channel of the Rio Grande. Both east and west of the crossing of the Palo Alto–Fort Texas road narrow ponds served as moats. Arista placed most of his army behind the Resaca. A three- or four-gun battery commanded the passage of the road and other guns occupied commanding positions to its west, or left. The bulk of the Mexican infantry defended the bank to the right of the road but other units moved into place among the artillery on the left. Arista's headquarters' tent stood in a small clearing about 500 yards behind the front to the left of the road. The Mexican commander stationed Torrejón further back and assigned Brigadier General Antonio Canales with his light cavalry and a pair of field pieces to watch a crossroad which led to the Mexican rear.

Arista had chosen well. The position was strong and could be held without extensive use of artillery—an important consideration because of the shortage of available ammunition. The bank of the Resaca itself formed a natural breastwork while the nearly impenetrable chaparral which surrounded it protected the flanks. In reality Arista's position was less favorable than it appeared. His army was too small for the position and therefore lacked sufficient reserves to contain any penetration of the defenses; his artillery had only limited arcs of fire both because of its location and the presence of detachments of Mexican infantry on the northern bank of the Resaca. Moreover, the chaparral broke up the Mexican units and destroyed the feeling of unit integrity which was important psychologically to the Mexican soldier.[31] Moreover, the troops were hungry. They had not eaten in twenty-four hours. In many cases they had lost confidence in their officers, notably Arista, because of the inactivity of the previous day. All of this combined to destroy the *esprit* of the Army of the North.

The Americans advanced in high spirits, buoyed by the successes at Palo Alto and a growing confidence that they could best any group of Mexicans they encountered. Taylor detailed the Artillery Battalion to guard the wagon park and set the rest of his force in motion at about two o'clock. Meanwhile, McCall's skirmishers felt their way cautiously down the road. Shortly after two o'clock they sighted the Mexican guns guarding the passage of the Resaca. Instantly the battery spoke and a half dozen Americans fell. The others retired. McCall's report of the incident reached Taylor at about three. He arrived an hour later. When McCall rode up to report, Taylor asked, "Well, Captain McCall, what have we here?"

"The Mexican Army, General, in full force."

"Where?" inquired Taylor.

"Between three and four hundred yards in front of you," McCall estimated.

"Is there a position for our artillery?"

"There is, General," McCall replied. "I will show them where to unlimber."

"Well," Taylor said, "you will move forward with the advance, bring on the engagement and then attack his flanks. I will push the regiments in to support you as they come up."[32]

Taylor ordered Ringgold's battery, now commanded by Lieutenant Ridgely, to work its way forward along the road. As Ridgely's guns moved into place McCall's men deployed in the chaparral on both sides of the road. Unfortunately, the obscured view of the Mexicans precluded rendering the usual support which the artillerymen expected. Even so, the artillerymen pushed their guns forward and drove off an attack by Mexican lancers. By showering the Mexican positions north of the Resaca with grapeshot the artillery drove the enemy back across the ravine.

As the different American units reached the battlefield, they took up

31. Taylor believed that Arista threw away his superiority in cavalry by taking a position in the "woods." ZT to Butler, June 19, 1846, in Yale: WA.

32. McCall to Captain B. R. Alden, June 5, 1846, Alden Family Papers, USMA.

positions in the chaparral with the 8th and 5th Infantry to the east and the 3d and 4th Infantry to the west of the road. The battle quickly became one of small units, at which the Americans excelled although not always easily. Some Mexican units, notably the 4th Infantry and the 2d Light Infantry, fought tenaciously but unsuccessfully. The American units on the right faced fewer foe and had the good fortune to strike a path which carried them west of the ponds and around the Mexican flank. Captain Robert D. Buchanan with ten men of the 4th Infantry seized one of the Mexican gun emplacements and beat off an attack by 150 enemy. Too few Mexicans manned that section of the line to contain the Americans who pushed through the chaparral. One group of mixed 3d and 4th Infantrymen under Captain Philip N. Barbour unexpectedly found themselves at Arista's headquarters clearing.

Meanwhile, Taylor, once again astride Old Whitey, watched the battle from a position along the road to the rear of Ridgely's guns. He was unaware of the successes on the right of the line and so reacted favorably to an urgent request from Ridgely for assistance in eliminating the Mexican guns confronting him. When Lieutenant Samuel G. French delivered the request, Taylor commented with irritation, "God, where is May? I can't get him up." Within ten minutes he had been found and given his orders. When he seemed uncertain of the orders, Taylor in frustration called out, "Charge, Captain, *nolens volens!*" (Whether willing or not.) Upon reaching the American guns May called to Ridgely, "Where are they? I am going to charge." Ridgely replied: "Hold on, Charlie, till I draw their fire." The American guns barked and drew a reply from the Mexican battery. Before the Mexican gunners could reload, May's men galloped down the road in a column of fours. The horsemen drove the gunners from their pieces but could not halt their horses until they were a quarter of a mile beyond the Mexican lines. The dragoons re-formed and returned through a hail of Mexican musketry which took heavy casualties. In repassing the battery they took several prisoners, including General Diaz de la Vega.[33] They re-formed and repeated the exercise a second time, taking even heavier casualties. All told, May's command lost six killed and ten wounded.

Each time the dragoons passed the guns the Mexicans returned and resumed fire. It was clear that only infantry could take and hold the position, so in exasperation Taylor turned to Colonel Belknap and ordered: "Take those guns, and by God keep them!" The 5th and 8th Infantry rushed through the crash of musketry to seize the battery. At some points

---

33. Despite May's claim to have captured de la Vega personally, the general was taken by a bugler. Samuel E. Chamberlain, *My Confession* (New York, 1956), 108–109.

the fighting became hand to hand. An order to Ker's squadron and the Artillery Battalion to join in the attack miscarried. They arrived only in time to pursue the fleeing Mexicans.

The success of the 8th and 5th Infantry attack was eased by the collapse of the Mexican line as a result of the turning of its left flank and the unexpected appearance of Barbour and his men. Arista took personal command of the cavalry from a reluctant Torrejón, attempted to salvage the situation with a charge down the road, but accomplished little besides helping some of the infantry escape. The Mexicans scattered, seeking a safe passage across the Rio Grande. Many panic-stricken soldiers brushed past Fort Texas and overwhelmed the guards at the main ferry crossing. Many of those who could not find passage on the lumbering ferryboat or scows hurriedly launched into the stream and tried to swim across, only to fall victim to swift currents. Arista and most of the cavalry crossed at one of the lower fords with less difficulty.

Arista officially reported 154 men killed, 205 wounded, and 156 missing, about 13 percent of his force of 3,758. The Americans buried about 200 Mexicans and seized eight artillery pieces, the colors of the Tampico Battalion, as well as Arista's correspondence and silver service. The American casualties were comparatively light: 49 dead and 83 wounded.[34] Taylor's men had fought what was little more than a series of small unit actions. They had fought them well, but on their own with at best only limited direction from their commander.

Although he still had Ker's squadron, Duncan's battery, and the Artillery Battalion uncommitted and fresh, Taylor did not push in pursuit of the broken Mexican army. The killer instinct which so often separates the

---

34. The sources for the description of the Battle of Resaca de la Palma are: ZT to AG, May 17, 1846, with enclosures, in *Senate Documents*, 29th Cong., 1st Sess., No. 388, pp. 6–26; McIntosh to Bliss, December 2, 1846, in *Mex. War Corres.*, 1102–1104; ZT to [Ann Wood], May 13, 1846, in Bixby Collection, MoHS; Childs to Belknap, May 12, 1846, in AGLR 1846, C-454 (M567/313); McCall to B. R. Alden, June 5, 1846, in Alden Family Papers, USMA; Alcaraz, *Other Side*, 50–55; Ampudia, *El Ciudadano . . . ante el tribunal*, 18–23; A. Doubleday, "From Mexican War to the Rebellion," 125–33; Samuel G. French, *Two Wars: An Autobiography* (Nashville, 1901), 51; Grant, *Memoirs*, 45–46; Henry, *Campaign Sketches*, 94–100; Oficial de Infantría, *Compaña contra los Americanos*, 15–20; Ripley, *War with Mexico*, I, 125–31; Blackwood, *To Mexico with Scott*, 50–51; Wilcox, *History of Mexican War*, 58–65; *Niles' Weekly Register*, LXX (1846), 251–53, 265; Albert G. Brackett, *History of the United States Cavalry* (1865; rpr. New York, 1968), 56–59; Brooks, *Complete History*, 137–47; Dawson, *Battles of the U.S.*, II, 451–53; Duncan, "Medical History," 88–89; Jenkins, *War Between U.S. and Mexico*, 112–17; Roa Bárcena, *Recuerdos*, I, 84–85; Theodore F. Rodenbough, *From Everglades to Cañon with the Second Dragoons* (New York, 1875), 514–15; Smith, *War with Mexico*, I, 169–76, 466–67; Smith and Judah, *Chronicles of the Gringos*, 67–71.

great general from the mediocre one was not one of the strong attributes of his character. In none of his victories did Taylor follow up on his battle-field success with a strong pursuit. The Artillery Battalion chased Arista's remnants but never made contact with any organized group. Neither did the Fort Texas garrison interfere with the disheartened, and largely disorganized, mass of men flowing past.[35] The Americans could not pursue across the river because they had no bridging equipment and Taylor had failed to have any substitute prepared. His solution was to propose a crossing in the vicinity of Barita using ships' boats from Conner's squadron.

On May 11 Taylor rode to Point Isabel to confer with Conner. Since he did not know the commodore, who had a reputation as somewhat of a stickler for protocol, Taylor put on his uniform. Conner, knowing the general's aversion to formal dress, wore civilian clothes. Both were embarrassed but quickly agreed to a joint assault on Barita. It occurred on May 17 but was overshadowed by the seizure of Matamoros.[36]

During the tenth Arista offered to exchange Thornton and Captain William J. Hardee for General la Vega. Taylor countered with a proposal to add all the men taken by Torrejón. The Mexican demurred but the final arrangement did bring fifty-one Americans back to the army and sent home most of the Mexican prisoners taken at Resaca de la Palma. La Vega and his staff were not included. They were sent to New Orleans to await their exchange.[37] While the prisoner exchange was being arranged, Arista pulled his troops out of Matamoros, and on the twelfth a council of war agreed to abandon the Rio Grande position but not upon the conditions which would trigger a retreat.[38]

Housekeeping duties occupied Taylor's time while he awaited the opportunity to cross the river and further instructions from Washington. He congratulated the Army of Occupation "upon the signal success which has crowned its recent operations against the enemy" and praised the Fort Texas garrison for its "distinguished service." On the twelfth he named the Point Isabel facility in honor of the president and five days later he renamed Fort Texas Fort Brown to honor her martyred former

35. Childs to Belknap, May 12, 1846, in AGLR 1846, C-454 (M567/313).

36. Captain J. Saunders to ZT, May 10, Wilson to Bliss, May 17, 1846, in AOLR, Box 2; AO Special Order 64, May 14, 1846, in AOGO, II (M29/9); Hamilton, *Taylor*, I, 192.

37. Arista to ZT, May 10, 1846, in AOLR, Box 2; AO Special Order 62, May 12, 1846, in AOGO, II (M29/2); Arista to Ministro de Guerra y Marina, May 13, 1846, in Castillo Negrete, *Invasión*, 193; Roa Bárcena, *Recuerdos*, I, 85.

38. Roa Bárcena, *Recuerdos*, I, 85; Alcaraz, *Other Side*, 57–58. See also Arista to Comandante General de Tamaulipas, May 18, 1846, in *Niles' Weekly Register*, LXX (1846), 296.

commander.[39] In the midst of the preparations for the crossing, Taylor came down with a fever which kept him in his tent during the fourteenth. Once he recovered he had to face the problem of the impending arrival of more volunteers than he could use. The potential influx of new regiments did not sit well with many of the regular officers, who felt overly confident of their own prowess. One exuberant lieutenant noted that it was "with great mortification that a majority of the officers learned, that Genl Taylor had made requisition for more troops. We felt that he had in a measure disgraced us by his inaction and apparent want of confidence in us."[40]

The complaints of his young braves were partially stilled by preparations to seize Matamoros and the mouth of the river. On the fifteenth Brevet Major William M. Graham of the 4th Infantry cut out some boats from the Mexican bank of the river. That morning the Army of Occupation received preparatory orders, but Taylor did not make the crossing then nor the next day when Graham failed in a second expedition. At noon on the seventeenth, a Mexican bugler sounded parley, and General Tomás Requeña delivered an armistice proposal. It called for a ceasefire until the outcome of rumored negotiations in process in Mexico City became known. Taylor, who knew of no negotiations, refused. Requeña then offered to surrender all public property in Matamoros if Taylor would forebear occupying the town. Taylor's answer was more bellicose than usual: "The city must capitulate. All [public] property must be surrendered; and only then may the Mexican army march out and retire." The Mexican negotiator asked for time to consider the demand but promised to have an answer by Taylor's three o'clock deadline.

The time passed without an answer, but Arista used it to complete his withdrawal. Taylor decided that not enough would be gained by a late afternoon crossing to offset its dangers and postponed the operation until the following morning. On the morning of the eighteenth he crossed on the boats seized by Graham and on others hammered together from lumber brought from Point Isabel. The dragoons and Walker's Texans followed. The first Americans to reach the southern bank realized that Arista's men had departed, and hastened to secure the ferry. Most of the Americans who followed rode it. Meanwhile, the local civil authorities, dressed in white and astride white horses, rode out to meet the advancing troops to surrender the city. Taylor refused to discuss terms but promised that civil laws would remain in effect and that women and property would be safe. In order to reduce the number of troops entering Matamoros, Taylor established his headquarters under a small tree outside the town.[41]

39. AO Order 59, 60, 62, May 11–17, 1846, in AOGO, I (M 29/1).
40. Brooks to [DeLorma Brooks], May 12, 1846, in William T. H. Brooks Papers, MHI.
41. Arista to ZT, May 17, 1846, in *Taylor, Scott Corres.*, 396–97; ZT to AG, May 18,

The American general must have appeared very strange to Mexicans used to the glitter of the uniforms that adorned their commanders. One young lieutenant in the 5th Infantry thought that Taylor looked like a Vermont farmer. He found him dressed in a big straw sombrero, a pair of enlisted men's trousers which were too short for him, a loose line coat, and a pair of "soldier shoes."[42] Nor did the American commander act as Arista had and ignore the plight of the injured Mexicans who could not accompany the retreating force. Taylor directed his surgeons to attend to the enemy wounded and personally contributed several hundred dollars to their support.[43]

As the Mexican army withdrew by a circuitous route to Monterrey, Taylor could look with justifiable pride on the accomplishments of his army. It had achieved all the tasks assigned it with conspicuous success. It controlled the lower Rio Grande valley, stood poised to advance deep into northern Mexico. These would be the first steps of what would prove to be a long march directed at conquering a peace. Public acclaim for the army's commander would soon echo from across the United States.[44] To many of his countrymen, he was the new Andrew Jackson, the American Cincinnatus, springing from the egalitarian frontier to demonstrate with simplicity of manner and natural dignity the superiority of the New World Anglo-Saxon. That little of this fitted Zachary Taylor mattered not at all; his image had been struck.

1846, in *Mex. War Corres.*, 297–98; to Wood, May 19, 1846, in William H. Samson (ed.), *Letters of Zachary Taylor from the Battle-Fields of the Mexican War* (Rochester, 1908), 3–5; ZT to [Ann Wood], June 9, 1846, in Bixby Collection, MoHS; AO Order 61, May 15, 1846, in AOGO, I (M29/1); R. Doubleday, *Journal of Barbour*, 61–64; Hamilton, *Taylor*, I, 193–94; James A. Huston, *The Sinews of War: Army Logistics, 1775–1953* (Washington, 1966), 139; Smith, *War with Mexico*, I, 178.

42. Charles S. Hamilton, "Memoirs of the Mexican War," *Wisconsin Magazine of History*, XIV (1930–31), 66.

43. Mary C. Gillett, "The Army Medical Department, 1818–1865," V, 14–15, MS in Center of Military History, Washington; Holman Hamilton, *The Three Kentucky Presidents* (Lexington, 1978), 24.

44. Polk sent Taylor's nomination for brevet major general to the Senate on May 25, the same day that a joint resolution of thanks was introduced in the House. Both cleared Congress three days later. James K. Polk, *The Diary of James K. Polk During His Presidency, 1845 to 1849*, ed. Milo Milton Quaife (4 vols.; Chicago, 1910) I, 428; *Congressional Globe*, 29th Cong., 1st Sess., 862, 867, 873–80.

CHAPTER IX

On to Monterrey

TAYLOR'S REPORTS of the ambush of Captain Seth
Thornton's patrol reached Washington on May 9 just as President James
K. Polk was wrestling with the problem of a response to the Mexican refusal to deal with the United States except on her own terms. In an unusual Sunday session the cabinet concurred in Polk's decision to ask for a
declaration of war. The president's war message was read to Congress
during Monday, May 11, along with a bill to provide money and 50,000
volunteers to conduct the war. The administration's political strategy was
masterful. By making opposition to the bill appear to be an unpatriotic
refusal of the arms needed by Taylor's troops to defend themselves, it cut
the ground out from under most of the Whig opposition. Because many
of the Whigs believed that the Hartford Convention in 1814, with its
overtone of disunion, had killed the Federalist party, the Whig party was
reluctant to resist Polk's call for war. After only a half-hour of limited debate, the House cleared the bill on the eleventh. The Senate followed on
the twelfth. Polk signed the bill the next day.[1]

Polk promptly conferred with his senior general, Major General
Winfield Scott. The president recognized the political need for immediate
military activity in order to use the short-term volunteers called by Taylor
from Louisiana and Texas as well as the necessity of appearing to assail
the Mexican aggressors. Scott viewed the situation from a military viewpoint and pointed out that the one-year volunteers would not reach the

1. James K. Polk, *The Diary of James K. Polk During His Presidency, 1845 to 1849*, ed.
Milo Milton Quaife (4 vols.; Chicago, 1910), I, 319–95; *Congressional Globe*, 29th
Cong., 1st Sess., 782–88, 791–804.

Rio Grande until early August, the middle of the rainy season. He proposed keeping the troops in the United States undergoing training until September. In Polk's view that was "too scientific and visionary." Despite those reservations, the president offered Scott command of the forces on the Rio Grande. The general apparently was surprised by the offer and had no campaign plans ready to offer.[2]

Scott delayed his departure for a mixture of reasons, some military, some political, and some stemming from a belief that "it was harsh and unusual for a senior, without reenforcement [sic], to supersede a meritorious junior." Although working fourteen-hour days, he found time to write a pair of letters which gave the president an excuse to relieve him of the Mexican command for political disloyalty. In one, Scott defended his delay in leaving for the front as the want of "a desire to place myself in the most perilous of all positions—*a fire upon my rear, from* [Democratic politicians in] *Washington, and the fire, in front, from the Mexicans.*" In a second letter he prophesied to Senator William S. Archer of Virginia that the administration would appoint no easterner, West Pointer, or Whig as an officer in the newly created Mounted Rifle Regiment.[3]

The administration's strategy was slow to develop. In many ways this was a natural result of the president's chosen method of graduated pressure and his preoccupation with the acquisition of California. That strategy ensured that the administration would not develop a true war plan until all else failed. From its point of view the twin victories north of the Rio Grande were but another effort to convince the Mexicans that negotiations were in their interest. To continue that pressure the initial plans merely called for seizure of the northern Mexican states. Their loss, Polk and his advisors assumed, would start negotiations. Moreover, they hoped to win the long desired settlement without mounting a major military effort. It is doubtful that Taylor understood the subtlety of Polk's plan, and the pressures under which the field commander found himself during the campaign tended to magnify his feelings of slight and justify his growing antipathy toward the president and his men.

Polk on May 14 directed his military leaders to start the northern

2. Polk, *Diary*, I, 395–96; Charles Winslow Elliott, *Winfield Scott* (New York, 1937), 420; Ivor Debenham Spencer, *The Victor and the Spoils: A Life of William L. Marcy* (Providence, 1959), 155; Justin H. Smith, *War with Mexico* (2 vols.; New York, 1919), I, 198–99.

3. Winfield Scott, *Memoirs of Lieut.-General Scott, LL.D.* (2 vols., 1864; rpr. Freeport, N.Y., 1970), II, 384–85; Scott to Marcy, May 21, 25, Marcy to Scott, May 25, Scott, Memorandum, May 25, 1846, in *Senate Documents*, 29th Cong., 1st Sess., No. 378, pp. 5–7, 10–12; Scott to Archer, February 6, 1846, in James K. Polk Papers, LC; Polk, *Diary*, I, 407–27; Smith, *War with Mexico*, I, 199–200.

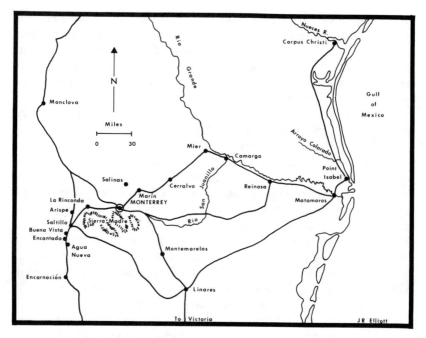

NORTHERN MEXICO

Mexican plan. To carry out the operations the War Department assigned 20,000 volunteers drawn from southern and western states.[4] Those instructions crossed a query from Taylor as to his future operations. He outlined his plan to move against Monterrey. The timing of his campaign, he cautioned, would depend upon the navigability of the river during the late summer since the operation depended on the establishment of a supply base at Camargo.[5]

While the discussions about future strategy took place in Washington, Taylor sent Lieutenant Colonel John Garland with the dragoons and two

4. Scott to ZT, May 18, 1846, in *Mex. War Corres.*, 446; Polk, *Diary*, I, 400; Charles Sellers, *James K. Polk, Continentalist* (Princeton, 1966), 422; Spencer, *Victor and Spoils*, 153.

5. ZT to AG, May 21, 1846, in *Mex. War Corres.*, 300. Marcy to ZT, May 28, 1846, *ibid.*, 282, requested Taylor's views on strategy.

companies of mounted Texans in pursuit of the retiring Matamoros garrison. Although the Mexican column was slowed by about 1,000 family members, camp followers, and other civilians, Garland did not make contact. His force was too small to engage and insufficiently provisioned to remain long in the field. It returned on the twenty-second with twenty-two Mexican stragglers and clear evidence that the Mexican force had abandoned the Rio Grande valley.[6]

When Taylor issued his call for Louisiana troops in the aftermath of Thornton's ambush, General Edmund P. Gaines, the commander of the Western Division at New Orleans, on his own, began requisitioning additional troops. Before he could be stopped he had sent six regiments of short-term volunteers from Louisiana and contingents from Missouri and Kentucky to the Rio Grande.[7] They totaled 11,211 men but arrived too late to contribute to the campaign on the Rio Grande. Moreover, they possessed little equipment, less discipline, and an immense disdain for training. Nor were they interested in extending their enlistments to a full year. In disgust, Taylor ordered them home on July 21.[8] More surprising, but in keeping with the volunteers' view of their rights, was the refusal of two Texas regiments to continue in service at Camargo at the onset of the Monterrey campaign. Colonel Albert Sidney Johnston's riflemen insisted that they had agreed to only three months' service and no amount of argument by their colonel could alter that determination. When a delegation called on Taylor, he attempted to shame them into staying by saying that he did not want any man in his force who did not want to be there. The regiment promptly voted to disband and only about 150 reenlisted.[9]

The influx of volunteers quickly overwhelmed the supplies held at Point Isabel, nearly depleting the stocks of wagons, tents, horseshoes, and medicines. Since their officers generally lacked even rudimentary knowledge of camp sanitation, diseases like dysentery and diarrhea swept through units. In some instances a third of the men in a regiment answered the sick call. Tents, when available, were fabricated from muslin because tent canvas could not be purchased in the United States.[10] Since

6. ZT to AG, May 24, 1846, *ibid.*, 301; William S. Henry, *Campaign Sketches of the War with Mexico* (New York, 1847), 113; José C. Valades, *Breve historia de la guerra con los Estados Unidos* (Mexico, 19), 120.

7. Gaines to AG, May 3, 1846, in AGRL 1846, 213 (M711/19); Marcy to ZT May 23, August 3, ZT to AG, July 1, 16, 1846, in *Mex. War Corres.*, 218, 315–18.

8. Marvin A. Kreidberg and Merton G. Henry, *History of Mobilization in the United States Army* (Washington, 1955), 75; AO Order 91, July 21, 1846, in AOGO, I (M29/1).

9. AO Special Order 126, August 22, 1846, in AOGO, II (M29/2); Henry, *Campaign Sketches*, 152; William Preston Johnston, *The Life of Gen. Albert Sidney Johnston* (New York, 1879), 135–36.

10. Holman Hamilton, *Zachary Taylor* (2 vols.; Indianapolis, 1941, 1951), I, 195; Erna

transportation did not exist to move the men upstream, they gathered in a series of camps at Point Isabel, on Brazos Island, and along the lower river.[11] The problems which the volunteers faced in the camps were not exclusively of their own making. Taylor, whose experience with such troops had been both limited and unfavorable, contributed substantially to the difficulties. He believed that "the great thing with volunteers was to keep them in good health & spirits, at all hasards [sic], & teach them a few simple & necessary maneuvers," but he quickly learned that his reinforcements, whether Gaines's three-months men or the twelve-months volunteers, were a notably unruly bunch. Neither Taylor, his staff, nor the citizen-officers devised adequate diversions for the energies of the men. As early as mid-May, when only a handful had joined, Taylor complained of their theft of Mexican cattle. It was only the first of many complaints. With few military duties to occupy their time, the men drifted into Matamoros to visit the gambling dens and bordellos which sprang up almost as soon as the troops arrived. The more intellectually curious visited local families and the cathedral in order to absorb some of their foreign flavor. A touring theatrical company which numbered a young Joe Jefferson among its members soon arrived to perform in the local theater before an unusually diverse audience of soldiers and civilians, many of whom had never before seen a stage production.[12]

President Polk recognized the damaging impact in Mexico of the overwhelming anti-Catholicism of the volunteers. After consulting the American Catholic bishops he arranged the assignment of two priests to Taylor's army. Although not formally appointed as chaplains, they performed that function as well as serving as liaisons with the local Catholic clergy and as a counter to Mexican religious propaganda. Secretary of War William L. Marcy followed up on the dispatch of the priests with a proclamation which he instructed Taylor to give wide circulation. It assured the Mexicans: "Your religion, your altars and churches, the property of your

---

Risch, *Quartermaster Support of the Army* (Washington, 1962), 264–65; Smith, *War with Mexico*, I, 206. In defense of the volunteers it should be pointed out that they were predominantly farm boys never before exposed to communicable diseases. Mary C. Gillett, "The Army Medical Department, 1818–1865" (MS at Center at Military History, Washington), V-2.

11. AO Special Order 71, May 22, 1846, in AOGO, II (M29/2); Smith, *War with Mexico*, I, 205–206.

12. AO Order 62, May 17, 1846, in AOGO, I (M29/1); Alan S. Downer (ed.), *Autobiography of Joseph Jefferson* (Cambridge, 1964), 55; Robert F. Lucid (ed.), *The Journal of Richard Henry Dana, Jr.* (3 vols.; Cambridge, 1968), I, 344; Hamilton, *Taylor*, I, 194–95; George Gordon Meade, *Life and Letters of George Gordon Meade* (2 vols.; New York, 1913), I, 91.

churches and citizens, the emblems of your faith and its ministers, shall be protected and remain inviolate."[13]

On May 30 the president congratulated Taylor on his victories and forwarded his brevet commission as major general. It was a friendly letter which showed none of the doubts about the general's ability or loyalty which would poison their relations later in the summer.[14] Marcy followed with news that Taylor would continue in command along the Rio Grande. The secretary's letter offered little strategic direction beyond suggesting the occupation of Monterrey, upon which Taylor had already settled. The aim of the administration's strategy, the secretary declared, was to "dispose the enemy to desire an end to the war." Since "a peace must be conquered in the shortest space of time practicable," he asked whether this could best be accomplished by an attack on Mexico City or by operations in northern Mexico. Were there sufficient supplies available locally, Marcy inquired, to support an advance inland?[15] The letter succinctly spelled out the principles that guided the administration as well as the dilemmas which it faced in achieving its objectives. Unfortunately, it appeared less clear when read in the humid atmosphere of the Rio Grande valley.

Scott added a gloss to the secretary's instructions. He estimated that 16,280 volunteers would reinforce Taylor's command but warned the Rio Grande commander not to accept any proposals for an armistice unless he was sure that it was "sufficiently formal and sincere." Even then, Scott reported, the president wished the cessation of fighting to be for only a limited time. The letter brought news of the dispatch of Colonel Stephen Watts Kearny's Army of the West to New Mexico and California and of the formation of an expedition at San Antonio, Texas, under Brigadier General John E. Wool to seize Chihuahua. Wool's force, Scott wrote, formed a part of Taylor's command.[16]

13. Polk, *Diary*, III, 104; Marcy to ZT, May 20, June 4, 1846, in SWMA, XXVI, 261, 289–90 (M6/26); Dom Aidan Henry Germain, *Catholic Military and Naval Chaplains* (Washington, 1929), 38–39; Sister Blanche Marie McEniry, *American Catholics in the War with Mexico* (Washington, 1932), 34–35, 54, 64–66. On the general question of anti-Catholicism see Ted C. Hinckley, "American Anti-Catholicism During the Mexican War," *Pacific Historical Review*, XXXI (1962), 121–37.

14. Polk to ZT, May 30, 1846, in *Mex. War Corres.*, 283; Marcy to ZG, May 30, 1846, in AGLR 1846, T-246 (M567/327). The Supplementary War Act of June 18, 1846, authorized an additional regular major general and two brigadiers. Taylor received the senior appointment while the one-star ranks went to Twiggs and Colonel S. W. Kearny. *U.S. Statutes at Large*, IX, 17; Francis B. Heitman, *Historical Register and Dictionary of the United States Army* (2 vols.; Washington, 1903), I, 949.

15. Marcy to ZT, June 8, 1846, in *Mex. War Corres.*, 324–25.

16. Scott to ZT, June 12, 15, 1846, *ibid.*, 325–27, 1328–29.

Taylor responded negatively to Marcy's request for strategic suggestions. He informed the Washington planners that the distances which had to be covered prohibited an attack on Mexico City from positions in the Rio Grande valley. Therefore, he recommended that operations in the north be confined to seizing the frontier states. In such an operation the capture of Chihuahua would be especially important since it was the commercial center for the area northwest of Monterrey.[17] In a private letter Taylor complained that the strategy had been formulated without consulting him and that he would have refused the command "could I have done so with propriety." The plan was "not in keeping altogether with my views, the number of men to be employed, as well as many other arrangements connected with it." He found the plan of campaign too extensive, the numbers "too great for the subsistence & means of transportation in the country they are to act in." Taylor believed the best strategy would be to secure the Rio Grande valley with the regulars and a few thousand six-months volunteers; hold the twelve-months men in training camps until the yellow fever season had passed; land at Veracruz; and attack the Mexican capital. Taylor also faulted Scott for not coming to the Rio Grande front as soon as he had been appointed to the command.[18]

Taylor's letters crossed one from Marcy, drafted by the president in consultation with Senator Thomas Hart Benton. It directed the field commander to take advantage of any neutrality or independence movements in the northern Mexican states. Polk again asked about the feasibility of a march from Monterrey to Mexico City but also inquired about Tampico (which Taylor had ruled out because of yellow fever) or Veracruz as possible points of departure.[19] Taylor replied that his political intelligence was limited but that he thought it too soon for internal divisions to develop. He added that he was attempting to conciliate the local populace but that the conduct of the volunteers complicated the efforts. If he could gather 10,000 men at Saltillo, south of Monterrey, Taylor prophesied that he would advance to San Luis Potosí, which he felt sure "would speedily bring proposals for peace." If such a move proved logistically impractical, he recommended occupation of the northern states followed by a landing at Veracruz. He dismissed the Tampico–Mexico City route as impractical.[20] In practice, further discussion of strategy involving the Army of Occupation had to await the completion of the Monterrey campaign, since it occupied Taylor's full attention.

Even before the instructions to strike inland reached him, Taylor com-

17. ZT to AG, July 2, 1846, *ibid.*, 329–32.
18. ZT to John Ewing, July 3, 1846, in Miscellaneous Papers, NYHS.
19. Marcy to ZT, July 9, 1846, in *Mex. War Corres.*, 155–58; Polk, *Diary*, II, 16–17.
20. ZT to Polk, August 1, 1846, in *Mex. War Corres.*, 336–38.

plained about his lack of transportation, especially steamboats. He ascribed the difficulties to the failure of the Quartermaster Department, headed by his long-time guardian angel Thomas S. Jesup, to provide steamers. It was not a fair charge since the delays owed as much to Taylor's failure to forecast his needs as they did to shortcomings in the Quartermaster Department. Major Charles Thomas, the depot quartermaster at Point Isabel, asked on his own for one or two river steamers on May 15. On May 24 Taylor raised the number to four vessels. None could be secured immediately at New Orleans but the quartermaster's agents secured eight river craft elsewhere. The first of them were en route to the Rio Grande by mid-June, so that twelve boats churned the muddy water of the river by late July.[21]

Wagons were another problem. The supply departments had few in reserve and could not secure additional ones until late summer. Taylor contributed significantly to the problem since he showed little concern about the condition of his supply train. In July only 175 wagons were in service out of the 300 on hand. The reason was primarily a shortage of draft animals. Lieutenant Colonel Henry Whiting, Cross's replacement as staff quartermaster, ultimately had to resort to draft oxen and pack mules to fill the deficiencies. Luckily, the latter could be secured locally.[22]

The civil authorities at Renosa, a river town about half way from Matamoros to Camargo, requested an American garrison on June 1 to protect it from marauders. Taylor readily agreed, dispatching Lieutenant Colonel Henry Wilson with a battalion of the 1st Infantry and a company of Texas Rangers.[23] Shortly afterwards the American army began its study of the routes to Monterrey. On June 12 Taylor directed Captain Benjamin McCulloch of the Texas Rangers to reconnoiter possible routes. The Texan returned ten days later to recommend that the army move via Camargo, since the path followed by Arista lacked both forage and water.[24] The report confirmed Taylor's own inclination toward the Camargo route.

The arrival of several steamboats permitted the initiation of the move

21. ZT to AG, June 10, 1846. Jesup Memorandum, n.d., *ibid.*, 547–50; Thomas to Bliss, June 1, 1846, in AOLR, Box 3; Risch, *Quartermaster Support*, 267–68.

22. Risch, *Quartermaster Support*, 268–71; Brainerd Dyer, *Zachary Taylor* (Baton Rouge, 1946), 189–91.

23. AO Special Order 78, June 4, 1846, in AOGO, II (M29/2); Wilson to Bliss, June 10, 1846, in AOLR, Box 3; Nathan Covington Brooks, *A Complete History of the Mexican War* (1849; rpr. Chicago, 1965), 163.

24. Samuel C. Reid, *The Scouting Expeditions of McCulloch's Texas Rangers* (Philadelphia, 1866), 43–56; Victor M. Rose, *The Life and Services of General Ben McCulloch* (Austin, 1958), 70–75; Charles Spurlin, "With Taylor and McCulloch Through the Battle of Monterey," *Texas Military History*, VI (1967), 214; Walter Prescott Webb, *The Texas Rangers* (Boston, 1935), 95–98.

to Camargo on July 6. That day the advance guard of the 7th Infantry departed Matamoros by steamer. It reached its destination on the four-teenth and linked up with other elements which had marched overland. The remainder of the 1st Brigade sailed on July 19 and the 3d Brigade on the twenty-eighth. In each case the waterborne troops were followed by the brigade train and artillery which moved by road.[25] On the next to last day of the month, Taylor, who had decided to use the half-trained volunteer regiments to protect his line of communication while employ-ing only the regulars and selected volunteer units for the Monterrey expe-dition, fixed their order of movement to Camargo.[26] Taylor himself left on August 4 and reached Camargo on the eighth.[27]

The forward movement of the volunteers came none too soon. In their view they had come to fight but there was no action. They became in-creasingly restive in the poor, hot, and humid camps along the river. "Vol-unteers are playing the devil," one regular complained, "and disgracing the country in Matamoros." Niles' Register explained the problem to its readers with considerable insight: "The graceless and lawless spirits, being the most difficult to control, join the ranks and carry with them their lawless propensities." The frustrations led to riots involving signifi-cant portions of entire units such as that between the Baltimore and Washington Battalion and the 1st Ohio over a catfish.[28] A more serious riot occurred in late August between the Georgia companies embarking on a steamer for Camargo. When Colonel Edward D. Baker of the 4th Illinois attempted to quell it he was wounded along with several of his men. Two Illinoisans and a Georgian died.[29]

25. ZT to AG, July 11, 1846, in Mex. War Corres., 397; Captain D. S. Miles to Bliss, July 8, 14, 1846, in Justin H. Smith Papers, XI, 42–44, 47–50, Latin American Collection, University of Texas, Austin; Henry, Campaign Sketches, 124–25; Bliss to Duncan, July 23, 1846, in James Duncan Papers, USMA.

26. Texas Brigade, Louisville Legion, Baltimore & Washington Battalion, Ohio Brigade, 2nd Kentucky, Mississippi, 1st Tennessee, Alabama, Georgia, and 2nd Pennsylvania regi-ments in that order.

27. Whiting to Jesup, July 23, ZT to AG, July 30, 1846, in Mex. War Corres., 401, 673; ZT to Wood, July 25, 1846, in William H. Samson (ed.), Letters of Zachary Taylor from the Battlefields of the Mexican War (Rochester, 1908), 30; AO Order 93, July 30, 1846, in AOGO, I (M29/1); ZT Will, July 20, 1846, in ZT(LC), ser 3, r 2; Henry, Campaign Sketches, 121.

28. Rhoda Van Bibber Tanner Doubleday (ed.), Journals of . . . Philip Norbourne Bar-bour (New York, 1936), 89; Niles' Weekly Register, LXX (1846), 326, LXXI (1846–47), 21; John R. Kenly, Memoirs of a Maryland Volunteer (Philadelphia, 1873), 47–48.

29. Wilbur G. Kurtz, Jr., "The First Regiment of Georgia Volunteers in the Mexican War," Georgia Historical Quarterly, XXVI (1943), 316–17; D. E. Livingston-Little, "Mu-tiny During the Mexican War: An Incident on the Rio Grande," Journal of the West, IX (1970), 340–45.

Camargo was one of those towns that most visitors wished to forget. It was shabby and had nearly been destroyed by earlier floods. The climate was worse. The wind almost never stirred; the heat reached 112 degrees Fahrenheit; and the humidity was scarcely bearable. The troops, unused to such a climate, easily succumbed to dysentery and diarrhea. Taylor's choice of the site for his staging point reflected his poor knowledge of the country in which he was operating. Mier, on the river upstream, and Cerralvo, inland, would have been healthier locations.[30] Both were on the route Taylor ultimately followed.

While waiting for the troops to gather, Taylor dispatched McCulloch and his rangers to disburse a group of Mexican irregulars based at China. The Texans missed their quarry but returned with additional information about routes to Monterrey.[31] Captain Duncan reconnoitered another road via Mier and Cerralvo in mid-August to determine the feasibility of establishing an advanced depot at Cerralvo. His report convinced Taylor that such a plan was entirely feasible.[32]

He set September 1 as the target date for the start of the Monterrey campaign. That was nearly the same date that Scott had prophesied in May. Taylor did not anticipate serious Mexican resistance but prepared to meet it if it arose. While awaiting Duncan's report on Cerralvo, Taylor organized his troops for the campaign. He established two divisions of regulars under Twiggs and Brevet Brigadier General William J. Worth and one of volunteers under Butler.[33] Taylor followed the reorganization with a grand review of the regulars.[34] Whether it was intended to impress the volunteers or any Mexican spies is not important since it undoubtedly accomplished both objectives.

Worth led the 1st Brigade of his division out of Camargo during the thirteenth. It escorted 180 wagons and 1,000 pack mules carrying 160,000 rations to stock the Cerralvo depot. The march was plain misery for the army. Swarms of frogs and insects bedeviled man and beast; the sun shown unrelentingly during the day, while at night the clammy chill

30. For descriptions of Camargo see E. Kirby Smith, *To Mexico with Scott*, ed. Emma Jerome Blackwood (Cambridge, Mass., 1917), 63; J. F. H. Claiborne, *Life and Correspondence of John A. Quitman* (2 vols.; New York, 1860), I, 240; Henry, *Campaign Sketches*, 152; Hamilton, *Taylor*, I, 200–201; Smith, *War with Mexico*, I, 211–12.

31. ZT to AG, August 10, 1846, in *Mex. War Corres.*, 408; Reid, *McCulloch's Rangers*, 78–82.

32. Rose, *McCulloch*, 91–93; Reid, *McCulloch's Rangers*, 96–102; John Frost, *The Mexican War and Its Warriors* (New Haven, 1848), 65.

33. ZT to AG, August 10, September 3, 1846, in *Mex. War Corres.*, 408, 411–19; to Wood, August 23, September 16, 1846, in Samson (ed.), *Letters of Taylor*, 46, 57; AO Order 98, 108, 111, 112, August 17, 28, 31, September 3, 1846, in AOGO, I (M29/1).

34. Edward J. Nichols, *Zach Taylor's Little Army* (Garden City, 1963), 129.

brought its own brand of discomfort. Many of the troops for the first time confronted the idiosyncrasies of pack mules. After camp had been broken up in the morning a detail remained behind to organize the tents and utensils into packages which could be carried by the mules. Tent poles, kettles, mess chests, and similar outsized items challenged the ingenuity of the men, who had also to contend with mules given to stampeding, rolling on their backs, or entangling their loads with tree limbs.

The route of march took the force along the Rio Grande to Mier and then roughly along the track followed today by Federal Highway 54. Each step of the way the distant pale blue summits of the Sierra Madres became clearer. The men reached Cerralvo on the twenty-fifth. In their trace followed Persifor Smith with the rest of Worth's division; next, Twiggs's divisions; and then Butler's volunteers. On September 5, Taylor and his staff joined the march. They reached the depot on the ninth. When the rear guard arrived on the thirteenth Taylor had 6,640 men.[35]

Cerralvo, a pleasant market town of 1,500 with white stone buildings and an abundant supply of good water, was the antithesis of Camargo. Lemon, orange, peach, fig, pomegranate, and pecan trees shaded houses and formed groves. Corn grew in abundance while cattle and sheep grazed in the surrounding fields.[36] Here the early arrivals rested and recovered from their march and the miasmas of the river valley.

Intelligence gathered by an especially effective spy indicated that Major General Pedro de Ampudia, once again commanding the Army of the North, would probably make a stand at Marín, about twenty-four miles from Monterrey.[37] Taylor warned his army to expect harassing attacks and ordered special security for the trains. On the eleventh he ordered the march to Monterrey resumed. The pioneers with their escort of dragoons and rangers would leave the next day and be followed at one day intervals by the 1st, 2d, and Volunteer divisions. The troops carried eight days' rations and forty rounds of buck and ball ammunition.[38]

The march from Cerralvo to Monterrey again took the troops through fertile country with plentiful water and striking scenery. It was also rela-

35. AO Order 109, August 29, ZT to AG, August 19, Whiting to Jesup, September 3, 1846, in *Mex. War Corres.*, 411–12, 680–81, 501–502; Worth to Bliss, August 25, 1846, in AOLR, Box 4; ZT to Wood, August 19, 1846, in Samson (ed.), *Letters of Taylor*, 41–43; Ulysses S. Grant, *Personal Memoirs of U. S. Grant*, ed. E. B. Long (Cleveland, 1952), 49–50; Hamilton, *Taylor*, I, 202.

36. Hamilton, *Taylor*, I, 203; Smith, *War with Mexico*, I, 229.

37. ZT to AG, September 12, 1846, in *Mex. War Corres.*, 421; Brooks, *Complete History*, 169.

38. AO Order 115, September 11, 1846, in *Mex. War Corres.*, 504–505. Buck and ball ammunition contained one musket ball and two buck shot. It was the standard musket cartridge issued to American troops.

tively uneventful, since Ampudia chose not to contest it. The only clash occurred on September 14, when McCulloch and a thirty-five-man patrol drove about 200 Mexican cavalry from the village of Ramos.[39] The American columns began gathering at Marín on September 15 and departed in a single column on the morning of the eighteenth. That evening Governor J. Pinckney Henderson arrived with the two-regiment Texas Division. By now Taylor seems to have realized that Monterrey would be defended.[40]

At about nine o'clock on the morning of September 19 Taylor followed his mounted Texan scouts onto the plain before the city. A 12-pounder cannonball greeted them. It passed over the general's head and two which followed whistled through the Texans, luckily hitting no one. The Americans then retired out of range to await the arrival of the rest of the army. Taylor selected a grove of walnut and pecan trees with plentiful good water for his camp. The Americans called it Walnut Springs. There Taylor's force of 7,230 (including 3,080 regulars) camped. They were supported by four field batteries, a pair of 24-pounder howitzers, and a single 10-inch mortar.[41]

Monterrey perched on the north bank of the swift-flowing Santa Clara River at the foot of steep, high spurs of the Sierra Madre. Approached across a relatively level plain from the north by roads from Marín and Monclova, it was dominated on the west by the heights of Mount Mitre and a lower, detached hill called Independencia, and the peaks of the Sierra Madre on the south and east. The main road to Saltillo followed the river west while a lesser track dropped through a break in the heights which created a small ridge called Federación that stood across the river from Independencia.

Mexican engineers rebuilt an unfinished cathedral on the plain into a citadel which covered the Marín and Monclova roads. To Americans the position was known as the "Black Fort." A redoubt and the unfinished Bishop's Place controlled Independencia, while a second redoubt and the small Fort Soldado perched on Federación Ridge. To protect the east end of the town the engineers fashioned Forts Tenería and Diablo[42] along with a strongpoint covering the stone La Purísima Bridge. As part of the preparations the houses along the eastern outskirts of the city had loopholes

39. Reid, *McCulloch's Rangers*, 177; Rose, *McCulloch*, 94–95; Webb, *Texas Rangers*, 102; Brooks, *Complete History*, 169–79.

40. ZT to AG, AO Order 119, both September 17, 1846, in *Mex. War Corres.*, 422, 506.

41. Hamilton, *Taylor*, I, 203–204; Smith, *War with Mexico*, I, 237–38; John Porter Bloom, "'Johnny Gringo' in Northern Mexico, 1846–1847," *Arizona and the West*, IV (1962), 239.

42. El Rincon del Diablo (The Devil's Corner) in Mexican accounts.

cut in their thick rubble walls and had sandbags piled atop the stone parapets on their flat roofs. Unfortunately for the defenders, the works required more men than the 7,303 Ampudia had available.

Ampudia planned to harass the American column and attack outlying garrisons, but General Antonio Canales, to whose irregular cavalry fell the assignment, refused to do so. On September 18 Ampudia recalled all of his cavalry, abandoning his best weapon and losing the chance to inflict possibly mortal wounds on the American expedition. Ampudia's decision to defend Monterrey was in direct contravention of orders from Santa Anna to fall back on Saltillo.[43]

A careful study of the Mexican defenses by American engineers under Brevet Major Joseph K. F. Mansfield concluded that it would be possible to cut the Saltillo Road and seize the heights west of the city. Such an assault would be difficult because of the fortifications that crowned them but it appeared less dangerous than attempting a frontal attack on the city's eastern defenses. Taylor called a council of war, which agreed to employ Worth's division to seize the western approaches while the remainder of the army demonstrated against the eastern ones. Whose plan this was is unclear. Bliss, Mansfield, and Worth are the strongest contenders. It is too complex, sophisticated, and radical to have been developed by Taylor, all of whose battle plans were relatively simple and extremely conservative.

At about 2:00 P.M. on Sunday, September 20, Colonel John C. Hays and 400 mounted Texans led a long column of blue-clad foot soldiers out of the American camp. It swung wide to avoid the guns of the citadel, but soon slowed its advance to fill ditches and cut through brush fences to make a path for the artillery. The movement could not be kept from Mexican eyes, and Ampudia, who correctly surmising the objective, sent a hundred men and two guns to strengthen Independencia. By six o'clock Worth's men had marched seven miles and reached a road which skirted the base of the hill.

Worth decided to await light before pushing further. His men spent a miserable, wet night without fire or shelter. On Monday morning, dawn crept through a densely clouded sky and a thick mist. The Americans arose and resumed their march. Just before the regiment reached the Saltillo road, two hundred or so scarlet-clad lancers struck the American advance guard. A counterattack and the arrival of American artillery scattered the horsemen to ensure Worth's men possession of Ampudia's line of communications.

Worth had little time to exult, although he assured Taylor: "The Town

43. Smith, *War with Mexico,* I, 230–36, 494; John S. Jenkins, *History of the War Between the United States and Mexico* (Auburn, 1851), 161–62.

is ours." The battery atop Independencia and the hitherto undiscovered redoubt on Federación opened fire. After some indecision Worth decided to storm Federación. By mid-afternoon the Americans had cleared the ridge and threatened the flank and rear of the city. Worth now turned his attention to Independencia. Brevet Colonel Thomas Childs led the mixed force of regulars and Texans who clawed their way up the steep face of the hillside during the early hours of Tuesday. As dawn's first light shattered the black of the night, they rushed the summit and drove out the defenders in a short hand-to-hand scuffle; but they were too exhausted to continue on to clear the garrison from the Bishop's Palace. Worth then committed most of the 2d Brigade. The 7th aided by a 12-pounder howitzer laboriously dragged up the mountainside. The Americans defeated a Mexican counterattack from the palace. The Mexicans then broke and by four o'clock the palace was in American hands. Worth now controlled the heights dominating the western portion of the city.

Meanwhile, Taylor with the rest of the army had begun a poorly coordinated attack on the eastern defenses of Monterrey. During Sunday, while Worth moved into position, Taylor had contented himself with a demonstration and an occasional shell from the mortar and the 24-pounder howitzers. Taylor appears to have learned little about the defenses of the eastern side of the town although Lieutenant George G. Meade had made a good map of them. Forts Diablo and Tenería plus some lighter works protected the eastern end of the city. Tenería represented a major obstacle to any attack. Its northern face was protected by the guns of the citadel, its south by the fortified tannery building which gave the position its name, and its throat by Diablo. On the other hand, neither Tenería nor Diablo were bombproof and could have been neutralized by a few well-placed mortar rounds. Why Taylor did not do so is uncertain. Before concluding that he had once again fallen victim to his antipathy towards the artillery, it should be remembered that he had no experience with mortars or with visually unimpressive works such as the two forts.

During Monday morning, at Worth's request to divert attention from his forthcoming attack, Taylor ordered his infantry to feint an attack against the citadel at seven o'clock. In preparation Major Mansfield surveyed the defenses at the eastern end of Monterrey. Taylor directed Lieutenant Colonel John Garland, commanding the 1st Division in the place of the ill Twiggs:[44] "Colonel, lead the head of your column off to the left, keeping well out of reach of the enemy's shot, and if you think, or you find, you can take any of them little forts down there with the bay'net you

44. Twiggs was incapacitated from an overdose of laxative.

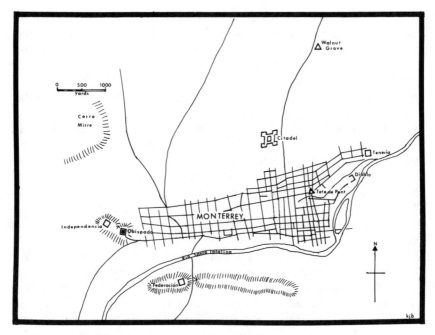

MONTERREY

better do it—but consult with Major Mansfield, you'll find him down there." Garland started off in the indicated direction with about 800 men from the 1st and 3d Infantry, the Baltimore and Washington Battalion, and Bragg's battery. When he encountered Mansfield the two devised a scheme of attack, which was difficult because the vegetation prevented any detailed survey of the ground.

Garland's men had to execute a right turn under fire to reach the part of the town Mansfield had selected for their assault. This unnerved the volunteer battalion. It broke and fled the field, losing its commander in the process. The regulars kept their composure and charged into the maze of streets west of Tenería in hopes of outflanking it. They soon lost their way and came under increasingly heavy musket and artillery fire. Accordingly, on Mansfield's recommendation, Garland disengaged.

Upon hearing the heavy firing, Taylor at about eight o'clock ordered Butler to reinforce Garland. In a blunder, three companies of the 4th Infantry which preceded the volunteers made an unsupported attack on

Tenería. They met such a withering fire that "almost in a moment" a third of the men fell. Brigadier General John A. Quitman's brigade led the volunteers. With great bravery and enthusiasm his men ran a mile-long gauntlet of fire as they marched toward a point to the left of that attacked by the regulars. When the Mexican fire appeared to waiver, Quitman's two regimental commanders, William B. Campbell of the 1st Tennessee and Jefferson Davis of the Mississippi Regiment, independently ordered their men to rush the work. The timing was perfect. A company of 1st Infantry under Captain Electus Backus had worked its way into a building about 130 yards from Tenería. Their fire when combined with an exhaustion of ammunition in the fort and the defection of its commander wrought panic among the defenders. They broke just as the first figures swarmed over the parapets.

The 1st Ohio accompanied by Butler and Taylor thrust into the city west of the newly captured position but had little success. Reinforced by other volunteers, the Buckeyes tried to storm La Purísima Bridge in an effort to get to the rear of Diablo. They failed. Nor could shelling by the American batteries dislodge the defenders. At about five o'clock Taylor ordered his troops out of the city, except for Tenería. The Monday assault brought no credit upon Taylor. He committed his troops piecemeal, thrust them unprepared and unplanned into house-to-house fighting; he placed his field batteries in narrow streets unable to maneuver or to shift fire, and he needlessly sent troops under the fire of the batteries at the citadel. Taylor lost 394 killed and wounded in the abortive assaults.

Taylor did not renew the attack on Tuesday. The Americans, cheered by the sight of their flag flying from Independencia, rested and treated their wounds. That night Ampudia, disheartened by the performance of his troops and worried by the cutting of his communications, withdrew his forces to his inner defenses around the grand plaza. While militarily sensible, the move accelerated the decline of Mexican morale.

At daybreak on Wednesday Quitman, whose brigade garrisoned Tenería, realized the Mexicans had moved from his immediate front. He began to expand the American position. When the Americans reached the inner defenses they encountered stiff resistance from Mexicans within and atop the strongly built houses and others manning barricades from which their fire swept the streets. It was difficult, dirty, and bloody work, but by mid-morning the American troops had developed techniques for clearing the houses, if not silencing the barricades. Most units burrowed from building to building while deploying sharpshooters on the roofs to command surrounding structures. Some units devised unusual means of safely crossing the streets and other open spaces. For instance, Jefferson

Davis' Mississippians built, but never tested, a mobile barricade of timbers, boxes, and saddles.

While the infantry worked their way through the city, an officer with a white flag appeared in front of one of Worth's outposts. He bore a letter from Francisco de Pablo Morales, the governor of the city, written at ten o'clock that morning. Morales requested that the noncombatants be allowed to leave. Worth forwarded the request to Taylor, who summarily rejected it. He recognized that acceptance would not only have suspended his attack but it would have had the effect of increasing the food available to the beleaguered garrison. By 3:00 P.M. the infantry had worked to within one square of the plaza. Inexplicably Taylor now ordered the men to withdraw. Ostensibly the reason was that they were tired and hungry. More probably, Taylor feared the confusion of a night counterattack and since he did not understand street fighting wanted his men out. It is also possible that he feared for their safety when the mortar began firing that night.

Throughout the fighting on Wednesday Taylor made no call on Worth for assistance. On hearing the heavy firing, Worth at 2:00 P.M., without orders, sent two columns into the city. They too worked to within one square of the plaza. Unlike Taylor, however, Worth did not pull out his men as dusk approached. During the night the mortar began firing from the city cemetery where it could not be reached by any of the Mexican guns. Despite a strong position, and an excellent opportunity for a sortie against one of the two separated American commands, Ampudia saw only his disadvantages.

At 11:00 P.M. the Mexican penned a short letter to his American counterpart proposing that the garrison be allowed to evacuate the city. Colonel Francisco R. Moreno delivered the request to Worth at about eight o'clock on Thursday morning, September 24. When he received it, Taylor refused the proposition and countered with a call for surrender on terms. He demanded an answer by noon. Before the time expired, Ampudia asked for a personal meeting with Taylor. The two met at one o'clock that afternoon. The Mexican assured the Americans that negotiators for the two nations were then meeting in Mexico City and announced that he felt no longer bound by his orders to defend Monterrey. The two commanders then agreed to form a joint commission to draw up articles of capitulation.[45]

45. The account of the Battle of Monterrey is based upon: ZT to AG, September 23, October 9, 1846, with enclosures, in *Senate Documents*, 29th Cong., 2nd Sess., No. 1, pp. 78, 83–108, *House Executive Documents*, 30th Cong., 1st Sess., No. 17, pp. 2–30; Ampudia to Ministro de Guerra y Marina, September 25, 1846, in *Niles' Weekly Register*, LXXI (1846–47), 166; Ampudia to ZT, September 23, ZT to Ampudia, September 24, to

Taylor appointed Worth, Henderson, and Davis as his negotiators. They met with General Tomás Requeña, José María Ortega, and former governor Manuel María Llano of Nueva Leon. The formal capitulation, signed that evening despite procrastination by the Mexican commander, generally followed the form suggested by Taylor. It provided for the surrender of the city and all public property except for the personal arms of the officers and men of the garrison and one field battery. Ampudia agreed to surrender the citadel on the following day and retire within a week south of a line from Rinconada Pass, Linares, and Parras. Taylor agreed to an eight-week armistice. Ampudia's men completed their departure from the city on the twenty-eighth. The conquest of Monterrey cost Taylor's force 122 men killed and 368 wounded, or 6.8 percent of its strength.[46]

The armistice and Taylor's motives for accepting it have been widely discussed. He believed he was following his instructions to achieve an

---

AG, September 25, 1846, in *Mex. War Corres.*, 345–49; Worth's reports in AOLR, Box 4; Brooks to [DeLorma Brooks], September 20, 1846, in William T. H. Brooks Papers, MHI; Webster to Thomas, September 26, 1846, in Smith-Kirby-Webster-Black-Danner Family Papers, Box 1, MHI; Ramon Alcaraz (ed.), *The Other Side*, trans. Albert C. Ramsey (New York, 1850), 70–79; Pedro de Ampudia, *Manifesto del General Ampudia á sus conciudadanos* (Mexico, 1847); Electus Backus, "Brief Sketch of the Battle of Monterey," and "Details of the Controversy . . . Battery No. 1 . . . ," *The Historical Magazine*, X (1866), 207–13, 255–57; Manuel Balboutin [*sic*], "The Siege of Monterey," *JMSIUS*, VIII (1887), 337–42; Jefferson Davis, "Autobiography" and reports, in Haskell M. Monroe, *et al.* (eds.), *The Papers of Jefferson Davis* (4 vols.; Baton Rouge, 1971–83), I, *lv–lvi*, III, 25–53, 62–76; Samuel G. French, *Two Wars: An Autobiography* (Nashville, 1901), 61–66; Luther Giddings, *Sketch of the Campaign in Northern Mexico* (New York, 1853), 170–82; Henry, *Campaign Sketches*, 189–216; Kenly, *Maryland Volunteer*, 105–31; Meade, *Life and Letters*, I, 132–37; Richard F. Pourade (ed.), *The Sign of the Eagle: A View of Mexico 1830 to 1855* (San Diego, 1970), 46–50; Manuel Balbontín, *La Invasión americana 1846 a 1848* (Mexico, 1883), 9–52; Brooks, *Complete History*, 174–89; Claiborne, *Quitman*, I, 243–55; Henry B. Dawson, *Battles of the United States by Sea and Land* (2 vols.; New York, 1858), II, 464–78; Lester R. Dillon, Jr., *American Artillery in the Mexican War, 1846–1847* (Austin, 1975), 27–30; Louis C. Duncan, "A Medical History of General Zachary Taylor's Army of Occupation in Texas and Mexico, 1845–1847," *Military Surgeon*, XXXVIII (1921), 91–97; Dyer, *Taylor*, 199–203; Hamilton, *Taylor*, I, 207–14; Jenkins, *History of the War*, 160–76; Smith, *War with Mexico*, I, 235–39, 497–501; George Winston Smith and Charles Judah (eds.), *Chronicles of the Gringos* (Albuquerque, 1968), 80–89; Isaac Ingalls Stevens, *Campaigns of the Rio Grande and of Mexico* (New York, 1851), 22–29; Hudson Strode, *Jefferson Davis, American Patriot* (New York, 1955), 164–67; Valades, *Breve historia*, 131–35; Edward S. Wallace, *General William Jenkins Worth* (Dallas, 1953), 87–103; Cadmus Marcellus Wilcox, *History of the Mexican War* (Washington, 1892), 91–110.

46. Davis, Memorandum of . . . capitulation, October 7, Articles of Capitulation, September 24, 1846, in Monroe (ed.), *Papers of Davis*, III, 22–24, 57–61; ZT to AG, September 28, 1846, in *Mex. War Corres.*, 424; Grant, *Memoirs*, 55; *Niles' Weekly Register*, LXXI (1846–47), 182.

early peace and to look with favor on sincere proposals for an end to the fighting. It was his misfortune to accept a truce just as the administration had concluded that nothing short of a further military campaign would bring serious negotiations—a decision not yet communicated to him. From a military point of view he found the arrangement very advantageous. His forces had suffered heavily in the poorly handled attacks on the eastern portion of the city; Twiggs's division was nearly out of action; Butler's had been mauled and its morale shaken; Worth's men were weary. Taylor himself understood little of city fighting but recognized that his force had to contend with a larger force of Mexicans, well dug in and adequately supplied. American food and artillery ammunition supplies were low and no easy replenishment available. To secure the key city of northern Mexico without further fighting and at the same time to achieve the armistice so desired by the administration was an opportunity no commander could reject. Taylor summed up his view in a letter to his son-in-law. "These terms," he wrote, "were liberal but . . . it was thought it would be judicious to act with magnanimity towards a prostrate foe, particularly as the president of the United States had offered to settle all differences between the two countries by negotiation, and the Mexican commander stating that said propositions he had no doubt would be favorably met by his got [sic] as their [sic] was a genl wish for peace on the part of the nation."[47]

If Taylor could exult over the seizure of Monterrey he could not over the recurring problem of the behavior of his troops. Probably the worst were the Texans, whose decade of warfare with the Mexicans made them particularly antagonistic. It was with a great feeling of relief that he released the two Texas regiments who had come with Governor Henderson. "With their departure we may look for a restoration of quiet and good order in Monterey," Taylor wrote the adjutant general, "for I regret to report that some disgraceful atrocities have been perpetrated by them." But the Texans were not the only outlaws. On October 5 a Mexican lancer riding down one of Monterrey's streets was shot without provocation by an American soldier. Taylor asked for instructions on how to try the man only to discover that no American laws applied and that he could only discharge the man and send him home.[48]

47. ZT to Wood, September 28, 1846, in Samson (ed.), *Letters of Taylor*, 61. See also ZT to AG, November 9, 1846, in *Mex. War Corres.*, 359–60. The armistice is discussed from various points of view in Eugene Irving McCormac, *James K. Polk* (1922; rpr. New York, 1965), 449–50; Dyer, *Taylor*, 206; Stevens, *Campaigns of the Rio Grande and Mexico*, 29–32; George Lockhart Rives, *The United States and Mexico, 1821–1848* (2 vols.; New York, 1913), II, 272–75; D. S. Miles to Polk, December 3, 1846, in James K. Polk Papers, LC; Hamilton, *Taylor*, I, 215–16.

48. AO Order 124, October 1, ZT to AG, October 6, 11, 1846, in *Mex. War Corres.*, 430–31, 508; Henry L. Scott, *Military Dictionary* (1862; rpr. New York, 1968), 659–60.

Captain Joseph H. Eaton, Taylor's courier, reached Washington with the preliminary report on the fall of Monterrey on Sunday, October 11. The president was thunderstruck. Taylor's armistice went far beyond his intentions and in his view violated express orders, although the historian is hard put to find them. Certainly the failure of the summer diplomatic peace offensive had made the arrangement counter-productive, as Polk recognized, but the slowness of communication with Taylor prevented him from knowing that. After consultation with the cabinet Polk had orders drafted canceling the armistice. Secretary Marcy in transmitting the order sensibly refrained from expressing censure.[49]

From the beginning to end the Monterrey campaign had been unfortunate. Its start was hampered by the rainy season and the descent of the mass of raw volunteers, plus the logistic problems, as much a result of Taylor's inability to foresee his future needs as they were shortcomings in the quartermaster's department. The use of Camargo as the advance base suggests an ill-informed decision, although none of the choices available lacked problems. The battle at Monterrey, despite flashes of brilliance by Worth and bravery by individuals, did not redound to Taylor's credit. Although one of Jefferson Davis' officers overstated the reaction when he claimed that "in Gen. Taylor nobody has any confidence, but all have confidence in Gen. Worth the next in command,"[50] it did reflect the natural initial reaction of men who had experienced Taylor's leadership in the fighting in the eastern part of the city. His inclusion of an armistice in the capitulation was, under the instructions which he had received, a reasonable action. It was his misfortune to have the rules changed without his knowledge.

49. Polk, *Diary*, II, 181–84; Marcy to ZT, October 13, 1846, in *Mex. War Corres.*, 355–57.

50. Rogers to wife, October 8, 1846, in Eleanor Damon Pace (ed.), "The Diary and Letters of William P. Rogers, 1846–1862," *SWHQ*, XXXII (1928–29), 265.

CHAPTER X

Buena Vista

THE FUROR over the Monterrey armistice brought into clearer focus Zachary Taylor's two-front war, or at least what he perceived to be one. Winfield Scott wrote him a friendly private letter in late September 1846 recounting various "plots" by the administration to build up a Democratic general as a presidential or vice-presidential candidate. Scott concludes with the wish that Taylor "will (as heretofore) defeat your enemies, both in *front* and *rear*."[1] It was a view of his position that Taylor began to adopt, not without provocation. Difficulties with the administration began to break into the open during the Monterrey campaign. Taylor's reluctance to recommend a strategy for victory and his failure to provide the Washington authorities with the intelligence they wished or to forecast his logistic requirements eroded the regard in which he was held in the White House. "Gen'l Taylor, I fear," Polk wrote in his diary after learning of his logistic derelictions from Quartermaster General Jesup, "is not the man for command of the army. He is brave but he does not seem to have resources or grasp of mind enough to conduct such a campaign." By mid-November the distrust had hardened into a conviction that Taylor would "not heartily . . . co-operate with the Government in prosecuting the war." Polk and his cabinet, however, realized that because of political implications they could not sack the general. The president believed Taylor to be the political puppet of the Louisiana Whig leader Baylie Peyton and of George W. Kendall, the publisher of the New

---

1. Scott to ZT, September 26, 1846, in Mrs. Chapman Coleman, *The Life of John J. Crittenden* (2 vols.; Philadelphia, 1871), I, 256–58.

Orleans *Picayune*.[2] Although both men became strong Taylor supporters, neither controlled the general nor manipulated his presidential boom.

On September 1–2 Secretary Marcy drafted new orders for his northern Mexican commander. They directed Taylor to seize the port city of Tampico following the end of the "sick" or yellow fever season. The Washington planners understood that a good road ran from there to the central Mexican center of San Luis Potosí, which was the probable next major American target. In asking for the information, Marcy assured Taylor, "It is not intended to weaken the force of your advancing column by any arrangements on the coast."[3]

Late in the month Marcy notified Taylor of the Mexican refusal to open negotiations. The secretary added some of the details of the Tampico expedition, which took on greater importance with the collapse of the diplomatic peace offensive. The force, to be composed of troops on the lower Rio Grande or from the States, would be commanded by Major General Robert Patterson, one of the newly appointed Democratic volunteer generals. He was a competent officer who would spend most of his service as a subordinate of Winfield Scott.[4] The Tampico expedition was one of the reasons that the administration was so disturbed by Taylor's armistice. Polk and his advisors wished to have the area in American hands before the Mexican congress met in December.[5]

On October 15 Taylor sent a long report on the difficulties of operations in northern Mexico. He voiced his opposition to Brigadier General John E. Wool's thrust from San Antonio to Chihuahua, arguing that Wool could not get his artillery through to the western city. Taylor estimated that he would need 20,000 men to extend his drive from Saltillo, south of Monterrey, to San Luis Potosí, as well as 5,000 more men to protect his communications. He concurred in the judgment that Tampico was the necessary supply base for such an attack or for one against Mexico City. Should the administration not want to commit itself to an attack on San Luis, Taylor recommended that the American forces hold the line of the Sierra Madres. The latter was his preference since the march to San Luis involved great difficulties and the unsettled nature of the Mexican government made any move a gamble. He believed that if an attack were to be made against Mexico City that it should be done by landing at Veracruz. Such an attack, he estimated, would require 25,000 men, at least 10,000

2. James K. Polk, *The Diary of James K. Polk During His Presidency, 1845 to 1849* (4 vols.; Chicago, 1910), II, 119, 139, 229, 236.

3. Marcy to ZT, September 2, 1846, in *Mex. War Corres.*, 339–40.

4. Marcy to ZT, September 22, 1846, *ibid.*, 341–42; ZT to AG, October 25, 1846, in *Senate Executive Documents*, 30th Cong., 1st Sess., No. 14, pp. 3–4.

5. Marcy to ZT, to Patterson, October 13, 1846, in *Mex. War Corres.*, 355–58.

of whom should be regulars. Before closing Taylor complained of the detaching of troops from his army without consulting him—a reference to the projected Patterson expedition to Tampico.[6]

Taylor need not have worried about the unappealing march to San Luis Potosí. The cabinet on October 20 concluded that he should not move beyond Monterrey and granted him authority to halt Wool's column. The Washington authorities concluded that Santa Anna's announcement of his support of the federalist constitution of 1826 had killed the hopes of a northern Mexican independence movement and made the occupation of Chihuahua no longer worth the effort. Moreover, if Wool were recalled it would permit Taylor to spare 2,000 men for the Veracruz operation. Realizing that the abandonment of active operations in the northern theater would disturb Taylor, Polk decided to send a special messenger to explain the change of policy. He chose Robert M. McLane, the son of the distinguished lawyer and statesman Louis McLane. Marcy's revised draft of the letter ordering the shift in strategy cleared the cabinet on the twenty-second.[7]

Meanwhile, another messenger reached Monterrey on November 2 carrying the orders to rescind the armistice. Taylor quickly notified the Mexican authorities of the cancellation, effective on the fifteenth, and ordered General Worth to seize Saltillo. Saltillo, the capital of the state of Coahuila, was as far as Taylor wished to advance. Possession of it, along with Parras on the west and Victoria on the east and possibly Tampico on the coast, would give him a strong defensive line, the core of which would be the Sierra Madres. He believed, as he wrote in a letter to Gaines which became a *cause célèbre* when released to the press, that the forces in northern Mexico should hold the line of the Sierra Madres while for the main thrust "we must go to Vera Cruz, take that place, and then march on the city of Mexico."[8] Not surprisingly, the Sierra Madre line came to be known popularly as "Old Zach's Line."

Worth's column accompanied by Taylor wound its way through the Pass of Rinconada and came out onto the plain before Saltillo. There fields bristled with wheat and oats and the lacy branches of apple and cherry trees signaled extensive orchards. The Americans entered the city on November 15 without resistance. Taylor remained only long enough to

6. ZT to AG, October 15, 1846, *ibid.*, 354.

7. Polk, *Diary*, II, 198–200, 204–205; Marcy to ZT, October 22, 1846, in *Mex. War Corres.*, 363–67.

8. ZT to AG, November 3, to Santa Anna, November 5, 1846, in *Mex. War Corres.*, 358–59, 437; ZT to Gaines, November 5, 1846, in *Niles' Weekly Register*, LXXI (1846–47), 342–43; AO Order 139, November 8, 1846, in AOGO, I (M29/1).

see Worth's men safely established and returned to Monterrey, arriving on the twenty-fourth.[9] Saltillo, in Taylor's mind, was a more satisfactory advance point for his forces than Monterrey. Not only was it an important political and commercial center but it commanded the approaches to Monterrey from the south. Any force advancing from San Luis Potosí, where Santa Anna had collected his main army, had to cross nearly 150 miles of semidesert to reach the American outpost. Moreover, the road to Parras at the center of a rich agricultural district to the west branched off at Saltillo. Its great drawback was that it extended the army's supply lines an additional fifty miles through country well suited to guerrilla operations.[10] Nevertheless, in seizing Saltillo Taylor had ignored express orders from Washington.

While Taylor accompanied Worth's men on their southward march, Robert McLane reached Monterrey with the orders to halt there. His instructions were to impress upon the general that the prohibition on further southward thrusts was based on the decision to concentrate on the Veracruz–Mexico City column and not a slap at him. Taylor was not mollified and viewed the orders as one more indication of the administration's hostility. He treated them as advisory and made no effort to pull Worth back from Saltillo.[11]

Meanwhile, Taylor held back on the Tampico expedition. Its need evaporated on November 14 when Commodore Conner's naval forces secured the town following the evacuation of its garrison.[12] The president interpreted the failure to launch the Tampico expedition as proof of Taylor's partisanship, noting in his diary: "I am now satisfied that he is a narrow minded, bigoted partisan, without resource and wholly unqualified for the command he holds." Taylor's insistence in sending only a small garrison to Tampico while pressing forward with his own plan of occupying Victoria as a counterpart to Saltillo did not enhance his standing with Polk.[13] Actually, the failure to comprehend Washington's desires partly re-

9. ZT to AG, November 15, 1846, *Mex. War Corres.*, 436; Justin H. Smith, *War with Mexico* (2 vols.; New York, 1919), I, 264–65.

10. Taylor's views were set forth in ZT to Gaines, November 5, 1846, in *Niles' Weekly Register*, LXXI (1846–47), 342–43; to AG, November 9, 1846, in *Mex. War Corres.*, 361; to E. G. W. Butler, October 1846, in Miscellaneous Collection, HM 21004, Huntington Library.

11. ZT to AG, November 12, 1846, in *Mex. War Corres.*, 374–76; Holman Hamilton, *Zachary Taylor* (2 vols.; Indianapolis, 1941, 1951), I, 227–28; Smith, *War with Mexico*, I, 350.

12. K. Jack Bauer, *Surfboats and Horse Marines* (Annapolis, 1969), 55–56.

13. Polk, *Diary*, II, 249–50; ZT to AG, November 25, December 8, 1846, in *Mex. War Corres.*, 378–79, 1379–81.

sulted from the slow speed of communications. Taylor still did not know that the Veracruz expedition had been ordered or that Patterson's force would form one of its divisions.

The long-delayed orders for Patterson's march finally appeared on November 28. As a result of shortages of transport and other complications the expedition did not set out until Christmas Eve.[14] While Taylor chafed at the restrictions placed upon him and demonstrated the pettiness of character which would surface on those occasions when he believed himself slighted or misused, the Veracruz expedition got under way. Polk overcame his dislike of Scott and chose him to lead the force. The general-in-chief left Washington November 24 carrying very broad orders and authority.[15] He realized the delicacy of his relations with Taylor and wrote him a conciliatory letter. "I am not coming, my dear General," he assured Taylor, "to supersede you. . . . But . . . I shall be obliged to take from you most of the gallant officers and men (regular & volunteers) whom you have so long and so nobly commanded." Those withdrawals were dictated by the approach of the yellow fever season, Scott wrote, and unfortunately would force Taylor to stand on the defensive until reinforcements reached him in the spring. Scott hoped, he added, to see Taylor before launching his attack but doubted he could visit Monterrey.[16]

Taylor's response, written on December 26 while he was en route to Victoria, was less than cordial. "When my presence shall be no longer required at Victoria," he huffed, "I propose unless otherwise instructed, to return to Monterey, which may be in early February. At all times and places I shall be happy to receive your orders and to hold myself and troops at your disposition."[17]

Meanwhile, General Wool's column reached Monclova, where he came under the limitations of Taylor's armistice. He asked for instructions, expressed his doubts about continuing to Chihuahua, and added: "I should be glad to join your forces." Wool's reservations about Chihuahua, as we have seen, coincided with Taylor's thoughts. He promptly directed Wool to move to Parras, from where the force could either join the main body or attack Zacatecas or Durango.[18]

14. Bliss to Patterson, November 28, 1846, in *Mex. War Corres.*, 383–84; Smith, *War with Mexico*, I, 360.

15. Polk, *Diary*, II, 241, 244–46; Marcy to Scott, November 23, 1846, in *Mex. War Corres.*, 372.

16. Scott to ZT, November 25, 1846, in *Mex. War Corres.*, 373. See also Marcy to ZT, November 25, 1846, *ibid.*, 374, which was equally conciliatory.

17. ZT to Scott, December 26, 1846, *ibid.*, 848. Taylor alleged that even then he did not know the object in sending Scott to Mexico. ZT to [Ann Wood], December 26, 1846, in William K. Bixby Collection, MoHS.

18. Wool to ZT, November 1, to Bliss, November 19, 1846, to AG, January 3, 1847, all

Santa Anna's intelligence of the American movements was good. He realized that with Taylor absent on his march to Victoria and Wool at Parras, apparently looking in the direction of Chihuahua, the time was ripe to strike Worth's exposed troops at Saltillo. His plan was to strike north about Christmas with a picked force while the rest of his forces threatened Victoria. Worth learned of the plan on December 16. He promptly appealed for help. General Butler at Monterrey immediately ordered reinforcements to Saltillo, and Wool had his entire force in motion toward there within two hours of receiving Worth's plea on December 17. Wool's men marched the 110 miles from Parras to the American camp south of Saltillo in four days. As soon as he learned of the American preparations, Santa Anna canceled his attack.[19]

Having established his advance post at Saltillo, Taylor belatedly turned his attention to the eastern end of his Sierra Madre line. The occupation of Victoria, he wrote Adjutant General Jones, would create a chain of posts from Parras to Tampico which he could direct from his headquarters at Saltillo.[20] On December 10 he issued warning orders for the march to Victoria by Twiggs's division. They left three days later. As he had done when he sent Worth to Saltillo, Taylor accompanied the column. The march proceeded uneventfully until it reached Montemorelos, where an express from Worth alerted Taylor to the rumored impending attack by Santa Anna. Taylor split his forces, sending Quitman's brigade forward to seize Victoria while he marched the remainder back to Monterrey so as to be in position to support Worth if the attack materialized. Once it was clear that Generals Butler and Wool had come to Worth's assistance, and that the danger of an attack was receding, Taylor retraced his steps. Leaving Monterrey two days before Christmas, he reached Victoria on January 4, 1847, six days after Quitman occupied it.[21] As the arrival of the yellow fever season along the Mexican coast approached, General Scott grew increasingly concerned about the slow appearance of the forces intended for his expedition. By the time he reached the Rio Grande in late December he had concluded that in order to make his schedule he would

in Letter Book XII, 199–203, 229, 269–70, John E. Wool Papers, NYSL; ZT to AG, November 27, 1846, in *Mex. War Corres.*, 377; Francis Baylies, *A Narrative of Major-General Wool's Campaign in Mexico* (Albany, N.Y., 1851), 18–19.

19. Worth to Bliss, to Wool, to Butler, all December 16, 1846, in AOLR, Box 5; Wool to Worth, December 21, 1846, in Letter Book, XII, n.p., Wool Papers; Wool to AG, January 17, 1847, in AGLR 1847, W-116 (M567/364); Smith, *War with Mexico*, I, 276, 357–58.

20. ZT to AG, December 8, 1846, in *Mex. War Corres.*, 1379–81.

21. AO Order 156, December 10, 1846, in AOGO, I (M29/1); ZT to AG, December 22, 1846, in *Mex. War Corres.*, 385–86; Quitman to Bliss, December 30, 1846, in AOLR, Box 5; Smith, *War with Mexico*, I, 359.

have to take most of Taylor's battle-hardened troops. Since Taylor's December 26 letter made amply clear Taylor's wish to avoid a face-to-face meeting, Scott as general-in-chief of the army had to issue the orders directing General Butler to send Worth's division to the Brazos Santiago and to have Patterson, Quitman, and Twiggs march to Tampico for embarkation.[22]

Worth's leading troops departed Saltillo on January 9. Twiggs's division marched out of Victoria on the fourteenth, followed on the fifteenth and sixteenth by Patterson with the brigades of Quitman and Brigadier General Gideon J. Pillow.[23] Taylor's army was now reduced to Wool's and Butler's commands, both composed almost entirely of volunteers and a handful of green units protecting the Rio Grande supply line. Together they totaled eight regiments of volunteer infantry, two of volunteer horsemen, two squadrons of regular dragoons, four batteries of field artillery, and the artillery garrison company at Monterrey.[24]

Taylor did not receive a copy of Scott's January 3 letter ordering the units to the coast until the fourteenth because the courier to whom it had been entrusted was waylaid and killed by Mexican guerrillas.[25] Taylor responded with predictable outrage. He would not have been bothered by Scott's relieving or superseding him, Taylor complained to his brother, but he was upset by the "extraordinary character" of the order which he viewed as designed to force him to surrender his command and leave Mexico. It is clear that Scott's actions had removed any doubts lingering in Taylor's mind that Scott and the administration were in league to destroy his political chances by so reducing his command that he would return home, thus appearing to desert his forces in the face of the enemy.[26]

To Scott, Taylor responded with equal vigor. He complained that the removal of troops from his command without his prior knowledge of the reasons suggested that he had lost the confidence of the government. Moreover, Taylor wrote, he was outraged and mortified at being stripped of most of the regulars and half of his veteran volunteers. It left him, he

22. Scott to ZT, to Butler, January 3, 1847, in *Mex. War Corres.*, 848–53.

23. Butler, Order 23, January 8, Worth to Scott, January 9, 1847, *ibid.*, 859–61; AO Order 3, 5, January 13–14, 1847, in AOGO, III (M29/2); Bliss to Twiggs, January 14, 1847, in AOLB 1847, p. 5.

24. ZT to AG, January 26, 1847, in *Mex. War Corres.*, 1097–99.

25. *Ibid.*; Thomas Kearny, *General Phil Kearny* (New York, 1937), 77.

26. ZT to J. P. Taylor, January 14, February 8, 1847, in ZT(LC), ser 2, r 1. See also ZT to Wood, January 26, February 9, 1847, in William H. Samson (ed.), *Letters of Zachary Taylor from the Battlefields of the Mexican War* (Rochester, 1908), 80–83, 85–87; ZT to Crittenden, January 26, 1847, in Coleman, *Crittenden*, I, 270–73; to R. F. Allison, February 12, 1847, in Yale: WA.

pointed out, with less than a thousand regulars and "such raw recruits as might be sent" to hold northern Mexico against 20,000 Mexicans.[27]

But it was for the War Department that Taylor reserved his most biting comments. He complained of "the extraordinary reserve manifested by the Department of War in not communicating to me the intentions of the Government, at least in regard to the withdrawal of so large a proportion of my command." Had he been "punctilious" he could have declined to release his troops pending an order from the president. He did not do so and regretted that the "President did not think it proper . . . to relieve me from a position where I can no longer serve the country with that assurance of confidence and support so indispensable to success." It made him fear, Taylor wrote, that he had lost the confidence of the government.[28]

Having fired a heavy barrage to protect his rear, Taylor turned his attention to restructuring his local defenses. He left Victoria on the sixteenth with an escort of Colonel Jefferson Davis' Mississippi regiment and the field batteries of Captains Braxton Bragg and Thomas W. Sherman. They reached Monterrey eight days later.[29] Taylor ignored Scott's directive to fall back on Monterrey and prepared to meet any Mexican advance before Saltillo.[30]

Santa Anna, who learned of the contents of the dispatch taken from the body of the waylaid courier, realized that he had an excellent opportunity to destroy the two American armies in detail. He could lead his Army of the North in overwhelming numbers against Taylor's depleted forces around Saltillo and destroy them with sufficient time to turn south and eliminate Scott's force either as it lay siege to Veracruz or as it attempted to move inland. It was Mexico's great opportunity to win the war on the battlefield.

Wool, commanding the American troops south of Saltillo, had already identified the Pass of Angostura, near the Hacienda de Buena Vista, as the best defensive position if he were attacked. He also picked up rumors in mid-January that large numbers of Mexicans had already arrived in the area.[31] He ordered increased patrols, especially by Colonel Archibald Yell's discipline-proof Arkansas Mounted Volunteers and Colonel Hum-

---

27. ZT to Scott, January 15, 1847, in *Mex. War Corres.*, 862–63.
28. ZT to AG, January 27, 1847, *ibid.*, 1101.
29. ZT to AG, January 26, 1847, *ibid.*, 1097–98.
30. Scott to ZT, January 26, 1847, *ibid.*, 864.
31. Lieutenant Irwin McDowell to Major J. P. Gaines and Captain Enoch Steen, January 15, 1847, in Letter Book, XI, 260, Wool Papers. The rumors were incorrect. The troops were Brigadier General J. Vicente Miñón's cavalry brigade, not a part of Santa Anna's main body.

phrey Marshall's Kentucky Mounted Volunteers. Both regiments had patrols swept up while asleep by Mexican cavalry.[32] Such incidents served to keep Wool, and Butler now at Saltillo, alive to the danger.

Unfortunately, Wool and Butler could not work together. Wool disdained the strategy Butler proposed and quite obviously was incensed at serving under a volunteer general. The clash came to a head when Butler proposed withdrawing to Monterrey. Wool objected vehemently and so antagonized Butler that he reduced the regular to command of a brigade. At this Wool appealed to Taylor "either to have me placed in my proper rightful position, or allow me to retire from a command where I can neither do justice to my country or myself."[33] Butler eased the problem by returning to Monterrey; Taylor solved it by appointing Butler to command of the rear area and then ordering him home to recuperate from his wound.[34]

Santa Anna's army, 19,525 men strong, began leaving San Luis Potosí on January 27. Its commander, escorted by a regiment of hussars, departed on February 2.[35] By January 29 Wool was convinced that a serious attack was near and called Taylor to Saltillo.[36] Not all of Wool's men viewed the situation to be as threatening as Wool did. Colonel John J. Hardin of the 1st Illinois, destined to be one of the heroes of the Buena Vista fight, for one, complained that Wool was too easily alarmed.[37] General Taylor, when he arrived on February 2, agreed. He did not believe that a large number of men could march across the arid country north of San Luis Potosí and assumed that most of the Mexican force had gone to Veracruz to confront Scott.[38] In order to improve the morale of his troops and convince the local Mexicans that the Americans would not withdraw, Taylor ordered an advance to Agua Nueva. He arrived there on February 5 with his escort, Davis' regiment, Bragg's and Sherman's batteries, and Brevet Lieutenant Colonel Charles A. May's squadron of dragoons. They were followed by Brigadier General Joseph Lane's Indiana brigade. By February 14 all of Wool's troops had arrived. Taylor had about 4,000 men

32. Wool to Yell, January 15, 25, to ZT, January 29, 1847, *ibid.*, 260–61, 273, 305.

33. Wool to ZT, January 20, 1847, in Yale: WA. See also Wool to Bliss, January 22, 1847, in Letter Book, XII, 295–305, Wool Papers.

34. Saltillo Order 199, January 23, 1847, in Smith-Kirby-Webster-Black-Danner Family Papers, Box 1, MHI; AO Order 6, 8, January 28, February 9, 1847, in AOGO, III (M29/2).

35. Manuel Balbontín, *La Invasión Americana, 1846 a 1848* (Mexico, 1883), 61–62; James Henry Carleton, *The Battle of Buena Vista* (New York, 1848), 227–31; Santa Anna, General Order, January 26, 1847, in AGLR 1847, T-259, encl. 19 (M567/362).

36. Wool to ZT, January 29, 31, 1847, in Letter Book, XI, 304, 306–307, Wool Papers.

37. Hardin to Ellen Hardin, January 31, 1847, in J. J. Hardin Correspondence, Hardin Papers, Chicago Historical Society.

38. ZT to AG, February 4, 1847, in *Mex. War Corres.*, 1109–10.

camped on the wide plain.[39] He showed no concern when the engineers reported that the site could be easily bypassed. The explanation appears to be that Taylor's attention centered on his own projected attack on San Luis Potosí rather than a possible Mexican counterstroke. Meanwhile, the Mexican army toiled northward across the miserable, parched countryside, 150 miles of it nearly a desert. Close to 3,000 men died or deserted before the force reached La Encarnación on February 17.[40]

That Santa Anna was north of the desert became evident when Ben McCulloch and a patrol of his Texas Rangers skirmished near La Encarnación with the Mexican vanguard on the sixteenth. Four days later McCulloch returned, rechecked the Mexican camp, and reported 20,000 men present.[41] Yet until McCulloch's report reached Agua Nueva, Taylor held to his belief that the Mexican threat was imaginary.[42]

Santa Anna led his army northward from La Encarnación on the twenty-first. It was a rugged march across thirty-six miles of nearly waterless country to Agua Nueva, and the Mexicans covered it without a halt for food or water. Before they rested thirty hours later most would have marched fifty miles.[43] During the morning of the twenty-first Taylor received two significant reports. One covered McCulloch's second reconnaissance of Encarnación; the other, from Brevet Lieutenant Colonel May, reported General José Vincente Miñón's troopers to be at La Hedando en route to cutting the Saltillo road behind the Americans. Agua Nueva was no longer tenable, no matter how much Taylor might wish to stand and fight there.[44] He had no choice and ordered the army to fall back to Buena Vista behind a screen of dragoons and Arkansas horsemen. Yell's men had a secondary responsibility of ensuring that the supply dump at Agua Nueva was evacuated.

39. ZT to AG, February 7, 1847, *ibid.*, 1110–11; Wool Order 214, February 8, 1847, in Order Book, XXXIV, 206, Wool Papers; Hamilton, *Taylor*, I, 231.

40. Smith, *War with Mexico*, I, 374, 381; Alfonso Trueba, *Legítima gloria* (Mexico, 1959), 33.

41. Walter Prescott Webb, *The Texas Rangers*, (Boston, 1935). 112; Victor M. Rose, *The Life and Services of General Ben McCulloch* (Austin, 1958), 113–15; Stephen B. Oates, "Los Diablos Tejanos: The Texas Rangers in the Mexican War," *Journal of the West*, IX (1970), 492. The actual number was 15,142. Smith, *War with Mexico*, I, 381. Santa Anna believed that his approach was betrayed by a deserter. Antonio López de Santa Anna, *The Eagle: The Autobiography of Santa Anna*, ed. Ann Fears Crawford (Austin, 1967), 92.

42. Wool to wife, February 20, 1847, in Wool Papers, Box 1.

43. Isaac Ingalls Stevens, *Campaigns of the Rio Grande and of Mexico* (New York, 1851), 18.

44. Samuel E. Chamberlain, *My Confession* (New York, 1956), 111, has a probably apocryphal account of a dispute between Wool and Taylor over the need to withdraw. It cannot be harmonized with other descriptions of the decision to retire to Buena Vista.

Colonel William R. McKee's 2d Kentucky Infantry and a portion of Captain John M. Washington's battery at La Encantada covered the withdrawal. When Taylor and Wool reached the Pass of Angostura[45] Taylor left his subordinate there, saying: "General, as you have reconnoitred the ground, and I have not, you will select the field of battle, and make such disposition of the troops on the arrival of the enemy as you may deem necessary."[46] Taylor led the Mississippi regiment, May's dragoons, and Sherman's and Bragg's batteries on to Saltillo to shore up its defenses against any assault by Miñón.[47] It is an interesting commentary on the perceptions of the moment that Taylor feared for the safety of his supply dump at Saltillo more than he did for that of his army taking its stand at Angostura.

The teamsters loaded supplies on their wagons amid much confusion at Agua Nueva. Their apprehensiveness increased at 11:00 P.M. when the pop of musketry began to be heard as the advance pickets clashed with the Mexican vanguard. Before long the Arkansans rushed past the old camp shouting that the Mexicans were close behind. The remaining teamsters and Yell's men quickly decamped. A few dragoons remained behind to set fire to the supplies abandoned in the rush to leave.

By daylight on February 22 all of the Americans had safely retired behind the defenses erected by Wool's men at Buena Vista. The location, whose defensive strength Wool had noted as early as December, offered great advantages to the Americans but to be exploited fully required a larger force than was available. The Agua Nueva–Saltillo road passed along a narrow ledge below a series of fingers stretching two to three miles from the cordillera on the east and broadening as they approached the mountains to form a narrow plateau. To the west of the road the land fell away to the broken gulley or arroyo of a nearly dry stream bed. The forty- to fifty-foot deep ravines between the fingers of the plateau offered substantial obstacles to any attacking force because they ran at right angles to its axis of advance. The arroyo was effectively impassable for any but small bodies of men. Wool concluded that the main effort of any attacking force had to be down the road and placed his strongest defenses there.

The American troops built a breastwork across the narrowest point in the pass to accommodate the eight guns of Washington's battery. Colonel

45. The battle called Buena Vista by the Americans and Angostura by the Mexicans was fought primarily in the vicinity of the pass rather than the Hacienda de San Juan Buena Vista about a mile and a half to the north.

46. Wool to [?], June 3, 1847, in Letter Book, XIV, 111, Wool Papers.

47. ZT to AG, March 6, 1847, in *Ann. Rpt. 1847*, 132–39; Carleton, *Buena Vista*, 12, 16–17, 19.

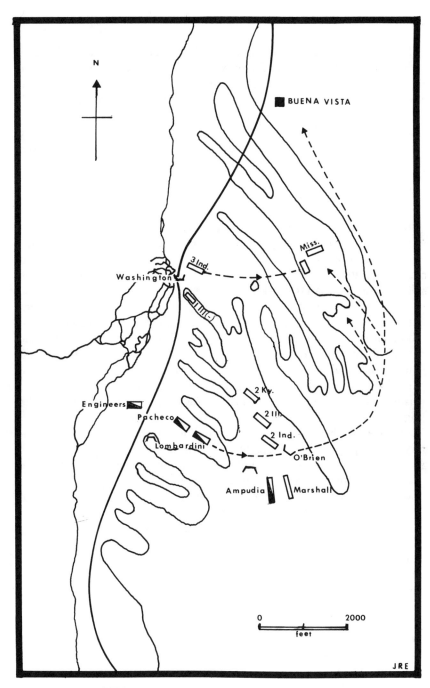

N

BUENA VISTA

Miss.

3 Ind.

Washington

2 Ky.

2 Ill.

2 Ind.

Engineers

Pacheco

Lombardini

O'Brien

Ampudia   Marshall

0   2000
feet

JRE

BUENA VISTA

McKee's 2d Kentucky took station on a hill immediately behind the guns while Colonel Hardin's 1st Illinois occupied a post atop the finger to the left and two companies manned a breastwork to the right. Wool stationed the 2d Illinois under Colonel William Bissell to the left of the Kentuckians. The reserve, General Lane's Indiana Brigade, and Captain Enoch Steen's squadron of dragoons formed a second line on the plateau. To the left of his second line, blocking the passage along the mountains, Wool placed the two regiments of mounted volunteers.

The Mexican advance guard reached Agua Nueva at 8:00 A.M., long after the last American had departed. The signs of the hasty evacuation and the apparent disorganization of Yell's horsemen as they rode off convinced Santa Anna that even if he had failed to surprise the American camp, he had at least caused them to stampede in panic. Allowing his troops time only to fill their canteens, the Mexican commander ordered an immediate pursuit. It was a tired and hungry Mexican army which plodded up the road toward Buena Vista.

Although he faced an immensely strong American position, Santa Anna had two substantial advantages. He had a numerical superiority of about three to one and a large number of cavalry who could exploit the gap between the American left and the mountains. Moreover, if he could emplace artillery on the mountainside it would command much of the American line on the plateau. The Mexican guns, however, could not easily reach Washington's battery because it stood in the shadow of the high ground.

Taylor with his escort reached Saltillo during the afternoon of February 21. Inspection convinced him that the garrison, Major William P. Warren's four-company battalion from Hardin's regiment and Captain Lucian B. Webster's pair of 24-pounder cannon, was adequate to protect the supplies being shifted from the dump at the Arizape mill outside of town. Allowing his men a short sleep, Taylor led them back to Buena Vista, arriving shortly after 9:00 A.M. on the following day.

At about 11:00, while his troops deployed, Santa Anna sent a formal surrender demand to Taylor. "You are surrounded by twenty thousand men," he wrote, "and cannot in any human probability avoid suffering a rout . . . I wish to save you from a catastrophe, and for that purpose give you this notice, in order that you may surrender at discretion." Taylor responded heatedly, but by the time his expletives had passed through Bliss's pen they simply said: "In reply to your note of this date summoning me to surrender my forces at discretion, I beg leave to say that I decline acceding to your request."

Inasmuch as the Mexican line of battle extended to the west of the road, Taylor deduced that Santa Anna had in mind turning his right flank.

He ordered McKee's regiment, Bragg's battery, and a company of Arkansas horses across the arroyo. Colonel William A. Bowles's 2d Indiana and a section of guns from Washington's battery under Lieutenant John P. J. O'Brien shifted southeastward along one of the fingers to block a Mexican advance around the base of the ridge. One infantry regiment could not close the entire gap to the mountains. When it became clear to Taylor that the Mexican light infantry under Brigadier General Pedro de Ampudia was working along the mountainside in an effort to turn the American flank, Wool, with Taylor's concurrence, sent Colonel Marshall with the bulk of his Kentucky horsemen, a battalion of riflemen under Major Willis A. Gorman of the 3d Indiana, and the rifle companies from Yell's regiment to counter the move. The horsemen dismounted at the foot of the slope and worked their way up on foot. The remainder of Yell's Arkansas horsemen moved forward to cover the base of the high ground.

At about 2:00 P.M., the Mexican howitzer fired on the American climbers but its shot fell short. It was the first shot of the battle. The leading Kentuckians reached their objective ahead of the Mexicans and opened an effective fire. Nevertheless, they could not drive off the larger contingent. At dusk the battle on the mountainside was a draw.

As the light of day faded, Taylor concluded that the situation around Buena Vista was in hand and left for Saltillo with Davis' regiment and May's dragoons. The fear of a descent by Miñón's horsemen on the supplies there still haunted Taylor. When the attack came it was easily turned back by the Saltillo garrison, as Taylor should have foreseen. His march there had only served to wear down the troops with him. The yo-yo marches to Saltillo demonstrated Taylor's uncertainty in the face of conflicting pressures and indicate that Taylor had not decided upon the critical point in his position. He did not recognize that so long as he could contain Santa Anna's main force he had little to fear from Miñón's light cavalry. It reflects his continuing overestimation of the value of cavalry which blinded him to their ineffectiveness against well-placed defenders such as Warren's men. As long as the garrison with its heavy artillery in the citadel remained behind their defenses the supplies in their care were safe. After detaching two companies of Mississippians and a 6-pounder to protect those supplies not yet evacuated from the Arizape mill, Taylor allowed his men to catch a short sleep. Shortly before dawn they again marched back to Buena Vista.[48]

Santa Anna employed the night hours to reshuffle his formation. He placed five 12-pounders on a small hill near the southern end of the

---

48. Miñón did not attack Saltillo during the twenty-third, although in withdrawing he passed close enough to be harassed by the garrison.

plateau. They were intended to support a diversionary attack against Washington's battery. The main attack would be delivered by the divisions of Major General Francisco Pacheco and Brigadier General Manuel María Lombardini supported by the five-gun battery under Brigadier General Manuel Micheltorena. The assault troops were ordered to form out of sight in the ravine at the south end of the battlefield preparatory to striking at the American center. While the two divisions deployed, 1,500 men climbed the mountain slopes to reinforce Ampudia. Their movement was detected by American observers during the predawn hours, so Wool dispatched Major Xerxes Trail with two companies of the 2d Illinois to reinforce Marshall. Wool also ordered Brigadier General Joseph Lane of the Indiana brigade to assume command of the left side of the line.

The night of February 22–23 had not been a pleasant one for either army. The weather was cold and toward morning a light rain soaked the troops, many of whom passed the night without blankets or fires. At daylight the Americans ate a cold breakfast, but the Mexicans had eaten their remaining rations for supper. The Mexican attack opened at 8:00 A.M. with the diversionary feint against Washington's guns. Colonel Santiago Blanco led an assault force composed of the 12th Infantry, Puebla Battalion, and the *Guarda Costa de Tampico* forward under the umbrella of shells from the Mexican artillery. The American gunners, ignoring the ineffectual Mexican counter-battery fire, turned back the attack.

Mexican strategy soon became clear. Wool awoke to the threat from Pacheco's and Lombardini's divisions whose advance swung like a broad axe toward the green and very skitterish 2d Indiana. The American commander sent Sherman's battery on to the plateau to support Bissell's regiment, which he ordered forward to reinforce Lane. Brevet Lieutenant Colonel Joseph K. F. Mansfield, the army's senior engineer, rode to the American right to fetch McKee's regiment and Bragg's guns. While these movements took place, Lane sent an additional four of Yell's companies onto the mountainside to reinforce Marshall.

As the two assault divisions came onto the plateau Micheltorena's battery opened fire on O'Brien's three exposed guns. The American artilleryman ordered his guns back to the protection of a small rise, from which General Lane directed him to move to the right of the 2d Indiana, intending to place Bissell's regiment to O'Brien's right. At 9:00 A.M. Lane, on Wool's order, directed the guns and the Hoosiers to move forward without waiting for the Illinoisans, apparently in hopes of gaining the top of the nearby ravine before the Mexicans could issue from it. Unfortunately, Colonel Bowles misunderstood what was intended and when O'Brien pushed forward sixty yards to fire point-blank at the oncoming Mexicans, ordered his regiment to retreat rather than advance in support.

As so often happens with raw troops, his men panicked and the unit lost all cohesion. O'Brien, left without support, had to abandon a 4-pounder whose team had been killed but salvaged his other two weapons. General Wool later claimed that had the 2d Indiana held ten minutes longer the Americans would have won an easy victory.[49]

The destruction of the 2d Indiana cleared the way for Pacheco's men to sweep away the few Americans on the west side of the plateau. Fearful of being cut off, the men in the mountains hastily withdrew. The cavalrymen reclaimed their horses and galloped, largely without organization, toward the supply dump at the hacienda of Buena Vista. Those who could not remount joined the infantry in a rapid withdrawal in the wake of the frightened men from the 2d Indiana.

Bissell's 2d Illinois and McKee's Kentucky regiment, supported by a six-gun battery drawn from Washington's, Bragg's, and Sherman's units, successfully withdrew before Lombardini's attack. It was a masterfully conducted movement, especially by Bissell, which exhausted the Mexicans. The Americans stabilized their line parallel to the road.

It was now approximately 9:00 A.M. but help was on the way. Taylor and the vanguard of the Mississippi regiment had reached the battlefield. Leaving Davis and the foot soldiers to organize a defense line near Buena Vista, Taylor hastened forward to confer with Wool. Whether Wool recommended a retreat is not clear but the preponderance of evidence suggests so. It would have been nearly disastrous to have attempted a withdrawal with an army composed almost entirely of green troops, as Taylor certainly realized. He refused even to consider retreat and established his command post on the finger of the plateau behind the Illinois regiments. He assigned Wool "the active duties of the field," which included rounding up the stragglers and exercising tactical control on the battlefield. Taylor contented himself with observing the battle but seldom interfered with his subordinate's arrangements. It is difficult to assess the psychological impact of Taylor's presence, but two considerations are important. The troops hated Wool, a tight-reigned martinet, while they loved the relaxed, unprepossessing Taylor. If nothing else, Taylor's appearance calmed the command group and through them helped stabilize the troops.[50]

49. One of the false charges made against Taylor during the 1848 presidential campaign was that he had used pages torn from bibles as wadding in the cartridges fired at Buena Vista. The story continued that when they were issued to the 2nd Indiana after it broke, Taylor shouted: "Now, you cowardly fools, let us see how you can advance the Gospel in Mexico." G. H. Crossman to H. A. S. Dearborn, October 29, 1848, in Yale: WA.

50. T. N. Parmalee, "Recollections of an Old Stager," *Harper's New Monthly Magazine*, XLVII (1873), 589, repeats a secondhand story attributed to Wool that he greeted Taylor by saying, "All is lost." It recounts Taylor's answer as: "Maybe so, General, we'll see." A some-

As the Mexican attack on the American center recoiled slightly under the hail of shrapnel from the American batteries on the plateau, Bissell's and McKee's men, joined by Hardin and four companies of the 1st Illinois, counterattacked. This so relieved the pressure on the center that Taylor ordered May's dragoons and a pair of 6-pounders to reinforce the position around the hacienda of Buena Vista. A third gun went to aid Davis, while Bragg with the fourth gun of his battery and Enoch Steen with his dragoons moved in the same direction in an effort to halt the fleeing men. Most of the fugitives were brought back into action by one agency or another. Colonel Bowles and a few of his men, for instance, attached themselves to the Mississippians. The largest group was intercepted by the 3d Indiana and formed into a provisional unit. It was during the efforts to rally the Hoosiers that Captain George Lincoln, one of Taylor's bright young assistant adjutant generals, was killed by a Mexican sharpshooter.

Colonels Marshall and Yell collected the majority of their troopers in front of the hacienda, forming them just in time to receive a stunning attack from the Mexican cavalry under Anastasio Torrejón, who had moved along the eastern edge of the plateau. The battle shattered the Arkansas regiment and cost Yell his life, but the resistance of the two regiments and a flank attack by May broke up the Mexican column before it reached the hastily organized defenses of the hacienda.

Santa Anna, smarting over the repulse of his attack on the center, pushed the assault against the American left since he had Pacheco's relatively fresh division available there. By now Davis' regiment had deployed on a finger of the plateau south of the hacienda. From there it appeared the command would soon be the target of a full division of infantry. Davis appealed for assistance. Wool sent the only unengaged American unit, Colonel James H. Lane's 3d Indiana. While awaiting reinforcement Davis moved his men down the finger, driving the Mexicans in his front before him. During the advance he was wounded in the heel but stayed in the saddle. When help took longer to arrive than he expected, Davis ordered his regiment back to a better defensive position. As the Mississippians

---

what similar, but less likely story, has Bliss reporting that the troops were whipped and Taylor replying, "I know it, but the volunteers don't know it. Let them alone, and see what they do." James Hobbs, *Wild Life in the Far West* (Hartford, 1875), 159. Taylor in his March 4, 1847, letter to E. W. G. Butler (in Allyn K. Ford Collection, r 5, MinnHS) says: "I was urged by some of the most experienced officers to fall back & take up a new position." On the other hand, Colonel Sylvester Churchill, a very knowledgeable observer, credited Wool with energy and coolness. Churchill to Willard, February 26, 1847, in Wool Papers, Box 5. See also Bragg to Lieutenant W. T. Sherman, March 1, 1847, in Grady McWhiney and Sue McWhiney (eds.), *To Mexico with Taylor and Scott, 1845–1847* (Waltham, Mass., 1969), 95.

arrived, the Hoosiers appeared on the adjoining finger to the west, about 200 yards south of Davis' position. Lane's men parried the initial Mexican thrust, fell back in good order, and after crossing the intervening ravine joined Davis. As the unplanned formation developed, the 3d Indiana stood immediately to the east of the ravine with its right flank company formed in a square to confront the Mexican lancers. To the left of the 3d regiment stood the provisional unit of refugees from the 2d Indiana and Marshall's command. On the far left was Davis' regiment. The Hoosiers and the Mississippians formed a slight V with the open end toward the Mexicans. The Mexican cavalry advanced cautiously but did not draw American fire until within fifty to eighty yards. The two American units then fired a massed volley into the head of the Mexican column which brought down hundreds of men and horses. The survivors broke. This was the turning point of the battle; at least Davis believed so and claimed that it proved his brilliance as a military leader. So intense was Davis' embrace of his self-proclaimed battlefield innovation that one Confederate wag insisted that "if ever the Confederacy perishes, it will have perished of a V."[51]

The effect of the destruction of the head of the column which struck the Mississippi and Indiana regiments and the defeat of Torrejón's assault on the hacienda of Buena Vista was to force the survivors back on the ranks following them. It turned the Mexican assault force into a milling mass of thousands of men and horses who fled back toward the mountains pursued by the surviving American horsemen, Davis' and Lane's regiments, and the artillery, which climbed the steep sides of the ravines to belch rounds of canister or grape at them. The Mexicans were trapped against the mountains.

Around noon a driving rain squall whipped across the battlefield for about fifteen minutes to drench the contestants and settle the dust. It bred a rainbow which spanned the battlefield. At about this time (the accounts are imprecise), a pair of Mexican officers who found themselves trapped behind the American lines devised a stratagem to escape. They hoisted a white flag and presented themselves as bearers of a garbled message from Santa Anna. Taylor ordered a cease-fire and sent Wool to discover what the Mexican wanted.[52] The American had to abandon his mission when the Mexican artillery continued firing. Whatever the motivation for the flag of truce, the lull in fighting allowed the trapped troops to escape.

51. Quoted in David Lavender, *Climax at Buena Vista* (Philadelphia, 1966), 203.

52. Wool's report claims that the cease-fire was caused by Taylor's using the break in fighting caused by the storm to send a surrender demand to the trapped Mexicans. If correct, and no other account mentions it, Santa Anna's message could have been an effort to understand the situation.

Santa Anna now reversed his strategy and ordered all the available men concentrated for a renewed attack on the American center. The assault was supported by three heavy 24-pounders manned by the San Patricio battalion.[53] It was a brilliant stroke. The American batteries which had saved the position during the earlier attacks had not yet returned from the left, the troops were weary from the morning's fight, and there were no reserves to commit.

Taylor seems not to have sensed that Santa Anna was preparing another assault but to have believed that the Mexicans were in retreat. He ordered the American center to keep up pressure on the enemy by seizing Micheltorena's artillery position. The men swept forward once again in a ragged line. Two guns under O'Brien were to the left of the 2d Illinois and a single gun under Lieutenant George H. Thomas was on their right. It was followed by the 1st Illinois and Kentucky infantry. Meanwhile, couriers rode off to hasten the arrival of the infantry and guns from the northern part of the field. Since the Mexicans appeared to be withdrawing, Taylor "left the plateau for a moment" to inspect the hospital and supply point on the road. But he remembered, "I was recalled thither by a very heavy musketry fire."

The two assault forces had run into each other. In the confused fighting that followed, O'Brien fought his guns until overrun; the 1st Illinois and Kentucky regiments both lost their colonels and the Kentuckians their lieutenant colonel.[54] The Mexicans closest to the road came under the fire of Washington's guns and their attack withered.

Atop the plateau the situation was desperate. Sherman's and Bragg's batteries arrived as fast as their tired horses could bring them. Taylor rode forward with Bragg and ordered the guns into battery without infantry support.[55] The fire of Bragg's and Sherman's guns, along with that of Thomas' piece, blasted gaps in the Mexican lines, but the intrepid attackers persisted. At one moment when Bragg's battery appeared in danger of being overrun, Taylor supposedly called out: "What are you using, Captain, grape or canister?"

"Canister, General."

"Single or double?"

53. How many members of the unit were actually deserters from the American army is unknown.

54. Henry Clay's son Henry, Jr.

55. There is no evidence to support the sometimes quoted statement that "Major Bliss and I will support you." It was explicitly denied by Bliss. John Pope, one of Taylor's aides, later recalled the exchange as: Bragg, "General, if I go into battery here I will lose my guns." Taylor responded, "If you do not, the battle is lost." Undated clipping from *National Tribune* in Yale: WA.

"Single."

"Well, double-shot your guns and give 'em hell."[56]

About the time that the van of the Mississippi and Indiana regiments ascended the ravine onto the battlefield the Mexican troops had absorbed all the punishment that they could take and began falling back. As dusk fell on a chilly February 23, the battered Americans still held the field. The Indiana regiments rested on almost the same site that the 2d Indiana had spent the previous night while the Illinoisans reoccupied their old works. Few men slept well. The cold penetrated to the marrow of their bones as they tried to sleep without blankets or fires. Wolves howled; wounded screamed and groaned. Vultures beat the air with their wings, while here and there horses moved restlessly amid the clinking and creaking of their harnesses.

During the night the Americans evacuated their wounded and received some reinforcements, but not enough to offset the loss of 272 killed, 387 wounded, and 6 missing, about 16 percent of the men engaged. The battle-weary Americans could look forward to as difficult a battle when fighting resumed at daylight as they had fought during the twenty-third. Indeed, Taylor's army had been saved by Santa Anna's strategy of massing his forces for a series of knockout blows. The delays inherent in such a strategy broke up the fight into a series of uncoordinated attacks which allowed Taylor and Wool to use their interior lines to rush troops, notably the field batteries, to the newly threatened portion of the field. It was this stellar performance of the field artillery at Buena Vista, more than at Palo Alto or in the fighting before Mexico City, that convinced American officers that the batteries could halt infantry attacks alone and led to their misuse in the early battles of the Civil War.[57]

Appearances on the battlefield can be as deceiving as elsewhere. Santa Anna actually faced worse problems than Taylor. His men were hungry, battle weary, and disheartened by their heavy losses and lack of success. The Mexican commander concluded that he could not ask his men to renew their attack and ordered a retreat. Mexican losses numbered 20 per-

56. The oft quoted "A little more grape, please, Captain Bragg" was undoubtedly a bowdlerized version concocted for the 1848 presidential campaign. For an extended discussion of what, if anything, Taylor said see Grady McWhiney, *Braxton Bragg and Confederate Defeat* (New York, 1969), 90–93. Taylor's statement in his report that Bragg's "first charge of canister caused the enemy to hesitate; the second and third drove him back in disorder, and saved the day" was a flight of literary fancy from the pen of his secretary William Bliss. The repulse of the Mexicans was more difficult than Taylor admitted, although later he did admit it was "much the severest I have witnessed." ZT to E. W. G. Butler, March 4, 1847, in Ford Collection, MinnHS.

57. See the discussion of the employment of artillery in Grady McWhiney and Perry D. Jamieson, *Attack and Die* (University, Ala., 1982), 36–38, 60–62, 116–17.

cent of Santa Anna's army: 594 killed, 1,039 wounded, and 1,854 missing. The Americans reported 321 of the latter had been taken prisoner.[58]

When day broke on February 24 the Americans were amazed to find that the Mexicans had retired. Taylor once again failed to pursue. He undoubtedly considered that his force was too small, too badly shaken from the previous two days, and too untrained to chase the rapidly retiring enemy, who appeared to have retained their organization and preponderance of numbers. The Americans spent the day resting and policing the battlefield. During the day Taylor dispatched Bliss to Agua Nueva to propose an exchange of prisoners. He hoped to secure the release of the men taken at Encarnación but failed, since they had already been sent back to San Luis Potosí and would undergo many months of additional captivity. The exchange of the others was accomplished the following day.[59]

During February 27 Santa Anna's army plunged southward again and

58. The account of the Battle of Buena Vista is derived from: ZT to AG, February 24, March 6, 1847, with enclosures, in *Ann. Rpt. 1847*, 97–98, 132–210; Wool to [?], June 3, 1847, in Letter Book, XIV, n.p., Wool Papers; Churchill, Tabular Report of Killed & Wounded, n.d., in ZT(LC), ser 2, r 1; Santa Anna to Ministro de Guerra y Marina, February 23, 27, 1847, in *Niles' Weekly Register*, LXXII (1847), 69, 80, 117–19; Ramon Alcaraz, (ed.), *The Other Side*, trans. Albert C. Ramsey (New York, 1850), 122–28; Balbontín, *La Invasión Americana*, 53–101; K. Jack Bauer, (ed.), "General John E. Wool's Memoranda of the Battle of Buena Vista," *SWHQ*, LXXII (1972–73), 111–23; Jonathan W. Buhoup, *Narrative of the Central Division, or Army of Chihuahua, Commanded by Brig. General Wool* (Pittsburgh, 1847), 111–27; Carleton, *Battle of Buena Vista*, 214–35; Chamberlain, *My Confession*, 114–31; Samuel Gibbs French, *Two Wars: An Autobiography* (Nashville, 1901), 73–83; William S. Henry, *Campaign Sketches of the War with Mexico* (New York, 1847), 307–77; Haskell M. Monroe, *et al.* (eds.), *The Papers of Jefferson Davis* (4 vols.; Baton Rouge, 1971–83), I, lv, iii, III, 123–63; [Benjamin F. Scribner], *Camp Life of a Volunteer* (Philadelphia, 1847), 60–65; George Winston Smith and Charles Judah, *Chronicles of the Gringos* (Albuquerque, 1968), 96–104; Isaac Smith, *Reminiscences of a Campaign in Mexico* (Indianapolis, 1848), 37–50; S. Compton Smith, *Chile Con Carne* (New York, 1857), 218–54; Isabel Wallace, *Life and Letters of General W. H. L. Wallace* (Chicago, 1909), 40–54; Baylies, *Narrative of Wool's Campaign*, 29–39; R. C. Buley, "Indiana in the Mexican War," *Indiana Magazine of History*, XV (1919), 299–305, XVI (1920), 46–57; Nathan Covington Brooks, *A Complete History of the Mexican War* (1849; rpr. Chicago, 1965), 205–23; Henry B. Dawson, *Battles of the United States by Sea and Land* (2 vols.; New York, 1858), II, 286–98; Brainerd Dyer, *Zachary Taylor* (Baton Rouge, 1946), 230–39; Hamilton, *Taylor*, I, 233–39; John S. Jenkins, *History of the War Between the United States and Mexico* (Auburn, 1851), 217–39; Lavender, *Climax at Buena Vista*, 173–213; McWhiney, *Bragg*, 78–90; Oran Perry, *Indiana in the Mexican War* (Indianapolis, 1908), 186–91, 308–11; Roswell Sabine Ripley, *War with Mexico* (2 vols.; New York, 1849), I, 158–89; Smith, *War with Mexico*, I, 384–400; Hudson Strode, *Jefferson Davis, American Patriot* (New York, 1955), 178–210; Trueba, *Legítima gloria*, 35–59; Herman J. Viola, "Zachary Taylor and the Indian Volunteers," *SWHQ*, LXXII (1968–69), 335–42; Ellen Hardin Walworth, "The Battle of Buena Vista," *Magazine of American History*, III (1879), 722–35; Cadmus Marcellus Wilcox, *History of the Mexican War* (Washington, 1892), 211–41.

59. ZT to AG, March 6, 1847, in *Ann. Rpt. 1847*, 132–41; to J. P. Taylor, in ZT(LC),

the American advance guard marched into Agua Nueva. Two days later Colonel William G. Belknap with a large force pushed onto Encarnación but found it evacuated except for about 300 wounded who had been abandoned in horrible conditions.[60] The lingering threat that the Mexican generalissimo might renew his offensive no longer confronted the American commander, but the threat to his supply lines from guerrillas continued.

Part of Santa Anna's strategy for his attack against Taylor's army called for the severing of the supply line between Monterrey and the Rio Grande by the cavalry brigade of Brigadier General José Urrea. On the twenty-fourth Urrea ambushed a mixed army-civilian supply caravan near Ramos, destroying it and killing most of the teamsters. The following day at Marín, Urrea besieged a battalion of Buckeyes en route to Monterrey, but they fought their way through to help. On March 7 Urrea struck a long wagon train near Cerralvo, which had to be rescued by a relief force from Camargo.[61]

The infestation of the road to the Rio Grande had two immediate effects. Colonel Samuel R. Curtis at Camargo, unaware of the defeat of Santa Anna but very much aware that communications to Monterrey were cut, on March 2 called upon Governor Henderson for 2,000 mounted Texans to assist in reopening the road. The precautionary request quickly blossomed, as rumors flew farther from Buena Vista, into the report of a disastrous American defeat. It caused Secretary Marcy to divert all available troops, even those intended as the follow-up units for Scott's expedition, to the Rio Grande.[62]

More immediate was Taylor's response. He arranged units to shield his communications and assigned protection of the road below Monterrey to the Kentucky horsemen. On March 15 Taylor led the dragoons, Bragg's battery, and Davis' regiment out of Monterrey on a search-and-destroy sweep against Urrea. It accomplished nothing despite their traveling as far as Marín. The experience, however, convinced Taylor he would need at least two regiments to keep the road clear. But in April the situation improved when Urrea withdrew to Victoria.[63]

ser 2, r 1. The trials of the Encarnación prisoners are detailed in [John A. Scott], *Encarnación Prisoners* (Louisville, 1848).

60. ZT to AG, March 1, 1847, in *Ann. Rpt. 1847*, 99; Baylies, *Campaign in Mexico*, 43; Chamberlain, *My Confession*, 137–39.

61. ZT to AG, March 22, 1847, in *Taylor, Scott Corres.*, 313–14; Colonel A. M. Mitchell to Bliss, February 26, Major Luther Giddings to Mitchell, March 16, 1847, in *Ann. Rpt. 1847*, 210–15.

62. Curtis to Henderson, March 2, 1847, in Henderson Family Papers, UTA; Polk, *Diary*, II, 444; Marcy to Brooke, March 22, 1847, in AGLS, XXIII, 381 (M6/27).

63. AO Order 14, March 3, 1847, AOGO, III (M29/2); Henry, *Campaign Sketches*,

Part of the problem that Taylor faced in protecting his supply columns was the willingness of the populace to support the guerrillas in their operations. This conjunction went far beyond patriotism, if indeed that term could be employed in mid–nineteenth-century Mexico, and much of Taylor's difficulty grew out of the behavior of his troops toward the locals. It was a recurring problem which had first surfaced during the early weeks on the lower Rio Grande. The causation was complex and scarcely one-sided. Many of the American troops, especially the western and southwestern volunteers, viewed Mexicans as lesser breeds; to others it was an excuse to give vent to their anti-Catholicism, while to others the activities of brigands who preyed upon unsuspecting Americans, as well as Mexicans, called for retribution.

Normal occupation problems resurfaced following Monterrey. Some of the enlisted men had secured horses and mules which they apparently rode while committing "the many outrages" on private Mexicans and their property. Taylor responded by ordering that private mounts of enlisted men be disposed of by the first of December. When he learned some men of the 1st Kentucky had wantonly shot a young Mexican boy, he proposed to send the regiment back to the Rio Grande but was disuaded by the regimental leaders, who promised to deliver the culprits. He followed this incident with a general order reminding his troops of the "great importance of respecting the rights of all Mexican citizens. The good faith of the country and of the army has been pledged to this Course and it is the intent of all to see that the reputation of neither be disgraced by scenes of plunder and marauding."[64] It was fine rhetoric but scarcely effective on much of the American army who viewed Mexicans as little better than Indians and enlistment as an opportunity to enjoy fun and games away from hometown eyes.

A much more serious incident arose just before the Battle of Buena Vista. Like many similar events, it had long-developing origins. Apparently some of the Arkansas troops had committed unspecified outrages on the women of the Agua Nueva ranch on Christmas Day. Some Mexicans retaliated on February 9 by brutally killing one of the Arkansans who strayed too far from camp. The following day a large group of men

---

329; Eleanor Damon Pace (ed.), "The Diary and Letters of William P. Rogers, 1846–1862," *SWHQ*, XXXII (1928–29), 279; ZT to AG, March 20, 24, 1847, in *Mex. War Corres.*, 1119–20, 1125. Taylor was "under the weather" for some weeks following his return to Monterrey, as the result of an infected insect bite or thorn. ZT to J. P. Taylor, April 25, 1847, in ZT(LC), ser 2, r 1.

64. AO Order 146, 149, November 27, December 2, 1846, in *Mex. War Corres.*, 512–13; ZT to Lieutenant Colonel J. Rogers *et al.*, December 1, 1846, in ZT(LC), ser 2, r 1; Dyer, *Taylor*, 211.

went looking for the murderers and in retaliation massacred a group of unarmed and probably unoffending Mexicans at Catana, about ten miles from the camp. When Colonel Yell could not, or would not, produce the culprits, Taylor ordered the two offending companies sent back to the mouth of the Rio Grande. The order was later stayed because of the service of the regiment at Buena Vista.[65]

In another aspect of his effort to pacify the countryside, Taylor on March 22 issued a Proclamation to the Inhabitants of Tamaulipas, Nuevo Leon, and Coahuila. It called upon them to maintain neutrality in the conflict and to avoid assistance to the guerrillas. To put teeth into the request, he instituted fines which would be levied on localities to pay for supplies destroyed nearby by guerrilla attacks.[66] Such a policy had the potential of eliminating much of the harassing of Americans that led to retaliation by hot-tempered volunteers, or allowed men bent on attacking the Mexican civilians to claim that they were merely retaliating.

The troubles were frequent. On March 28 a company of Texas Rangers and teamsters massacred twenty-four Mexicans near Ramos, apparently in retaliation for the February attack on the wagon train. It provoked exactly the kind of response that Taylor hoped to counter with his proclamation. General Antonio Canales, the leading guerrilla leader in northern Mexico, called upon all Mexicans to take up arms on penalty of being shot as a traitor. General Ignacio Mora y Villamil, the senior Mexican commander in the north, also protested. To the latter Taylor responded with a hot letter pointing out that he had not approved of the outrages and assailed the activities of the Mexican guerrillas, especially "the murder and subsequent mutilation of unarmed drivers" as "an atrocious barbarism unprecedented in the existing war." The atrocity problem, Taylor pointed out to the adjutant general, was almost entirely caused by the volunteers.[67]

Guerrilla attacks on the vulnerable communications links to the Rio Grande continued. Taylor himself led a counter sweep along the road by a mixed command but it failed to bring the enemy to battle. The inability of heavy, slow columns tied tightly to the road network to locate and force light, fast-moving enemy forces to fight was a problem which would torment Taylor and a great many other commanders through the years. The

65. ZT to AG, June 4, 1847, with enclosures, in AGLR 1847, T-352 (M567/362); Chamberlain, *My Confession*, 86–88; [G. N. Allen], *Mexican Treacheries and Cruelties* (Boston, 1848), n.p.; AO Order 24, 30, April 2, 11, 1847, in AOGO, III (M29/2).

66. ZT, Proclamation, March 22, 1847, in *Mex. War Corres.*, 332–33.

67. ZT to AG, May 23, Mora to ZT, May 10, ZT to Mora, May 19, 1847, in *Taylor, Scott Corres.*, 328–32; Canales, Proclamation, April 4, 1847, in *Niles' Weekly Register*, LXXII (1847), 199; ZT to Wool, May 19, 1847, in Wool Papers, Box 5.

tactics employed by Taylor proved no more successful than similar "search and destroy" tactics would in Viet Nam a century and a quarter later. To combat guerrillas successfully an occupying force must create conditions which turn the allegiance of the local populace away from the guerrillas and harass the guerrilla in his own sanctuaries. Such a program, as Winfield Scott proved along the route from Veracruz to Mexico City, will assure relative security to the countryside.[68]

While dealing with the guerrillas who infested his supply lines, Taylor had to contend with what he grew to believe was an even more pernicious enemy, the administration. On March 3 he penned a strong reply to Secretary Marcy's January 27 letter taking him to task for the November letter to General Gaines. Taylor pointed out in his defense that he had not intended the letter for publication and objected to the harshness of Marcy's rebuke. "I have sought," he wrote, "faithfully to serve the country by carrying out the rules and instructions of the Executive; but it can not be concealed that, since the capture of Monterey, the confidence of the Department, and, I too much fear, of the President, has been gradually withdrawing, and my consideration and usefulness correspondingly diminished."[69]

The general came to believe that the cause of his disfavor was his potential candidacy rather than the administration's unhappiness with the Monterrey armistice or the Gaines letter. In Taylor's view, the antagonism manifested itself in the administration's refusal to give him sufficient troops to permit an offensive against San Luis Potosí.[70] The reasons for the delay in reinforcing Taylor were more complex than he was willing to admit. The time of enlistment of the twelve-month volunteer regiments was about to expire, but recruiting for the new regiments was slower than expected. Moreover, the priority for reinforcements was Scott's Mexico City column.

In late April, upon the decision on the apportionment of the ten new regiments of regulars recruited for the duration of the war, four regiments, an infantry brigade under Brigadier General Enos D. Hopping, and the 3d Dragoons were assigned to Taylor's command.[71] Taylor hoped that he might launch his offensive before the departure of the twelve-months volunteers in May but concluded that the possibility was slight.

68. Frederick A. Wislizenus, *Memoir of a Tour to Northern Mexico* (1848; rpr. Glorieta, N. Mex., 1969), 80; ZT to AG, April 20, 21, 1847, in AGLR 1847, T-239 (M567/362), *Niles' Weekly Register,* LXXII (1847), 302.

69. ZT to Marcy, March 3, 1847, in *Mex. War Corres.,* 809–10.

70. ZT to J. P. Taylor, April 22, 1847, in ZT(LC), ser 2, r 1.

71. Jones, Circular, April 29, Marcy to ZT, May 4, 1847, in AGLS, XXIII, 608, 633 (M565/15).

"The Honl. Secretary of War seems determined not to correspond with me," he complained, "but to withhold all information which might be communicated through the adjt. genls. office."[72]

The administration recognized the political danger in leaving Taylor apparently neglected in northern Mexico. Secretary Marcy suggested appointing him second in command to Scott but leaving him in the north. The president overruled that suggestion because he did not want Taylor to supersede Major General Robert Patterson, a good Democrat if not a native-born American, should anything happen to Scott. As a result the orders to Taylor merely granted him discretionary authority to advance on San Luis Potosí should conditions appear favorable.[73] By May all possibility of an offensive vanished with the discharge of the twelve-months men, very few of whom would reenlist. Taylor concluded that he lacked the strength to attack and that San Luis Potosí was valueless except as a base for future operations toward Queretaro. Nevertheless, since he wished to have his men ready for an advance if called upon, Taylor established a training camp at Mier under Colonel William G. Belknap to prepare the new regiments for field service.[74]

As the frustration of enforced idleness boiled, so did Taylor's desire to escape from Mexico. "I am heartily tired of this war," he wrote his daughter. "I will not remain longer in this country than duty and honor compel me. I hope to leave it in the fall, peace or no peace." In mid-July he wrote his second in command that he expected the northern army to be inactive during the summer, since he had received only one company from the five new regiments that had been promised. An early September start of the long-delayed attack on San Luis Potosí was the best that Taylor could foresee. By then he expected that Scott would have concluded an armistice. Taylor subsequently told Wool that he was convinced that Santa Anna would make peace so long as Scott did not have to take Mexico City but feared a prolonged war if he did. The United States, Taylor believed, could not accept a territorial settlement that failed to conclude the Rio Grande boundary, New Mexico, and upper California.[75] His thinking had come a great distance from his opposition to the annexation of Texas.

72. ZT to Wool, April 28, 1847, in ZT(LC), ser 2, r 1.

73. Polk, *Diary*, III, 14–15; Marcy to ZT, May 6, 1847, in *Taylor, Scott Corres.*, 311–12.

74. ZT to AG, May 9, 28, June 16, 1847, in *Mex. War Corres.*, 1134–36, 1177–78, *Taylor, Scott Corres.*, 336–38; AO Order 48, 68, May 9, June 16, 1847, in AOGO, III (M29/1); Jones to Brooke *et al.*, May 21, 1847, in AGLS, XXIV, 740–55 (M565/150).

75. ZT to [Ann Wood], June 23, 1847, in Bixby Collection, MoHS; ZT to Wool, July 14, September 18, 1847, in Yale: WA. See also Wool to ZT, July 12, 1847, in Miscellaneous Collection, HM 27496, Huntington Library.

The administration quickly embraced Taylor's suggestion that the northern forces remain on the defensive and on July 15 ordered him to send all troops who could be spared to reinforce Scott. The immediate effect was to divert twenty-four newly formed companies to Veracruz. Taylor added an additional 2,957 men from his own force.[76]

The inactivity frustrated his command, especially the volunteers, who had joined to fight Mexicans not to perform camp and occupation duties. The problem erupted in a mutiny in the North Carolina regiment at Saltillo in mid-August. Wool intervened harshly and discharged two lieutenants and a pair of privates for their part. Although their cashiering was sustained by Taylor, the officers were later restored by Polk.[77] Given the lack of contact with Mexican forces, the physical limitations of the area, and the decision to keep the northern forces on the defensive, the irritation of the volunteers at their occupation role is understandable. What is less comprehensible is the failure of Taylor and Wool, both experienced commanders, to devise activities to keep the troops employed.

The inactivity did not mean that the guerrilla attacks had ceased, although they decreased as a result of the added protection given the supply columns. On September 7 a group of Canales' men raided Mier and seized $25,000 to $26,000 in goods. They were pursued by a mixed force of 3d Dragoons and civilians who reclaimed the stolen property and killed fifteen Mexicans.[78] Another dragoon patrol engaged a guerrilla force about five times its size near Màrín in early November. The Americans not only fought their way out of the trap but killed Mucho Martinos, one of the best of the guerrilla commanders. The dragoon success was quickly followed by a raid on the guerrilla base near Ramos by Texas horsemen. Taylor reported that the operation freed communications between Monterrey and Camargo of further threats.[79] As part of his effort to retard hostilities between the occupiers and the occupied, Taylor in late September authorized the trial of Mexicans accused of murder and other major offenses against Americans before military commissions. Even more effective were the administration's October instructions to seize and

76. Marcy to ZT, July 15, 1847, in *Taylor, Scott Corres.*, 383–84; Jones to ZT, July 16, AGLS, XXIV, 1048 (M565/15); to Scott, September 25, 1847, in Office of the Adjutant General (NA, RG 94), Letters to Generals in the Field and to State Governors, I.

77. Proceedings of Court of Inquiry, in *Senate Executive Documents*, 30th Cong., 1st Sess., No. 62; Wool to ZT, August 18, 1847, in Letter Book, XIV, 203–204, Wool Papers; Marcy to ZT, October 25, 1847, in *Taylor, Scott Corres.*, 398–400.

78. Captain John Butler to E. G. M. Butler, [September] 9, 1847, in AOLR, Box 5; Belknap to Bliss, September 9, 1847, in *Taylor, Scott Corres.*, 388–80; *Niles' Weekly Register*, LXXIII (1847), 88.

79. ZT to AG, November 7, 1847, in *Taylor, Scott Corres.*, 401–402; Albert G. Brackett, *History of the United States Cavalry* (1865; rpr. New York, 1968), 121.

hold as prisoners of war all who assisted the guerrillas and to intensify the levying of contributions on the local populace for any incidents in their locale.[80]

Taylor had little opportunity to carry out the new occupation policies. On October 4 he requested a six months' leave of absence. It was approved on November 6, but before the authorization reached Mexico, Taylor completed his departure preparations. On the eighth Taylor, Wool, and their staffs left Monterrey for Mier. They embarked on the *Major Brown* for the short voyage to Camargo, where they arrived on the thirteenth. After a review of the garrison they parted two days later. Wool returned to Walnut Springs, outside of Monterrey, while Taylor boarded the *Colonel Cross* for the trip to Matamoros. The two-day trip must have been less than enjoyable for Taylor, who complained about the constant shaking of the boat. At Matamoros on the twenty-fifth he formally transferred command to Wool and proceeded to the Brazos Santiago, where on November 26 he boarded the steamer *Monmouth* for New Orleans.[81]

The small side-wheeler reached the Southwest Pass of the Mississippi on November 30 and Taylor transferred to the larger *Mary Kingsland* for a leisurely trip to the Crescent City. On board he was greeted by a welcoming committee who entertained the hero at a dinner, and en route upstream the vessel stopped for an hour at Maunsel White's plantation. On December 2 the steamer stopped again, this time at the barracks below New Orleans where Mrs. Taylor and other members of the family came on board. The following day the *Mary Kingsland* delivered her passengers to the New Orleans levee. That evening the city honored Old Rough and Ready with a large banquet. Part of the festivities included the presentation of the sword which had been authorized by the Louisiana legislature.[82]

The Taylors departed New Orleans on December 5 for Cypress Grove.[83] Taylor's career as an active field soldier was over. He nominally continued his command in Mexico until taking over the Western Division in July 1848. He held that assignment until his formal resignation prior to as-

80. AO Order 109, September 29, 1847, in AOGO, II (M29/2); Marcy to ZT, October 11, 1847, in *Taylor, Scott Corres.*, 377–78.

81. ZT to AG, October 4, November 2, 23, Jones to ZT, November 6, 1847, in *Taylor, Scott Corres.*, 390–91, 397, 400–401, 403–404; ZT to Wood, October 27, 1847, in Samson, *Letters of Taylor*, 147; Hamilton, *Taylor*, I, 248–49; ZT to Wood, November 17, 1847, in Andre DeCoppet Collection, Princeton University Library; AO Order 132, November 25, 1847, in AOGO, III (M29/2).

82. *Niles' Weekly Register*, LXXIII (1847–48), 240, 257; Dyer, *Taylor*, 253–54; Hamilton, *Taylor*, I, 249.

83. *Niles' Weekly Register*, LXXIII (1847–48), 257.

suming the presidency. Taylor returned home a great hero. In the public mind he was the architect and leader of the victories at Palo Alto, Resaca de la Palma, Monterrey, and Buena Vista. It was an unearned reputation. Taylor was a successful battlefield commander because he faced opponents whose tactical abilities and nerves were less than his and because his army in the early battles contained well-trained, self-confident subordinates. Taylor demonstrated little tactical virtuosity or the instinct great commanders have for a final crushing blow. More than anything else, Taylor's performance, especially when his activities were questioned by his superiors, illuminated his petulance. He easily rationalized objections as political attacks and suggestions as traps.

CHAPTER XI

The Soldier Becomes a Politician

THERE IS a long tradition in the United States, as in most other nations, that successful military leaders become serious contenders for political office. Despite the antimilitary tradition which many Americans loudly proclaimed, most politicians throughout the nation's history have utilized military titles whenever possible. Since three major military figures from previous wars had moved into the presidency, many if not most politicians assumed that the leading hero or heroes of the clash with Mexico would follow in their footsteps. Thus, the administration frantically searched for a Democrat to assign to a major command in order to offset the potential candidacies of Winfield Scott, a known Whig, and Zachary Taylor, a suspected one.[1] The soldier-politician tradition ensured that many political leaders hastened to curry the favor of Taylor immediately after his successes along the Rio Grande.

The earliest person to comment on Taylor's political attractiveness was Secretary of War William L. Marcy. He noted in his diary upon receiving the first reports of the victories in Texas that they made Taylor a leading candidate of the nomination in 1848. Going a step further, Thurlow Weed, newspaper editor and powerful behind-the-scenes Whig leader, seized upon a chance meeting with Taylor's brother, Lieutenant Colonel

---

1. The senior Democrat in the regular army was Brigadier General John E. Wool, but he attracted no political attention although his party affiliation was well known to Secretary Marcy.

Joseph P. Taylor, on a Hudson River steamer to determine the general's political leanings. On learning that the two Taylors were pro-Clay and anti-Jackson, Weed pointed out the potential for a candidacy. Sensing an opportunity to play kingmaker, Weed seized the moment to counsel the general. He suggested the younger Taylor advise his brother to avoid statements on political issues and ignore political letters. Following his return to Albany, Weed began his campaign. He wrote in the Albany *Argus* that one or two more victories would ensure the White House should Taylor so desire.[2]

A political phenomenon of the time was the organization of meetings of local politicians to promote potential candidates for national office. At worst they were efforts to establish primacy on a campaign bandwagon and at best a genuine response to local enthusiasms. Since such movements were frequently organized outside normal party structures, the meetings were commonly called popular or mass meetings. On June 11 a meeting on the Revolutionary War battlefield of Trenton made what is apparently the first of many nominations of Taylor as the "people's candidate" for the presidency. Taylor's response to the efforts to draw him into the political ring was astonishment. A candidacy, as he wrote his brother after hearing of Weed's interest, "seems to me too visionary to require a serious answer. Such an idea never entered my head, nor is it likely to enter the head of any sane person."[3] Taylor's refusal to view the presidential boom seriously, his insistence that common courtesy required him to answer all letters, and a proclivity for writing politically unwise letters puzzled practical politicians like Weed and caused them to step back from an immediate, public embrace of his candidacy.

Much of the discussion of Taylor's political attractiveness revolved around the uncertainty of his party affiliation, not a surprising concern about a man who had never voted and had eschewed public political statements. J. Watson Webb, later to be one of Taylor's strongest supporters, dissuaded a New York City mass meeting from a premature nomination by arguing that the general's political principles were as yet too little known.[4]

2. T. M. Marshall, "Diary and Memoranda of William L. Marcy, 1849–1851," *AHR*, XXIV (1919), 455; Harriet A. Weed (ed.), *The Autobiography of Thurlow Weed* (Boston, 1884), 571–72.

3. Joseph G. Rayback, *Free Soil* (Lexington, 1970), 34; Weed, *Autobiography*, 573. See also ZT to Wood, June 21, 30, July 25, 1846, in William H. Samson (ed.), *Letters of Zachary Taylor from the Battlefields of the Mexican War* (Rochester, 1908), 13, 21–22, 29–32.

4. Rayback, *Free Soil*, 35; Glendon G. Van Deusen, *The Jacksonian Era* (New York, 1959), 250–51.

The most important advice Taylor received during the early summer of 1846 came from his old friend Senator John J. Crittenden of Kentucky. He congratulated Taylor on his battlefield successes and took note of the support building up for a Taylor presidential candidacy. He counseled against returning home until "peace shall crown all your dangers, & place your fame beyond all accident of war."[5] Crittenden's political advice was undoubtedly that of a friend but it did betray more than a hint of interest in a Taylor candidacy. As such, it shattered the senator's longstanding alliance with Henry Clay and reflected a reluctant conclusion that Clay had acquired too many political enemies to be elected. To Crittenden, Taylor represented the best hope of a Whig victory in the 1848 presidential election. It did not mean that Crittenden, nor the other Whig leaders who followed him into the general's camp, necessarily concurred in many of the general's policies, although Crittenden and Taylor seldom diverged in their political principles.

In his July responses to well-wishers, Taylor continued to deny interest in the presidency. "I am not and shall never be an aspirant for that honor," he wrote one friend. "My opinion has always been against the elevating of a military chief to that position." To another he insisted that "We must have a statesman," and he confided to his son-in-law that his ambition was to hold "some unimportant command in a pleasant position for a few years after peace is restored" and his hope that the Whig nomination would go to Scott. Although Taylor into the early fall continued to express his lack of political aspirations and to assert that his sole concern was to bring the war to a rapid close, by mid-September a note of antagonism toward the administration over its perceived hostility emerged. It appeared initially in his response to Crittenden's July note, a letter which has been seen as the start of the Crittenden-Taylor political alliance which led to the White House.[6]

Taylor considered the order to stop at Monterrey to be politically motivated. He was realistic enough to recognize that growing support for his presidential candidacy, even if he did not embrace it himself, antagonized the administration. Nor was the support universal despite the appearance

5. Crittenden to ZT, July 5, 1846, in John Jordan Crittenden Papers, UKL. The letter, written in Scott's office, was carried by Crittenden's son Thomas who joined Taylor's staff as a civilian volunteer.

6. ZT to J. T. Van Alen, July 17, 1846, quoted in Holman Hamilton, *Zachary Taylor* (2 vols.; Indianapolis, 1941, 51), II, 39; to N. Young, July 18, 1846, in ZT(LC), ser 2, r 1; to Wood, July 31, August 4, 1846, in Yale: WA, Samson (ed.), *Letters of Taylor*, 34; to Crittenden, September 15, 1846, in Mrs. Chapman Coleman (ed.), *The Life of John J. Crittenden* (2 vols.; Philadelphia, 1871), I, 251−56; George Rawlings Poage, *Henry Clay and the Whig Party* (Gloucester, 1965), 154.

of spontaneous local Taylor or Rough and Ready clubs. Few Democratic politicians evinced more than a passing interest in the war hero, even before his Whig credentials were established, nor did he develop a following among his fellow professional officers. The abolitionist press, as might be expected, shrilly assailed the candidacy as that of an ignorant military man and large-scale slave owner who personified an unrighteous cause. The controlling factor, however, was Taylor's own belief expressed in an October letter to Nathaniel Young that the time for any open drive for the nomination was premature.[7] Supporting the efforts of his partisans to keep his image before the nation were the presentation gifts which flowed into Taylor's tent at Monterrey, each duly noted in the press. During November, for instance, the "Citizens of Jefferson County, Kentucky" presented a silver pitcher and the Louisiana state legislature authorized the acquisition of a presentation sword.[8]

Despite the news of Monterrey and the reports of seizure of New Mexico and California which circulated prior to the fall elections in 1846, the results were disheartening to the administration. The public, which had generally accepted even if it did not welcome the war, was not emotionally prepared for as long a conflict as appeared to be developing or for one which required as great a commitment of men and resources. The Whig successes in the mid-term elections led Daniel Webster to assure Thurlow Weed that "with prudence, moderation, & discretion, the Whigs can hardly lose their present ascendancy."[9] Taylor, had he read those words, would have heartily agreed.

In December a group of young Whig congressmen led by Alexander H. Stephens of Georgia formed a Taylor club. The charter members of the Young Indians, as they were called, included Stephens, Robert Toombs of Georgia, W. Ballard Preston, Thomas S. Flournoy, and John S. Pendleton of Virginia, Henry A. Hilliard of Alabama, and a pair of northerners, Truman Smith of Connecticut and Abraham Lincoln of Illinois. The number grew rapidly. By March Lincoln could claim that fourteen other northern Whig congressmen supported Taylor's candidacy. Most had been Clay supporters who had concluded that the Great Compromiser was no longer electable. One of them later wrote that the Whigs were a minority party who would lose the 1848 elections if they chose Daniel Webster, John McLean, or Winfield Scott, the leading alternatives to Tay-

7. ZT to Wood, November 10, 1846, in Samson (ed.), *Letters of Taylor*, 67; to Young, November 27, 1846, in ZT(LC), ser 2, r 1; Hamilton, *Taylor*, I, 217–18; Frederick Merk, *Manifest Destiny and Mission in American History* (New York, 1963), 100.

8. Washington, D.C., *National Intelligencer*, November 10, 14, 1846.

9. Webster to Weed, November 16, 1846, in Weed Papers, Rush Rhees Library, University of Rochester.

lor or Clay. With Taylor at the head of their ticket he was confident that the party would win.[10] The Young Indians' timing was excellent. It coincided with Taylor's decision to accept a nomination if offered.[11] He still considered himself a nonpartisan candidate and was attracted to the idea of his nomination by a series of "no party" meetings.

The rising call for Taylor's nomination, especially among Whigs, sounded like a dissonance in the ears of the radical, abolitionist Whigs. The editor of the Concord, New Hampshire, *Independent Democrat* developed an unusual picture of the general as "one of the greatest slaveholders in the United States" who, the paper charged "raises babies for the market and makes merchandize of his fellow men! He has a hundred mothers, with or without their babies, for sale in the shambles. He furnishes creole virgins for the 'hells' of New-Orleans, and riots on the ruins of souls for whom the Man of Sorrows died."[12]

Joshua Giddings made a more moderate, but more accurate, thrust toward the Taylor supporters when he observed that they "oppose the war, but lend their whole energy to prosecute our Conquest in Mexico. . . . They advocate the encouragement of free labor, but pledge themselves to vote a President whose whole intent is vested in slave power." One of Giddings' correspondents lent color, if not light, to the content when he wrote: "To kill women and children and hurry men unprepared to eternity because they refuse to give up their land now free in order that, we may cover it with slaves, are certainly high qualifications for the highest office in the gift of a free nation of professing Christians."[13] Equally illustrative of the hostility to a possible Taylor candidacy was Senator Thomas Corwin's observation that the general's qualifications consisted of "sleeping forty years in the woods and cultivating moss on the calves of his legs."[14]

In late January the New York *Express* published Taylor's "Line of the Sierras" letter to General Gaines. It was not a letter intended for publication and just why Gaines released it is unclear. Polk's reaction was ex-

10. William J. Cooper, Jr., *The South and the Politics of Slavery, 1828–1856* (Baton Rouge, 1978), 245; Myrta Lockett Avary (ed.), *Recollections of Alexander H. Stephens* (New York, 1910), 21–22; Rayback, *Free Soil*, 38; Smith to [?], May 17, 1848, in Miscellaneous Manuscripts, Yale: M&A; Lincoln to V. F. Linder, March 22, 1846, in Roy P. Basler (ed.), *The Collected Works of Abraham Lincoln* (8 vols.; New Brunswick, N.J., 1953), I, 45.

11. ZT to Wood, December 10, 1846, in Samson (ed.), *Letters of Taylor*, 76.

12. Concord, N.H., *Independent Democrat*, December 17, 1846, quoted in Merk, *Manifest Destiny and Mission*, 100.

13. Giddings to Charles Francis Adams, December 23, 1846, and Columbus Delano to Giddings, both quoted in John H. Schroeder, *Mr. Polk's War, American Opposition and Dissent, 1846–1848* (Madison, 1973), 135.

14. Van Deusen, *Jacksonian Era*, 252.

plosive. He complained that the letter assailed the administration, uttered uninformed complaints, and published plans of the campaign. He upbraided Gaines for its leak but was convinced it was a political move planned by Taylor, which it was not. On the twenty-sixth the cabinet agreed that Secretary Marcy should condemn Taylor's conduct, which he did in a strong letter the following day.[15]

While the administration struggled with Taylor's perceived insubordination, Congress considered recognition for the Army of Occupation and its commander over the Monterrey victory. Representative William M. Cocke, a freshman Democrat from Tennessee, introduced a resolution of thanks on January 29. Following a short debate over wording the measure passed the following day by a vote of 103 to 67. The Senate began consideration on February 3 but soon wrangled over the House's inclusion of a statement disavowing approbation of the armistice. That evoked a strong defense of the general by Crittenden. Finally the Senate by a 26 to 23 vote accepted Webster's proposal for a simple resolution of thanks and the authorization of a gold medal for Taylor. After some debate the House accepted the revised resolution.[16]

Meanwhile, Crittenden formally took himself out of contention for the presidential nomination and added his respected voice to those counseling against the Whigs' bringing forward any candidate so far ahead of the election. Delay, which allowed the popular support for a Taylor campaign to build, suited the proponents of the general's candidacy. The Kentucky senator assured Taylor in February that the public indeed recognized the position into which he had been cast by the administration's shift of emphasis to Scott's expedition. Crittenden noted the controversy between the two soldiers and stressed that it should be settled before the political damage became irretrievable. Not all Whigs agreed with Crittenden's conservative strategy. In New York City, John Jay Hyde, the editor of a pro-Taylor political paper, recruited James Watson Webb to the cause and proposed a campaign to create local Taylor clubs.[17]

It was the victory at Buena Vista in February 1847 which for many Whigs, and not a few Democrats, turned Taylor from one of several po-

15. James K. Polk, *Diary of James K. Polk During His Presidency, 1845 to 1849* (4 vols.; Chicago, 1910), II, 353–55, 357; Marcy to ZT, January 27, 1847, in *Mex. War Corres.*, 391–92.

16. *Congressional Globe*, 29th Cong., 2nd Sess., 293, 295–96, 315–16, 433, 558.

17. Crittenden to G. B. Kinkead, January 10, to ZT, February 1847, in Coleman (ed.), *Crittenden*, I, 268–69, 278–80; Hyde to Webb, January 10, 1847, in James Watson Webb Papers, Box 2, Yale:M&A; Calhoun to T. G. Clemson, May 6, 1847, in J. Franklin Jameson (ed.), "Correspondence of John C. Calhoun," *Annual Report of the American Historical Association for the Year 1899* (Washington, 1900), 728–29.

tential candidates into the leading one. It verified his status as a genuine hero able to extract from a green and outnumbered army the battlefield performance to be expected of free American citizens. Calhoun predicted that he would be "the popular [nonparty] candidate." Yet, Taylor's growing acceptance by the moderate leaders of the northern wing of the Whigs engendered a greater opposition from the radical, abolitionist wing. The radicals encouraged other candidates to enter the race and to pledge support for the Wilmot Proviso. Acceptance of the Proviso with its prohibition on slavery in the territory to be acquired from Mexico became the litmus test for the antislavery Conscience Whigs.[18]

Wilmot's resolution sparked countermoves by the extreme southern partisans. In February 1847 Senator John C. Calhoun introduced a series of resolutions which embodied the extreme southern position on slavery extension: Territories were the "joint and common property" of all the states. Moreover, he held, Congress lacked authority to deprive a state of its "full and equal rights" in the territories or to limit the freedom of the citizens of a territory in the formation of a constitution. He followed the resolutions with a suggestion for southern unity to protect the section's interests. Although the initial response among southern Democrats was positive, the idea rapidly lost momentum in the face of a current of opinion which held that it was merely a tactical move in a quest for the presidential nomination.[19]

During the fall of 1847 Vice-President George M. Dallas advanced a proposal which took the northern Democrats off the tynes of the Wilmot Proviso dilemma.[20] He suggested that the question of slavery be left to the inhabitants, an idea later popularized by Senator Lewis Cass as Popular Sovereignty. It had the twin advantages of being a sensible and moderate solution and of allowing its supporters to avoid taking a stand on the Wilmot Proviso. Taylor would subsequently take it one step further by suggesting that the former Mexican lands be admitted as states without passing through the territorial apprenticeship.

Even after Buena Vista Taylor continued to stand aside from the political campaign, complaining to E. W. G. Butler in a letter which received wide publicity that his name was being brought forward without his consent.[21] The general assured Crittenden later in the month, "I have no aspirations for civil office of any kind" and that he merely wished to bring an

18. Frederick J. Blue, *The Free Soilers* (Urbana, 1973), 40–42.
19. Ernest McPherson Lander, *Reluctant Imperialists: Calhoun, the South Carolinians, and the Mexican War* (Baton Rouge, 1980), 71–79; Rayback, *Free Soil*, 28, 30–33.
20. Rayback, *Free Soil*, 115.
21. ZT to Butler, March 4, 1847, in *Niles' Weekly Register*, LXXII (1847), 135.

end to the war.[22] Even so, the support for his presidency grew. In March William H. Seward boasted that Taylor "writes better than he fights," with the result that he was rapidly becoming not just a candidate but a winner.[23]

April brought further strides in the Taylor boom. The anti-Clay faction of Kentucky Whigs began to coalesce around his banner while on April 1 James Watson Webb's New York *Courier and Enquirer* became the first northern Whig paper to come out for his candidacy. The New Orleans *Bulletin* followed on April 7. Even such a stalwart Clay supporter as the Louisville *Daily Journal* readily predicted that Taylor would be elected. By the end of the month *Niles' Weekly Register* could report a raft of public meetings which nominated Old Rough and Ready. They continued throughout the summer and fall. The increase in activity was a direct outgrowth of the publicity generated by the Battle of Buena Vista.[24]

Nor was interest in Taylor as a candidate limited to Whigs. Joseph E. Davis commented to his brother that if the general would repudiate the extreme Whig positions "many of the Democrats would rejoice at an opportunity to vote for him."[25] Indeed, in March the Pennsylvania Democratic state convention deadlocked on its presidential and vice-presidential nominations when Senator Simon Cameron pronounced Taylor was a Democrat and endorsed him. Cameron subsequently established his brother as editor of the pro-Taylor Lancaster *Sentinel* and led a People's Convention in Harrisburg in late June which endorsed the general's candidacy.[26]

The Baltimore *Bulletin* advanced similar sentiments when it suggested that Taylor was a political independent, "a true follower of Gen. Washington." Moreover, the paper reported, rumors had reached the city that Calhoun would support the general. There was nothing to the rumors, of

22. ZT to Crittenden, March 23, 1847, in John J. Crittenden Papers, X, r 5, LC. See also ZT to Wood, April 22, 1847, in Pequot Collection, M 748, Beinecke Rare Book and Manuscript Library, Yale University.

23. Seward to wife, March 31 [sic], 1847, in Frederick W. Seward, *Seward at Washington as Senator and Secretary of State* (New York, 1891), 42.

24. Poage, *Clay & Whig Party*, 157; James L. Crouthamel, *James Watson Webb, A Biography* (Middleton, Conn., 1969), 107; Seward, *Seward at Washington*, 43; William H. Adams, *The Whig Party of Louisiana* (Lafayette, La., 1973), 163; Betty Carolyn Congleton, "Contenders for the Whig Nomination in 1848 and the Editorial Policies of George D. Prentice," *Register of the Kentucky Historical Society*, LXVII (1969), 122–23; *Niles' Weekly Register*, LXXII (1847), 112, 128.

25. J. E. Davis to Jefferson Davis, April 16, 1847, in Haskell M. Monroe *et al.* (eds.), *The Papers of Jefferson Davis* (4 vols.; Baton Rouge, 1971–83), III, 356.

26. Philip Shriver Klein, *President James Buchanan* (University Park, Pa., 1962), 196; Henry R. Mueller, *The Whig Party in Pennsylvania* (New York, 1922), 143–45.

course, and Joseph Taylor probably came as close as anyone to reading his brother's mind when he wrote Thurlow Weed in April that he did not think the general was concerned about the election. He added that he did not believe Taylor would accept nomination unless it was offered "by the spontaneous wishes of his fellow-citizens."[27]

The first national party to query Taylor about carrying its colors in 1848 was the Native American. He was approached by an unnamed New Jersey nativist but responded negatively, stressing his refusal to become a candidate during the war. Taylor had refused for at least two reasons. At that point in the development of his thinking about the presidency he did not want a partisan nomination, and even if he had, the Native Americans were so controversial as to be counter-productive. As a result the Native Americans merely conferred their recommendation, rather than a nomination, in September.[28] As it turned out, they supported Taylor in the election, playing a significant role in Pennsylvania.

Henry Clay, whose interest in the nomination was not great in the early spring, wrote to one of his supporters that the Taylor candidacy was not surprising and that he preferred Taylor to any other military man, although he did not favor electing one without experience beyond the military. Others were less charitable. Horace Greeley conceded merely that "Old Rough would get along tolerable well with good advisors but it is all a lottery about that."[29] The candidacy received a not unexpected boost in May when former secretary of war John Bell pronounced for Taylor. Bell viewed the soldier as a moderating force within Whig ranks and a counter to Clay's close ties to the free-state elements of the party.[30] Actually the Taylor boom peaked in the late spring and receded as news of Scott's victories began to dominate popular attention. The shifting acclaim permitted combinations of political opponents to Taylor to form, spurred in part by his tendency to make impolitic comments.

What was happening to Taylor's thinking about a candidacy is rather simple. His antagonism toward the administration festered because of what he perceived as a carefully calculated and politically motivated effort to drive him from active service. As his animosity grew his resis-

27. *Niles' Weekly Register*, LXXII (1847), 112; Taylor to Weed, April 24, 1847, in Weed, *Autobiography*, 574.

28. *Niles' Weekly Register*, LXXII (1847), 334, 340, and LXXIII (1847–48), 62; Oliver Otis Howard, *General Taylor* (New York, 1892), 295–96; Mueller, *Whig Party in Pennsylvania*, 144–45.

29. Clay to Adam Beatty, April 29, 1847, in Henry Clay Letters, UKL; Van Deusen, *Jacksonian Era*, 253. See also Clay to Daniel Ullman, May 12, 1847, in Calvin Colton (ed.), *The Private Correspondence of Henry Clay* (New York, 1856), 541–43.

30. Joseph Howard Parks, *John Bell of Tennessee* (Baton Rouge, 1950), 229.

tance to a candidacy shrank. Increasingly, Taylor viewed himself as a nonpartisan figure attracting support from all parties and believed that if he were to be nominated it should not be by one of the established parties.[31] "I will not say I would not serve if the good people of the country should think it proper to elect me," he wrote Dr. Wood, but sensibly noted that the time was inauspicious for his coming or being brought forward as a candidate. Taylor's insistence on a nonpartisan nomination caused his first political stumble. It made him receptive to an editorial written by James W. Taylor in his Cincinnati *Signal*, a free-soil paper. The newspaper urged the election of the general provided he agreed to extend the Northwest Ordinance's prohibition on slavery to the land to be acquired from Mexico. Taylor replied in mid-May with an oft-reprinted letter reiterating his refusal to enter the presidential race until the conclusion of the war and restating his declination to state his political opinions until then. Unfortunately, he also added a comment that he approved in a general way the sentiments expressed in the editorial. It is not clear to what position Taylor thought he was agreeing, but many southern Whigs interpreted the statement as a commitment to the Wilmot Proviso and departed from the Taylor banner.[32]

The response was a mistake only if one believes Taylor was attempting to put together a personal coalition or looking toward the Whig nomination. For that to be true, as some historians have suggested, it assumes that Taylor was capable of more dissembling than his personality or mental agility permitted. This is no reason to doubt his sincerity in insisting that he was not a candidate nor to question the genuineness of his often repeated, if naïve, statement that he would serve only if "by the spontaneous move of the people."[33]

The disclaimers do not mean that Taylor lacked advice to keep a low

---

31. Taylor's shift from outright opposition to a nomination to an active candidacy for the Whig designation passed through many of the same stages as that of the only other professional soldier to occupy the White House. See Robert H. Ferrell (ed.), *The Eisenhower Diaries* (New York, 1981), 138–216.

32. ZT to Wood, May 9, July 13, 1847, in Samson (ed.), *Letters of Taylor*, 91–100, 114–14; to J. P. Taylor, May 9, to Nathaniel Young, May 13, 1847, in ZT(LC), ser 2, r 1; to Crittenden, May 15, 1847, in Crittenden Papers, XI, r 6, LC; to J. W. Taylor, May 18, 1847, in *Niles' Weekly Register*, LXXII (1847), 288; Chaplain W. Morrison, *Democratic Politics and Sectionalism* (Chapel Hill, 1967), 97; Brainerd Dyer, *Zachary Taylor* (Baton Rouge, 1946), 271–72; Hamilton, *Taylor*, II, 43.

33. ZT to Wood, May 30, 1847, in Samson (ed.), *Letters of Taylor*, 102–103. See also ZT to Gentleman in Lansingburgh, N.Y., May 29, and to an unnamed individual in West Baton Rouge, May 1847, in *Niles' Weekly Register*, LXXII (1847), 193, 333; to J. P. Taylor, June 4, 24, 1847, in ZT(LC), ser 2, r 1; to A. P. Merrill, June 20, 1847 in *New York Times*, February 1, 1931.

profile and avoid commenting on political issues. Nor did he need that advice since he firmly believed that as long as he was on active duty in Mexico he was precluded from public partisan comment. Nor did the reluctance of Taylor discourage Whigs who saw in him an alternative to an unelectable Henry Clay, as a southerner who would help protect the section against antislavery and other northern biases. The Taylor boom fitted in well with the efforts of Truman Smith, the administratively minded Connecticut congressman, to form a national Whig organization to support whatever candidate received the nomination. Smith, who was backed in his endeavors by Weed and Crittenden, favored Taylor. He soon brought Stephens' Young Indians into the organization.[34]

The drumfire of support continued. In June the Maryland Whig gubernatorial convention endorsed his candidacy, yet Taylor continued his posture of discomfort at having his name mentioned. He insisted that "gladly would I hail the nomination of a sound, just and upright statesman." To James C. Harvey in Washington he admitted that he had never voted but would have cast his ballot for Henry Clay in 1844 had he done so.[35] Taylor's reluctance to embrace either party was no surprise to those close to him. As Jefferson Davis pointed out, "the General has always referred to the strict Jeffersonians school as the one in which he had been taught, and the elements there acquired as the basis of his political opinions." He believed in strict construction and state sovereignty, and had a strict integrity and an utter contempt for intrigue. Davis insisted that Taylor was neither a Whig nor a Democrat.[36]

From the broader Whig viewpoint the existence of a Taylor candidacy, whether sanctioned by the candidate or not, was valuable. It allowed the party to avoid the onus of opposition to the war effort, which could be equated with treason. During the mid-term elections for the 30th Congress, which occurred over the nine months from March to November 1847, the administration lost ten House seats in the south and four in the north. The Whig gains in the south resulted from the party's candidates' success in painting the Democrats with the tar of the Wilmot Proviso. The tactic forced the regular southern Democrats to compromise with the Calhoun wing in a move which naturally alienated a substantial group of voters, who were in turn attracted to the Whigs because of both the

34. ZT to J. P. Taylor, May 29, 1847, in ZT(LC), ser 2, r 1; Arthur C. Cole, *The Whig Party in the South* (Washington, 1913), 126–31; Cooper, *South & Politics of Slavery*, 249–50; Hamilton, *Taylor*, II, 63.

35. *Niles' Weekly Register*, LXXII (June 19, 1847), 256; ZT to Harvey, June 4, 1847, in Gratz Collection, Case 4, Box 38, HSPa.

36. Davis to Robert J. Walker, June 29, in Monroe *et al.* (eds.), *Papers of Davis*, III, 419–20.

party's clear anti-Proviso stand and the potential of a southern Whig president.[37]

During the summer of 1847 Calhoun openly forecast the breakup of the traditional parties and prophesied the demise of the administration regardless of the success of the Taylor candidacy. A counterpoint came from Jefferson Davis, who assured Simon Cameron that he expected Taylor to get the Democratic nomination. He believed that irrespective of the party under whose banner Taylor ran that he would carry the South.[38]

While the general continued to respond to questions about his positions with a simple statement that he had found little time to study such questions and did not aspire to the presidency, he wrote his son-in-law that he was willing to run to keep Scott or Lewis Cass from being elected.[39] In private he was equally willing to take stands. After a particularly vitriolic attack on Scott, he outlined his political beliefs for Jefferson Davis. He opposed the government's borrowing money during peacetime but thought Congress should decide whether the revenues necessary to operate the government should be raised by taxation or through tariffs. Reestablishment of a national bank he viewed as a dead issue for the immediate future. The Wilmot Proviso "is a mere bugbare, & amounts to nothing. Will soon fade and be looked upon as a seven days wonder." Congress will not permit slavery in any territory taken from Mexico, Taylor believed, because Mexican law forbade it. "So far as Slavery is concerned, we of the south must throw ourselves on the constitution & defend our rights under [it] to the last, & when arguments will no longer suffice, we will appeal to the sword, if necessary to do so. I will be the last to yield one inch." Taylor reiterated his disinterest in the presidential nomination, assuring Davis, "[I] can truly say that I feel more interest in the recovery of your wound, & in the termination of this war . . . than I do of being president of the U. States."[40]

By early August, Taylor was willing to admit openly that his sympathies lay with the Whigs, whom he considered closer to Jefferson's ideals than the Democrats. While still denigrating his qualifications for the

37. See Brian G. Walton, "The Elections for the Thirtieth Congress and the Presidential Candidacy of Zachary Taylor," *JSH*, XXXV (1969), 191–94; Cooper, *South & Politics of Slavery*, 235; Michael F. Holt, "Winding Roads to Recovery: The Whig Party from 1844 to 1848," in Stephen E. Maizlish and John J. Kushma (eds.), *Essays on American Antebellum Politics, 1840–1860* (College Station, Tex., 1982), 134–69.

38. Calhoun to Clemson, July 8, 1847, in Jameson, "Correspondence of Calhoun," 735; Davis to Cameron, July 26, 1847, in Monroe *et al.* (eds.), *Papers of Davis*, III, 434–35.

39. Compare ZT to Dr. C. L. Wilcox *et al.*, July 20, 1847, in *Niles' Weekly Register*, LXXIII (1847–48), 63, and ZT to Wood, same date, in Samson (ed.), *Letters of Taylor*, 116–19.

40. ZT to Davis, July 27, 1847, in Monroe *et al.* (eds.), *Papers of Davis*, III, 440–49.

presidency, Taylor admitted that he would serve if elected. He still insisted, however, that his nomination must be by a nonpartisan popular convention. In accordance with his Jeffersonian principles, Taylor assured his correspondents that if elected he would govern in strict accordance with the Constitution. But the general still did not take his candidacy seriously. He did not believe, he wrote his brother, that there would be another president elected from a slaveholding state, especially a slaveholder. Moreover, he would stand aside if he were sure Henry Clay could be elected. To Dr. Wood he wrote that he would prefer to remain in the army in command of the Western Division or retire in preference to becoming president, since "I do not care a fig about the office."[41]

From the perspective of western New York, one of Weed's correspondents suggested that: "If Taylor keeps writing letters Clay will be nominated." Later he opined that "the blossoms of Genl Taylor's popularity are falling under the foot of Presidential letter writing." William H. Seward put it even more strongly: "I did not think General Taylor's popularity so easily shaken. If I judge from what I hear it is already ended."[42]

The damage done by Taylor's pen, especially the letter to James Taylor of the *Sentinel*, caused Crittenden to suggest very strongly that the general refrain as far as possible from committing himself on political issues. Most of those writing Taylor for his opinion, Crittenden sensibly advised him, were enemies hoping to trap him into impolitic statements. Crittenden's agent, Taylor's brother Joseph, played on the general's ego by reminding him that it was the politicians who opposed his candidacy while the people favored it. In a comment which would be echoed later by other outsiders to the Washington establishment he recommended that if elected his brother "call around [him] young and talented men" who would support him instead of posturing to improve their own political status. The letter crossed one from Taylor to Crittenden in which the general repeated his willingness to withdraw if he were convinced Clay would win the election.[43] Since most of his supporters, including Crittenden, were men who viewed Taylor as the winner which Clay could not be, the letter must have caused some wry amusement.

41. ZT to J. R. Ingersoll, August 3, to Dr. F. S. Bronson, August 15, 1847, in *Niles' Weekly Register*, LXXIII (1847–48), 83, 407; to Jefferson Davis, September 18, 1847, in Monroe *et al.* (eds.), *Papers of Davis*, III, 478–87; to Brantz Mayer, September 25, 1847, in Gratz Collection, Case 2, Box 22; to J. P. Taylor, September 1847, in ZT(LC), ser 2, r 1; to Wood, September 14, 1847, in Samson (ed.), *Letters of Taylor*, 130.

42. Seth C. Hawley to Weed, September 7, 13, Seward to Weed, September 15, 1847, all in Weed Papers.

43. J. P. Taylor to ZT, September 8, 1847, in ZT(LC), ser 2, r 1; to Crittenden, September 15, 1847, in Crittenden Papers, XI, r 6, LC; Albert D. Kirwin, *John J. Crittenden* (Lex-

Despite his occasional naïveté, Taylor sometimes showed a surprising grasp of political realities for a man who professed no study of the subject. In late September, as he prepared to leave Mexico, he commented to Dr. Wood that both the tariff and other economic concerns were dead issues. He reiterated to Jefferson Davis his view that the Wilmot Proviso was "at best a trifling affair" since the North would not agree to the addition of any territory south of the Missouri Compromise line and defeat any treaty which included it. The pressure for a Clay nomination, he believed, came from those who sought a means of stopping a Taylor candidacy and he was unsure of the degree of Clay's own involvement. In any event, Taylor questioned whether a slaveowner, or even a resident of a slave state, could be elected. He explained later to Crittenden: "I should not be surprised if Mr. Calhoun & his friends take a course in regards to Slavery, which may have the effect of uniting the people of the non-Slaveholding States, on a candidate for the presidency from some one of said states."[44]

There was considerable merit in Taylor's suspicion of a proslavery vs. abolitionist split among the Democrats. John Van Buren, the leader of New York's radical Barnburners offered support if Taylor would reaffirm the anti-Wilmot stand of the *Sentinel* letter. Taylor, having been burned once, hedged.[45] His suspicion of a revived Clay candidacy proved correct on November 13. Clay in a strong speech at Lexington attacked the administration for precipitating the war and called upon Congress to declare that the objectives of the conflict excluded extension of slave territory. Although he might have strengthened his candidacy further by an open support of the Wilmot Proviso, the speech restored Clay's candidacy and delivered a major blow to Taylor's march toward the nomination. The Kentuckian soon added a hint that he would support Seward for vice-president but reserved the final decision on his candidacy until spring.[46] In December Taylor thought that Clay would win the nomination and have either Cass or James Buchanan as his Democratic opponent. The soldier confided to his friends, however, that he did not believe Clay could

ington, 1962), 208. See also ZT to Clay, November 4, 1847, in Colton (ed.), *Private Correspondence of Clay*, 548–49.

44. ZT to Wood, September 27, October 12, 1847, in Samson (ed.), *Letters of Taylor*, 134–35, ZT(UKL); to Davis, September 18, 1847, in Monroe *et al.* (eds.), *Papers of Davis*, III, 478–89; to Crittenden, November 1, 1847, in Crittenden, XI, r 6, LC.

45. Morrison, *Democratic Politics & Sectionalism*, 97.

46. *Niles' Weekly Register*, LXXIII (1847–48), 197–200; Carl Schurz, *Henry Clay* (2 vols., 1899; rpr. New York, 1968), II, 290–92; Van Deusen, *Jacksonian Era*, 254; Glendon G. Van Deusen, *The Life of Henry Clay* (Boston, 1937), 386–89. Clay's interest in Seward coincided with the New Yorker's conclusion that Taylor was the most likely nominee. Seward to Weed, December 14, 1847, in Weed Papers.

even unite the Whigs, while he would gain support from not only Whigs but also Democrats and Nativists.[47] This is one of the few instances in which Taylor permitted himself, even in private, to promote his own candidacy. Even his sniping at Clay did not prevent Taylor from keeping on good personal terms with the Great Compromiser. On December 28 he wrote a stiff but friendly reply to Clay's invitation to visit Ashland. He had to remain near Baton Rouge in case the war resumed, Taylor wrote, and added that Mrs. Taylor was then in "feeble health." At the end of April, Taylor penned a longer letter to Clay justifying his own candidacy. The general wrote that he believed that Clay, Crittenden, Justice John McLean, and Senator John M. Clayton were better prepared for the presidency than he was but that he had allowed his name to be entered when assured that Clay was not a candidate and that no other Whig could win. Taylor repeated his oft-spoken promise to support Clay if the Kentuckian received the nomination.[48]

Taylor's doubts about the broad acceptance of Clay were justified. Congressman Washington Hunt reported to Thurlow Weed from Washington: "It is agreed on all hands, amongst our friends here, that Mr. Clay *cannot* be our candidate." The southern wing of the party, Hunt prophesied, would promote Taylor as a moderate. Since the north had no candidate, it had no choice but to support the war hero. Thomas Corwin, whose abolitionist credentials were impeccable and who could have led the radical wing of the party, in January declined to enter the contest. He feared that his candidacy would split the party into pro- and antislavery camps as it had nearly done at the Ohio state convention.[49]

The reception that Taylor received after his return from Mexico convinced him that Clay's supporters had abandoned their favorite and that Clay was no longer a serious candidate. Therefore, the general explicitly informed Crittenden that he would remain a candidate. At the same time, he assured the Kentuckian that he would continue to give questions about the Wilmot Proviso "the go by." Meanwhile, the nomination meetings by both Whig and nonpartisan groups continued in Alabama, Louisiana,

47. ZT to Davis, December 31, 1847, in Monroe *et al.* (eds.), *Papers of Davis*, III, 383; to [?], December 16, 1847, in ZT(LC), ser 2, r 1; to Brown, December 18, 1847, in Orlando Brown Papers, KHS. The letter to Davis freed him to follow his own political interests during the presidential election. Subsequently Taylor urged Davis to act in the way he believed best for himself "without regard for my advancement . . . I have your advancement more at heart than my own." ZT to Davis, July 10, 1848, in Jefferson Davis Papers, LC.

48. ZT to Clay, December 28, 1847, April 30, 1848, in Colton, *Private Correspondence of Clay*, 550–51, 557–59.

49. Hunt to Weed, December 26, 1847, in Weed Papers; Norman A. Graebner, "Thomas Corwin and the Election of 1848," *JSH*, XVII (1955), 171; Rayback, *Free Soil*, 161–62.

Kentucky, and New York.[50] Taylor was quizzed in mid-January 1848 by a group of prominent local Whigs at a dinner in New Orleans in which he confirmed his acceptance of the traditional Whig stand on protective tariffs and internal improvements. He pronounced himself in favor of a Rio Grande border and acquisition of a part of California.[51]

Shortly after his return from the New Orleans dinner Taylor suffered an attack of rheumatism in his leg, the first time that malady had struck him. It confined him to the house for five weeks.[52] While Taylor remained at the small house on the reservation at Baton Rouge, he sent Richard to take charge of the plantation at Cypress Grove, where later in the year he installed a steam sawmill. It proved to be such a successful assignment that Taylor in May 1850 agreed to finance his son's purchase of Fashion Plantation for $120,000.[53]

On February 7 Alexander H. Stephens introduced a resolution of thanks and an award of a gold medal to Taylor for the Buena Vista victory. It passed the House immediately by a vote of 181 to 1. After slight amendment in the Senate it cleared the House again on May 4 and was signed by President Polk five days later.[54]

Taylor emerged as the front-running Whig contender for the presidential nomination when it became clear that Clay's almost quixotic thrust toward the nomination had not lived up to its initial expectations. Horace Greeley and a handful of other moderates who were especially disturbed by the prospect of a soldier in the White House attempted to develop John McLean as an acceptable alternative for those who doubted the ability or the desirability of Taylor. The western New York Congressman Nathan K. Hall surveyed the possible alternatives and concluded that the likely nominee should Taylor and Clay falter would be either Clayton or Millard Fillmore.[55] The antiextensionists who came to form the core of the McLean faction hoped to promote deadlock at the Whig convention which would permit the nomination of McLean or some

50. ZT to Crittenden, January 3, 1848, in Crittenden Papers, XI, r 6, LC; Malcolm C. McMillan, "Taylor's Presidential Campaign in Alabama, 1847–1848," *Alabama Review,* XIII (1960), 91; *Niles' Weekly Register,* LXXIII (1847–48), 339, 393.

51. Adams, *Whig Party in Louisiana,* 166. Similar sentiments appear in ZT to J. P. Taylor, January 19, 1848, in ZT(LC), ser 2, r 1.

52. ZT to Davis, April 20, 1848, in Monroe *et al.* (eds.), *Papers of Davis,* III, 662–73.

53. ZT to J. P. Taylor, March 10, 1848, to Richard Taylor, May 9, June 12, W. W. Hill to ZT, May 17, 1850, in ZT(LC), ser 2, r 1.

54. *Congressional Globe,* 30th Cong., 1st Sess., 304, 725–27; Francis B. Heitman, *Historical Register and Dictionary of the United States Army* (2 vols.; Washington, 1903), I, 949. The gold medal was not struck and delivered until July 1849. Crawford to ZT, July 7, 1849, Office of the Secretary of War (NA, RG 107), Letters Sent to the President, V, 13 (M127/5).

55. Seward to Weed, January 22, 1848, in Weed Papers; Hall to R. S. Colt, February 15, 1848, in Colt Collection, HSPa. See also Seward, *Seward at Washington,* 62; Rayback, *Free*

other acceptable candidate such as Seward. While Greeley's opposition to Taylor is not itself important, it is instructive in illustrating some of the causes of antipathy to the general. Greeley listed eight objections: 1) "He is deplorably vague on the *Slavery* question"; 2) he opposes the Wilmot Proviso; 3) the "Peace-men" will not support him; 4) the Old Whig areas will not give him strong support; 5) he will lose Ohio and is weak in Indiana, Connecticut, Vermont, and New Jersey; 6) "All the rotten, run-down, locked-out and used-up of both parties are his original friends"; 7) his election will open up patronage to the army; and 8) he will not understand political activities.[56] In the context of 1848, vagueness on slavery was more of an asset than a liability since there was no national, or even sectional, consensus on how to deal with the issue. Greeley's concern about Taylor's weakness as a candidate among some anti-administration factions and in some of the traditional Whig states was valid but more than offset by the war hero's popularity elsewhere. The fears over patronage were legitimate although based on a lack of understanding of the general.

The hope for a Taylor-Clay deadlock at the convention was a forlorn one at best and by mid-February was dead. Clay ceased active campaigning, although he refused to withdraw because of Taylor's noncommittal positions and a fear that withdrawal "would lead to a prostration of the Whig party."[57] The Clay candidacy became a central issue when the Kentucky Whigs met on February 21–22 to select their delegates to the Philadelphia convention and the nominee for governor. Crittenden demonstrated his statesmanship by securing the election of a slate of delegates overwhelmingly favorable to Taylor but without a formal endorsement, and this satisfied the Clay supporters. The convention, in order to prevent a split over the gubernatorial nomination, selected Crittenden without his knowledge or candidacy. Crittenden had little choice but to accept the nomination although it deprived Taylor of the presence in Washington of his most sagacious advisor and effectively stilled one of the voices of moderation within the administration's limited group of supporters.[58]

By mid-February the Taylor campaign was in full stride. Abraham Lin-

Soil, 1–9; and Francis P. Weisenberger, *The Life of John McLean* (Columbus, 1937), 124–32.

56. Blue, *Free Soilers*, 50; Robert J. Rayback, *Millard Fillmore* (Buffalo, 1959), 179; Glyndon G. Van Deusen, *Horace Greeley, Nineteenth Century Crusader* (Philadelphia, 1953), 119–20; Horace Greeley, *Recollections of a Busy Life* (New York, 1868), 211; Greeley to A. H. Wells, May 23, 1848, in Miscellaneous Papers, NYHS.

57. Clay to H. T. Duncan, February 15, 1848, in Colton (ed.), *Private Correspondence of Clay*, 554.

58. Kirwin, *Crittenden*, 21–13; Rayback, *Free Soil*, 149. See also ZT to Mrs. Chapman Coleman, April 2, 1848, in ZT(UKL).

coln predicted that it would gain the Whigs an additional congressional seat from normally Democratic Illinois. Even so, Taylor still spoke in non-partisan terms. He wrote his son-in-law that "if I occupy the White House, I must be untrammelled & unpledged, so as to be president of the nation & not of a party." He would, he insisted, decline nomination by a party convention.[59] The anniversary of Buena Vista, with its happy coincidence with the birthday of the nation's first president, brought Taylor mass meetings in New York City, Cincinnati, Harrisburg, and Philadelphia. Meanwhile, Alexander H. Stephens engineered a Taylor nomination by the Georgia Whig state convention, which was soon followed by similar action in Virginia and Tennessee.[60]

Nevertheless, Henry Clay's candidacy refused to die. Clay himself was enthusiastically received in Philadelphia and New York in late February, which revived his hopes. In late 1847 Daniel Webster also tested the waters of a possible campaign, but it was poorly handled and his effort never developed into a serious obstacle to Taylor's drive. In part the Webster campaign failed because of the capture of the Massachusetts party by the Cotton faction led by Abbott Lawrence.[61]

In spite of what he conceived of as a strong Clay campaign, Taylor refused a request from Truman Smith that he state his Whig principles more explicitly than he had yet in public.[62] The refusal reflected both his nonpartisan stand and his continuing ambivalence about the nomination. In mid-March he still insisted that he could support Clay if the latter won the Whig nomination. Later in the month Taylor again voiced his preference for some other candidate although admitting that he was willing to accept the nomination if it were offered.[63]

On April 10, to nearly everyone's surprise, Clay formally announced his candidacy. Why he chose the late date and ignored the evident weakness of his support is not clear. It probably reflected the pressure from the

59. Lincoln to T. S. Flournoy, February 17, 1848, in Basler (ed.), *Collected Lincoln*, I, 452; ZT to Wood, February 18, 1848, in Samson (ed.), *Letters of Taylor*, 152–55.

60. *Niles' Weekly Register*, LXXIII (1847–48), 408; Crouthamel, *Webb*, 107–108; Dr. J. K. Mitchell, Call for Convention, December 28, 1847, in Meredith Family Papers, HSPa; *Great Whig Demonstration in Favor of the Nomination of Gen. Taylor to the Presidency* (Philadelphia, 1848); Van Deusen, *Clay*, 389; Roger C. McCrary, "Georgia Politics and the Mexican War," *Georgia Historical Quarterly*, LX (1976), 223.

61. Kirwin, *Crittenden*, 214; Claude Moore Fuess, *Daniel Webster* (2 vols.; Boston, 1930), II, 173–78, 184; Kinley J. Brauer, *Cotton Versus Conscience* (Lexington, 1967), 216–17; Richard N. Current, *Daniel Webster and the Rise of National Conservatism* (Boston, 1955), 153.

62. ZT to J. P. Taylor, March 10, 1848, in ZT(LC), ser 2, r 1.

63. ZT to Orlando Brown, March 15, 1848, in ZT(KHS); to Crittenden, March 25, 1848, in Crittenden Papers, XI, r 6, LC.

antimilitary candidate faction who recognized that the strongest alternative to Taylor would be Winfield Scott. Many of the antimilitarists had initially supported McLean, but his candidacy had not developed nor had those of other alternatives like Webster or Corwin. So volatile was Whig politics that John Bell wrote that a dark horse with a moderate stance such as Crittenden could be nominated. Taylor believed that the nomination was likely to go to Clay or Scott.[64]

While the anti-Taylor forces debated their strategies, the general's advisors concluded that a declaration of acceptance of Whig principles was imperative if Taylor was to secure the nomination and turn back Clay's thrust with its threat of northern radicalism. During April 11 Bliss, then in Washington, conferred with the congressional Taylor bloc and probably also with Jefferson Davis. Bliss returned to Baton Rouge eleven days later with a draft of a letter, only to learn that Logan Hunton, James Love, and Baylie Peyton in New Orleans had proposed a similar solution. The suggestions were well timed since they crossed another Taylor letter, this time to the Richmond *Republican*, reiterating his nonparty stand.[65] Although the Washington proposal had been drafted by Crittenden with assistance by Stephens and Toombs, Bliss chose not to substitute it for the one prepared by the New Orleans trio. Their letter, drafted by Hunton after Love convinced Taylor that he had to abandon the insistence on an independent nomination, was nominally addressed to John Allison. It included the declaration, "I am a Whig but not an ultra Whig." While Taylor insisted on the inclusion of a statement that he would be a president independent of party, he promised to limit his vetoes to "cases of clear violation of the Constitution" since "the personal opinion of the individual who may happen to occupy the executive chair ought not to control the action of Congress upon questions of Domestic policy." He would, therefore, follow Congress on questions of the tariff, currency, and internal improvements.[66] The letter accomplished its objective. It convinced the doubters that Taylor was a Whig and would carry the party's banner openly if nominated. By late May most observers accepted the probability of a Taylor nomination.[67]

64. Van Deusen, *Clay*, 390; Hamilton, *Taylor*, II, 72–75; Parks, *Bell*, 231; ZT to Davis, April 20, 1848, in Monroe *et al.* (eds.), *Papers of Davis*, III, 662–73.

65. Hamilton, *Taylor*, II, 77, 79, 81; Rayback, *Free Soil*, 155–56.

66. Stephens to A. M. Coleman, October 13, 1870, in Coleman (ed.), *Crittenden*, I, 194; Kirwin, *Crittenden*, 218–20; Cooper, *South & Politics of Slavery*, 250–51; Hamilton, *Taylor*, II, 77–81, includes the text of the letter; Joseph G. Rayback, "Who Wrote the Allison Letters," *MVHR*, XXXVI (1949), 62–63; ZT to J. P. Taylor, May 15, 1848, in ZT(LC), ser 2, r 1; J. P. Taylor to Weed, April 28, 1848, in Weed Papers.

67. Cooper, *South & Politics of Slavery*, 251; Lincoln to E. B. Washburne, April 30,

The Taylor campaign, like others in the period, had occasional problems with sabotage such as assaults upon its meetings by groups of troublemakers. After a series of unfortunate problems in New York City, Robert Toombs visited the city and contacted Isaiah Rynders, a Taylor admirer and gang leader. At a meeting on April 27 at Lafayette Hall, Rynders and some of his toughs policed the hall. When heckling began, they marked the backs of the troublesome men and when commanded to "Put him out" they tossed the hecklers into the street.[68]

Although it appears to have held little interest for Taylor, the Democrats held their nominating convention at Baltimore on May 22–25. The meeting began with a credentials fight centered upon the New York delegation. Both Hunker (conservative) and Barnburner (radical) slates arrived. Seeking to prevent the bolting of either group, the convention voted to seat both factions. The Barnburners refused to accept the arrangement, so no New York delegation participated; Lewis Cass received the nomination on the fourth ballot. In an effort to offset Taylor's military image the Democrats settled upon Major General William O. Butler for vice-president. His choice also served as a sop to the party's radical wing. The platform called for strict construction of the Constitution, denial of federal support for internal improvements, and revenue tariff. It was silent on slavery, although an effort to insert a plank supporting slavery in the territories failed decisively. The effect was to establish Cass's doctrine of popular sovereignty as the party's position. In his acceptance speech the nominee carefully avoided any sensitive issues.[69]

Cass was a strong candidate. He had a long and distinguished political career as governor and senator from Michigan, secretary of war, and minister to France and was recognized as one of the most able of American politicians of his era. He had established a strong military reputation during the War of 1812 which the Democrats hoped would combine with that of Butler to overcome Taylor's fame. The Democrats could also take solace in the fact that Taylor faced probable dissension within Whig ranks if he secured the nomination. In late May the Conscience Whigs led by Charles Francis Adams agreed to bolt if the convention turned to the

---

1848, in Basler (ed.), *Collected Lincoln*, I, 467; ZT to Webb, May 16, 1848, in Webb Papers, Box 2; Hunt to Weed, May 31, 1848, in Weed Papers; George Penn to M. M. Marmaduke, June 2, 1848, in Sappington Papers, MoHS.

68. Avary, *Recollections of Stephens*, 23–24; Crouthamel, *Webb*, 108.

69. Van Deusen, *Jacksonian Era*, 249–50; Richard C. Bain, *Convention Decisions and Voting Records* (Washington, 1960), 37–40; Kirk H. Porter and Donald Bruce Johnson, *National Party Platforms, 1840–1968* (Urbana, 1970), 10–12; W. G. L. Smith, *The Life and Times of Lewis Cass* (New York, 1856), 652–53; Andrew C. McLaughlin, *Lewis Cass* (1899; rpr. New York, 1980), 241–45.

slave-owning Taylor. Whether they would ally with the Liberty-party abolitionists or attempt to make common cause with the Barnburners was left for future decision.[70]

In early June the Whigs began to gather in Philadelphia for their nominating convention. Taylor agents, including most of the "Congressional Whigs," greeted them. The Taylor men argued that he alone was electable and when confronted by strong anti-Taylor delegates strove to deflect them to the weaker candidates and away from Clay. It was a well-conducted campaign.

When the convention opened on the seventh in the Chinese Museum on Ninth Street, Clay's supporters appeared to be in control of the mechanics. Temporary chairman Henry White, president pro tempore John A. Collier of New York, and temporary secretary James Harlan of Kentucky were all Clay supporters. So was the permanent chairman, John M. Morehead of North Carolina. Yet when the question of the proxy given by the absent Texas delegation to their Louisiana counterparts arose, it was settled in favor of Taylor. There were problems during the day with the gallery. The convention managers had not adequately controlled the issuance of spectator tickets during the first day and the onlookers tended to be unruly. They widely applauded or hissed and booed speakers and generally made a nuisance of themselves. Thereafter, tickets were more circumspectly issued.

The convention settled down to its real business on the eighth. There was a short flare-up when a Scott delegate attempted to introduce a rule requiring the nominee to agree to follow the decisions of the convention and to promote the Whig party. It was patently a slap at Taylor's independent stance but was ruled out of order by the chairman. When the nominations began Lewis D. Campbell of Ohio nominated Scott, Asahel Huntington offered Webster, Edward Kent put forward Taylor, N. Bowditch Blunt of New York added Clay, and the Delaware delegation contributed Clayton. McLean's name was also put forward but Samuel Galloway of Ohio promptly withdrew it, to the consternation of many of the delegates who had no advance warning of the Buckeye's refusal. Judge Lafayette Saunders deflected the argument that Taylor was not a Whig by effective use of the general's promise to support whomever the convention nominated.

On the first ballot Taylor had a clear lead with 111 votes but it was clearly as a sectional candidate. All but 26 of the votes came from the South. Only 17 votes came from northern states and 9 from the north-

70. Brauer, *Cotton Versus Conscience*, 223–25; Cheryl Haun, "The Whig Abolitionists' Attitude Towards The Mexican War," *Journal of the West*, XI (1972) 271.

west. Clay had 97 votes, chiefly from New York; Scott stood third with 43 votes, almost half of them in Ohio. Webster followed with a bloc of 22 votes almost exclusively from New England, while six votes were scattered elsewhere. On a second ballot that day, Taylor picked up 7 votes, but Clay slipped to 86, and Scott added 6 for a total of 49. Webster held firm at 22. Nearly half of the shift came from Pennsylvania, where 4 Clay votes changed to Scott and 1 to Taylor.

The Clay forces secured an adjournment to permit them to apply a tourniquet to the hemorrhaging of their delegates. They worked well into the night but seem to have done more damage than good. The Taylor managers, notably Truman Smith and Reverdy Johnson, proved more adept and more successful. When the third ballot was counted on the ninth, Taylor's count rose to 133. It resulted from three delegates each shifting from Clay in Connecticut, Maryland, and Pennsylvania along with a scattering from elsewhere. Clay's decline continued. He slipped to 74 while Scott rose to 54. Daniel Webster still held on to 17 votes in New England, and 1 Delaware vote continued for John Clayton. But the conclusion was clear. Taylor needed only 7 more votes for the nomination. On the fourth ballot they shifted. Taylor received 171 votes, Scott 60, Clay 35, and Webster 14. It has to be viewed as a southern victory, since the core of Taylor's support came from below the Mason-Dixon line and southern Whigs had dominated the campaign organization. Even on the final vote Weed's tightly controlled New York delegation supported Scott with 14 votes to 6 for Taylor. A proposal to make the nomination unanimous collapsed when Charles Allen, one of the Massachusetts Conscience faction, announced that his delegation would not agree.

In the confusion which followed, Allen also proposed adoption of the Wilmot Proviso. That was promptly ruled out of order, much to the relief of most of the members of the convention, who clearly recognized that any statement on the slavery issue would weaken their chances in November. The convention then moved to take up the vice-presidential nomination. Since Taylor had given no indication of his personal preference the choice was wide open. Thomas Ewing of Ohio, William Woodbridge of Maryland, George Evans of Maine, T. Butler King of Georgia, Abbott Lawrence and Robert C. Winthrop of Massachusetts, Andrew Stewart, John Sergeant, and Thomas M. Kennan of Pennsylvania were nominated along with Millard Fillmore, Seward, Governor John Young, Hamilton Fish, and J. Watson Webb of New York. Lawrence, Fillmore, Ewing, and Seward were the leading contenders despite Seward's having already withdrawn. Ewing's name was also taken out of the contention by the Ohio delegation in a surprise move. That left the choice between Fillmore and Lawrence, who was reportedly prepared to contribute $100,000 to the campaign if nominated. The latter was not acceptable to the Clay faction, and thus Fillmore's choice was ensured. He was nominated by John A. Collier, an obscure New Yorker, apparently without clearing the move with either Fillmore's or Taylor's manager. Collier implied that Fillmore was a Clay supporter, which he was not, and therefore his nomination would be a form of reconciliation. Once the favorite sons were eliminated after the first ballot the nomination quickly went to Fillmore, 173 to 87, since he was acceptable to both the Clay and Taylor factions.

Despite his modern unfamiliarity, Fillmore was a national figure in 1848, albeit a secondary one. He had been chairman of the House Ways and Means Committee and a serious contender for the vice-presidential nomination in 1844. That he played only a minor role in New York politics was a result of his opposition to the dominant Seward-Weed faction. The nomination did not sit well with the latter. Seward complained that Fillmore's nomination meant that "a faction apparently opposed to the New York leader [would be] in the general council of the Whigs of the Union."[71]

Once the vice-presidential candidate had been chosen and the final housekeeping resolutions adopted, the convention adjourned. It made no effort to adopt a platform, since most delegates recognized that to do so would probably split the party. That evening a few of the delegates and a great gathering of onlookers adopted a resolution which passed for an unofficial platform. It applauded Taylor as a candidate who would bring "Peace, Prosperity, and Union" to the nation while supporting the Constitution. But it offered no specifics. More substantial, however, was the statement of the radical Conscience wing that it refused to accept a Taylor nomination and would support another candidate.[72]

News of the nomination reached Taylor by a roundabout route. Telegraph carried it to Memphis, where the captain of the appropriately named side-wheeler *General Taylor* had his vessel ready. She sped downstream with flags flying, signal guns firing, and her crew cheering each passing vessel. The formal notification came from Chairman Morehead. When Taylor had not acknowledged it by June 28, Morehead wrote

71. Seward to Weed, June 10, 1848, in Weed Papers.

72. The account of the Whig convention is drawn from: Bain, *Convention Decisions and Voting Records*, 41–43; Porter and Johnson, *Platforms*, 14–15; Dyer, *Taylor*, 283; Hamilton, *Taylor*, II, 89–97; Van Deusen, *Jacksonian Era*, 255–56; Greeley, *Recollections*, 21, 252; Malcolm C. McMillan (ed.), "Joseph Glover Baldwin Reports on the Whig Convention of 1848," *JSH*, XXV (1959), 370–82; Rayback, *Free Soil*, 194–200; Mueller, *Whig Party in Pennsylvania*, 148; Van Deusen, *Clay*, 392; Cooper, *South & Politics of Slavery*, 252; Rayback, *Fillmore*, 186; Holman Hamilton, "Abraham Lincoln and Zachary Taylor," *Lincoln Herald*, LIII (Fall 1951), 17; Holt, "Winding Roads," 126.

again. It developed that Taylor had not received the original letter because it had been sent collect. The general had earlier instructed the Baton Rouge postmaster not to deliver mail sent with postage to be collected, so Morehead's letter resided in the dead letter pile of the post office until late July when it was finally rescued and acknowledged by Taylor.[73]

The general had become the candidate in spite of himself. If he had not been drafted by the public at large, as he had initially required, he certainly had been drafted by Whigs searching for a winner. Taylor was undoubtedly honest when he insisted that he did not wish the office and believed that other men were better qualified—so long as they were not Polk, Marcy, or Scott. To suggest that he was an adept schemer who promoted himself astutely, as some authors have, is to credit Zachary Taylor with capacities he did not possess. He was a rather quick tempered, unimaginative individual, who was often slow to make up his mind but tenacious in his opinion once he had done so.

Taylor's campaign for the nomination, to the degree that he planned it at all, began as an effort to gain revenge for what he perceived were slights and attacks by the administration and by Winfield Scott. As one reads his political correspondence from the fall of 1846 down to the Whig convention in 1848, one cannot avoid being impressed by the consistency of Taylor's reactions to all efforts by politicians to draw him into active campaigning. He did not wish to satisfy them although his responses showed a growing political sophistication.

73. Morehead to ZT, June 10, 28, 1848, in ZT(UKL); ZT to Morehead, July 15, 1848, in *Niles' Weekly Register*, LXXIV (1848), 69; Hamilton, *Taylor*, II, 117–18; Frederick Way, Jr., *Way's Packet Directory, 1848–1983* (Athens, Ohio, 1983), 183. There is an alternative tradition that the news was brought by the steamer *Ringgold* (*ibid.*, 394). Upon learning of the mixup on the notification letter, Seward quipped: "The Candidate was very Rough and quite Unready, in refusing a nomination for the Presidency from a Whig Convention because it was not *post paid*!" Seward to Weed, July 24, 1848, in Weed Papers. Fillmore accepted his nomination on June 17 and soon afterwards wrote a friendly letter to Taylor expressing his appreciation at joining the ticket. Fillmore to Morehead, June 17, to ZT, June 26, 1848, both in ZT(UKL).

CHAPTER XII

The General Becomes President

ZACHARY TAYLOR accepted the Whig nomination with the same set of assumptions that had brought him the selection. He did not intend to canvass the country actively; nor could he, since he remained on active duty throughout the campaign as the commander of the Western Division.[1] He believed that if the people wanted him to be chief magistrate they would vote for him; if not, they would vote for someone else. In either case he would serve in whatever post they assigned. The general truly did not care whether or not he was elected president.

The decision not to campaign must have cheered his advisors immensely, considering Taylor's proclivity for political *faux pas*. It coincided with the emerging Whig strategy of keeping a low profile and relying on the name of Old Rough and Ready to attract the necessary votes. For a party already battered by the rocks of sectionalism no other course was possible which did not lead to disaster. The program worked out by the Taylor campaign strategists led by Truman Smith called for party speakers to flood the country excoriating the Democrats and extolling Taylor without mentioning concrete legislative proposals. "We shall have a most overwhelming, glorious, triumph," predicted Abraham Lincoln, who

---

1. See ZT to Crittenden, July 1, 1848, in Mrs. Chapman Coleman (ed.), *The Life of John J. Crittenden* (2 vols.; Philadelphia, 1871), I, 314.

239

concluded that Taylor would draw support from Barnburners, Native Americans, Tylermen, and disappointed Locofocos.[2]

Congress resumed its session during the hot Washington summer. Both parties maneuvered for advantage but accomplished little beyond defining more strongly than ever the sectional split. The southerners, whether Democrat or Whig, made clear their insistence on the opening of the newly acquired territory to slavery, utterly ignoring the impracticality of the system in nearly all of the area. Northern radicals continued to insist upon total exclusion of slavery from the new territories, failing to recognize that climate and economics were on their side. Northern moderates and a handful of men from the slaveholding areas sought the politically acceptable solution which the polarization of the issue made nearly unobtainable. As a result most congressional activities were aimed at establishing a representative's or senator's record more often than they represented genuine effort to solve the problem.

Even before Congress resumed its sessions, the radicals combined to create a new party and nominate a third major candidate. On June 10 the Massachusetts Conscience Whigs called a meeting of anti-Taylor and anti-Cass men to gather at Worcester later in the month. At about the same time Ohio Free Soilers met in Columbus. A similar meeting in Utica, N.Y., nominated Martin Van Buren and led to a call for a general convention of antislavery groups at Buffalo in early August.[3] The call came in the face of the existence of the Liberty party, whose stature as the original antislavery party had been fully documented in the 1840 and 1844 elections. The party had nominated John P. Hale of New Hampshire, but its leadership, notably Salmon P. Chase, was willing to abandon a separate campaign if a broader coalition could be formed. About 465 Free Soilers, Liberty party men, Barnburners, Conscience Whigs, and advocates of other reforms gathered in Buffalo on August 9. The Whigs struck a bargain with the Barnburners and Free Soilers. In return for acceptance of Martin Van Buren as the presidential nominee they received a voice in the group's platform and the designation of Charles Francis Adams as vice-presidential candidate. The group took the name of the Free Soil party.[4] The Free Soil candidacy proved to be a great assistance to

2. Lincoln to W. H. Herndon, June 12, 1848, in Roy P. Basler (ed.), *The Collected Works of Abraham Lincoln* (8 vols.; New Brunswick, N.J., 1953), I, 477.

3. Cheryl Haun, "The Whig Abolitionists' Attitude Towards the Mexican War," *Journal of the West*, XI (1972), 271; Glendon G. Van Deusen, *The Jacksonian Era* (New York, 1959), 257; Kinley J. Brauer, *Cotton Versus Conscience* (Lexington, 1967), 259; John Nevin, *Martin Van Buren* (New York, 1983), 584–85. See also C. F. Adams to William Walker, June 14, 1848, in Miscellaneous Papers, NYHS.

4. Van Deusen, *Jacksonian Era*, 258–59; Joseph G. Rayback, *Free Soil* (Lexington,

the Taylor campaign since it siphoned off appreciably more Democratic votes in the North than it did Whig.

One middle-western democrat complained to Howell Cobb that the Taylor nomination was "a Southern Whig trick . . . to catch up others than Whig votes in the South." Elsewhere, the Whigs collected other allies. In Pennsylvania, for instance, the local Whig leaders struck a deal with Lewis C. Levin of the Native American movement. In return for Native American support of Taylor, the Whigs lent their support to Levin's candidacy for the House.[5] Taylor also secured the neutrality, if not the active support, of his leading Whig opponents. Henry Clay in late June formally announced his acceptance of the action of the convention but refused to endorse Taylor as a good Whig. Winfield Scott's response was that since Taylor did not "frankly accept the nomination as a Whig . . . I shall at least be indifferent."[6] The congressional session became increasingly partisan. Senator Henry S. Foote, a combative Mississippi Democrat, belittled Taylor's promise to avoid excessive use of the veto. Senator John M. Clayton of Delaware, Taylor's most consistent defender in that body, responded that the nominee would support the voice of the people. Clayton on July 12 suggested that the Senate appoint a committee to write a bill settling the status of slavery in the territories. Six days later he proposed that Oregon be permitted to retain its antislavery laws while Congress prohibited any legislation on the subject in California or New Mexico. The effect of such a law would be to force a slave in the latter two territories to sue to determine his status and throw the onus of any decision on the courts. The plan drew considerable support. Proslavery senators favored it in the belief that Congress had no authority to prescribe the policy on slavery in a territory, while some antislavery legislators argued that the Mexican antislavery laws would still apply. The bill passed the Senate on July 27 by a vote of 33 to 22; the slave-state senators supported it 23 to 3, while the free-state ones opposed 19 to 10. On a motion of Alexander Stephens', the bill was promptly tabled in the House by a 129 to 97 vote. The free-state congressmen provided 112 of the negative

1970), 186–94; Kirk H. Porter and Donald Bruce Johnson, *National Party Platforms, 1840–1968* (Urbana, 1970), 13–34; Frederick J. Blue, *The Free Soilers* (Urbana, 1973), 63, 72–80; Nevin, *Van Buren*, 585–89.

5. Thomas Smith to Cobb, July 27, 1848, in Ulrich B. Phillips (ed.), "The Correspondence of Robert Toombs, Alexander H. Stephens, and Howell Cobb," *Annual Report of the American Historical Association for the Year 1911* (Washington, 1913), 112; Holman Hamilton, *Zachary Taylor* (2 vols.; Indianapolis, 1941, 1951), II, 111.

6. Clay to Committee, June 28, Scott to Clay, July 16, 1848, in Calvin Colton (ed.), *The Private Correspondence of Henry Clay* (New York, 1856), 566, 571; Clay to R. L. Houghton, July 4, 1848, in Miscellaneous Papers, NYHS.

votes. The effect of the defeat in the House was the shattering of the efforts for a compromise.[7]

During July Taylor became increasingly disturbed by efforts of some of the more partisan Whigs to circumscribe his freedom by demanding commitments to particular party doctrines. It came at the same time that former secretary of the Treasury Thomas Ewing counseled that he make no replies at all to inquiries about his beliefs. Ewing's suggestion was an effort to prevent Taylor's making further gaffes like those which plagued the campaign for the nomination. The kind of letter which Ewing feared was Taylor's assertion to a Mr. Lippard of Philadelphia that he was not a "party candidate." What Taylor meant, he explained to William C. Rives, was to bring the country back to the principles of Thomas Jefferson, a condition which the general viewed as above partisanship. Taylor also complained about the patronage problem, which as early as July brought a deluge of letters from office seekers who flooded him with assurance of their good will and claims for appointment. This led him to conclude that if elected he would stand aside from the dispensing of offices.[8]

Throughout the political maneuverings, Taylor continued serving as commanding officer of the army's Western Division with his headquarters at Baton Rouge. The demands of command were few, largely administrative matters such as recommendations for the locations of posts in Texas and requesting the stationing of single companies at New Orleans and Baton Rouge.[9] This not only permitted him time for political activities but it allowed him to make short visits to Cypress Grove and elsewhere. In late June Taylor visited New Orleans to accept a special medal from the Louisiana legislature in commemoration of the Buena Vista battle and to receive delegations of supporters.[10] During late August and early September Taylor took his family on a vacation to a small cottage on the water-

7. David M. Potter, *The Impending Crisis, 1848–1861* (New York, 1976), 74–75; Haun, "Whig Abolitionists," 270; Arthur C. Cole, *The Whig Party in the South* (Washington, 1913), 126; Clement Eaton, *Jefferson Davis: The Sphinx of the Confederacy* (New York, 1977), 68–69; Joseph P. Comegys, *Memoir of John M. Clayton* (Wilmington, 1882), 164–65; *Congressional Globe*, 30th Cong., 1st Sess., 898–99, 927.

8. ZT to Webb, July 23, 1848, in James Watson Webb Papers, Yale: M&A; to Lippard, July 24, 1848, in *Niles' Weekly Register*, LXXIV (1848), 165; to Rives, July 26, 1848, in William C. Rives Papers, Box 78, LC; to Edward Kent, July 27, 1848, in Miscellaneous Papers, HM 23148, Huntington Library; to William Holdredge, July 29, 1848, in William H. Seward Papers, Rush Rhees Library, University of Rochester; Rayback, *Free Soil*, 270.

9. ZT to AG, July 13, 19, 31, 1848, in AGLR 1848, T-305 (M567/394), AGRR, XXIV, T-339 (M711/21), ZT(LC), ser 2, r 1.

10. Governor Isaac Johnson to ZT, June 30, 1848, in ZT(UKL); ZT to L. T. Wilson *et al.*, July 7, 1848, in ZT(LC), ser 2, r 1; William H. Adams, *The Whig Party of Louisiana* (Lafayette La., 1973), 172. On July 3, President Polk forwarded the congressional gold medal struck in honor of the Monterrey victory. Polk to ZT, July 3, 1848, in ZT(UKL).

front in East Pascagoula, Mississippi, near the mouth of the Singing River.[11]

During the late fall Taylor prepared for the marriage on December 5 of his youngest daughter Betty to William W. S. Bliss, known to the Taylor family as "Perfect Bliss." Surprisingly, we have no description of the wedding. The bride, however, was universally described as a charming and lovely young woman who had grown into a smart and unspoiled twenty-two year old. She had acquired a very good education for the times and had sharpened it during her father's absence in Mexico by serving as her mother's companion and keeper of the household accounts. Taylor, who had grown dependent on and fond of Bliss, did not oppose this marriage. Clearly, Betty and Perfect Bliss were a particularly well-matched pair.[12]

Part of the concern that troubled Taylor's supporters was the continuing accusation that he was not truly a Whig. Contributing substantially to the misapprehension was his response to the dissident South Carolina Democrats who offered a Taylor–W. O. Butler slate. Taylor acknowledged the nomination in a friendly letter which merely promised he would do his best if elected, a response which left the unfortunate implication that he was comfortable with some Democratic policies. Fillmore was so disturbed by the "poor Whig" charge that he wrote Taylor in mid-August to point out the dangers. Others believed that a second Allison letter was needed to correct the course of the campaign. Among them were the three promoters of the first letter, Baylie Peyton, Logan Hunton, and Alexander C. Bullitt. They seem to have conferred in New Orleans during late August and Bullitt may also have met with Taylor there about September 1. We do know that on September 4 Bullitt traveled to East Pascagoula, where Taylor signed a second letter addressed to John Allison. Its author is not known but probably reflects the common effort of Taylor and Bullitt. In the missive Taylor complained that he had been misrepresented and misunderstood. He pointed out that all who served with him in Mexico knew that he was a Whig in principle. Moreover, while in Mexico he had been nominated by popular assemblies of Whigs, Democrats, and Native Americans but had declined all of them so as not to appear partisan. Taylor continued that he was not a partisan candidate but would be the president of all the people. He promised not to impose indiscriminate, politically motivated personnel changes nor to coerce Con-

11. ZT to AG, August 22, 1848, in AGRL, XXIV, T-392 (M711/21); Hamilton, *Taylor*, II, 21.

12. William H. Samson (ed.), *Letters of Zachary Taylor From the Battle-Fields of the Mexican War* (Rochester, 1908), xii; Hudson Strode, *Jefferson Davis, American Patriot* (New York, 1955), 209; Hamilton, *Taylor*, II, 25–26, 136. After Bliss's death in 1853 she married Philip Dandridge of Winchester, Va.

gress with vetoes of constitutional legislation. It was, Taylor later promised Crittenden, the last letter he would write during the campaign.[13]

During the last two months of the campaign Crittenden took charge. He deployed speakers like a general and with a skill and deftness which would have done credit to Thurlow Weed. At the same time he maintained a massive correspondence with lieutenants like Truman Smith, Reverdy Johnson, Abbott Lawrence, Alexander Stephens, and Robert Toombs. Lincoln, for instance, spoke in Massachusetts and Illinois; Clayton in the Middle Atlantic states; and Seward in New York, New England, the middle states, and Ohio, where his abolitionist credentials made him a useful counterbalance to the Free Soilers.[14] Also contributing to the growing strength of the Taylor campaign was Daniel Webster's belated endorsement on September 1. It was lukewarm because the Massachusetts statesman merely regarded Taylor as less dangerous than Cass, who had opposed both the Webster-Ashburton and Oregon treaties and had supported war with Mexico, and whom Webster considered to be a rash partisan of Manifest Destiny. Van Buren and the leaders of the Free Soil party had destroyed their image in Webster's eyes by voting for the annexation of Texas.[15] It is indicative of the lack of partisanship in Taylor's personality that he showed little pique at the limited support he received from Webster and Clay.[16] It is also characteristic that he sought neither their support nor their advice while president.

Taylor showed more than normal circumspection in responding to letters from Clayton and Truman Smith requesting comments on a rumored expedition, supposedly supported by the administration, to seize northern Mexico. Taylor responded with a letter supporting the upholding of the neutrality laws and voicing his opposition to the acquisition of

13. Rayback, *Free Soil*, 269, 274–75; ZT to W. B. Pringle, August 9, 1848, in *Niles' Weekly Register*, LXXIV (1848), 165; Fillmore to ZT, August 19, 1848, in ZT(UKL); ZT to Allison, September 4, 1848, in Hamilton, *Taylor*, II, 121–24; Joseph G. Rayback, "Who Wrote the Allison Letters," *MVHR*, XXXVI (1949–50), 71; ZT to Crittenden, September 23, 1848, in Miscellaneous Papers, NYHS.

14. Albert D. Kirwan, *John J. Crittenden* (Lexington, 1962), 232–33; Basler (ed.), *Collected Lincoln*, II, 1–9, 11–14; Mary Wilhelmine Williams, "John M. Clayton," in Samuel Flagg Bemis and Robert H. Ferrell (eds.), *American Secretaries of State* (18 vols.; New York, 1927–72), VI, 3; Thornton Kirkland Lathrop, *William Henry Seward* (Boston, 1896), 55–56.

15. Richard N. Current, *Daniel Webster and the Rise of National Conservatism* (Boston, 1955), 155–56; Claude Moore Fuess, *Daniel Webster* (2 vols.; Boston, 1930), II, 191. See also Webster to R. M. Blatchford, September 18, 1848, in Fletcher Webster (ed.), *The Private Correspondence of Daniel Webster* (2 vols.; Boston, 1857), II, 285–86.

16. See ZT to George Lunt, November 17, 1848, in Louis A. Warren Lincoln Library and Museum, Fort Wayne, Indiana; to Clay, November 17, 1848, in Colton (ed.), *Private Correspondence of Clay*, 580–81.

any additional Mexican lands but forbade publication of the letter since he felt "it may be construed by my enemies as an assault on the authorities at Washington." Apparently, Clayton and Smith were responding to confused rumors of efforts to support a revolt in Yucatan in which a number of discharged veterans of the fighting in Mexico participated with at least the silent assent of the Polk administration.[17]

The efforts of various southern politicians to develop unity undoubtedly assisted the Taylor campaign in the region. Although directed at creating and maintaining a defense of the section's interests, especially slavery, the effort weakened the attachment of many Democrats to their party and eased their concern at following the Whig banner. This type of thinking had made possible the nomination of the Taylor and Butler ticket by the South Carolina dissidents.[18]

As events developed, however, the election turned on voting in the North. Balloting occurred on November 7, when for the first time the entire nation went to the polls on the same day. Either for that reason or because of voter disenchantment, the turnout was light. Only 2,880,572 men voted. They represented less than 13.1 percent of the total population of 22 million, or 77.1 percent of the eligible voters. Four years earlier the percentages had been 13.8 and 82.4 for these categories. Taylor carried all of New England except Maine and New Hampshire, the three Middle-Atlantic states, and the four border ones. In the South he carried four (Florida, Georgia, Louisiana, and North Carolina) of the seven. He carried no western state. He carried 671 counties but lost 747 to Cass and 31 to Van Buren. Nevertheless, Taylor held a plurality of the popular vote with 1,360,099 as opposed to 1,220,544 for Cass and 291,263 for Van Buren. The latter was on the ballot of only seventeen of the thirty states. Nevertheless, the Free Soil ticket outpolled Cass and Butler in Massachusetts, New York, and Vermont. The electoral vote added up to Taylor 163, Cass 127, and Van Buren 0.

Taylor carried four states that Clay lost in 1844: Georgia, Louisiana, New York, and Pennsylvania, worth 78 electoral votes, plus the new state of Florida with 3 votes. He lost the 23 votes of Ohio. The critical area for Taylor was the Middle-Atlantic, where he ran 12,000 votes ahead of Clay despite a nearly 14,000 vote drop in New York. Without the votes of

17. ZT to Clayton, September 4, October 2, 1848, in John M. Clayton Papers, II, 261–62, 264, LC. For the Yucatan mercenaries see Nelson Reed, *The Caste War of Yucatan* (Stanford, 1961), 111; Edward S. Wallace, *Destiny and Glory* (New York, 1950), 35–52.

18. For a good discussion of the unity efforts see Philip May Hamer, *The Secession Movement in South Carolina* (Allentown, Pa., 1918), 22–37; William J. Cooper, Jr., *The South and the Politics of Slavery, 1828–1856* (Baton Rouge, 1978), 264–66.

	1848 Popular Vote			1848 Electoral Vote		1844 Popular Vote			1844 Electoral Vote	
	Taylor (Whig)	Cass (Demo.)	Van Buren (F.S.)	W.	D.	Polk (Demo.)	Clay (Whig)	Birney (Liberty)	D.	W.
Alabama	30,482	31,363	0		9	37,740	26,084	0	9	
Arkansas	7,588	9,300	0		3	9,546	5,504	0	3	
Connecticut	30,314	27,046	5,005	6		29,841	32,832	1,943		6
Delaware	6,421	5,898	80	3		5,996	6,278	0		3
Florida	3,116	1,847	0	3		Not yet state				
Georgia	47,544	44,802	0	10		44,177	42,100	0	10	
Illinois	53,047	56,300	15,774		9	57,920	45,528	3,570	9	
Indiana	69,907	74,745	8,100		12	70,181	67,867	2,106	12	
Iowa	11,084	12,093	1,126		4	Not yet state				
Kentucky	67,141	49,720	0	12		51,988	61,255	0		12
Louisiana	18,217	15,370	0	6		13,782	13,083	0	6	
Maine	35,125	39,880	12,096		9	45,719	34,378	4,836	9	
Maryland	37,702	34,528	125	8		32,676	35,984	0		8
Massachusetts	61,070	35,281	38,058	12		52,846	67,418	10,860		12
Michigan	23,940	30,687	10,389		5	27,759	24,337	3,632	5	
Mississippi	25,922	26,537	0		6	25,126	19,206	0	6	
Missouri	32,671	40,077	0		7	41,369	31,251	0	7	
N. Hampshire	14,781	27,763	7,560		6	27,160	17,866	4,161	6	
New Jersey	40,015	36,901	829	7		37,495	38,318	131		7
New York	218,603	114,318	120,510	36		237,588	232,482	15,812	36	
N. Carolina	43,550	34,869	0	11		39,287	43,232	0		11
Ohio	138,360	154,775	35,354		23	149,117	155,057	8,050		23
Pennsylvania	185,513	171,176	11,263	26		167,535	161,203	3,138	26	
Rhode Island	6,779	3,646	730	4		4,867	7,322	107		4
S. Carolina	Electors apptd. by legislature				9	Electors apptd. by legislature			9	
Tennessee	64,705	58,419	0	13		59,917	60,030	0	9	
Texas	4,509	10,668	0		4	Not yet state				
Vermont	23,122	10,948	13,837	6		18,041	26,770	3,954		6
Virginia	45,124	46,586	9		17	49,570	43,677	0	17	
Wisconsin	13,747	15,001	10,418		4	Not yet state				
TOTAL	1,360,099	1,220,544	291,263	163	127	1,337,243	1,299,062	62,300	170	105

Pennsylvania and New York, Taylor would not have been elected. The voters of the two industrial states reacted quite differently. In Pennsylvania the Whig alliance with the strong Nativist faction combined with popular reaction against the Walker Tariff to bring out 38,000 more voters than four years earlier, and the Whig total increase by 24,000 votes. In New York 32,000 fewer voters visited the polls than in 1844 but the defectors to the Free Soilers were 9:1 Democrats. No states shifted in New England although both major parties lost support, the Democrats at twice the rate of the Whigs.

Taylor carried the Border States, as Clay had, with a plurality of about 28,000 votes, more than twice the Whig majority four years before. Taylor swept four of the seven Deep South states with a majority of over 12,000 votes, two-thirds of it coming from the Whig stronghold of North Carolina. Nevertheless, the regional total represented a shift of 25,000 votes from 1844 and moved both Georgia and Louisiana into the Whig column. It was in the great arc of western states stretching from Ohio to Arkansas and Texas that Cass ran best. He carried all of the western states with a regional plurality of nearly 49,000 votes. Only one of them, Ohio, had supported Clay four years earlier. The Free Soil defections in the Buckeye State were the critical factor, drawing heavily from the Whigs, whose vote dropped over 16,000. How badly Taylor was hurt in Indiana and Missouri by the memories of his castigation of their soldiers is unclear, since he outpolled Clay in both states.[19]

Whether Taylor voted for himself is not certain. The New Orleans *Weekly Delta* on November 27 published a story describing a discussion between the president-elect and a stranger who did not initially recognize him, during which Taylor reputedly claimed: "I did not vote for General Taylor; and my family, especially the old lady is strongly opposed to his election."[20] Neither did the Taylor victory appeal to the outgoing president. Polk confided to his diary that the results were "to be deeply regret-

19. Hamilton, *Taylor*, II, 131–34; Van Deusen, *Jacksonian Era*, 260–61; Rayback, *Free Soil*, 279–302; Bureau of the Census, *Historical Statistics of the United States* (Washington, 1960), 685–689; Edgar Allan Holt, "Party Politics in Ohio, 1840–1850," *Ohio Archaeological and Historical Publications*, XXXVIII (1929), 281–318; Edwin H. Price, "Election of 1848 in Ohio," *ibid.*, XXXVI (1927), 255–90; W. G. L. Smith, *The Life and Times of Lewis Cass* (New York, 1856), 657–58; Randolph Campbell, "The Whig Party of Texas in the Elections of 1848 and 1852," *SWHQ*, LXXIII (1969–70), 19, 21; Andrew C. McLaughlin, *Lewis Cass* (1899; rpr. New York, 1980), 259–61; William E. Gienapp, "Politics Seem to Enter Into Everything," in Stephen E. Maizlish and John J. Kushma (eds.), *Essays on American Antebellum Politics, 1840–1860* (College Station, Tex., 1982), 18; Thomas B. Alexander, "The Dimensions of Voter Partisan Constancy in Presidential Elections from 1840 to 1860," *ibid.*, 72–73.

20. Quoted in Adams, *Whig Party of Louisiana*, 181.

ted," since Taylor was "without political information and without experience in civil life." The Tennessean thought the general "wholly unqualified for the station" and feared that he would be manipulated by devious Whig politicians. Nor was Polk alone in fearing Taylor would be a captive of his advisors. Lieutenant Thomas Williams, who was part of Scott's official family, concluded that since he "cannot conceive that one man could be more indebted to another than T[aylor] is to B[liss]," the success of the administration would depend on the quality of the men around the president. Williams feared that they would be incompetents.[21]

Not all Democrats, however, viewed Taylor in such negative terms. Vice President George M. Dallas considered the president-elect to be "an observing & reflecting man . . . vastly superior in natural endowment and public service" to men like James Buchanan. "Taylor," he concluded, "is a man of Providence" who may "for some purposes be greater than Washington or Jackson." Unfortunately for the historian, Dallas did not specify those purposes. Even George Bancroft, a partisan Democrat to the ends of his fingers, admitted, "Taylor is, I believe honest and firm; but he is a decided Whig."[22]

More interesting, but no better defined than the dynamics of his victory, were Taylor's political beliefs on the eve of the organization of his administration. Taylor insisted that they were fundamentally Jeffersonian but he never defined closely what he thought the term encompassed. It can be inferred, however, that he took it to be a government based upon a broad electorate with a limited concentration of power in the central administration. He believed in the supremacy of the legislative branch in domestic areas but took seriously the constitutional provisions placing foreign affairs in the hands of the president. As he often said, he did not believe that a president should be presumptive and veto a bill merely to stop legislation with which he did not agree. The veto, he held, should be reserved for the prevention of enactment of unconstitutional legislation. Nor did he plan a wholesale removal of government workers appointed by the outgoing administration.

Upon the more immediate issues, he believed that the reestablishment of the Bank of the United States was no longer feasible, no matter how close it might be to the hearts of many Congressional Whigs. Time would prove him correct. Unlike many of the eastern and northern Whigs, Taylor opposed a protective tariff, wishing to limit it to a source of revenue

21. James K. Polk, *The Diary of James K. Polk During His Presidency, 1845 to 1849*, ed. Milo Milton Quaife (4 vols.; Chicago, 1910), IV, 184; Williams to Hitchcock, November 8, 1848, in Ethan Allen Hitchcock Papers, Box 2, LC.

22. Roy F. Nichols (ed.), "The Library, the Mystery of the Dallas Papers," *The Pennsylvania Magazine of History and Biography*, LXXIII (1949), 480–81; M. A. DeWolfe Howe, *The Life and Letters of George Bancroft* (2 vols.; New York, 1908), II, 40–41.

only. There, as in the Bank of the United States controversy, his southern and agrarian sympathies were evident. He broke with many southerners, however, in favoring internal improvements. That deviation from the traditional view of his region undoubtedly reflected the experience of an army officer long assigned to the frontier.

Taylor believed that slavery should be protected where it existed but not extended. Unlike most southerners he recognized the damaging effect on national unity of any effort to extend it into the territory acquired from Mexico. Whether Taylor realized that slavery as an economic system was incompatible with the new territory is not certain, but no one should have misread his devotion to the preservation of the Union. Whether the attachment arose from his army service or from even deeper convictions is irrelevant. It existed and came to be the driving principle of the administration.

In keeping with his Jeffersonian principles, Taylor intended to have his cabinet represent all sections and the "great interests" of the nation.[23] As a result he planned to limit the membership geographically and to seek out men who fitted his concept of interests. Taylor wished to delay his final choices until he could consult with Crittenden, to whom he would offer the position of secretary of state. But in practice selecting the cabinet proved to be particularly difficult. The president-elect seems to have tentatively decided upon Horace Binney, a noted but semiretired lawyer, as attorney general; Abbott Lawrence as secretary of the Treasury; and Clayton, although his portfolio was unsettled. Taylor kept his own counsel, causing Clayton to complain that: "Strange as it may seem, yet to this moment nothing is known [in Washington] directly from General Taylor about his cabinet." By that time, however, Taylor had decided upon the geographical apportionment of the cabinet and allotted seats to New England, Pennsylvania, Delaware, Kentucky or Tennessee, Georgia, and Virginia or North Carolina.[24]

The secrecy and caution with which Taylor made his cabinet selections mirrored his aversion to the whole problem of patronage. His repugnance to job seekers did not prevent them from making their availability known. Some genuinely hoped to be of service to the new administration while others openly sought positions with sufficient salaries to pay off their debts.[25] Although Joseph Taylor pointed out that "nobody knows or can know anything about [the cabinet] until the Prest. announces," many

23. ZT to Webb, November 2, 1848, in Webb Papers, Box 2.
24. Seward to Weed, November 29, 1848, in Weed Papers, Rush Rhees Library, University of Rochester; Clayton to David Ullmann, January 6, 1849, in Historical Society of Delaware; A. T. Burney to Crittenden, January 12, 1849, in John J. Crittenden Papers, XIII, r 7, LC; Hamilton, *Taylor*, II, 137–39; Nichols, "Mystery of the Dallas Papers," 481–82.
25. Seward to Weed, November 29, 1848, in Weed Papers.

people believed that Crittenden held the key. In their eyes he was the power broker of the new administration as well as the leading internal statesman of the Whig party. When it became clear to the Whig politicians in Washington that Taylor would not engage in the traditional political maneuvering associated with the installation of a new administration, Alexander Stephens, among others, urged Crittenden to come to Washington to help select the new administration.[26] Crittenden refused for reasons of his own, growing out of both his knowledge of the president-elect and an unwillingness to be the behind-the-scenes power in the administration. Why he shrank from the latter role has never been satisfactorily explained.

In early January Taylor rebuffed a Crittenden suggestion that he announce he would not seek a second term. Apparently the Kentuckian assumed that such a statement would relieve the president-elect of substantial pressures and consolidate Whig support, but Taylor refused to consider the idea. He responded more positively to another proposal, this one from his friend Albert T. Burnley, to establish an administration newspaper in Washington. They settled upon Alexander C. Bullitt as its editor.[27] Less successful in the long run was Taylor's encounter with Henry Clay. They met by accident at the Baton Rouge landing, but their short social conversation did nothing to close the political distance between them. There is little evidence to suggest that the president-elect even understood the political advantage to be derived from a conciliatory gesture toward Clay or any of the other old-line Whig leaders.[28]

The slow pace of preparations for the transfer of power disturbed many Whigs. Daniel Webster complained: "It is strange that there should be nobody here [in Washington] by this time possessing General Taylor's confidence. Many things require attention before the 3d of March . . . I fear that neither he nor those about him take a proper view of the state of things, and of what the future requires to be attended to now."[29] Taylor, more than any president before him and all but a handful since, was a true outsider to the Washington political scene. He had few close friends, personal or political, who were intimately acquainted with the power structure in the city. Indeed, like a number of his mid–twentieth-century

26. Coleman, Crittenden, I, 328–29; Seward to Weed, February 27, 1849, in Frederick W. Seward, Seward at Washington as Senator and Secretary of State (New York, 1891), 100.
27. Burnley to Crittenden, January 12, 1849, in Crittenden Papers XIII, r 7, LC; Hamilton, Taylor, II, 170; Kirwan, Crittenden, 226.
28. Clay to T. B. Stevenson, January 31, 1849, in Colton (ed.), Private Correspondence of Clay, 584; Hamilton, Taylor, II, 141.
29. Webster to R. M. Blatchford, February 4, 1849, in Webster, Private Correspondence, II, 295.

successors, Taylor had made a virtue of that absence. Part of the preparation for the departure for Washington involved Taylor's formal resignation from the army and his transfer to command of the Western Division
to Major General Edmund P. Gaines. The selection of the latter as the
new division commander was formally made by Secretary of War William
L. Marcy on December 15. Six days later Taylor signed his resignation,
effective February 28, 1849. On January 8 Bliss wrote Gaines that Taylor
expected to depart about the twenty-fifth and would transfer command
then. Gaines responded with a gratuitous letter of advice which included
counsel to hold at least one open house a week in Washington at which all
who wished to see the president could present themselves and their problems. As it developed Polk accepted Taylor's resignation effective January
31. The reason for the earlier date is not clear.[30]

Taylor formally surrendered command of the Western Division on
January 23. Before boarding the steamer *Princess Jr.* for Cypress Grove,
he said good-bye to his neighbors at the Spanish Cottage in Baton Rouge.
The writer and artist Thomas B. Thorpe spoke for the local well-wishers,
to whom Taylor responded with great feeling. The president-elect traveled
from Cypress Grove to Vicksburg on the packet *Saladin*, whose captain
had enticed him on board before the arrival of a second vessel with the
official delegation. From Vicksburg the Taylor party rode the side-wheeler
Tennessee to Nashville. That proved to be an eventful passage when below Memphis the steamer broke her rudder and had to be succored by a
passing craft. The accident so delayed the steamer that at Cairo, Illinois,
the welcoming crowd saluted the wrong vessel. When the *Tennessee* did
arrive it was 3:00 A.M. and Taylor had gone to bed. The locals were so
incensed at his failure to appear that they had a three-gun salute fired as
the packet left the landing "to make sure and waken him up."

The Taylor party left Nashville in the *Daniel Boone*, but at the mouth
of the Tennessee River they transferred to the larger *Courtland*, which
had a second craft lashed alongside to accommodate the overflow of local
dignitaries. On reaching Louisville, Taylor and his escort landed in order
to partake of a formal banquet at the Louisville Hotel. Immediately afterwards the party resumed their trip on the Kentucky River packet *Sea
Gull*, which carried them to Frankfort. They reached the Kentucky capital on February 15.[31]

When the *Sea Gull* arrived at 10:00 A.M. she was greeted by an artil-

30. Bliss to Gaines, January 8, 1849, in WDLB, XI, 45; Gaines to ZT, January 11, Jones
to ZT, January 2, 1849, in ZT(UKL).

31. Hamilton, *Taylor*, II, 144–45; William Owsley to Vance, February 8, 1849, in
William R. Vance Correspondence, Filson Club; Frederick Way, Jr., *Way's Packet Directory,
1848–1983* (Athens, Ohio, 1983), 379.

lery salute and a throng of people crowding the waterfront. Taylor was welcomed to the statehouse by Crittenden with a short speech and presented to the legislature. A general reception followed at the First Presbyterian Church. When Taylor and Crittenden finally were able to talk, the latter made it clear that he would not abandon the governorship. Neither man ever explained the decision but it is reasonable to believe that Crittenden wished to avoid the charge of a corrupt bargain which dogged Clay when he joined the administration of John Quincy Adams. Crittenden pressed Taylor to add Robert P. Letcher to the cabinet, probably as postmaster general. But Taylor refused to consider it because of his belief that cabinet posts were allotted to states, not to men. Since Kentucky, in the person of Crittenden, had turned down an offered post, she would have to go to the end of the line while other states had their turn. The failure to name Letcher was a mistake. He was a balanced and politically astute individual with a noted good humor. His presence would have added strength and political acumen to an administration which was notably deficient in its understanding of the workings of the federal government as it functioned during the mid–nineteenth century.

Taylor departed on the *Sea Gull* at noon on February 16. At Carrollton he transferred to the *Ben Franklin No. 8* for the trip to Cincinnati. The voyage was eventful and, for Taylor, painful. At Madison, Indiana, he was struck by a trunk being loaded on board and received a bruised side. Despite miserable weather marked by high winds and low temperatures, Taylor was welcomed to Cincinnati by a great reception, during which he suffered an injured hand. Before leaving Cincinnati he telegraphed Clayton, offering him the post as secretary of state which Crittenden had refused. Taylor embarked on the fast sidewheeler *Telegraph No. 2* intending to continue upstream to Pittsburgh but found the ice floes too much. The steamer had to abandon her voyage at Captina Island near Moundsville, Virginia. Her passengers, including Taylor, walked to the village where they procured sleighs. On the twentieth a reported 10,000 people welcomed the president-elect to Wheeling.[32]

The following day Taylor and his party left for Washington. They journeyed by sleigh and coach along the icy Cumberland Road to Cumberland, Maryland, arriving during the twenty-second. By now the president-elect had a cold to add to his injuries. After a reception and night's sleep at Cumberland, the party boarded the train for Baltimore. At 4:00

32. Way, *Packet Directory*, 48, 114, 119, 352, 389, 414, 422, 446, 448; Kirwan, *Crittenden*, 238–40; William O. Lynch, "Zachary Taylor as President," *JSH*, IV (1938), 283; Hamilton, *Taylor*, II, 145–46. See also J. C. Hall to Clayton, February 16, 1849, in Clayton Papers, III, 407, LC.

P.M. the next day they reached the Relay House, where Taylor received welcoming committees from Baltimore and Washington and was reunited with his brother Joseph. Joining them there also was Colonel Bliss, his wife, Mrs. Taylor, and Dr. Wood, all of whom had come overland. About 3,000 Baltimorians gathered around the hotel to honor the visitor who, to one in the crowd, looked like a "much fatigued" old man. Later in the evening Taylor boarded the train to complete the trip to Washington.

Once again the guns roared, bonfires blazed, and a huge crowd lined the way from the Baltimore and Ohio Station to the Willard Hotel. Yet when Taylor appeared briefly on the hotel's balcony many in the crowd mistook him for Navy Department clerk John Boyle. The cold, the injuries, and the rigors of the trip tired him. Taylor sensibly rested during the twenty-fourth and twenty-fifth. He received few, if any, visitors outside of the family.[33]

Between noon and 1:00 P.M. on February 26 Taylor visited the White House to pay his respects to President Polk. It solved a protocol problem which had confounded Polk's cabinet. They could not decide whether to call on the president-elect before he visited the White House. Taylor spent about half an hour with the president and accepted an invitation to dine at the White House on Thursday, March 1. He then returned to the Willard to receive callers. That afternoon they included Secretary of State Buchanan, Alexander H. Stephens, Webster, and the diarist Philip Hone.[34]

They found an undistinguished looking man. One caller likened him to "the plain, respectable, painstaking ordinary citizen." Another observer reported: "If you should see him on a load of hay—taking it to market—you would imagine him perhaps a farmer—worth a good substantial property. But as for scholarship—statesmanship or any other pursuit requiring a high order of intellect—he must be destitute of. . . . His eye is the only thing noticeable. It indicates considerable firmness and keeness of perception."[35]

Taylor continued to receive callers during the twenty-seventh. They included the remainder of Polk's cabinet and Vice-President Dallas. The latter was disappointed. "If he has any intellectual greatness," he commented, "physiognomy is a cheat." The joint congressional committee charged with notifying the president-elect of the election results also

33. Hamilton, *Taylor*, II, 146–47; James Todd to wife, February 26, 1849, in Miscellaneous Papers, HSPa.

34. Hamilton, *Taylor*, II, 149; Eugene Irving McCormac, *James K. Polk: A Political Biography* (1922; rpr. New York, 1965), 736; Polk, *Diary*, IV, 358.

35. Nichols, "Mystery of the Dallas Papers," 515; E. P. Hollister to W. M. Black, March 11, 1849, in Hagaman Collection, MoHS.

called. Jefferson Davis, who was a member, relayed Taylor's formal acceptance and wish to be inaugurated on March 5. Seward and Fillmore
called, hoping to discuss the cabinet selections. They learned that Taylor
had already settled upon his choices, relying upon the advice of Crittenden, which Seward viewed as being at once "honest, misconceived,
and erroneous." But, he added, "General Taylor relied upon it implicitly."
It was also an inauspicious start for the uneasy alliance between the New
York Whig factions. During the evening of the twenty-seventh Taylor was
guest of honor at a dinner given by Speaker of the House Robert C.
Winthrop.[36]

The conferences continued during the twenty-eighth, although Taylor
took time to visit Georgetown during the afternoon to make a short address. Apparently because his exertions had tired him too much, Taylor
did not attend the levee given at the White House that evening by
the Polks. The following morning Cass called but what the two men
discussed is not recorded. Taylor also met for half an hour with Seward.
That evening the president-elect joined about forty people at the White
House. Among the Polks' guests were Mrs. Dallas (her husband was kept
at the Capitol presiding over a late Senate session), Cass, Fillmore, the
cabinet along with Mrs. Robert Walker, Marcy, and Isaac Toucey, Supreme Court Justice and Mrs. John Catron, Senator and Mrs. John Bell,
Jefferson Davis, and Colonel and Mrs. Bliss. Taylor sat on Mrs. Polk's
right and Cass on her left. The evening went well and lasted until 10:00
or 11:00 P.M.[37]

On Sunday, March 4, 1849, the Thirtieth Congress adjourned.[38] It had
not settled the question of the organization of the new territories nor the
whole issue of sectional rights. Those problems and a host of others
awaited both the Thirty-first Congress and the new administration. It was
an administration more poorly prepared than most to handle the diver-
gent pressures. Zachary Taylor, the outsider, arrived in Washington with

36. Hamilton, *Taylor*, II, 149; Robert McElroy, *Jefferson Davis, the Unreal and the Real*
(2 vols.; New York, 1937), I, 111; Seward, *Seward at Washington*, 100–101; John M.
Belohlavek, *George Mifflin Dallas, Jacksonian Patrician* (University Park, Pa., 1977), 132.
Clayton's draft of the statement to be read to the notification committee by Taylor is in the
Clayton Papers, VIII, LC.

37. Hamilton, *Taylor*, II, 150; Polk, *Diary*, IV, 358–59; Fillmore to Gilbert Davis, January 22, 1853, in Frank H. Severance (ed.), *Millard Fillmore Papers* (2 vols.; 1907; rpr. New
York, 1971), II, 337; Seward to Weed, March 1, 1849, in Seward, *Seward at Washington*, 101.

38. There is a legalistic argument that because the swearing in of Taylor did not occur
until March 5 that the nation lacked a president from 1:00 P.M. on March 4 until Taylor's
oath. George H. Haynes, "President of the United States for a Single Day," *AHR*, XXX
(1924–25), 310.

an especially naïve assumption that good intentions and a genuine dedication to the common good would triumph. Moreover, he arrived with an administration less well formed and policies less well defined than any other man elected to the nation's highest office.

CHAPTER XIII

Domestic Affairs

THE FIFTH of March, 1849, dawned gusty and cold in Washington. The frosty, humid wind off the Potomac cut through the coats of the multitude of spectators and officials moving toward the Capitol for the inauguration of Zachary Taylor as the nation's twelfth president. The formal proceedings at the Capitol were spelled out in a document drawn up by a Committee on Arrangements composed of Reverdy Johnson, Jefferson Davis, and John Davis. More informal celebrations were planned for the evening, when Whigs could celebrate their return to power for the first time since the death of William Henry Harrison in 1841.

The president-elect arose in his room at Willard's Hotel, dressed warmly, and ate breakfast. Meanwhile, the proceedings began. The Senate sergeant-at-arms opened his chamber's doors at ten o'clock. The ladies' gallery immediately filled, as did the space allocated to the press. At eleven the Senate assembled to witness the administration of the oath to its new members. By now the gallery was so tightly packed that three women fainted. At 11:30 Vice-President George M. Dallas and Vice-President-elect Millard Fillmore entered the chamber arm in arm. The latter swore his oath and addressed the senators. It was a brief talk which called for patriotism during the sectional crisis. The justices of the Supreme Court and the diplomatic corps, resplendent in their dress uniforms, then filed into the Senate, taking their seats to the left and right of the vice-president. The outgoing secretaries of state and navy as well as the attorney general followed.

While the Senate attended to its constitutional duties, a cavalcade of a hundred mounted marshals made its way to the Willard. At about eleven o'clock Taylor, escorted by Speaker Robert C. Winthrop and Mayor William W. Seaton of Washington, took their staff in an open carriage drawn by four gray horses. The procession continued on to the Irving Hotel where President Polk awaited. He entered the carriage for the ride to Capitol Hill. The heavy crowds in the streets delayed the parade of vehicles for almost three-quarters of an hour. During the trip Polk understood Taylor to say that California and Oregon were too distant to become states and their inhabitants would be better served by independence. There is no evidence to indicate that Taylor really believed that to be the case, which suggests that Polk misunderstood what his successor said. The ride convinced Polk that Taylor "is . . . a well meaning old man. He is, however, uneducated, exceeding ignorant of public affairs, and I should judge of very ordinary capacity." That judgment, long held by Polk, indicated their face-to-face meetings had produced no amelioration.[1]

The procession finally reached the Capitol at about 12:30. The Senate promptly adjourned and its members joined the Supreme Court justices and the diplomatic corps in following Taylor to the East Portico. From there he could look across a crowd of 10,000 people to the artillery battery which stood poised to salute its new commander-in-chief. After the initial ceremonies on the platform, Taylor was introduced and delivered an address which one observer commented "was remarkable only for its brevity, simplicity, good idiomatic English, and the absence of great promises in high sounding phrases."[2]

The inaugural address was a statement of Taylor's philosophy of severely limited presidential leadership. He looked to Congress, he said, "to accept such measures of conciliation as may harmonize conflicting interests and tend to perpetuate that Union which should be the paramount object of our hopes and affections." He would support any action directed to that end. "Chosen by the body of the people under the assurance that my Administration would be devoted to the welfare of the whole country, and not to the support of any particular section or merely local interest, I this day renew the determination to maintain to the extent of my ability the Government in its original purity." He continued, promising to "make honesty, capacity, and fidelity" the prerequisites for appointment or continuation in government service. All in all, it was an address notable for its failure to offer a solution to the sectional division or the territorial question, or to suggest any other programs. Following the

1. James K. Polk, *Diary of James K. Polk During His Presidency, 1845 to 1849*, ed. Milo Milton Quaife, (4 vols.; Chicago, 1910), IV, 374–76.

2. Nathan Sargent, *Public Men and Events* (2 vols.; Philadelphia, 1875), II, 342.

address Chief Justice Roger B. Taney administered the oath of office. The artillery fired its salute. The two presidents departed together and Taylor accompanied Polk back to the Irving Hotel before continuing on to the White House.

That evening the Whigs celebrated with three balls. Taylor and Fillmore drove through a snowstorm to attend each. The initial stop was at Carusi's Saloon at 11th and C streets, where the military held their ball. Then they continued on to the Washington Assembly Rooms in the Jackson Hall on Pennsylvania Avenue where the Democrats were gathered. At about 11:45 P.M. they reached the main gathering at City Hall. It had been organized by a group of 230 sponsors who included Lincoln and Robert E. Lee. The band played "Hail Columbia" as the president appeared and four to five thousand people stood and turned toward the door hoping to catch a glimpse of the man of the hour. Taylor moved around the room speaking to various political and diplomatic dignitaries. If the descriptions of the overcrowding of the hall are accurate it must have been difficult even for the president to move about. Mrs. Taylor stayed away from the festivities but the winsome Betty Bliss was much in evidence, striking in a white gown with a single flower in her dark hair. Taylor stayed about two hours. The crowd so filled the City Hall chamber that several women fainted. Moreover, the rooms set aside for eating proved to be too small and food in short supply. When the celebrants sought their wraps the cloakrooms lost all semblance of order. Lucky was the man who could reclaim his hat or his lady's coat.[3]

Since Mrs. Taylor did not feel strong enough to sit through state dinners or stand in long receiving lines, Betty Bliss agreed to serve as the official hostess in her mother's stead. Mrs. Taylor, however, was not a recluse nor did she avoid informal entertaining. She met frequently with friends like the perceptive and charming Fanny Calderón de la Barca, the wife of the Spanish minister, and Varina Davis. The first lady always participated in the informal family dinners to which a few friends were in-

3. Description of the inaugural ceremonies can be found in: "Arrangements for the Inauguration of the President Elect, on the Fifth of March, 1849," in Department of State (NA, RG 59), Miscellaneous Letters March 1–April 30, 1849 (M179/117); Washington, D.C., *National Intelligencer*, March 6, 1849; Holman Hamilton, *Zachary Taylor* (2 vols.; Indianapolis, 1941, 1951), II, 155–61; Holman Hamilton, *Prologue to Conflict* (Lexington, 1964), 14; Allan Nevins, *Ordeal of the Union: Fruits of Manifest Destiny* (New York, 1947), 229; Oliver Otis Howard, *General Taylor* (New York, 1892), 315–23; Brainerd Dyer, *Zachary Taylor* (Baton Rouge, 1946), 307–309; Robert J. Rayback, *Millard Fillmore* (Buffalo, 1959), 194–99. Taylor's address is in James D. Richardson (ed.), *A Compilation of the Messages and Papers of the Presidents* (20 vols.; New York, 1897–1922), VI, 2543–44; Fillmore's is reprinted in Frank H. Severance (ed.), *Millard Fillmore Papers* (2 vols., 1907; rpr. New York, 1971), I, 287–88.

vited. As a devout Episcopalian, Mrs. Taylor nearly every day attended service at St. John's Episcopal Church across Lafayette Park from the White House. Moreover, she enjoyed gathering members of her family about her. They included Joseph Taylor's teenage daughter Rebecca, then in school in Georgetown, various nieces and nephews, and her own grandchildren. For them Mrs. Taylor's sitting room was the center of activity in the White House. It surprised few who knew her that the White House frequently resounded to the gaiety of dances and children's parties.

Taylor's own association with the society of Washington was not appreciably limited despite Mrs. Taylor's abhorrence of large gatherings. The president occasionally joined in the capital's social events, as in May 1850 when he was among the three hundred people "of historical fame" who attended the wedding of Secretary of the Interior Thomas Ewing's daughter Ellen to Brevet Captain William Tecumseh Sherman of the army. Frequently, also, Taylor walked in the White House grounds shaking hands with tourists who gazed through the fence or patted "Old Whitey" as he grazed there.[4]

Taylor so despised patronage that he refused to participate in the distribution of offices to his friends, supporters, or deserving party faithful. He assigned that responsibility to his cabinet, the first time that a president had done so. The pressure on many of the cabinet, notably Clayton, who was the acknowledged senior patronage dispenser, was more than they were capable of withstanding. Indeed, the administration did not initially know how many patronage posts it had to fill, since Polk took the Executive Journal with him when he left the White House. The number of Democrats removed was relatively high for the period, although most served outside of Washington.[5]

The administrative principles followed by Taylor as chief executive bore a strong resemblance to those adopted by the other two soldier–presidents. He, as they had, readily delegated well-delineated authority to individual subordinates. The cabinet members, in effect, were his brigade and division leaders responsible for the day-to-day activities of their com-

4. Lady Emmeline Stuart-Wortley, "American Nobilities," *Harper's New Monthly Magazine*, III (1851), 387; Ishbel Ross, *First Lady of the South* (New York, 1958), 58, 60; Hamilton, *Taylor*, II, 171–72; William H. Samson (ed.), *Letters of Zachary Taylor from the Battle-Fields of the Mexican War* (Rochester, 1908), ix; W. T. Sherman to P. F. Smith, August 4, 1850, in Miscellaneous Letters, HSPa.

5. George W. Parry, "A Century of Cabinet Ministers," *Magazine of American History*, XXIII (1890), 397; Eugene Irving McCormac, *James K. Polk, a Political Biography* (1922; rpr. New York, 1965), 720; Carl Russell Fish, "Removal of Officials by the Presidents of the United States," *Annual Report of the American Historical Association for the Year 1899* (2 vols.; Washington, 1900), I, 78; Richardson Dougall and Mary Patricia Chapman, *United States Chiefs of Mission, 1778–1973* (Washington, 1973), 7–165.

mands and for recommending actions to be taken by the entire administration. As a commander it was his responsibility to oversee their activities but not to interfere unless disaster threatened. As field leader Taylor had made use of councils of war to collect advice and seems to have regarded his cabinet meetings in a similar fashion. As an experienced commander, Taylor recognized that men who proved unequal to their assignments had to be replaced. This he was willing to do, but neither in the field nor in Washington did he ruthlessly exercise the power.

Since the cabinet played a critical role in his administrative formulations, its selection consumed a great amount of Taylor's time prior to his arrival in the White House. John M. Clayton took the State Department. He was a distinguished fifty-two-year-old Delaware lawyer and politician who had been educated at Yale and the Litchfield Law School. He had a reputation as a *bon-vivant* and a six-foot-tall, slightly portly figure to support the claim. His twinkling gray eyes shown from beneath black brows but white hair topped his head. Actually, he was badly worn down by the deaths of nearly all his close relatives and was fast becoming an alcoholic. His polished manners, brilliant conversation, and intellect seemed to fit him perfectly for the post, but experience proved otherwise. He was too kind-hearted and unselfish to be a good administrator and too indolent to lead the cabinet. Moreover, Taylor relied so heavily on him for nondiplomatic activities, such as patronage, that it magnified his natural shortcomings.[6]

Taylor's initial choice for secretary of the treasury had been the distinguished Philadelphia lawyer Horace Binney, but he had shown no desire for the post and the Pennsylvania Whig congressional delegation supported Andrew Stewart. The president, seemingly acting on the suggestion of Clayton, chose instead William M. Meredith. He was a fifty-year-old Philadelphia lawyer and local politician, little known nationally. He proved to be an admirable selection and became one of the strongest members of the cabinet.[7]

The selection of Meredith as secretary of the treasury disrupted Taylor's plans for a Navy Department head. He offered the post to Abbott

6. Anson Phelps Stokes, *Memorials of Eminent Yale Men* (2 vols.; New Haven, 1914), II, 207, 209; Franklin Bowditch Dexter, *Biographical Sketches of the Graduates of Yale College with Annals of the College History* (7 vols.; New Haven, 1885–1912), VII, 738–40; Joseph P. Comegys, *Memoir of John M. Clayton* (Wilmington, 1882), 23–159; Mary Wilhelmine Williams, "John M. Clayton," in Samuel Flagg Bemis and Robert H. Ferrell (eds.), *American Secretaries of State* (18 vols.; New York, 1927–72), VI, 4–10.

7. *Dictionary of American Biography*, XII, 548; Roy F. Nichols, "The Library, the Mystery of the Dallas Papers," *Pennsylvania Magazine of History and Biography*, LXXIII (1949), 516; Hamilton, *Taylor*, II, 163.

Lawrence but the Massachusetts manufacturer, peeved at being passed over for the Treasury post, refused the Navy assignment. T. Butler King of Georgia, one of the congressional specialists in naval affairs, hoped for the appointment but was vetoed by Robert Toombs and Howell Cobb. The Navy post ultimately went to William Ballard Preston, whom Taylor had initially slated for attorney general. He had to be dropped as the chief legal officer when former senator William Archer protested his weakness as a courtroom lawyer. Nevertheless, Preston was a responsible if not brilliant administrator who served Taylor loyally. He was a forty-three-year-old Virginian, a lawyer, and an experienced politician. More interested in politics than the navy, he was passionately concerned with solving the sectional issue. His sponsorship by Alexander H. Stephens and Toombs undoubtedly led Taylor to assume that he had more influence among southern leaders than proved to be the case.[8]

Crittenden suggested Toombs be given the War Department. He refused and joined Stephens in recommending the appointment of George W. Crawford. Taylor quickly concurred. The secretary of war designate was a fifty-year-old Georgia lawyer and former governor with a reputation as a superior administrator to whom no hint of scandal attached. He developed only limited influence within the administration and controlled only minimal patronage outside of it. Crawford's service would be marred by the controversy which developed over his involvement in the Galphin claims.[9]

Senator Reverdy Johnson of Maryland, who had campaigned extensively behind the scenes for the job, received the attorney general assignment at Clayton's suggestion after Preston proved unqualified. A noted constitutional lawyer, Johnson may have been the hardest-working member of the cabinet. His was a stepchild office with so few assistants that he had to write his own briefs and to argue the government's cases in person before the Supreme Court. Because of his quick mind and uniform courtesy his service as the government's chief legal officer was highly successful. He was a distant relative of Mrs. Taylor but the relationship played no role in his appointment.[10]

When Meredith P. Gentry of Tennessee declined to leave the House of Representatives to assume the postmaster general's position, Taylor tentatively assigned it to Thomas Ewing. But that plan was upset by other re-

8. Harold D. Langley, "William Ballard Preston," in Paolo E. Coletta, Robert G. Albion, and K. Jack Bauer (eds.), *American Secretaries of the Navy* (2 vols.; Annapolis, 1980), I, 243–44, 254; Hamilton, *Taylor*, II, 165; Hamilton Andrews Hill, *Memoir of Abbot Lawrence* (Boston, 1884), 83.

9. Hamilton, *Taylor*, II, 164; *DAB*, IV, 520.

10. Hamilton, *Taylor*, II, 165–66; *DAB*, X, 113.

fusals to leave the House, this time by Truman Smith and John Davis, who refused the newly created post of head of the Home (later Interior) Department, as did Abbott Lawrence. Ewing then was shifted to Interior. He was an old warhorse of a politician who had served in the Senate as early as 1830 and had been Harrison's secretary of the Treasury. A successful lawyer in his native Ohio, he had brought up William T. Sherman, who would marry his daughter Ellen. Ewing was a strong believer in the spoils system, which he installed in the Interior Department.[11]

The postmaster general appointment, for which Crittenden had proposed Robert P. Letcher, went to former representative Jacob Collamer of Vermont. Although recommended by a legislative caucus, Collamer is probably the least-known member of the cabinet. He was considered plodding and narrow by some contemporaries but perceptive and commonsensical by others. Inasmuch as he disliked patronage politics, he was an odd choice for a post which included in its duties bestowing the nation's postmasterships as rewards for party fealty. Consequently he was often bypassed by other cabinet members when they were dispensing posts.[12]

The selections were generally respectable, solid appointments. Collamer and Preston were probably the weakest. Collamer, who had the most patronage jobs to dispense, found it very difficult to replace postmasters whose only sin was that they were Democrats. Preston was upright, honorable, and not without innovative ideas, but he was a poor administrator and very ignorant of the navy. He is supposed to have been surprised to learn that vessels were hollow and to have confused the boatswain of the ship-of-the-line *Pennsylvania* with her commander. Meredith and Ewing were better than competent men for their offices. Crawford was a successful secretary of war until his usefulness was destroyed by the Galphin Claims scandal. Clayton should have been the leader of the cabinet but he was a poor administrator, indecisive, and a difficult colleague. The ablest member was Reverdy Johnson. Four of the seven men were southerners but only Crawford came from the cotton-growing area. The group was heavy with pro-bank and pro-tariff Whigs (Clayton, Meredith, Ewing, and Collamer) but they never succeeded in nudging Taylor in either direction. Unfortunately, most of the cabinet were also men of limited influence in Congress, and this became the nearly fatal weakness of the administration.[13]

11. Hamilton, *Taylor*, II, 163–64; *DAB*, VI, 237–38; Hill, *Lawrence*, 83.

12. Hamilton, *Taylor*, II, 165; *DAB*, IV, 300.

13. Hamilton, *Taylor*, II, 151–52, 162–66; Edward M. Steel, Jr., *T. Butler King of Georgia* (Athens, Ga., 1964), 69–70; [T. N. Parmalee], "Recollections of an Old Stager," *Harper's New Monthly Magazine*, XLVII (1873), 586–87; Myrta Lockett Avary (ed.), *Recollections*

Patronage overshadowed all else during the first months of the administration. Since they had to decide upon both replacements and hirings, the individual cabinet members were forced to devote large blocks of time to minor decisions when they should have been learning the intricacies of their departments. Although historians have focused much attention on the failure to find a place for Abraham Lincoln and the firing of Nathaniel Hawthorne from his sinecure in the Salem customshouse, these were both minor incidents which draw attention only because of the subsequent stature of the men involved.[14]

New York presented particularly difficult patronage problems for the administration since Vice-President Fillmore was part of the anti-Weed faction of the Whig party. The Weed group was represented in Albany by Governor Hamilton Fish and in Washington by Senator William H. Seward. Although Seward and Fillmore struck a deal over patronage during the early days of the administration, that did not prevent Seward from moving rapidly to cultivate the president and to gain influence in the cabinet through Clayton and Preston. The arrangement between the New York Whig factions foundered in late 1849 over the appointment of Hugh Maxwell as collector of the port of New York, a major patronage plum. The selection had been made by Taylor himself in an effort to avoid having to side with either Seward or Fillmore, but the former thought it an overly great concession to the vice-president.[15] By the latter part of March Seward could assure Weed that while he had yet to "ascertain the way upstairs through the kitchen of the White House" he had reached an understanding with some members of the cabinet on patronage. Seward's growing control of patronage caused Fillmore to fear for his standing with the

of Alexander H. Stephens (New York, 1910), 24; Dyer, Taylor, 310–17; Mrs. Chapman Coleman (ed.), The Life of John J. Crittenden (2 vols.; Philadelphia, 1871), I, 344; Albert D. Kirwan, John J. Crittenden (Lexington, 1962), 250–51; Charles M. Wiltse, John C. Calhoun, Sectionalist, 1840–1850 (Indianapolis, 1951), 394–95.

14. Both are discussed at length in Hamilton, Taylor, II, 209–14. In Lincoln's case it is clear that he muffed his chances for an appointment as commissioner of the Land Office and turned down the opportunity to become governor of Oregon. Hawthorne lost his appointment when the collectors changed.

15. ZT to Clayton, March 20, 1849, in Dreer Collection, HSPa; Fillmore to Edward Everett, July 11, 1849, in Millard Fillmore Papers, r 15, Buffalo and Erie County Historical Society; Glendon G. Van Deusen, William Henry Seward (New York, 1967), 114; [Parmalee], "Recollections," 587–88; Avary (ed.), Recollections of Stephens, 25; Thurlow Weed Barnes, Memoir of Thurlow Weed (Boston, 1884), 175; Hamilton, Taylor, II, 168–70. Seward to Weed, March 7, 1849, in Weed Papers, Rush Rhees Library, University of Rochester, denies that there was a patronage agreement. The background of the Fillmore-Seward split is explained in Henry J. Carman and Reinhard Luthin, "The Seward-Fillmore Feud and the Crisis of 1850," New York History, XXIV (1943), 166–69. See also ZT to Fish, June 26, 1849, in Hamilton Fish Papers, XIV, LC; Seward to ZT, October 19, 1849, Weed Papers.

president. In mid-December he met with Taylor for an hour-and-a-half session and emerged convinced that the chief executive remained well-disposed toward him.[16]

By April Clayton was so overwhelmed by patronage decisions that he began a campaign to entice Crittenden to Washington to take over the problem. He even suggested that Crittenden replace him, which the Kentuckian quickly refused. Crittenden suggested, however, that Orlando Brown be added to the administration as the advisor on patronage. Although appointed commissioner of Indian affairs, he devoted most of his attention to other matters during a year in Washington. In addition Brown quickly became one of Taylor's confidants, although his moderating influence could not prevent the split that developed between Taylor and Congress. Almost as soon as he reached the capital Brown called John Letcher to assist. Crittenden delayed the latter's departure from Kentucky until September because he wanted to be sure that Taylor, then on a tour, was in residence when he arrived. The former congressman, Crittenden wrote Clayton, "is full of good sense & wholesome counsel & may be the means of strengthening your hands & promoting your objects."[17]

Even Whigs with scant claim on the administration pressed for consideration. Henry Clay, for instance, asked that his son James Brown Clay be given a diplomatic post. He was named *chargé d'affaires* in Lisbon.[18] The overwhelming concentration on patronage caused former president Polk to charge that the new administration seemed to have spent all its time dispensing jobs.[19] Moreover, the president's policy of keeping out of the patronage dispensing led Abraham Lincoln to complain that it made him appear to some people as a weak leader. He should, the former Whig congressman suggested, occasionally appear to say "I take the responsibility."[20]

In the meantime Winfield Scott had shifted the headquarters of the army to New York. He felt that it would eliminate much potential friction with Taylor. Retired chief of engineers General Joseph G. Swift and Philip Hone prevailed upon Scott to visit Washington March 14 to make a formal call on the president. Although Hone reported that the meeting went

16. Seward to Weed, March 24, 1849, in Weed Papers; Fillmore to H. K. Hall, December 18, 1849, in Fillmore Papers, r 16.

17. Kirwan, *Crittenden*, 256; Hamilton, *Taylor*, II, 173; Brown to ZT, June 4, 1849, in Orlando Brown Papers, KHS; Crittenden to Clayton, August 15, September 1, 1849, in John M. Clayton Papers, VI, LC.

18. Clayton to ZT, May 12, 1849, copy in possession of the Henry Clay Papers Project, University of Kentucky; Dougall and Chapman, *Chiefs of Missions*, 126.

19. Polk to J. Y. Mason, May 17, 1849, in Clift Collection, Box 1, Yale:M&A.

20. Lincoln to Clayton, July 28, 1849, in Roy P. Basler (ed.), *The Collected Works of Abraham Lincoln* (8 vols.; New Brunswick, N.J., 1953), II, 60.

well, Scott returned to New York, much to Taylor's apparent pleasure. Lieutenant Thomas Williams observed that "any advantages gained by greater proximity to the fountain of affairs would be more than counter-balanced by the personal differences between Gen. S. and Gen. Taylor." He believed, quite correctly, that if Scott returned to Washington "the mutual repugnance between them would be more likely to be fostered by their political friends . . . than to be diminished, much less cured."[21] Scott, whose common sense could often be overshadowed by his temper, in this instance was quite sensible and remained in New York throughout the entire Taylor administration. This ensured that there would be no contest between the two great American military figures of the age or their notable egos. Nor did the ill-feeling between the two military heroes prevent cooperation on one notable occasion. Scott recommended the appointment of Nathan W. Brown, the son of Major General Jacob Brown, as a paymaster. It was an unusual appointment but argued by Scott and others on humanitarian grounds, since Brown undertook to support both the family and the widow of his predecessor, who were "left without the means of subsistence, a widow and nine children." Brown was appointed a paymaster major in September and rose to serve as paymaster general of the army after the Civil War.[22]

At no place does Taylor's lack of political experience show more clearly than in his failure to recognize the necessity of creating a substantial bloc of congressional supporters. Even if his objective, as some historians have argued, was to forge a new political party, he could not hope to achieve success without cultivating a group of supporters in Congress who would ensure that his program received publicity, if not passage. Yet, so unaware of the problem was the president that to many he appeared to go out of his way to alienate those Whigs who could have been expected to assist the administration in crafting a program attractive to a majority of the members of the legislative branch. So poor was the relationship with the Congressional Whigs that Henry Clay complained in 1850: "I have never before seen such an Administration. There is very little co-operation or concord between the two ends of the avenue. There is not, I believe, a prominent Whig in either House that has any confidential intercourse with the Executive."[23]

21. Charles Winslow Elliott, *Winfield Scott, the Soldier and the Man* (New York, 1937), 598–99; Williams to Hitchcock, June 4, 1849, in Ethan Allen Hitchcock Papers, Box 2, LC.

22. Crawford to ZT, August 28, 1849, in ZT(LC), ser 2, r 1; Francis B. Heitman, *Historical Register and Dictionary of the United States Army* (2 vols., 1903; rpr. Urbana, 1965), I, 253.

23. Clay to James Harlan, March 16, 1850, in Calvin Colton (ed.), *The Private Correspondence of Henry Clay* (New York, 1856), 604. See also William J. Cooper, Jr., *The South and the Politics of Slavery, 1828–1856* (Baton Rouge, 1978), 275.

If there is any explanation beyond ignorance or pique it is Taylor's naïve belief that domestic policy was primarily a responsibility of the legislature and not a fit area for presidential intervention. His often-stated belief that he had been elected as a nonpartisan chief executive whose actions and proposals would attract popular and congressional support because of their obvious merit further complicated his relations with Congress. The inability of Congress in the absence of presidential leadership to arrive at a politically acceptable settlement to many issues was a possibility which Taylor seems never to have considered before taking office. By the time he realized that his preconceived notions of Washington did not fit reality, the opportunity for the formation of an administration bloc in Congress had evaporated. Moreover, Taylor's failure to recognize the political weakness and isolation of his cabinet as well as the degree of his own alienation of congressional leaders ensured scant consideration of his ideas for solving the great domestic issues of the day.

A good example of Taylor's inability or unwillingness to cement relations with the old Whig leadership was his treatment of Henry Clay. The president followed up the chance meeting on the Mississippi with a letter on May 28 in which he repeated his friendly feelings. Clay, for his part, was willing to forget any rancor over the nomination and ready to support the administration if it did not diverge too far from his definition of Whig principles. The Kentuckian quickly discovered that his stand was easier to maintain in the abstract than in practice, since the administration appeared to go out of its way to slight him politically. Although invited to dinner at the White House, Clay complained late in 1849, "I have been treated with much consideration by the President and most of his cabinet; but I have had yet no confidential intercourse with the President."[24] The same treatment was the fate of most other old-line Whig leaders like Webster, Winthrop, or John Bell. The president entertained extensively, both privately and publicly, without discrimination between his supporters and others. He was more discriminating in his choice of advisors and relied on few outside of his cabinet and his small personal circle.

Taylor did recognize the value of a friendly newspaper in Washington. Even before leaving Louisiana he had accepted Albert T. Burnley's proposal to establish an administration mouthpiece. The *Republic* began operations in June with Alexander C. Bullitt, formerly an editor of the New Orleans *Picayune*, and John N. Sargent, who had previously worked

24. ZT to Clay, May 28, 1849, in Henry Clay Papers, XXVI, r 6, LC; to Mrs. J. B. Clay, December 15, 1849, in Colton (ed.), *Private Correspondence of Clay*, 592. See also Glyndon G. Van Deusen, *The Life of Henry Clay* (Boston, 1937), 393–94.

for J. Watson Webb on the New York *Courier & Enquirer*, as editors. While the paper normally supported the administration and frequently served as its spokesman, editorial loyalty was sometimes limited by Burnley's desire to reestablish a single comprehensive political group similar to the Republican party of the Era of Good Feeling. The arrangement worked reasonably well until the spring of 1850 when Bullitt, a Clay supporter who had swung to Taylor, refused to condemn the efforts to arrange a compromise settlement of the territorial dispute. In May 1850 the administration, following its open break with Clay, forced his resignation and replacement by the Tennessean Allen A. Hall.[25] Whether Hall would have built more support for the administration's program than Burnley did is debatable. The short time left in Taylor's period in office prohibits any judgment.

The concentration of the administration on the minutiae of government, like patronage, had to give way to more weighty concerns. During July reports of renewal of attacks by the Seminoles left in Florida began to reach Washington. The settlers in South Florida panicked and appealed to the president to authorize the calling out of volunteers. Even Brigadier General David E. Twiggs, who commanded the district, was swept up by the excitement, although he reported that the Indians had purchased only 120 rifles since 1842 and could put only 300 braves in the field. Taylor, true to character, refused to be stampeded. He directed Secretary Crawford to reinforce Twiggs but declined to call out the Florida militia. The president suspected, correctly as matters developed, that the peninsula did not face a general uprising. Indeed, closer investigation showed that the trouble had been the work of five young men. The difficulties were peacefully settled by the Indian agents on the scene and by a delegation of western Seminoles who arrived to calm tempers.[26]

Nor was Florida the only area bothered by Indians. The western border of Texas had traditionally suffered harassment by the plains Indians, notably the Commanche. Taylor had frequently encountered the problem during his command of the 1st Military District and of the Western Division. In August 1849 Henry L. Kinney, the Corpus Christi magnate, excitedly complained that Indian raiders had killed at least two hundred people, kidnapped women, and done $40,000 damage to property in the area between Mier and Corpus Christi. He followed that with a list of thirty-nine people who had been killed, wounded, or kidnapped from the

25. George Rawlings Poage, *Henry Clay and the Whig Party* (Gloucester, Mass., 1965), 187; Fayette Copeland, *Kendall of the Picayune* (Norman, 1943), 123n; Avery O. Craven, *Growth of Southern Nationalism* (Baton Rouge, 1953), 98.

26. Hamilton, *Taylor*, II, 183–84; *Senate Executive Documents*, 31st Cong., 1st Sess., No. 49.

Corpus Christi area alone since March. Kinney asked that a garrison be stationed at Corpus Christi. Taylor, whose policy was one of noninterference with the commander on the scene, did not alter the dispositions made by Brigadier General George M. Brooke. Although he disbelieved Kinney's claims, Brooke subsequently federalized three companies of Texas Rangers. They pacified the frontier.[27]

More serious was the outbreak of cholera in New York and New Orleans during December 1848. By May it extended as far north as Kenosha, Wisconsin, having killed 10 percent of the population in St. Louis and nearly as many in Cincinnati. Before it died out in New York City during August, 5,017 people died. Early in July Taylor proclaimed Friday, August 3, as a day of fasting and prayer over the cholera victims. It was one of the earliest, if not the first, national days of thanksgiving proclaimed in the country. In Taylor's mind the celebration undoubtedly held little religious significance. He was not a churchman, either formally or privately, insofar as surviving evidence allows us to judge. He never formally joined a church and seems not to have attended services with any regularity. Nevertheless, the day of thanksgiving drew attacks from free thinkers as "political religious canting" not sanctioned by the Constitution or law. Most Americans supported the plan. Throughout the country businesses closed for the day and churches held prayer sessions. Nonchurchgoers joined in celebration with a day of relaxation and drinking.[28]

Despite the danger from cholera the president decided to leave the oppressive heat and humidity of Washington. Traditionally, most federal officials took vacations during the summer months, leaving only a skeleton force to operate the government. Taylor needed a vacation. By mid-summer he was, one visitor recorded, "put down considerable."[29] Moreover, a sojourn away from Washington served as a mechanism for a president to reinforce his political standing. The trip, nominally to add to his knowledge of the North, was planned as a leisurely jaunt westward through central Pennsylvania to Erie and then a swing east through Buffalo, central New York, and Albany before crossing into New England to visit Boston before returning south via New York City and Philadelphia.[30] The journey started on August 9 when the presidential party went by special train to Baltimore and York. As the train entered Pennsylvania, Governor

27. Hamilton, *Taylor*, II, 185; Kinney to ZT, August 25, 1849, in ZT(LC), ser 2, r 1. The numbers were undoubtedly exaggerated.

28. Charles E. Rosenberg, *The Cholera Years* (Chicago, 1962), 101–24.

29. W. A. T. Brooks to DeLorma Brooks, July 20, 1849, in William T. H. Brooks Papers, Military History Institute, Army War College.

30. See the extensive correspondence, mostly invitations, preceding the trip in ZT(LC), ser 2, r 1.

William R. Johnston boarded it to escort the travelers through his state.

Throughout Pennsylvania, Taylor was greeted by enthusiastic crowds and feted by local dignitaries. The travels and the festivities fatigued the old warrior, who suffered from the midday heat and found little relief at night. By the time he left Harrisburg on the thirteenth, Taylor was visibly weak. Complications soon followed. Diarrhea and vomiting struck him at Carlisle on the thirteenth. Dr. Wood, who accompanied him, put Taylor to bed and prescribed medicines which seemed to cure the illness by the next morning. The president, however, concluded that his affliction was caused by the hard local water and suggested that they hurry out of the limestone district. The trek carried the little party westward to Pittsburgh. There on the eighteenth Taylor made a long speech during which he proclaimed his support for specific duties, a clear signal of his embrace of protectionism. The statement followed advice which he had received from Andrew Stewart and drew applause from Clayton, who predicted it "will produce a great effect in Pennsylvania."[31]

From the iron center the party turned north to Mercer, where the president met with a delegation of Whigs from across the border in Warren, the center of Ohio's free-soil area. During the discussion, he assured the Buckeyes that: "The people of the North need have no apprehension of the further expansion of Slavery," implying that the Whigs would henceforth be the major antislavery party. While it is quite possible that Taylor was considering the formation of a new party drawing its support from nationalists, protectionist Whigs, fiscal conservatives, and slavery nonexpansionists, there is little evidence to support the argument that it had yet occurred. It is more likely that Taylor still thought in terms of altering the alignment of the Whig party.[32]

At Waterford, south of Erie, during the night of Friday, the twenty-fourth, vomiting and diarrhea again hit Taylor. He continued on to Erie, where Dr. Wood put him to bed with the "shakes." The president spent a sleepless night and missed a torchlight parade in his honor. The next day he worsened and ran a fever. Dr. Wood called in Navy Surgeon William Maxwell Wood, stationed in Erie, for consultation. When Taylor showed no improvement on the twenty-eighth they moved him into Surgeon Wood's house and sent for Mrs. Taylor. The president began to throw off his ailment the next day, having conquered both his fever and his shakes. This so relieved Mrs. Taylor, and Mrs. Wood who accompanied her

31. Stewart to ZT, August 8, Clayton to ZT, August 13, 1849, *ibid.*; C. B. Penrose to Meredith, August 1849, in Meredith Family Papers, HSPa.

32. Troy, N.Y., *Daily Whig*, September 8, 1849. The argument that Taylor's objective was the creation of a new party is best set forth in Michael F. Holt, *Conflict, Consensus, and the Coming of the Civil War* (New York, 1978).

mother, that they turned around in Baltimore and returned to the White House. So rapid, in fact, was Taylor's recovery that his advisors concluded that he could resume the trip on Saturday, September 1.

On the twenty-ninth the president was strong enough to transact business, sending a telegram to Secretary Clayton concerning diplomatic problems in Cuba. It crossed a message from the cabinet entreating Taylor to abandon the trip for the sake of his health. The president, vice-president, Dr. Wood, A. C. Bullitt, and other members of the party departed Erie on the steamer *Diamond* during September 1, bound for Niagara Falls. But the president was still weak and could scarcely walk to his carriage on disembarking that evening. Fillmore and Dr. Wood hustled him into bed at the nearby Eagle House. He rallied rapidly and on the third visited Goat Island and drove across the newly constructed suspension bridge of Charles Ellet to Canada. The following day Letcher and Peyton arrived to lend their support and advice.[33]

Taylor wished to follow his original schedule but was talked out of it by the doctors and others in his entourage. The party left Niagara Falls on Wednesday, September 6, and boarded the Lake Ontario side-wheeler *Bay State* at Lewiston for the trip to Oswego. There Weed's lieutenants became highly visible as escorts, to the exclusion of the vice-president's partisans. Taylor rode the Oswego and Syracuse Railroad to its terminus, where he spoke briefly and spent the night. He continued by train on to Albany. Governor Fish welcomed him at the densely packed Albany station. That evening the president joined a group of local notables at a state dinner in the governor's mansion. The activities left Taylor so weary he could scarcely be heard by the crowd which called for him to address them from a window.

The president left Albany on the handsome and large night steamer *Isaac Newton*, arriving in New York on Friday morning in time to breakfast with Simeon Draper. He took the train to Philadelphia, where Secretary of the Treasury Meredith and Attorney General Johnson joined him for the steamer trip through the Chesapeake and Delaware Canal to Baltimore, where Taylor spent the night with his brother Joseph. He returned home on Saturday and began a rapid recovery. He appeared fully recovered by the time Congress reconvened in December.[34]

Despite its shortened duration and the clear evidence of the frailty of the president's health, the Pennsylvania trip had substantial political sig-

---

33. Troy, N.Y., *Daily Whig*, August 14–September 8, 1849; W. S. A[llen?] to Clayton, August 29, 1849, in Clayton Papers, VI, LC; Clayton to ZT, August 29, 1849, in ZT(LC), ser 2, r 1; Bullitt to Orlando Brown, September 5, 1849, in A. C. Bullitt Papers, KHS.

34. Hamilton, *Taylor*, II, 224–27.

nificance. It confirmed for those who cared to study Taylor's words how far he had developed from the naïve soldier-planter who entered the White House only six months before. No longer did he view himself as a neutral figure surveying the field of political combat indifferent to the identity of the victorious faction. The Pittsburgh speech placed him squarely in the camp of the northern wing of the party and his comments at Mercer further solidified his identification with it. Taylor had consciously forsaken his heritage and his home constituency, but the reason is less evident. In part it mirrors the growing influence on him of the northern abolitionists like Seward as well as the president's dissatisfaction with the support of moderates like Crittenden and Bell. Very clearly Taylor was being pushed into the embrace of the northerners by the intransigence and harsh rhetoric of the southern radicals as well as the understanding that the votes which would enact his ideas on the proper steps to maintain the Union had to come from the northern Whigs. Taylor's transformation was gradual and tied directly to the developments described in Chapter XV.

When he had recovered sufficiently from the effects of his foray into Pennsylvania, Taylor considered visiting New England, New York, and Philadelphia, but soon abandoned the idea. He decided instead to visit Baltimore in mid-October in order to attend the state fair and cattle show. With little advance warning the president arrived on October 10 and established himself in Barnum's City Hotel. He made three trips to the fair grounds, one of them to view a plowing match, which the newspapers reported he watched with an expert's eye. He also visited the fair of the Maryland Institute and attended a banquet in his honor, at which he spoke a few impromptu but very eloquent words. The president returned to Washington on the evening of Friday, the twelfth.

Taylor so obviously enjoyed himself at Baltimore and responded so positively to the crowds that some onlookers were convinced that he had already decided to seek a second term.[35] They may have been correct but little concrete evidence supports them. Indeed, what Francis Preston Blair and others took for an intoxication with the political life may have been little more than a farmer's exuberance at exposure to a good agricultural exhibition.

The president made another excursion away from Washington in February 1850, although it was primarily ceremonial and clearly less enjoyable than the Baltimore sojourn. It involved a trip to Richmond, Virginia, to participate in the cornerstone laying of the Washington monument there. He left Washington on February 21, making the steamer trip to

35. *Ibid.*, 238–41.

Aquia Creek in company with George Washington Parke Custis. They were met at Aquia by a committee from the Virginia legislature and taken by train to Richmond, where he was welcomed at the capitol and made a short speech reiterating his devotion to the Union. Governor John B. Floyd honored the president with a ball at which former president John Tyler and his wife were present. The young and beautiful Mrs. Tyler attracted more attention than Taylor, who was described by one of the ladies present as an "indifferent specimen of the Lord of Creation . . . looking neither like the President of a great nation nor a military hero." Taylor played no role in the cornerstone laying beyond listening to the addresses of Governor Floyd and assorted masonic officials. During his trip back to Washington on February 23 Taylor used a dinner in Fredericksburg as the opportunity to caution the southern firebrands against secession.[36]

The threat of disunion, against which Taylor warned in Fredericksburg, was real and its prevention became the overriding concern of his administration. It so overwhelmed other issues that they no longer mattered. Neither Taylor nor Congress viewed the traditional questions like tariffs, the bank, internal improvements, or land policy as matters of consequence except to those to whom they appeared in sectional colors.

36. ZT to [Eleanor Parke Custis Lewis], [March 1850], in ZT(LC), ser 2, r 1; Hamilton, *Prologue to Conflict*, 71; Robert Seager II, *And Tyler Too* (New York, 1963), 355; Howard, *Taylor*, 346–47.

CHAPTER XIV

Foreign Relations

THE FOREIGN relations of the United States were in relatively good condition when Zachary Taylor moved into the White House. The United States faced no major diplomatic problem and only a relative handful of minor ones. The Polk administration had handled its stewardship of the nation's foreign contacts with adroitness and success. Whether its successor would be as effective was uncertain. Neither the president nor Secretary of State John M. Clayton had experience in dealing with foreign governments nor had either played any substantial role in formulating policies for dealing with foreign concerns. Both had maintained a general interest in foreign matters but they had concentrated primarily on domestic concerns.

In foreign relations, as in most other aspects of his administration, Taylor followed his army pattern of assigning responsibilities and not interfering unless forced to by the missteps of his subordinates. Whereas it is clear from the surviving record that the president paid close attention to foreign developments, there is little evidence of his direct involvement in either policy formation or diplomacy. He early discovered that a world view very similar to his own shaped the directions given American foreign policy by Clayton. As a result Taylor effectively abandoned control of foreign relations to his secretary of state although it appears that he expected to be and was consulted on major matters such as the negotiations with Britain over Central America and the steps to contain Narciso López' filibustering expeditions. The surviving record does not indicate that Taylor played a substantial role in selecting the diplomats sent abroad. Although he certainly was involved in the selection of Abbott Lawrence for the London Legation and was consulted in the other major appointments, the president treated the foreign assignments as patronage plums to be left in the hands of the cabinet.

One common belief shared by Taylor and his secretary of state was the conviction that the history of the preceding half century had demonstrated the superiority of the American and his socioeconomic-political system. In their view the United States had arrived at that point in her history where the European autocrats had to respect her, even if they did not like the jingoistic bumptiousness of her policies and the ill-mannered actions of some of her leaders. Nowhere was this American disdain of the old order more pronounced than in her reaction to the European revolutions of 1848. Nor was this mere Fourth of July oratory; the wave of German and Irish immigrants which rose to unprecedented heights during the 1840s strengthened the normal American embrace of those who proclaimed their attachment to liberty and republicanism. The Taylor administration, like the mass of Americans, was easily swept up in the euphoria of a movement which proclaimed its objective to be the removal of the yoke of autocracy from the masses of Europe.

The Polk administration had responded to the wave of revolutions with cautious support. In February of 1849 it allowed the North German Confederation, which it had supported and whose naval cadets it had trained, to purchase the trans-Atlantic steamer *United States,* which was to be converted to a warship at the New York Navy Yard. This was not an uncommon arrangement, and no one would have thought much of it had not war broken out between the Confederation and Denmark. But then the neutrality laws came into effect and they forbade the outfitting of belligerent vessels in American ports.

On March 19, at the president's direction, Secretary of the Navy W. Ballard Preston ordered official assistance terminated and work stopped. When the German minister, Baron Friedrich Ludwig von Roenne, protested, Clayton pointed to the neutrality legislation and later forwarded the formal opinion of Attorney General Johnson which stated that continued work was illegal. At Clayton's request, Preston also investigated rumors that American officers were being employed by the Confederation. He determined that the men being employed were former officers. The *United States* departed New York on May 31 still flying the American flag. She was legally handed over to the North German Confederation in England and assumed the name *Hansa.* In August 1849 the Navy Department also ordered discharge of Prussian midshipmen undergoing training on vessels of the Mediterranean Squadron.[1] The administration had handled a small tempest well and smoothly.

1. Most of the correspondence is in *Senate Executive Documents,* 31st Cong., 1st Sess., No. 1, pp. 18–57. See also Preston to Clayton, April 5, 1849, in LEA, VI, 60 (M472/3);

Despite its actions concerning the *Hansa*, the Taylor administration, like its predecessor, supported the efforts of the 1848 revolutionaries in Germany to establish a national government. By the time the Whigs took office that government was on its last legs, the new American government's good wishes notwithstanding, and Clayton could only recall Minister Andrew Jackson Donelson. The collapse of the revolutionary movement in Germany hastened the emigration of a substantial number of moderates and liberals to the United States, but their political impact on their new homeland came well after the close of Zachary Taylor's tenancy in the White House.

One other remnant of the revolutions of 1848 which had not yet played itself out was in Hungary. The profession of democracy by the Hungarian rebels gained them the support of the American public, much as it had the German nationalists at Frankfort. In June 1849 A. Dudley Mann, an experienced diplomat then in Paris, received orders to make a secret visit to Hungary to appraise the prospects for the revolutionaries. If they appeared promising, Clayton told his agent, the United States would quickly recognize the new government, since Taylor wished his nation to be the first to do so. Inasmuch as the Hungarian state was crushed by Austrian and Russian troops before Mann could make his visit, the United States took no formal action to recognize it. Nevertheless, the obvious support of the rebels by the American government roused the indignation of the Austrian *chargé d'affaires* in Washington, Baron Johann von Hülsemann. The Austrian protested orally and frequently that the United States was interfering in his nation's domestic affairs. It took all of Clayton's considerable diplomacy to keep Hülsemann's complaints verbal. So sensitive did the administration consider the issue that Taylor did not send copies of Mann's instructions and reports to the Senate until March 1850.[2] By then the matter had only academic interest since the revolt had been crushed.

A second and more serious international dispute arose with France. During the Mexican War two incidents involving Frenchmen had arisen. In one a Frenchman, Alexis Port, had purchased from American occupa-

to Captain Hiram Paulding, August 13, 1849, in *NASP:NA*, II, 343; Harold D. Langley, "William Ballard Preston," in Paolo E. Coletta, Robert G. Albion, and K. Jack Bauer (eds.), *American Secretaries of the Navy* (2 vols.; Annapolis, 1980), I, 244–45; Bernard C. Steiner, *Life of Reverdy Johnson* (New York, 1970), 35; Cedric Ridgely-Nevitt, *American Steamships on the Atlantic* (Newark, Del., 1981), 146; Mary Wilhelmine Williams, "John M. Clayton," in Samuel Flagg Bemis and Robert H. Ferrell (eds.), *American Secretaries of State* (18 vols.; New York, 1927–72), VI, 16–18.

2. Williams, "Clayton," 16. The message and documents were published as *Senate Executive Documents*, 31st Cong., 1st Sess., No. 43. In mid–nineteenth-century diplomatic practice the senior diplomat assigned to a minor nation often carried the rank of *chargé d'affaires* rather than minister.

tion authorities in Veracruz 500 bales of improperly seized tobacco which he resold for a $4,500 profit. When the error was discovered the Americans reclaimed the tobacco and refunded Port's money with interest. The Frenchman was not satisfied. He also wanted to be paid $1,000 for the lost profit. On instructions from the French Foreign Ministry, the French minister Guillaume Tell Levalée Poussin pressed Port's case. When Clayton turned down the request for additional money, Poussin persisted. Clayton responded with an ill-tempered note pointing out that it was not the responsibility of the United States Government to guarantee the profit on a speculation in which there was more than a hint of collusion. The Frenchman hotly replied that it was surely more honorable to pay a debt than to avoid payment by branding "the character of an honest man." That infuriated Clayton still more and he showed the letter to Taylor. The president too found the language highly offensive and authorized a complaint to French Foreign Minister Alexis de Tocqueville unless Poussin softened his words. He did and the matter subsided.

Relations might have returned to their normal routine level had not Poussin very belatedly decided to protest the actions of Commander Edward W. Carpenter of the USS *Iris* in salvaging and then holding the French merchantman *Eugénie* off Veracruz during the latter stages of the war. When Clayton evaded the issue of the detention of the vessel Poussin replied with a note that went far beyond acceptable diplomatic practice and constituted grounds for his expulsion. Clayton complained through Richard Rush, the retiring American minister to France. The French government agreed to replace the inept Poussin, but in a letter to Clayton, Foreign Minister Tocqueville suggested that some of the latter's language had also been undiplomatic. The secretary misconstrued the note as a refusal to replace Poussin and began a hot exchange of correspondence with Tocqueville. It grew so fierce that in September 1849 Secretary Preston warned his Mediterranean Squadron commander to prepare for a break in diplomatic relations. Nor did the arrival of the new American minister, William C. Rives, in November improve matters. Although Rives strove to quiet the riled diplomatic waters and to reestablish cordial relations with the French, Clayton's refusal, at Taylor's behest, to retreat from his insistence on the recall of Poussin snarled any settlement. Evidently the president viewed the French actions as assailing American integrity and as a failure to abide by diplomatic practice. The French Foreign Office, in turn, postponed the formal reception of the American diplomat although that did not inhibit their dealing with him.

The refusal to receive Rives seemed to Taylor further proof of the iniquity of the French government. He concurred in a suggestion by Clayton that Rives be instructed to leave Paris if he were not received within a week of the arrival of the orders. Although the administration proved willing even to go to war over the fancied insult, matters never reached that stage because domestic considerations caused Louis Napoleon to replace the French cabinet on November 7. A new foreign minister was able to sweep the dispute into the office trash bin and treat Rives in a normal manner. When Poussin's successor reached Washington during the spring of 1850 he was cordially received and memories of the dispute quickly faded.[3]

More productive of international good will was Clayton's agreement to cooperate in the search for the lost British arctic explorer Sir John Franklin by asking American whalers to assist. It was followed by more concrete action. In January 1850 the president, upon the recommendation of a navy board, requested that Congress authorize an American search expedition. Henry Grinnell, a New York ship owner, offered to provide a pair of vessels if the government would man and supply them. Congress agreed. Unfortunately, the expedition under Lieutenant Edwin J. DeHaven of the navy found no clues to the disappearance of the British party.[4]

Another of the administration's inherited diplomatic troubles lay with Portugal. It involved various claims for damages suffered by American citizens as a result of actions of the Portuguese government. They extended as far back as 1814 when the privateer *General Armstrong* was assailed and destroyed by a British squadron in the harbor of Fayal in the Azores and the 1828 seizure of money from the ship *Shepherd*, which Portuguese courts had held was illegally confiscated. Clayton attempted to bring pressure on the Portuguese by writing the senior American diplomat in Lisbon, *Chargé d'Affaires* George W. Hopkins, that it would be Lisbon's responsibility if the United States resorted to "ulterior measures" to gain redress. Hopkins was directed to warn the Portuguese government that the president would lay the results of the appeal before Con-

3. Williams, "Clayton," 19–31; Brainerd Dyer, *Zachary Taylor* (Baton Rouge, 1946), 349–52; Holman Hamilton, *Zachary Taylor* (2 vols.; Indianapolis, 1941, 1951), II, 187–90; Henry Blumenthal, *France and the United States* (Chapel Hill, 1970), 219; Preston to Commodore C. W. Morgan, September 15, 1849, in *NASP:NA*, II, 343–44. Tocqueville does not mention the incident in his memoirs. Blumenthal notes that the Taylor ladies had reservations about the reputation of Mme. Poussin. However, what role their concern played is uncertain.

4. Lady Jane Franklin to ZT, April 4, Clayton to Lady Franklin, April 25, 1849, in Joseph P. Comegys, *Memoir of John M. Clayton* (Wilmington, Del., 1882), 180–86; Commodores Lewis Warrington, C. W. Skinner, and Joseph Smith to Preston, June 12, 1849, Preston to DeHaven, May 15, 1850, in *NASP:NA*, IX, 243–49; James D. Richardson (ed.), *A Compilation of the Messages and Papers of the Presidents* (20 vols.; New York, 1897–1922), VI, 2563–64; Langley, "Preston," 250. See also *Senate Executive Documents*, 31st Cong., 1st Sess., No. 8.

gress but that he wished to avoid a suspension of diplomatic relations. It was a strong statement that Hopkins delivered, along with a demand for a reply on the oldest cases by October 1.

The Portuguese response beat the deadline but was hardly satisfactory. It rejected the *General Armstrong* claim and merely promised to investigate the others. Taylor lashed out at the response in his 1849 annual message as a "matter of profound regret" and grave character but took no further action. In March 1850 Secretary Clayton instructed Hopkins' successor James B. Clay to insist Portugal stop its procrastination and settle the claims. He was to demand his passports and leave Lisbon if the Portuguese continued to delay. To enhance the impact of the demand it was sent to Commodore Charles W. Morgan, the commander of the Mediterranean Squadron, for delivery by one of his warships. Clay received the instructions on June 21 and when the Portuguese agreed only to arbitration he asked for his passports.[5] By then the Taylor administration had ended.

The administration evinced no overwhelming interest in embracing the Monroe Doctrine, despite the president's earlier strong backing of the measure. Clayton, in view of his biographer, was "not always convinced of the efficacy of the Monroe Doctrine." He pointedly informed one Latin American diplomat that the president had not adopted the doctrine when he entered office. Clayton explicitly renounced the Polk Corollary and welcomed British and French intervention on Hispaniola in an effort to halt the incipient war between Haiti and the Dominican Republic. Nevertheless, he warned the Dominicans that the United States would oppose the establishment of a French protectorate over the strife-torn republic. Neither did the administration have any interest in acquiring Cuba. Even so, Clayton feared a possible British purchase of the island, never a serious threat, and on August 2, 1849, he instructed Minister Daniel M. Barringer to warn Spain that transfer to another power would bring war.[6]

But as events proved, the greatest difficulty arising over Cuba originated within the United States. Many southerners looked toward it as the most logical slaveholding area to be added to the Union. The acquisition of the island, in their view, would bring at least one new slaveholding state into the nation. Such an addition would partially correct the northward list which had developed in Congress, especially as it became increasingly clear that California would apply for admission as a free state. The prospect of additional slave territory prompted some radical south-

5. Dyer, *Taylor*, 353–54; Hamilton, *Taylor*, I, 190–91; Williams, "Clayton," 34–36.
6. Dexter Perkins, *A History of the Monroe Doctrine* (Boston, 1963), 96; Charles H. Brown, *Agents of Manifest Destiny* (Chapel Hill, 1980), 40.

erners to support filibustering expeditions aimed at overthrowing the Spanish power on the island. Some northerners, including former secretary of state James Buchanan, sought annexation simply to prevent the island from falling into British hands.

In early August 1849 the Spanish minister, Don Angel Calderón de la Barca, complained to the State Department that Narciso López, a Venezuelan-born former Spanish general and Cuban landowner, was gathering an expedition to invade Cuba. López had planned an uprising during the summer of 1848 but had been frustrated by the Polk administration's interest in purchase of the island. After the change of administrations he approached several Americans, including General William J. Worth, Jefferson Davis, and Robert E. Lee, about leading an invasion. All refused.

During the early summer of 1849 López chartered three vessels to carry his men. The force of about 600 gathered at Round Island, near Pascagoula, Mississippi. On August 8 Clayton ordered U.S. Attorney Logan Hunton at New Orleans to investigate. The following day Secretary of the Navy Preston directed the Home Squadron to institute a patrol off the Mississippi coast. On the eleventh Taylor, then in Harrisburg, Pennsylvania, on his ill-starred trip into the North, signed a proclamation warning of the expedition and threatening punishment to anyone violating the neutrality law and withdrawing protection from anyone involved in the attack. It was a strongly worded document which could have left no question about the position of the administration.

Commander Victor M. Randolph in the sloop of war *Albany* promptly blockaded Round Island while the federal authorities at New York seized two of López' vessels and those at New Orleans sequestered the third. The prompt action by the navy and the officials in New York and New Orleans had its effect. By the first of September the roughnecks whom López had recruited began to leave the island and Randolph successfully talked the last into leaving on the ninth.[7] The administration had greater success than most of its predecessors in enforcing the neutrality legislation. Unlike the Jackson administration, for instance, which could not get local courts to act against violators, the Taylor administration was able to secure convictions in New Orleans.

7. Robert Granville Caldwell, *The López Expeditions to Cuba, 1848–1851* (Princeton, 1915), 50–56; Brown, *Agents of Manifest Destiny*, 42–51; Louis N. Feipel, "The Navy and Filibustering in the Fifties," *United States Naval Institute Proceedings*, XLIV (1918), 769–79; Williams, "Clayton," 37–40; Langley, "Preston," 251; Hamilton, *Taylor*, II, 199–201; Richardson, *Messages & Papers*, VI, 2545–46; *NASP:NA*, II, 125–27. The orders and reports are reprinted in *Senate Executive Documents*, 31st Cong., 1st Sess., No. 55.

As the defusing of the López threat was successfully accomplished, a new and potentially more dangerous confrontation with Spain developed. On August 18 Clayton informed the president, then sick in Erie, Pennsylvania, that he had information that Carlos de España, the Spanish consul in New Orleans, was implicated in the abduction of Juan García, a Cuban who claimed American protection. Moreover, the Spanish authorities in Havana, where García had been spirited, refused to allow the American consul to visit him. Despite his indisposition from his illness, Taylor on August 29 ordered Clayton to take "the most decided measures . . . to demand the release of García." The instructions, which ordered Clayton to take action even without presidential sanction, were superfluous since the Spanish authorities at Havana had changed their minds and had acceded to the American demands eleven days earlier.[8]

Despite the success in preventing López' expedition, Taylor warned the Senate of "repeated attempts . . . under the direction of foreigners enjoying the hospitality of this country to get up armed expeditions in the United States for the purpose of invading Cuba."[9] Among the expeditions was a second force raised by López. In late April and early May 1850 his three chartered vessels evaded the watchful eyes of the American and Spanish authorities to slip to sea. The expedition seized Cardenas, Cuba, on May 19 but suffered sixty-six casualties and attracted no support. López and most of the survivors fled. They were chased by a Spanish warship into Key West, where they surrendered to the local authorities. "I have nabbed López," a happy Clayton told the president.[10] The filibusterers were subsequently released by mistake, but their leaders were apprehended and brought to trial. Unlike a year earlier, the efforts to have the men convicted of violation of the anti-filibustering statute collapsed in the face of the overwhelming pro-López feeling in New Orleans. No jury would convict. It was a performance that must have reminded many in the city of the similar problems faced by Andrew Jackson when trying to enforce the neutrality laws during the Texas Revolution.

Spanish naval patrols meanwhile had seized the other two vessels and charged their crews and passengers with piracy. Fifty-two of the fifty-four prisoners were American citizens. When requests for their release proved unsuccessful, the Navy concentrated the frigate *Congress*, sloops-of-war *Albany* and *Germantown*, and the steamer *Saranac* at Havana. The

8. Clayton to ZT, August 18, ZT to Clayton, August 29, 1849, in John M. Clayton Papers, VI, LC. The official correspondence is reprinted in *Senate Executive Documents*, 31st Cong., 1st Sess., No. 13. Taylor subsequently lifted the exequatur of the consul. Richardson (ed.), *Messages & Papers*, VI, 2588.

9. Richardson (ed.), *Messages & Papers*, VI, 2585.

10. Clayton to ZT, June 9, 1850, in Clayton Papers, IX, LC.

American consul and Commander Randolph of the *Albany* presented the demand for the release of the Americans. The governor general refused, arguing that the men were pirates and properly should be tried in Spanish courts, and denied permission for the American officials to visit the prisoners. Taylor, exasperated at the delay in securing the release of the men, ordered Commodore Charles Morris to Havana. It is not at all certain why he expected Morris to accomplish what others on the scene had failed to achieve. Anyway, by the time Morris reached Cuba the Americans there, notably Captain Isaac McKeever of the *Congress*, had secured the surrender of all but ten of the Americans. They were tried and convicted but pardoned by the queen of Spain as a gesture of friendship.[11]

As potentially dangerous as the relations with Spain might have been, those with Britain were more sensitive. The administration's policy toward Britain was controlled by at least two somewhat conflicting attitudes. Taylor never expressed himself clearly but Clayton, like most Whigs, was a firm advocate of Anglo-American friendship. Nevertheless, the administration faced an apparently resurgent British imperialism in Central America. Even if the president and secretary of state had reservations about the universality of the Monroe Doctrine, Clayton, at least, had long supported the construction of a transisthmian canal. The most promising project was the American Atlantic and Pacific Ship Canal Company formed by Cornelius Vanderbilt and other American capitalists to construct a river, lake, and canal route across Nicaragua. It was stymied by the British support of claims of sovereignty by the Miskito Indians over the Atlantic terminus at Greytown (San Juan del Norte). The Americans on the scene and the Nicaraguans, with considerable validity, assumed an imperialist plot when the local British authorities summarily seized the port. Only later did it become known that the responsibility did not extend all the way back to London.

The rush of events in Central America upset a plan by Clayton and Taylor to delay diplomatic selections until June, by which time the bulk of the domestic patronage would have been dispensed. In April, however, they selected the untrained twenty-seven-year-old former newspaperman and would-be archaeologist E. George Squier to assume responsibility for United States interests in Central America as *chargé d'affairs* in Guatemala. His instructions directed the negotiation of commercial treaties

11. Brown, *Agents of Manifest Destiny*, 57–70; Caldwell, *López*, 58–82; Feipel, "Navy & Filibustering," 1010–27; Hamilton, *Taylor*, II, 368–71; Langley, "Preston," 252–53. The correspondence generated by the López expeditions can be found in William R. Manning (ed.), *Diplomatic Correspondence of the United States, Inter-American Affairs, 1831–1860* (12 vols.; Washington, 1932–39), II, 69–71, 77–80, 429–43, 470–73, and in *Senate Executive Documents*, 31st Cong., 1st Sess., Nos. 13 and 57.

with the Central American states and the securing of protection from Nicaragua for the canal company.

Before the new diplomat could arrive, his predecessor Elijah Hise, on June 21, 1849, negotiated a far-reaching agreement with Nicaragua. It granted in perpetuity a transit right-of-way across the country and authorized American fortification of the route. But it also committed the United States to guarantee the independence of the Central American state, and that gave Clayton and Taylor pause in view of the conflicting claims to the Greytown entrance for the canal. Moreover, Hise's treaty went beyond any commitment into which they wished to enter and threatened to bind their hands in any negotiations with Britain. Taylor withheld the treaty, despite a call for it from the Senate in January, on the grounds that Hise had not been empowered to negotiate it. The agreement did not resurface because Squier negotiated a replacement.

Shortly after his arrival, Squier achieved a less far-ranging treaty. It provided for continuation of the rights granted the canal company, joint Nicaraguan-American protection of the route, and explicit recognition of Nicaraguan sovereignty over the canal. Squier suspected that his British counterpart, Frederick Chatfield, had plans to block construction of the waterway. The suspicions seemed proven when Chatfield demanded settlement of some British claims against Honduras which would have granted Britain control of the Gulf of Fonseca, the Pacific outlet of the projected canal. On September 28 Squier secured the temporary cession of Tigre Island to the United States, but before the arrangement could be formalized the island was seized by a British landing party on October 16, 1849.[12]

From the beginning of his term Clayton recognized that the most effective settlement of the Central American dispute would be by direct negotiation with Britain. His objective was to dislodge the Britannic foothold in Central America, a difficult maneuver since the British occupation of Belize had long been recognized by the United States and any British retrenchment would force them to surrender their protectorate over the Miskito Indians. Yet a safe, American-controlled crossing of the isthmus was obligatory if secure communications with California were to be maintained.

On May 2, 1849, he instructed George Bancroft, still occupying the legation in London, to sound out Foreign Minister Lord Palmerston on British intentions and to warn him that unilateral British control of a

12. Mary Wilhelmine Williams, *Anglo-American Isthmian Diplomacy, 1815–1915* (Washington, 1916), 48–66; Williams, "Clayton," 41–44; Richard W. Van Alstyne, "British Diplomacy and the Clayton-Bulwer Treaty," *Journal of Modern History*, XI (1939), 149–50; Perkins, *History of the Monroe Doctrine*, 95; Richardson (ed.), *Messages & Papers*, VI, 2569–78.

transisthmian route would be unacceptable. If discussions did not gain British withdrawal, Bancroft was directed to deliver the protest in writing. Although his meetings with the British foreign secretary were inconclusive, Bancroft detected enough movement to justify his refraining from issuing the warning.

By mid-summer Clayton realized that the terms of the Hise treaty would soon become known in London and that the nearly completed Squier arrangement would further complicate negotiations. Unfortunately, minister-designate Abbott Lawrence could not leave for London for some weeks because of pressing private business. As a stopgap Clayton arranged that the new minister to France, William C. Rives, would visit London en route to his permanent station. The secretary directed Rives to explain American aims and intentions to Palmerston. The Britisher had learned of the Hise treaty by the time Rives arrived in September and after hearing an explanation of the American position was disposed to be reasonable. Both Rives and Lawrence recognized the British willingness to negotiate and so informed Washington.

The American diplomats proposed that the United States and Britain jointly guarantee the independence of the three Central American states of Nicaragua, Honduras, and Costa Rica. As a part of the arrangement they suggested that Nicaragua should buy the Miskito claims to land along the canal route. Clayton on October 20 instructed Lawrence to "place the whole negotiation on the broad basis of a great highway for the benefit of mankind, to be dedicated, especially by Great Britain and the United States, to the equal benefit and advantage of all the nations of the world that will join us in entering into these proposed treaty stipulations with the state of Nicaragua."

Unfortunately appearances were more propitious than the reality. Britain, while willing to join in guaranteeing the neutrality of the canal and renouncing any aim of colonization in Central America, was put off by the terms of Squier's treaty and unwilling to surrender her protectorate over the Miskito Indians. In the United States, public opinion was convinced that the seizure of Tigre Island offered proof of British ulterior motives. The administration, however, was willing to seek an accommodation. British *Chargé d'Affaires* John F. Crampton reported, after a meeting with Clayton and Taylor, that the Americans were willing to forgo the Hise treaty if they could secure British agreement to joint abandonment of claims to Nicaragua. The president, noted Crampton, wished the matter arranged "to the honour and advantage of both Countries."[13]

13. Comegys, *Clayton*, 191–92; Van Alstyne, "British Diplomacy," 151–52; Williams, *Anglo-American Isthmian Diplomacy*, 67–88; Williams, "Clayton," 45–50, 52–53; Hamilton, *Taylor*, II, 193–98.

For reasons that are not recorded but probably because Palmerston also wished the discussions moved to Washington, Crampton's successor was the highly regarded diplomat Sir Henry Lytton Bulwer, who was also a confidant of the foreign secretary. Even so, he arrived with very general and vague instructions about the Central American problem and no directions at all about the Tigre Island incident. Bulwer, nevertheless, accepted Clayton's proposal that the two men settle upon a preliminary draft of *projet* before further consulting their superiors. Whether Clayton intentionally kept Taylor in the dark about the discussions or whether the president chose to ignore them is not clear. The former is out of character for both of the two men but the latter would be in keeping with Taylor's military training.

The draft was finished on February 3. It was dispatched to Britain for Palmerston's approval and given to Taylor and the cabinet for their agreement. The Americans found the wording too imprecise to ensure the evacuation of the British from the Miskito coast. Complicating matters from the administration's vantage point was a January 28, 1850, call by the Senate for the instructions and correspondence concerning the Central American negotiations. Taylor refused to provide them, arguing quite plausibly that the negotiations were still in progress. Bulwer, whose instructions did not go that far, refused to modify the treaty to encompass an explicit renunciation of the protectorate. It appeared that a settlement was out of reach of the diplomats.

Clayton, convinced that the negotiations had reached an impasse, took the offensive. He threatened annexation of Central America if the British insisted on maintaining the guardianship of the Miskitos. As a step to increase the pressure on the British he had Taylor send the Squier and Hise treaties to the Senate on March 19. The bundle also contained Squier's arrangements with El Salvador as well as those signed by Hise with Guatemala. Taylor's covering letter cast the British moves as efforts to establish control over the canal route.

The British government surprised the Americans by being less rigid than expected and willing to accept any arrangement which did not disturb their Miskito protectorate. Bulwer offered to write a note to Clayton which would disavow any desire to use the protectorate for aggressive moves. Once again Britain, as she had in 1846, showed a willingness to accommodate even extreme American demands which did not compromise a substantial English political objective. Taylor, who had been quietly observing the negotiations but keeping aloof from them, now became disturbed by the British concern over the protectorate. He insisted that Clayton formally notify Bulwer that the United States did not recognize the Miskito title to the Nicaragua coast. The secretary did so on April 6. After extensive negotiations in which Bulwer successfully protested the tone of the letter, it was withdrawn and the two diplomats agreed upon an ambiguous self-denying statement whch they inserted into the treaty as Article I. It was necessarily vague. As Bulwer wrote Clayton coincident with the exchange of ratifications, Britain had no intention of surrendering Belize or of renouncing the protectorate over the Miskitos, although she was willing to curtail further advances. Clayton chose to settle for the promise of no further expansion of British control but dared not broadcast the fact because of the ammunition it would provide to the rhetorical Columbiads in the Senate. Clayton cleared the revised text with various Senate leaders and signed it on April 19.[14]

The treaty provided for the mutual renunciation of unilateral control of any ship canal that might be built and the neutralization of the route. Both governments disclaimed any intent to exercise dominion over any part of Central America or special rights along the canal route. The agreement linked the two nations as protectors of the canal during construction and afterwards as well as guarantors of the freedom of the waterway from blockade in time of war. The signatories also promised to use their good offices to keep Central American peace. They further agreed to extend the provisions of the treaty to Tehuantepec or Panama in the event a canal was built across either isthmus. A final provision required that the current option for construction of a canal through Nicaragua had to be exercised within one year. Taylor's message transmitting the text to the Senate, on April 22, presumably written by Clayton, called the document a commercial alliance. "It will," the president insisted, "secure in future the liberation of all Central America from any kind of foreign aggression." That, Taylor claimed, had been one of the objectives in negotiation of the treaty. He then formally rejected the extension of Manifest Destiny into Central America.

Technically the submission was for advice only, but since Clayton had kept the Senate leadership well-informed of the negotiations the treaty quickly passed to formal consideration. Despite some resistance from Anglophobe members of the body the Senate ratified the document on May 22 by a vote of 42 to 11. The formal exchange of ratifications on July

14. Williams, *Anglo-American Isthmian Diplomacy*, 89–97; Comegys, *Clayton*, 190; Van Alstyne, "British Diplomacy," 153–57; Paul R. Varg, *United States Foreign Relations, 1820–1860* (Lansing, 1979), 222–23; Richardson (ed.), *Messages & Papers*, VI, 2569–78; Hamilton, *Taylor*, II, 357–67. The correspondence relating to the negotiations in Central America and with Britain are in Manning (ed.), *Diplomatic Correspondence*, III, 36–63, 311–536, V, 731–55, VII, 33–63, 297–400, and in *House Executive Documents*, 31st Cong., 1st Sess., Nos. 42 and 75.

4 was fated to be Zachary Taylor's last act of state.[15] The relative ease with which Clayton's treaty cleared the Senate stands in stark contrast to the inability of the administration to secure acceptance of its domestic program. It demonstrates the destructive effect which the failure to develop a congressional spokesman had for the administration. The fault must rest squarely on the president, who simply eschewed that unpleasant task.

While the Senate debated ratification, the two negotiators exchanged notes attempting to clarify the meaning of their obfuscations. They accomplished little beyond leaving a bad taste in the mouths of many historians. The treaty became, as one of them wrote, "perhaps the most unpopular treaty in the history of the United States." Contemporaries decried it as thwarting the southward expansion of the country and of violating the Monroe Doctrine by permitting Great Britain to keep her Central American possessions.[16] Yet, the Clayton-Bulwer Treaty was one of these landmark agreements which charted the course of the nation's foreign relations. The inclusion of the self-denying clause, so damned by contemporaries, signified the abandonment of Manifest Destiny by the United States just as it also marked a de facto British acceptance of the primacy of American interests in Central America and a ratification of the Monroe Doctrine. Even if the treaty did not eliminate British presence in the region it raised a substantial barrier to any further expansion of her influence. Moreover, the Clayton-Bulwer Treaty, like the Webster-Ashburton and the Oregon treaties which preceded it, represented a giant stride in the development of the great Anglo-American alliance of the late nineteenth and twentieth centuries.

While the negotiations with Britain moved slowly toward their settlement, the administration took other steps to support the construction of communication lines to the Pacific settlements. Some American investors, as had the Polk administration, viewed the route across the Isthmus of Tehuantepec in southern Mexico as the preferred crossing to the Pacific. They secured the rights to build a canal or rail passage. On September 18, 1849, Clayton ordered Minister Robert F. Letcher to negotiate a convention for the protection of their rights and property. After consulting with British and Mexican officials, Letcher received authority in April 1850 to sign a multinational treaty guaranteeing the neutrality of the line. The ne-

15. Williams, *Anglo-American Isthmian Diplomacy*, 97–100; Comegys, *Clayton*, 197–99; Van Alstyne, "British Diplomacy," 157–65; Richardson (ed.), *Messages & Papers*, VI, 2580–82.

16. Samuel Flagg Bemis, *The Latin American Policy of the United States* (New York, 1967), 106. See also Samuel Flagg Bemis, *A Diplomatic History of the United States* (New York, 1965), 247–52; Richard W. Van Alstyne, *The Rising American Empire* (Chicago, 1965), 158–61; Williams, *Anglo-American Isthmian Diplomacy*, 102–109.

gotiations resulted in the June 1850 Letcher-Pedraza Convention which provided for a neutralized route but one which would be protected by the United States on the request of Mexico. The passage remained unbuilt until the twentieth century because the prospective builders objected to some of the provisions in the agreement.[17] Nevertheless, the Tehuantepec negotiations demonstrated the depth of the commitment of the Taylor administration to the development of a transisthmian route to California.

As a part of her movement to free trade, Britain in 1849 opened her ports to American trade. Merchants in both the mother country and in Canada brought the London government under pressure to negotiate reciprocal concessions from the United States. Taylor noted the repeal of the British Navigation Acts in his 1849 State of the Union message but offered no comparable concession in return. On June 26 Clayton rejected a British proposal for a reciprocity treaty. The Quebec authorities persisted and on May 7, 1850, Taylor forwarded to the Senate correspondence with Bulwer over a proposal to open the St. Lawrence and the Canadian canals to American citizens upon passage of a reciprocity law by the United States. Both actions developed from efforts of Canadian Governor-General Lord Elgin to promote free navigation and low tariffs for Canadian goods in the United States. Elgin considered the actions indispensable as a means of combating economic pressures for annexation to the United States following the loss of Canadian preferential duties in Britain in 1846. Although the second British proposal came late in the life of the administration while the attention of both the White House and the Congress were fixed upon the sectional struggle, there is no reason to expect that it would have received serious attention. Clayton and Taylor were too firmly welded to protectionism to make an exception for Canada, especially when the emerging administration strategy for the 1852 elections centered on winning states like Pennsylvania where the tariff issue was critical.[18]

The Far East attracted little attention from the administration, which at first glance seems unusual for a Whig government. Normally the Whigs could be counted upon to support overseas commerce, and the Far East in the decade and a half before the Civil War represented one of the areas of growth for American trade. The explanation appears to be that American interests there were under no attack. Nevertheless, the administration did recognize the value of supporting an expansion of American commerce

17. J. Fred Rippy, "Diplomacy of the United States and Mexico Regarding the Isthmus of Tehuantepec, 1848–1860," *MVHR*, VI (1920), 507–11.

18. H. C. Allen, *Great Britain and the United States* (New York, 1958), 446–48; Bemis, *Diplomatic History*, 299–300. See also *House Executive Documents*, 31st Cong., 1st Sess., No. 46.

into areas not yet penetrated. During the summer of 1849 the State and Navy departments jointly prepared the dispatch of Joseph Balestier to the Orient as special agent and envoy to Cochin China and Southeast Asia.[19] Although the initiation of the efforts to enlarge trading opportunities in southeast Asia were initiated by the Taylor administration, most of Balestier's activities occurred after it left office.

The lack of significant diplomatic activity by the Taylor administration outside of the Clayton-Bulwer Treaty makes it difficult to evaluate its handling of foreign relations. Taylor and Clayton faced their few substantial international complications on a reflexive basis. They neither established a broad policy within which they directed American negotiations toward a well-defined objective nor did they settle upon any set of common principles to serve as guides. The lack of any discernible unified foreign policy in part reflected a quiet period in American diplomacy, but even more it demonstrated the limitations of both the president and the secretary of state. Neither demonstrated any talent for the formulation of foreign policy and the lack of a coherent administration policy offers a strong argument that Taylor assigned that portion of the field to the secretary of state and in keeping with his military training refrained from interfering.

19. Preston to Clayton, August 21, 1849, LEA, VI, 125 (M472/3). The correspondence relating to the mission is printed in *Senate Executive Documents*, 32nd Cong., 1st Sess., No. 38, pp. 3–92, and in *NASP:NA*, III, 377–420.

CHAPTER XV

The President Faces Disunion

THROUGHOUT ALL of the discussions of his candidacy Zachary Taylor insisted that he would be a president of all the people. Most of his contemporaries as well as historians since assumed that the statement was little more than a disclaimer of political partisanship. It clearly was intended as such, but Taylor also viewed the president as a figure above regionalism or class. The threat of disunion against which he spoke so eloquently at Fredericksburg was real and by the winter of 1849/50 had become his overriding concern.

The crisis had deep and complex origins in the sectional differences of the nation and in the fears of many southerners that their section no longer could politically protect its interests. They feared the domination of economic policy by the newly forged alliance of the northeastern and old northwestern states as well as the assaults on a stable southern culture growing out of the abolitionist movement and other small antitraditional groups in the North and West. These fears caused some southerners to look to a separate southern confederation as the logical ultimate defense of a strictly southern culture.

To a soldier like Taylor who had spent nearly a half century in service to national security, the idea of division of the Republic was an anathema. His motivation for joining the service had been patriotism for the nation, not for his native section. Moreover, his years of frontier service led him to distrust the motivations of locally oriented politicians. Too often he had seen them support local interests, particularly those of the land speculators, at the expense of the Indians and others having prior claims to an area. This was a common concern of sensitive army officers and is an undercurrent in much of Taylor's reaction to the politics of the frontier. It can be seen as one thread in the development of a program for his administration to follow in New Mexico. In California events had their own dynamics which derived only limited guidance from Washington.

The conquests of the Mexican lands proved to be a mixed blessing which inflamed the sectional strife. The newly acquired territory naturally divided into three large areas. The first was an ill-defined region which had formed the Mexican state of Nuevo México. It was largely unsettled except for scattered Indian pueblos, villages, and camps and the Mexican settlements around Santa Fe and Tucson. To the north of New Mexico was the territory commonly referred to as Utah, which had been settled during the Mexican conflict by Mormons and called by them the State of Deseret. The third area was that formerly occupied by the Mexican state of Alta California stretching along the Pacific Coast from the Mexican border to Oregon. Only California held a substantial population; most of those were late arrivals whose primary concern was the discovery of gold.

Both New Mexico and California were ruled by military governments which had been established as wartime expedients and could not be legally replaced until congressional action established some form of civilian rule. Utah, held securely in the grasp of its Mormon settlers, offered a different and less pressing problem. The Californians, in particular, chaffed under military rule. As early as November 1848 the naval and military commanders there concluded that unless a civilian government was formed anarchy would follow. Nevertheless, they decided to await the arrival of Brevet Major General Bennet Riley, the new commander of the Tenth (California) Military District. An unofficial popular meeting called at San Jose in mid-December 1848 proposed a convention to gather the following month to form a provisional civilian government. Similar gatherings followed in Sonoma, Sacramento, Monterey, San Diego, and in the gold fields.[1] When Congress assembled in 1849 Representative William Ballard Preston, soon to join Taylor's cabinet, proposed granting statehood to California forthwith. It was a reasonable and statesmanlike solution but needed support from both sides of the Mason-Dixon line for passage. The necessary southern support evaporated when northern congressmen added an antislavery amendment. An effort by John Bell to se-

---

1. Donald C. Biggs, *Conquer and Colonize* (San Rafael, Calif., 1977), 155–56, 163–66; Neal Harlow, *California Conquered* (Berkeley, 1982), 327.

cure Senate adoption of a similar bill also failed because of southern opposition.[2]

Unaware of the foot shuffling in Washington, Brevet Major General Persifor F. Smith, the commander of the newly created Pacific Division and Riley's immediate superior, accepted the idea of a de facto provisional civil government in the area although he ignored the call for a convention.[3] The Taylor administration, on assuming office, settled upon immediate statehood. The population in the region met the constitutional requirements for admission and immediate progress to statehood had immense political advantages. Since Congress had but to pass upon the new state's constitution, the members could avoid taking sides on the slavery issue; or so it appeared to the administration. The administration concluded that a special agent should be sent to California to hasten the adoption of a constitution. It was a plan, in keeping with Taylor's thinking, which had earlier been proposed by a number of individuals including Preston, Clayton, and Representative (former colonel) Edward D. Baker. The agent was Representative T. Butler King. His instructions, issued by Clayton on April 3, were disingenuous even by mid–nineteenth-century standards. "You are fully possessed of the President's views," they read, "and can, with propriety suggest to the people of California the adoption of measures best calculated to give them effect. These measures must, of course, originate solely with themselves." The commanders in California were also instructed to follow King's "advice and counsel in the conduct of all proper measures within the scope of these instructions." The administration confidently concluded that its plans would win admission of a "free and Whig" California, as Clayton wrote Crittenden.[4]

King and his party sailed from New York by steamer to Chagres, crossed the isthmus, and boarded the first Pacific Mail steamer for San Francisco. Their mission was largely completed even before they arrived.

2. *Congressional Globe*, 30th Cong., 2nd Sess., 477–78, 562, 605–609, A253–55, 279–81; William J. Cooper, Jr., *The South and the Politics of Slavery, 1828–1856* (Baton Rouge, 1978), 272–73, 377–78.

3. Smith to AG, March 15, 1849 in *Calif. & N. Mex.*, 712. Secretary Crawford, before learning of Smith's actions, directed him to accept a de facto civil government. Crawford to Smith, April 3, 1849, *ibid.*, 273.

4. Clayton to King, April 3, 1849, *ibid.*, 9–10; Preston to Commodore T. apCatesby Jones, April 2, 1849, in Office of Naval Records & Library (NA, RG 45), Area File, A-9 (M625/286); Baker to Clayton, March 20, 1849, in Roy P. Basler (ed.), *The Collected Works of Abraham Lincoln* (8 vols.; New Brunswick, N.J., 1953), II, 38; Robert W. Johannsen, *Stephen A. Douglas* (New York, 1973), 265; Edward M. Steel, Jr., *T. Butler King of Georgia* (Athens, Ga., 1964), 73; Arthur C. Cole, *The Whig Party in the South* (Washington, 1913), 155; Holman Hamilton, *Zachary Taylor* (2 vols.; Indianapolis, 1941, 1951), II, 177–78.

On June 3 Riley, as the military governor, called a constitutional convention to meet at Monterey on September 1. King arrived the next day and promptly confirmed the administration's concurrence.[5] Riley had acted under pressure from an unofficial San Francisco assemblage which in early June issued an "Adress to the People of California" calling for a convention at San Jose in mid-August. Riley ignored the call but on August 1 he authorized the election of local officials.[6]

The Monterey Convention met on September 1 but did not gather a quorum until the third. It sat until October 12, but King, who had been stricken with dysentery, did not attend. The constitution that emerged from the deliberations was modeled on those of Iowa and New York and repeated their clear prohibitions on slavery. The California document was ratified on November 13 by a popular vote of 12,061 to 811, and Riley formally transferred civil authority to the new government on December 20.[7] The scene now returned to Washington, where Congress had to decide whether and when to honor the California request for statehood. To help speed matters along, King left San Francisco on the Pacific Mail Line's steamer *Oregon* on January 1, 1850, in company with California's two congressmen-designates. They reached New York on the Panama steamer during February 7.[8]

Even as the administration set in motion the drive to secure statehood for California it faced a more difficult challenge in New Mexico. Texas had laid claim to the region around Santa Fe as early as 1836 although the Lone Star authorities had never been able to enforce their dominion. In January 1847 Governor J. Pinckney Henderson reasserted the claim. He reminded the Washington authorities of it in protesting against the establishment of any territorial government on lands that the Texans considered theirs. President Polk responded with soothing words which the Texans interpreted as an assurance that the military government in Santa Fe was merely a temporary wartime expedient. While the exchange of letters was in process the Texas legislature created four counties in the re-

5. Preston to W. H. Aspinwall, to Ringgold, April 3, 1849, in Area File, A-9 (M625/286); Riley, Proclamation, June 3, 1849, in *Calif. & N. Mex.*, 776–79; Theodore Grivas, *Military Governments in California, 1846–1850* (Glendale, Calif., 1963), 206; Biggs, *Conquer & Colonize*, 171; Holman Hamilton, *Prologue to Conflict* (Lexington, 1964), 16; Harlow, *California Conquered*, 323; Steel, *King*, 74.

6. Riley to Jones, June 30, 1849, in *Calif. & N. Mex.*, 748; Biggs, *Conquer & Colonize*, 171–72.

7. Riley, Proclamations, October 10, December 20, 1849, in *Calif. & N. Mex.*, 846–62; *Congressional Globe*, 31st Cong., 1st Sess., 966; Avery O. Craven, *Growth of Southern Nationalism* (Baton Rouge, 1953), 58; Biggs, *Conquer & Colonize*, 184–87; Steel, *King*, 75; Grivas, *Military Governments*, 219–20; Harlow, *California Conquered*, 340–51.

8. Steel, *King*, 76.

gion between the Rio Grande and the Nueces. In March 1847 it added a fifth county embracing most of the New Mexican territory included in the 1836 claim.[9]

Brevet Lieutenant Colonel John M. Washington, commander of the forces in New Mexico and military governor of the region, reached Santa Fe on October 10, 1848. His appearance coincided with the gathering of a convention which petitioned Congress for territorial status, primarily as a means of protecting the inhabitants against the Texas claims to area. Two days later the Polk administration effectively established the Rio Grande as the dividing line between Texas and New Mexican jurisdiction by instructing the Santa Fe commander to respect any civil government established east of the river by the Texas authorities.[10]

Judge Spruce M. Baird reached Santa Fe on November 10 to establish Texan authority in the area, but Colonel Washington refused to recognize his commission. The two were still at a stalemate when the Taylor administration took office. The first instructions sent by Secretary of War George W. Crawford changed nothing. They merely noted that the administration did not expect Texas to attempt to extend its control into New Mexico east of the Rio Grande.[11]

On the fourth of July, Baird and Washington formalized their stand-off. The Texan agreed to suspend his activities and the soldier promised not to take any action which would prejudice the Texas claims. Later in the month Taylor, probably as a result of a complaint by Texas Governor George T. Wood about Colonel Washington's stance, realized that the Polk policy had never been altered. The cabinet considered possible courses of action and settled upon an order to the Santa Fe commander to defend the area against any attack and to counter any assertion of Texas control until Congress acted.[12] Taylor and the cabinet in effect held that the question of Texas boundaries was a federal matter since the territory

9. William Campbell Binkley, "The Question of Texas Jurisdiction in New Mexico Under the United States, 1848–1850," *SWHQ*, XXVII (1920–21), 3–7; Kenneth F. Neighbors, "The Taylor–Neighbors Struggle Over the Upper Rio Grande Region of Texas in 1850," *ibid.*, LXI (1957–58), 434–38. Most of the significant documents are reprinted in *Senate Executive Documents*, 31st Cong., 1st Sess., Nos. 60 and 67, and *House Executive Documents*, same Congress, Nos. 65, 66, and 82.

10. William A. Keleher, *Turmoil in New Mexico, 1846–1868* (Santa Fe, 1952), 37; Binkley, "Texas Jurisdiction," 13; William Campbell Binkley, *The Expansionist Movement in Texas* (Berkeley, 1925), 156–57; Marcy to Commanding Officer, Santa Fe, October 12, 1849, in *Calif. & N. Mex.*, 261.

11. Crawford to Commanding Officer in New Mexico, March 26, 1849, in *Calif. & N. Mex.*, 272–73; Binkley, "Texas Jurisdiction," 9–11.

12. Binkley, "Texas Jurisdiction," 12; Neighbors, "Taylor–Neighbors Struggle," 438–39; Thomas Ewing Memoir, February 16, 1864, in Ewing Family Papers, XVIII, LC.

in dispute had been surrendered to the national government by the Treaty of Guadalupe-Hidalgo. Moreover, they did not accept the Texas claim, which was based upon an unexecuted law, although they recognized that Congress might do so if it wished.

A group of Americans living in Santa Fe drafted a series of resolutions on August 22 calling for a convention to meet September 24 to consider the area's political future. The call received the blessing of acting governor Lieutenant Colonel Benjamin L. Beall. The convention met September 24–26, adopted a territorial constitution, petitioned Congress for territorial status, and elected both a governor and a delegate to Congress.[13]

While the New Mexicans awaited the results of their petition to Congress, the administration shifted ground. By mid-November Taylor had decided to support statehood. This had several advantages. By avoiding territorial status for the area such an arrangement served to reduce the impact of the slavery issue in Congress by placing the site of the decision in New Mexico, not in the chambers of the national legislature. Congress would have only to accept or reject a state constitution which reflected the expressed will of the inhabitants. This, Taylor assumed, would appeal to Congress. He was wrong. He had misread the degree to which Congress had been polarized by the slavery issue. The president also believed that the acquisition of statehood by New Mexico would defuse the boundary dispute by allowing it to be settled in the courts.

Major (Brevet Lieutenant Colonel) George A. McCall, en route to duty in Santa Fe, was called to Washington and instructed by Secretary Crawford to urge the New Mexicans to apply for statehood. McCall also joined Indian Superintendent James S. Calhoun as the administration's political deputies in New Mexico. The action came none too soon. In late December, Texas moved to reiterate her territorial claims. Newly installed governor P. Hansborough Bell asked his legislature for authority to use military force if necessary to establish civil government in Santa Fe as well as agreement to send a commissioner to Washington in an effort to raise money to pay the state's debt by selling the land north of 36°30′ to the federal government. On the last day of the year the legislature created four counties out of the old Santa Fe jurisdiction. Robert S. Neighbors, dispatched to organize the new governments, carried out part of his assignment at El Paso during February but was blocked from further action by the opposition of the Santa Fe authorities.[14]

Neighbors reached Santa Fe in early April but it was too late for him to head off the move for statehood. Brevet Colonel John Munroe, Washing-

---

13. Binkley, "Texas Jurisdiction," 16–17; Loomis Morton Ganaway, *New Mexico and the Sectional Controversy, 1846–1861* (Philadelphia, 1976), 26. The proceedings of the convention are reprinted in *Calif. & N. Mex.*, 93–104.

14. Crawford to McCall, November 12, 19, 1849, in *Calif. & N. Mex.*, 280–81,

ton's successor as military governor, in keeping with the instructions carried by McCall, set May 15 for the meeting of the constitutional convention. By the twenty-fourth the gathering had adopted an antislavery constitution which was ratified by a popular vote of 8,381 to 39.[15] The constitution and the petition for admission were promptly sent to Washington, where they became but one factor in complex congressional maneuvering.

Nor were the Californians and New Mexicans alone in believing the time ripe for statehood. The Mormons in Utah, as reported by Taylor's agent the Indian superintendent John Wilson, feared that the establishment of a territorial regime would place them under the control of Gentiles. That very fear had driven them initially to Utah. Therefore, in March 1849 they drew up a constitution for the State of Deseret. It encompassed all the territory between the Sierra Nevada and Rocky Mountains north of Mexico and south of Oregon, plus an outlet to the sea in southern California. Whether the Salt Lake City leaders seriously expected the admission of a Mormon fiefdom of that size is uncertain. It was unlikely because of the widespread animosity toward them and their polygamy. Nevertheless, Taylor for a while did consider proposing a state which would combine both California and Utah.[16]

More realistic was the expectation that Congress would create a Mormon territory, an action which gained support from both the administration and the Mormon leadership. Wilson, on instructions from Washington, assured the Mormons that any territorial government would have friendly leadership and that the administration would support their claim to an outlet at San Diego.[17] Although the governing arrangement for Utah played only a minor role in the deliberations that led to the Compromise of 1850, that legislation established its territorial status and landlocked boundaries.

The administration's efforts to solve the vexing territorial questions were deeply entwined in the growing threat of southern secession. The

George Archibald McCall Papers, LC; George A. McCall, *Letters from the Frontiers During Thirty Years' Service in the U.S. Army* (1868; rpr. Gainesville, Fla., 1974), 485–86; Hamilton, *Prologue to Conflict*, 17, 47; Binkley, "Texas Jurisdiction," 18–19, 22–24; Neighbors, "Taylor–Neighbors Struggle," 432, 443–46. See also Colonel John Munroe to Major J. Van Horne, December 28, 1849, in *Senate Executive Documents*, 31st Cong., 1st Sess., No. 56, pp. 4–5.

15. Binkley, "Texas Jurisdiction," 27–30; Neighbors, "Taylor–Neighbors Struggle," 448–56; McCall to Bliss, May 21, June 11, 1849, in McCall Papers; to Crawford, July 15, 1849, in McCall *Letters*, 522.

16. Wilson to ZT, April 12, 1849, in ZT(LC), ser 2, r 1; Hamilton, *Prologue to Conflict*, 18, 20.

17. [Wilson] to ZT, December 24, 1849, in Ewing Family Papers, Box 53, LC; Johannsen, *Douglas*, 266.

danger from southern radicalism first became serious in the later stages of the Thirtieth Congress. In January 1849 John C. Calhoun suggested a caucus of southern senators and congressmen to devise a mechanism to protect the interests of the South in the argument over the admission of California. Some Whigs viewed the call in purely political terms, as an attempt "to disorganize the Southern Whigs and either to destroy Genl. Taylor in advance or compel him to throw himself in the hands of a large section of the democracy of the South." But more valid is the modern interpretation that "At heart the address legitimated the need for southern separatism on the ground that the North was bent on demanding emancipation and racial equality." The California issue accelerated the conflict.[18] The traditional southern political sensitivity also produced a Virginia call for a meeting to consider "the mode and measure of redress" if the Wilmot Proviso became law. Florida pledged in January to join other states in a common defense of southern interests. Such actions, which went well beyond any earlier steps, led Clayton to lament, "My soul sickens at the threats to dissolve the Union."[19]

Nor did the presence of a southern president in the person of Zachary Taylor slow the movement toward secession. As the spring turned into summer Whig candidates in the South who failed to align themselves with Calhoun found votes scarce. The strengthening of southern nationalism affected some of Taylor's original supporters. Both Robert Toombs and Alexander H. Stephens, for instance, increased the distance between them and the president until it became unbridgeable. In South Carolina a meeting of unhappy politicians in May 1849 suggested that the state cooperate with others of a like mind in the South and Southwest while the governor placed the state on a "military footing." In October a large, but unofficial, gathering in Jackson, Mississippi, issued a call for a convention of dissatisfied southerners at Nashville, Tennessee, on June 3, 1850. The main complaint of the southerners remained, as it had been for the past two years, the threat of passage of the Wilmot Proviso. As Avery Craven has pointed out, most southerners, like rural-agricultural peoples elsewhere, were orthodox and conservative. They viewed the Wilmot Proviso as "a deliberate act of aggression against their legal rights," and this affront angered even moderates.[20]

18. Robert Toombs to Crittenden, January 3, 1849, in Ulrich B. Phillips (ed.), "The Correspondence of Robert Toombs, Alexander H. Stephens, and Howell Cobb," *Annual Report of the American Historical Association for the Year 1911* (Washington, 1913), 139; James MacGregor Burns, *The Vineyard of Liberty* (New York, 1982), 470–72.

19. David M. Potter, *The Impending Crisis, 1848–1861* (New York, 1976), 88–89; Cole, *Whig Party in South*, 150.

20. Potter, *Impending Crisis*, 88; Avery O. Craven, *Civil War in the Making* (Baton

The southern fire-eaters were matched in ferocity, if not in numbers, by the northern radicals, mostly abolitionists. Just as Calhoun's call to defend southern interests attracted support from both of the major parties, the spread of antiextensionist feelings brought a joining of forces between the Democrats and the Free-Soilers of 1848 in New England, New York, Ohio, and Illinois. Joshua R. Giddings, the famed Ohio antislavery Whig, turned a convention in Cleveland, ostensibly celebrating the Northwest Ordinance, into a gathering of abolitionist zealots. The alliance of Democrats and Free-Soilers in the Old Northwest, an area of normal Whig weakness, represented a major threat to the success of the administration's programs.[21] It was one of the developments which led to the president's increasing alliance with the Seward-Weed faction in the Northeast and his courting of the protectionists in Pennsylvania.

It is especially difficult for modern observers, knowing what happened in the succeeding months, to realize how dangerous the situation appeared during the winter of 1849/50. Representative (former colonel) William H. Bissell did not overstate a consensus when he wrote in January, "The Union is in real, imminent peril. There is no use in denying the fact." The depth of the North-South split was apparent as soon as the Thirty-first Congress met on December 3, 1849. From the beginning of the session the southern feeling was so violent that some northern congressmen complained that it involved open talk of secession. In the Senate the 34 Democrats easily controlled the organization over the opposition of 24 Whigs and a pair of Free-Soilers. The House, in contrast, was effectively deadlocked with 111 Democrats, 105 Whigs, and 13 Free-Soilers. Moreover, the sectional split of the two major parties prevented either from functioning as a unit. Further confusing matters, the Thirty-first Congress was the first in American history in which the president's party controlled neither house. After taking four ineffective ballots on the third in which Democrat Howell Cobb led Whig Robert Winthrop for speaker, the House settled into a deadlock which lasted through 63 ballots. Not until December 21 was Cobb finally elected. The White House played no role in the maneuvering in the halls and rooming houses of Capitol Hill.[22]

Meanwhile, Robert Toombs sought private assurances from the presi-

Rouge, 1968), 39, 45; Thelma Jennings, *The Nashville Convention* (Memphis, 1980), 6–103; Philip May Hamer, *The Secession Movement in South Carolina, 1847–1852* (Allentown, Pa., 1918), 38–59; Hamilton, *Taylor*, II, 299–32.

21. Hamilton, *Taylor*, II, 232–33; Edgar Allen Holt, "Party Politics in Ohio, 1840–1850," *Ohio Archaeological and Historical Publications*, XXXVIII (1929), 358–66.

22. *Congressional Globe*, 31st Cong., 1st Sess., 1–6, 8–18, 35–39, 43–48, 51, 65–66; Hamilton, *Taylor*, II, 247–52. Bissell's quote is from George Fort Milton, *The Eve of Conflict* (Boston, 1934), 51.

dent that he would veto the Wilmot Proviso should it pass Congress. Taylor responded that "he would give no pledges either way" but left little doubt in Toombs's mind that he would sign the measure so abhorrent to the South.[23] Undoubtedly Taylor would have accepted the Proviso if it reached him for approval, but he did not consider that a likely prospect. By this time he was deeply involved with his own project to bypass the slavery issue through immediate statehood for California and New Mexico. Luckily for his peace of mind, Toombs did not know that at the same time William H. Seward was boasting that he had secured control over the direction of the administration. "The President," he told Weed, "will be put on the North side of the Mason & Dixon line, and he will not flinch from any duty."[24] Seward's claims reflected his bias more than it did any substantial shift in Taylor's views.

Taylor was appalled at the southern talk of secession and viewed the question of slavery in the new territories as an unfortunate tempest buffeting the ship of Union. He was, as he had been ever since he considered the issue, a unionist and had his own program for solving the crisis. It differed substantially from that of Seward and the northern radicals. But that would change, for as southern intransigence grew and as Taylor's temper and pettiness affected his stand, he moved closer to Seward and the radicals.

On Christmas Eve Colonel Bliss carried Taylor's annual message to Capitol Hill. It was the administration's first and only integrated policy statement. It began with a survey of international relations, noting the elimination of trade restrictions with Britain as a result of the Reciprocity Treaty, the enforcement of the neutrality laws during the Schleswig-Holstein War, and the failures of the revolutions of 1848 in Europe. The president then reviewed the current state of relations with Spain and Central America and the steps taken to suppress filibustering expeditions against Cuba.

More interesting to most members of Congress were the president's domestic proposals. He recommended the admission of California and New Mexico to statehood when they applied. Their government, he insisted, should be "in such form as to them shall seem most likely to effect their safety and happiness." This was a clear adoption of popular sovereignty. He cautioned Congress: "With a view to maintaining the harmony and tranquillity so dear to all, we should abstain from the introduction of those exciting topics of a sectional character."

23. Potter, *Impending Crisis*, 87, 89; William O. Lynch, "Zachary Taylor as President," *JSH*, IV (1938), 280n; Milton, *Eve of Conflict*, 50; Hamilton, *Taylor*, II, 255.

24. Seward to Weed, December 3, 1849, in Weed Papers, Rush Rhees Library, University of Rochester.

Taylor then passed to the question of the tariff, mildly suggesting an "adjustment on a basis which may augment the revenue." He recommended a return to specific duties rather than the ad valorem levy which had been imposed by the Walker Tariff in 1846. But he looked to "the wisdom and patriotism of Congress for the adoption of a system which may place home labor at least on a sure and permanent footing and by due encouragement of manufactures give a new and increased stimulus to agriculture and promote the development of our vast resources and the extension of our commerce." Not surprisingly, Congress found the issue too prickly to settle while sectional strife divided the body. The same lack of action greeted Taylor's suggestion of unspecified modifications in the subtreasury system and his call for the establishment of an agricultural bureau in the Interior Department. The suggestion for a survey of railroad routes to the West Coast and for the geological and mineralogical exploration of the gold areas of California would ultimately bear fruit but not during Taylor's administration.

The president supported the proposals of his service secretaries for the retirement of old or disabled officers. It must have come as no surprise to those who knew him that Taylor added kind words for Secretary Crawford's proposals for correction of the over-utilization of brevet rank and the shifting of staff officers into the line. In keeping with his pre-election stand, Taylor rejected the concept that the president was a "direct representative of the people," arguing instead for a balance of powers between the branches of government. He then added, clearly as a second thought, a promise to preserve the Union, proclaiming: "Whatsoever dangers may threaten it, I shall stand by it and maintain it in its integrity."[25]

Taylor's message is an interesting document from several viewpoints. The style is so ponderously rhetorical as to be conspicuously unlike his normal writing. Though there is no direct evidence, it seems to have been a committee work with Clayton, Meredith, Bullitt, Ewing, Letcher, and Taylor all sharing credit. Its mixed paternity is clearly evident in its variegated style and the famed solecism: "We are at peace with all the nations of the world, and seek to maintain our cherished relations with the rest of mankind." The reason for hanging the defense of the Union statement at the end of the document like a pendant diplomatic seal has never been satisfactorily explained. It had undoubtedly been added as a response to southern rhetoric. Thomas Hart Benton later claimed that it grew out of a request by Calhoun to Clayton that the message be silent on

25. James D. Richardson (ed.), *A Compilation of the Messages and Papers of the Presidents* (20 vols.; New York, 1897–1922), VI, 2547–62. The message is reprinted with its appended documents as *House Executive Documents* No. 5 and *Senate Executive Documents* No. 1, 31st Cong., 1st Sess.

the subject. Why it was not placed more logically is another question. In general, the message demonstrated how much political naïveté had chipped off Taylor during his first nine months in office. Conversely, it offered little warning of the prickliness that he would show during the next half year. Reaction to the message was predictably mixed. Daniel Webster thought it merely a "good Whig Document" but attached little importance to its contents. From the other side of the aisle Thomas Hart Benton concluded that it did demonstrate the president's concern about the threats to the Union.[26]

Taylor's call for calm had little effect. On the thirteenth Toombs heatedly responded to a speech by Seward and advanced to the brink of open advocacy of secession. He proclaimed, to the applause of most of the southern Democrats, and not a few Whigs: "You seek to drive us from the territories of California and New Mexico, purchased by the common blood and treasure of the whole people, and abolish slavery in this District, thereby attempting to fix a national degradation upon half of the states of the Confederacy." If the North succeeded, he thundered, "I am for disunion."[27]

The Mormon proposal for statehood proved to be the pry bar that opened the box of congressional argument over governments in the former Mexican lands. On December 27 Stephen A. Douglas presented the Deseret statehood memorial. It promptly brought calls for the president to report on the appointment of governors in California and New Mexico. Taylor submitted the documents on January 21, 1850, but pointed out that he had not replaced the military governments because Congress had not authorized it. The president described the King mission to California and reaffirmed his support of statehood for both regions. He again suggested, as he had in the annual message, that the courts could settle the New Mexico boundary question once it was granted statehood.[28] Although Taylor saw instant statehood as a means of avoiding the whole question of slavery in the territories, his proposal was politically unfortunate, for it had the effect of placing him in opposition to the extension of the Missouri Compromise line and to popular sovereignty at the territorial stage. Both had substantial support among the moderates upon whom Taylor had to depend if his program was to prevail.

26. Hamilton, *Taylor*, II, 256, 258–59; Webster to F. Haven, December 25, 1849, in Daniel Webster, *The Writings and Speeches of Daniel Webster* (16 vols.; Boston, 1903), XVI, 527; Thomas Hart Benton, *Thirty Years View* (2 vols.; New York, 1854–56), II, 740.

27. *Congressional Globe*, 31st Cong., 1st Sess., 27–28; Ulrich Bonnell Phillips, *The Life of Robert Toombs* (New York, 1913), 68–70; Potter, *Impending Crisis*, 94; William Y. Thompson, *Robert Toombs of Georgia* (Baton Rouge, 1966), 57.

28. *Congressional Globe*, 31st Cong., 1st Sess., 86–87; Richardson (ed.), *Messages & Papers*, VI, 2564–68; *Calif. & N. Mex.*, 1–3.

The Senate requested essentially the same information on January 7, to which the president responded on the thirtieth. He insisted that the military in Santa Fe had not interfered with the Texas efforts to establish courts there. It was technically correct, although the resistance to the spread of Texan authority was clear.[29] While awaiting Taylor's report the Senate continued its debate. Senator Benton introduced a bill to reduce the size of Texas which was promptly sent to the Judiciary. The same day, January 16, Senator Henry S. Foote's proposed establishment of territorial governments in California, New Mexico, and Utah was tabled, as was a proposal from Senator Henry Dodge to split up Texas. The Senate debate on California ranged back and forth across the aisles, and above and around other activities throughout most of January.[30] It frightened many of the older and more moderate politicians. Various individuals and groups sought to devise compromises which would cool the heated passions.

Henry Clay once again turned his fertile mind toward a possible solution. Despite illness, he trudged through the Washington streets on the stormy night of January 21 to visit Daniel Webster. The two huddled before the fire in Webster's library and produced a compromise to save the country.[31] Clay introduced the result on January 29 in a series of resolutions. The first called for the organization of territories without regard to slavery. Clay argued realistically that the system was impractical in such arid areas. His second resolution granted California free choice over slavery, which guaranteed that it would become a free state. His third proposal was for the federal government to assume the debt to the Republic of Texas in return for the state's relinquishing its claim to New Mexico. The fourth resolution provided for the abolition of slave trade, but not slavery, in the District of Columbia. The fifth suggestion was the passage of a stronger fugitive slave law, long desired by the South. The final action would be a declaration of the freedom of the interstate slave trade. Collectively the proposals, all of which had been offered individually earlier by other senators, were an effort to secure an "amicable arrangement of all questions in controversy between the free and the slave States, growing out of the object of slavery."[32]

29. *Congressional Globe*, 31st Cong., 1st Sess., 110; *Senate Executive Documents*, 31st Cong., 1st Sess., No. 24.

30. *Congressional Globe*, 31st Cong., 1st Sess., 165–71, 176–85, 210–13.

31. Irving H. Bartlett, *Daniel Webster* (New York, 1978), 245; Robert F. Dalzell, Jr., *Daniel Webster and the Trial of American Nationalism, 1843–1852* (Boston, 1973), 173; Claude Moore Fuess, *Daniel Webster* (2 vols.; Boston, 1930), 204–205; Glendon G. Van Deusen, *The Life of Henry Clay* (Boston, 1937), 399.

32. *Congressional Globe*, 31st Cong., 1st Sess., 244–52; Craven, *Growth of Southern Nationalism*, 71; Hamilton, *Prologue to Conflict*, 53–55; George D. Harmon, "Douglas

Clay defended his compromise in a long speech during February 5–6. He was so ill with a cold that he had to be assisted up the steps of the Capitol. When he arose a thermometer in the Senate Chamber stood at one hundred degrees. Nevertheless, he spoke for three hours that afternoon and an hour and forty-five minutes the following morning. It was a stirring speech. The Kentuckian pointed out that while the Wilmot Proviso dealt only with territories in which slavery would not be practical, his offer to Texas was a good bargain and the rest of his proposal balanced. He insisted that continuation of slavery in the District of Columbia was a concession to the South and the elimination of the slave trade there a concession to the North. While the interception of fugitive slaves was a constitutional responsibility of all states, the formal recognition of interstate slave trading was a further concession to the South. Although he did not stress it, the effect of Clay's proposal was to tilt permanently the free/slave-state balance in the Senate in favor of the North in return for concessions to the South which placed the institution of slavery on a firmer legal basis than it had formally possessed. The latter was an effort to placate the southern wing of the Whigs whose votes were necessary to pass the compromise. Few of them were supporters of the Kentuckian, who they generally believed had allied himself with the antislavery faction of the party, but time would prove that very few viewed Clay's plan as adequate protection of southern interests. The Senate debated Clay's resolutions until April but the arguments shifted few votes.[33]

During mid-February Taylor gave the debaters some factual basis for their flights of rhetoric. On the thirteenth he forwarded the text of the California constitution. The next day Senator Foote proposed sending the constitution and all slavery proposals to a select committee of thirteen.[34] That precipitated another round of the prolix profundity so much a part of the mid-century legislature. While orators thundered for the edification of their brethren and editors declaimed to a largely disinterested populace, some statesmen groped toward a compromise. Clay had already offered his thoughts. Webster still believed that the split between Clay and Taylor could be resolved and the Whigs be brought into the nearly solid phalanx needed to promulgate a workable settlement.

---

and the Compromise of 1850," *Journal of the Illinois State Historical Society,* XXI (1928–29), 464; Carl Schurz, *Henry Clay* (2 vols., 1899; rpr. New York, 1968), II, 330–35; Van Deusen, *Clay,* 399–400.

33. *Congressional Globe,* 31st Cong., 1st Sess., 301, 334–775, A115–27; Hamilton, *Prologue to Conflict,* 55–59; Hamilton, *Taylor,* II, 278–86; Schurz, *Clay,* II, 335–38; Van Deusen, *Clay,* 400–402.

34. *Congressional Globe,* 31st Cong., 1st Sess., 461–63; Richardson (ed.), *Messages & Papers,* VI, 2570.

A second, mixed group of Whigs and Democrats composed of Toombs, Cobb, Stephens, the Kentucky Democrat Linn Boyd, Illinois Whig John A. McClernand, Illinois Democrat William A. Richardson, and Ohio Democrat John K. Miller met on February 19 and agreed upon a package including the admission of California as well as open (*i.e.*, without limitation on slaveholding) territories and opposition to abolition in the District of Columbia.[35]

Toombs and Stephens along with Thomas L. Clingman of North Carolina called on the president on February 23. Apparently they wished to argue for the compromise worked out by the Toombs group but found Taylor adamantly opposed to open territories as too high a price to pay for the admission of California. In arguing their case the three southerners seem to have suggested that if a similar compromise were not adopted the southern states would secede. Taylor's anger flared. He accused them of threatening rebellion and announced he would take the field in person to put down any insurrection.[36] Some insight into Taylor's planned steps in case of southern secession appear in his comment to Horace Mann that he would levy an embargo on the offending states and blockade southern harbors.[37] The action was reminiscent of Andrew Jackson's response to the Nullification Controversy of 1833 and was essentially that which Abraham Lincoln would attempt to follow in 1861.

The same day as the collision between the southerners and Taylor, other southern Whigs pressed upon Webster the need for a compromise. The following day he dined with Stephens, Toombs, Clay, and the Free-Soil leader John P. Hale, but the outlines of a compromise remained elusive. Webster wrote his son on the twenty-fourth, "I know not how to meet the present emergency, or with what weapons to beat down

35. Richard N. Current, *Daniel Webster and the Rise of National Conservatism* (Boston, 1955), 161; Thompson, *Toombs*, 61; Alexander H. Stephens, *A Constitutional View of the Late War Between the States* (2 vols.; Philadelphia, 1868–70), II, 202–204.

36. Both the date and details of the meeting are uncertain. None of the participants left an account, although Thurlow Weed and Hannibal Hamlin claimed to have arrived at the White House immediately following it and to have found Taylor fuming. It is possible that the two men recounted different incidents since Hamlin's account, written in his old age, is plainly garbled. See John T. Hubbell, "Three Georgia Unionists and the Crisis of 1850," *Georgia Historical Quarterly*, LI (1967), 314; Thompson, *Toombs*, 61–62; Phillips, *Toombs*, 82; H. Draper Hunt, *Hannibal Hamlin of Maine* (Syracuse, 1969), 63; Thurlow Weed Barnes, *Memoir of Thurlow Weed* (Boston, 1884), 178; Hamilton, *Taylor*, II, 300–301; Milton, *Eve of Conflict*, 50. Hamlin's account is in Hamlin to Weed, August 10, 1876, in Weed Papers. Ann R. M. Hampton to Jane H. Hampton, January 26, 1850, in Miscellaneous Papers, HSPa, recounts a similar example of Taylor's exploding at a caller.

37. Hamilton, *Prologue to Conflict*, 70; Brainerd Dyer, *Zachary Taylor* (Baton Rouge, 1946), 382. See also an unattributed letter to the editor of the *Tribune*, February 23, 1850, New York *Tribune*, February 25, 1850.

the Northern and Southern follies. . . . I have poor spirits and little courage."[38]

Yet the way to safety was beginning to be delineated. The first steps were led by an unlikely guide. On February 25 Foote proposed the creation of a committee of fifteen to study the whole sectional issue. The importance of placing the solution in the hands of a blue ribbon commission was amply illustrated in a speech given by Toombs in the House two days later. He softened his rhetoric not at all in demanding southern rights and attacking the admission of California as a free state.[39]

During the last day of February Senator John Bell offered an alternative compromise, more in line with Taylor's ideas than Clay's. It proposed placing the Texas border at the Trinity River with the area further west and below the Thirty-fourth Parallel to form a new state. It would be free or slave as its inhabitants desired. Bell proposed to match the new state with one carved from Texas. He also suggested that the Lone Star State sell the land west of the Colorado River to the federal government as a means of generating the funds needed to pay off the debts of the Texas Republic. The newly acquired federal lands, Bell held, could be attached to New Mexico until such time as they attracted enough settlers to permit admission as a state. The status of slavery in the region, Bell would leave to the inhabitants.[40] It was a less sweeping proposal than Clay's but too complicated for the times.

John C. Calhoun was dying of consumption but rallied sufficiently to make a final thrust for the South. He barely struggled into the Senate chamber, walking on the arm of former governor James Hamilton, and was too weak to deliver his speech, which was read for him by James M. Mason of Virginia. It argued that the concessions offered by Clay gave the South insufficient protection. The North, Calhoun pointed out, already had a preponderance of population and with the admission of California would have the majority in the Senate also. That would give northern politicians the congressional strength to enact the protective tariffs, adopt cheap land prices, and finance internal improvements opposed by the South. Moreover, northern political parties catered to abolitionism. In Calhoun's view the South must have stronger, constitutional guaranties of

38. Herbert Darling Foster, "Webster's Seventh of March Speech and the Secession Movement, 1850," *AHR*, XXVII (1922), 258–59; Webster to Fletcher Webster, February 24, 1850, in Webster, *Writings*, XVI, 534.

39. *Congressional Globe*, 31st Cong., 1st Sess., 418, 424–28, A198–200; Thompson, *Toombs*, 62; Phillips, *Toombs*, 75–78.

40. *Congressional Globe*, 31st Cong., 1st Sess., 436–39; Joseph H. Parks, "John Bell and the Compromise of 1850," *JSH*, IX (1943), 340–42, and *John Bell of Tennessee* (Baton Rouge, 1950), 244–46.

its rights than proposed by Clay.[41] As he had so often before, the great southern political theorist expressed clearly the fears of his section. The reality of geography was that all of the land suitable for slavery in the United States had already entered the Union as states.[42] Although the South had lost the population race and could no longer protect its interests in the House of Representatives, the numerical equality of free and slave states so carefully crafted in the Missouri Compromise would be destroyed forever by the admission of California as a free state. To the mind which spawned the concept of concurrent majorities, it was logical to seek a constitutional sanctification of sectional rights.

Webster moved rapidly to respond to his longtime rival. For the Massachusetts sage the maintenance of the conservative alliance between northern men of property and southern plantation owners was the great imperative. It required the preservation of the Union. On March 7 Webster arose in the Senate to deliver one of the most memorable speeches ever heard by that body. "I do speak today, not as a Massachusetts man, nor as a Northern man, but as an American. I speak for the preservation of the Union," he intoned. During the next three hours Webster pleaded for tolerance, arguing that both the North and the South had benefited from the Union. Slavery, he reminded his southern listeners, would not succeed in California and New Mexico. Therefore, he would not support the empty rhetoric of the Wilmot Proviso. Abolitionism, he reminded the northern hotheads, had been counterproductive, but he reminded southerners that the violence of the northern press was not a federal issue. Webster reminded his listeners, however, that fugitive slaves were an issue that could be solved by federal legislation. He admitted that he had no solution for the greater issue of slavery although he personally would support colonization.[43]

It was Webster's last great speech but it failed to stir the winds of compromise. Although Webster's words attracted favorable popular response they rallied few if any northern Congressional Whigs. Northern antislavery men, to whom the idea of strengthening the fugitive slave law was an anathema, greeted the speech as the final evidence of "the fall of an archangel." Webster's call for moderation was predictably viewed by south-

41. *Congressional Globe*, 31st Cong., 1st Sess., 450–55; Hamilton, *Prologue to Conflict*, 71–74.

42. See Charles W. Ramsdell, "The Natural Limits of Slavery Expansion," *MVHR*, XVI (1929), 154–55.

43. *Congressional Globe*, 31st Cong., 1st Sess., 640–43; Hamilton, *Prologue to Conflict*, 76–78; Foster, "Webster's Seventh of March Speech," 262; Current, *Webster*, 161; Dalzell, *Webster & Nationalism*, 177–95; Bartlett, *Webster*, 246–50; Fuess, *Webster*, II, 210–17.

ern radicals as just another attempt to shackle the South to the wagon of northern exploitation. From their opposed vantage points both Jefferson Davis and William H. Seward assailed Webster's arguments in unforgiving speeches. Seward's attack was particularly unfortunate since he chose to express his personal sentiments rather than those of the administration. As the Whig senator closest to the president he was the natural spokesman for the administration on Capitol Hill. Had he chosen moderation or, at least, offered some hope of a compromise the crisis might have been ended in March instead of stretching on into summer. The harshness of Seward's words so disturbed Taylor that he stuttered in excitement and had Bullitt print a disclaimer in the *Republic*.[44]

During mid-March Stephen A. Douglas' Committee on Territories struggled to craft an acceptable territorial compromise. After working closely with Toombs, Stephens, and other southern leaders, Douglas reported out a bill on March 25 which called for the admission of California as a slave state and the establishment of the territories of New Mexico and Utah without any slavery stipulation. The bill also provided for settlement of the Texas boundary question.[45] Before discussion could shift to the substance of the Douglas proposal, however, the debate was diminished by the loss of John C. Calhoun. Although he had been too weak during the final weeks of his life to exercise much restraint over the southern fire-eaters, Calhoun's death ensured that the cleavage in southern ranks would widen since his very presence had been a restraining influence.

When the Senate returned from its recess in respect to Calhoun, tempers were frayed. On April 17 during a confrontation between Benton and Foote the latter pulled a pistol from his coat and pointed it at the Missourian, who he said was threatening him. They were quickly separated but the incident reminded everyone how close to a flashpoint was the temperature in the Senate.[46]

The next day the Senate adopted the proposal made in February by Foote that the California constitution and all of the slavery proposals be referred to a select committee of thirteen, composed of three Whigs and

44. *Congressional Globe*, 31st Cong., 1st Sess., 496, 502–503, A286; Foster, "Webster's Seventh of March Speech," 264; Schurz, *Clay*, II, 341; Glendon G. Van Deusen, *William Henry Seward* (New York, 1967), 122–25; Frederic Bancroft, *The Life of William H. Seward* (2 vols.; New York, 1900), I, 243–52; Hamilton, *Prologue to Conflict*, 84–86; [T. N. Parmalee], "Recollections of an Old Stager," *Harper's New Monthly Magazine*, XLVII (1873), 589; Hamilton, *Taylor*, II, 321–22.

45. Harmon, "Douglas & Compromise of 1850," 467–72; Johannsen, *Douglas*, 274; Van Deusen, *Clay*, 403; Stephens, *Constitutional View*, II, 204; *Congressional Globe*, 31st Cong., 1st Sess., 592–93. McClernand introduced a companion bill in the House.

46. William Nesbit Chambers, *Old Bullion Benton* (Boston, 1956), 460–62; Elbert B. Smith, *Magnificent Missourian* (Philadelphia, 1957), 270–71.

three Democrats from each section and chaired by Clay. The northern Whigs were James Cooper (Pennsylvania), Webster, and Samuel S. Phelps (Vermont); the southern Whigs: Bell, John M. Berrien (Georgia), Willie P. Mangum (North Carolina); the northern Democrats: Cass, Jesse D. Bright (Indiana), Daniel S. Dickinson (New York); the southern Democrats: Solomon W. Downs (Louisiana), William R. King (Alabama), and James M. Mason (Virginia). The men were all experienced, thoughtful individuals who had the confidence of their peers. Four—Clay, Webster, Bell, and Cass—had been or would be presidential candidates.[47]

Very little is known about the deliberations of the group. But worth noting was Foote's comment that: "The gentlemen who composed that committee did rise above influence; they did forget their party, absorbed as they were in patriotic solicitude for their country's welfare and honor." He went on to note that "Clay, Cass, and Webster, on the altar of their country's happiness, sacrificed everything like personal rivalry, disregarded everything like party ascendancy and success of faction, uniting themselves as a band of brothers, standing shoulder to shoulder in support of their common country." Some of the impetus for the final settlement came from outside the committee; several modern scholars give great credit to Stephen A. Douglas. Be that as it may, the final proposal as it appeared on May 8 was very close to that originally suggested by Clay. One bill established California as a free state, created the territories of Utah and New Mexico without reference to slavery, and provided for the purchase of the Texas claims to New Mexico. The second strengthened the fugitive slave act, and the third forbade the shipment of slaves to the District of Columbia for sale or transshipment.[48]

During April an incident occurred which deepened the split between Taylor and Clay. Relations between the two men had been correct but not cordial since the election. The president had apparently consciously excluded Clay from any role as an advisor. The reason has long been debated by historians without resolution and undoubtedly lies in the psyche of Taylor. He was not a man who easily accepted the honors bestowed on others or who was comfortable in the presence of those whom he perceived to have greater influence or standing. Moreover, he was quick to take offense and display his formidable temper, but unlike most people with quick tempers he tended to hold a grudge. It is, therefore, arguable that Taylor kept Clay at arm's length for several reasons. The first was cer-

47. *Congressional Globe*, 31st Cong., 1st Sess., 769–75.

48. *Ibid.*, 944–49; W. G. L. Smith, *The Life and Times of Lewis Cass* (New York, 1856), 695–96; Milton, *Eve of Conflict*, 68; F. H. Hodder, "The Authorship of the Compromise of 1850," *MVHR*, XXII (1936), 525–36.

tainly a desire to demonstrate his independence; the second was more subjective: to show that the administration was capable of managing the country on its own. Third, it demonstrated pique at the Kentuckian for his continued opposition to the Taylor nomination. The president's annoyance was further strengthened when Clay, deep in thought, passed Taylor on the street and did not speak. The latter assumed that he had been cut and took umbrage despite Clay's apology and explanation that he had not seen the president.[49]

The flare-up with Clay coincided with some shifts of power within the administration. Although the evidence is mostly circumstantial, it seems probable that Taylor had concluded that he must forge a new coalition to head off the threat of disunion. Abandoning his political ties to the South, he shifted to an alliance with the northern unionists. Most were antislavery men but that apparently played only a limited role in the new alignment. Seward played a major role in Taylor's alliance with the northerners. He had not only cultivated the president but had won his confidence and friendship. Seward's rise not only froze Fillmore from influence but it shifted to him control of all patronage in the North. Clayton, Meredith, and Preston supported the move, reasoning that it would remove any northern competition to Taylor's renomination in 1852 while opening the way for Seward to seek the presidency in 1856. Since Taylor during the Pennsylvania tour had hinted at a transformation of the Whigs into the moderate antislavery party, the plan looked to some observers like nothing less than the use of Seward to win over the northern antislavery faction while Taylor held on to southern unionists. It was a bold plan which in many ways presaged the efforts after 1856 by the former Whigs to mold the Republican party into an amalgam of moderates.[50] Whether the plan had yet received the president's blessing is not evident from the surviving record, but probably it had not. Nevertheless, the opposition of the administration to the compromise was unmistakable. Whether motivated by a jealousy of Clay, a genuine belief in the superiority of the two-state plan, mulish resistance to a proposal which was not his, or the arguments of antislavery proponents like Seward, Taylor refused to bargain with the congressional leaders. The reaction of the old Whig leadership is instructive. Webster, for instance, while professing to wish the administration well, insisted upon his independence and adamantly refused to champion the White House.[51]

49. Dyer, *Taylor*, 383. See also Van Deusen, *Clay*, 404; Hamilton, *Taylor*, II, 333.

50. Bancroft, *Seward*, I, 216; Phillips, *Toombs*, 65–66; Robert J. Rayback, *Millard Fillmore* (Buffalo, 1959), 199–200. See also Toombs to Crittenden, April [23], 1850, in Mrs. Chapman Coleman (ed.), *The Life of John J. Crittenden* (2 vols.; Philadelphia, 1871), I, 364–66.

51. Webster to J. P. Hall, May 18, 1850, in Webster, *Writings & Speeches*, XVI, 539–40.

After May 8 the debate in both houses shifted to a discussion of the Compromise. By June 11, fifty-eight speakers had addressed the House. Thirteen were in complete agreement with the proposal and six leaned toward it. Nineteen others supported the president's proposals while five diehards argued for the Wilmot Proviso and four wished to extend the Missouri Compromise line. Another nine were inclined to extending the Missouri line but objected to the notion of a compromise. The remaining two took no position. The Senate debate included a two-hour comparison of the Compromise to the administration's plan on May 13 by Clay and an unsuccessful effort by Davis to prohibit the territorial legislatures from interfering with slavery. The balance in the Senate was close. Webster concluded in mid-May that the Compromise hung on the vote of six southern senators. Clay on May 21 attacked the president's plan as one solving only a single issue, California, and leaving four others untended. The speech was not an intemperate attack but it signified Clay's final break with the administration. The White House's reaction was immediate. It appeared in a violent editorial in the *Republic* which excoriated the Kentuckian for shattering the Whig support for Taylor's plan and of acting out of a desire for personal glory. When Bullitt resisted printing the attack he was sacked at the behest of the White House.[52]

On June 13 Seward castigated Texas for her threats to use force to exert her claim over parts of New Mexico. It brought a sharp retort from Foote that the New Yorker was "panting" for a Civil War. Four days later Taylor assured the Senate that no orders had been given to the military officers in Santa Fe to prevent the exercise of Texas authority. The president again seized the opportunity to argue that the boundary question should be settled by "some competent authority." But Taylor at the same time privately told Lieutenant Alfred Pleasanton, bound for Santa Fe, that he would take the field in person in New Mexico if necessary to keep the Texans at bay. Some southerners, Taylor insisted, were plotting a Civil War. He firmly believed that the disunion movement must be arrested, peacefully if possible but by force if necessary. Daniel Webster, however, was probably correct when he observed that Taylor simply did not understand the political impact of Americans shedding American blood.[53]

52. *Congressional Globe*, 31st Cong., 1st Sess., 941–1178, A612–16; Hamilton, *Prologue to Conflict*, 99–100, 104, and *Taylor*, II, 333–35; Van Deusen, *Clay*, 406; Milton, *Eve of Conflict*, 69; Potter, *Impending Crisis*, 104; Craven, *Growth of Southern Nationalism*, 98, 100; Webster to Havens, May 18, 1850, in Webster, *Private Correspondence*, II, 369. On June 1 Senator John H. Clarke of Rhode Island identified nineteen northern or border senators as opposed to the Compromise. A similar estimate was made by Lewis Cass on June 13. Holman Hamilton, "Democratic Senate Leadership and the Compromise of 1850," *MVHR*, XLI (1954), 406.

53. *Congressional Globe*, 31st Cong., 1st Sess., A815–18; Bancroft, *Seward*, I, 274; Richardson, *Messages & Papers*, VI, 2586; Pleasanton to Weed, September 22, 1876, in

Taylor, the observer must remember, lived in a simplistic, black and white world in which a transgression of law, written or unwritten, had to be dealt with by immediate and strong action. That such an action could be counterproductive in some situations was a concept which Taylor found foreign.

Despite the intensity of rhetoric in Washington, the grassroots pressure for southern separation declined in the spring of 1850. The Nashville Convention, so boldly called during the preceding fall, met on June 3–12. Only nine states dispatched delegations and many of them were small and undistinguished. The gathering demonstrated that while the southern political leadership could agree on the need to defend the section's rights it could not agree on what those rights actually were.[54]

By mid-June Vice-President Fillmore concluded that the compromise would pass the Senate but had not decided how he would vote if he had to break a tie. The indecision soon vanished. About the first of July he warned the president that he would vote for the Compromise. The vice-president insisted, however, that he would do so for patriotic reasons, not pique over his loss of influence within the administration.[55] Fillmore's independence was one more indication of the disintegration of the team that Taylor had installed a year earlier. Another was the resignation, written on June 18 but probably never delivered, of Clayton. It was a move expected by many who knew him. The Delaware lawyer was unhappy as an administrator and had been worn down by the demands of leadership of the cabinet. Moreover, he needed to return to his private affairs. Nor was Clayton the only advisor whose departure was imminent. The president on June 28 requested Orlando Brown's resignation as commissioner of Indian affairs.[56] Brown had come to Washington to serve as Crittenden's agent on patronage but had proven less successful than the Kentuckian had anticipated. Moreover, Taylor wished to fill the position with a commissioner better attuned to the job.

As the struggle over the Compromise intensified in the Congress and the administration moved to realign itself for its second phase, Taylor, it appears, was in good spirits. But the president did not remain unruffled

---

Barnes, *Memoir of Weed*, 180; Webster to Havens, September 12, 1850, in Webster, *Writings & Speeches*, XVIII, 388.

54. Potter, *Impending Crisis*, 104; Craven, *Growth of Southern Nationalism*, 95–97; Jennings, *Nashville Convention*, 135–66; St. George L. Sioussat, "Tennessee, the Compromise of 1850, and the Nashville Convention," *MVHR*, II (1915), 347.

55. Rayback, *Fillmore*, 235, 237; Henry J. Carman and Reinhard Luthin, "The Seward-Fillmore Feud and the Crisis of 1850," *New York History*, XXIV (1943), 176.

56. Clayton to ZT, June 18, 1850, in John M. Clayton Papers, IX, LC; ZT to Brown, June 28, 1850, in ZT(KHS).

for long. On July 1 a group of southern Whig congressmen concluded that they should protest the administration's alliance with the northerners before openly breaking with the White House. They selected Charles M. Conrad, Humphrey Marshall, and Toombs, all original Taylor supporters, to remonstrate with the president. The three visited the White House that evening. They warned Taylor that his demand for the admission of both California and New Mexico and his menacing attitude toward Texas would drive the southern Whigs into opposition. The president responded with the very practical argument, which undoubtedly reflected the advice that Seward and his allies in the cabinet had proffered, that he could not afford to lose eighty-four votes from northern Whig congressmen to hold twenty-nine southern ones. Taylor warned the southerners that he would order the army to defend the New Mexico border if Texas attempted to alter it. When Secretary Crawford learned of the threat he insisted he would not sign such an order; Taylor responded he would sign it if necessary.[57]

The president considered sending a special message to Congress defending his plan and discussed the tactic with Seward. It is not clear how far the project developed, although Seward delivered a defense of Taylor's plan in the Senate on July 2.[58] The following day Alexander Stephens tried to dissuade Taylor from his course. With Toombs and two other southerners, he called on the president but found him immobile, Taylor's usual position when he met with opposition. Shortly after leaving the president, Stephens and Toombs encountered Secretary Preston on the steps of the Treasury Building. Hoping to gain support, they warned the navy secretary that Taylor would be impeached if he attempted to use federal troops in New Mexico. Preston asked, "Who will impeach him?" To which Stephens replied, "I will if nobody else does." Still exercised by the president's course, Stephens wrote a letter which appeared in the July 4 *National Intelligencer*.[59] It warned that the South would support Texas in any clash with the federal authorities over New Mexico.

On the same day as Taylor's meeting with Stephens, John Bell, who was the administration's most consistent supporter in the Senate, began a long speech which continued into the sixth. He assailed the Compromise bill

57. Frederick W. Seward, *Seward at Washington as Senator and Secretary of State* (New York, 1891), 141; J. F. H. Claiborne, *Life and Correspondence of John A. Quitman* (2 vols.; New York, 1860), II, 32–33; Thompson, *Toombs*, 67–68; Hamilton, *Taylor*, II, 380–81.

58. Bancroft, *Seward*, I, 275–78; *Congressional Globe*, 31st Cong., 1st Sess., 1330; Cole, *Whig Party in South*, 167.

59. Myrta Lockett Avary (ed.), *Recollections of Alexander H. Stephens* (New York, 1910), 26; Hubbell, "Three Georgia Unionists," 315; Phillips, *Toombs*, 84; Thompson, *Toombs*, 68, 83.

as "a piece of political joinery" and insisted that a broader settlement was needed. Therefore, he supported the president on the admission of California and New Mexico. He argued, as did Taylor, that admission as a state would end the controversy over slavery in the two areas.[60]

While the Senate continued to debate the Compromise, the House moved to a much more embarrassing problem for the administration. It involved activities of Secretary of War Crawford prior to his joining the cabinet. Crawford since 1833 had been the counsel in the Galphin Claims case. The claims were those of a colonial Indian trader in Georgia who in 1775 received a certificate from the colonial government for land in compensation for losses. The state of Georgia ignored the claim after the Revolution but the Treaty of New Echota contained a provision transferring responsibility for Cherokee-related claims to the federal government. In 1839 a Senate committee concluded that the Galphin Claim was a responsibility of Georgia, but in August 1848 Congress reversed itself and approved payment. Polk's secretary of the Treasury, Robert J. Walker, paid the principal of $9,700 but refused interest. Crawford, as lawyer for the claimants, then made a claim for interest. It was not acknowledged by the Treasury until after the change of administrations. Reverdy Johnson as attorney general ruled that interest was due and Meredith paid $191,352.89. It embarrassed Crawford, who received half of the payment as his fee. He only belatedly told Taylor of his involvement but, apparently correctly, insisted that he had not influenced the settlement.[61] The House then investigated the payment. Its committee reported that neither Crawford, Johnson, nor Meredith were guilty of any deliberate wrongdoing but recommended against payment of the interest. On July 9 a resolution of disapproval passed the House but was never considered in the Senate.[62] The move against the three cabinet members coincided with Taylor's acceptance of proposals from Weed and others that the cabinet be revamped. Edward Stanly of North Carolina would replace Crawford at the War Department; John Bell return to the cabinet as attorney general in the place of Johnson; and Governor Hamilton Fish of New York become secretary of the Treasury. Clayton's successor in the State Department would be Crittenden.[63] Had such changes been made, it would have given

60. *Congressional Globe*, 31st Cong., 1st Sess., 1334, 1342, 1349; Parks, *Bell*, 253–56; Parks, "Bell & Compromise of 1850," 348–52.

61. William P. Brandon, "The Galphin Claim," *Georgia Historical Quarterly*, XV (1931), 114–70; Bernard C. Steiner, *Life of Reverdy Johnson* (New York, 1970), 35; Hamilton, *Taylor*, II, 345–47.

62. Hamilton, *Taylor*, II, 347–52; Thompson, *Toombs*, 67; *Congressional Globe*, 31st Cong., 1st Sess., 1019–1360 *passim*.

63. Harriet A. Weed (ed.), *Autobiography of Thurlow Weed* (Boston, 1884), 590–91;

Taylor one of the strongest cabinets ever assembled. Crittenden, Bell, and Fish were extremely able and dedicated men who had great strength of character. Moreover, when combined with a president who had passed from his initial naïve belief in a nonpolitical chief executive to at least the glimmering of a recognition of the necessity for political leadership in the White House, the prospects for a strong, positive administration appeared promising.

Rayback, *Fillmore*, 236; Dyer, *Taylor*, 334–35; W. T. Sherman to P. F. Smith, August 4, 1850, in Miscellaneous Papers, HSPa; Hamilton, *Taylor*, II, 355–56, 382.

CHAPTER XVI

The President Is Dead

BEFORE THE cabinet shifts could be made, or the territorial question be brought to a settlement, the fates intervened. Thursday,
the Fourth of July, 1850, dawned sunny, hot, and humid. Taylor joined the
cabinet on the shaded platform near the unfinished Washington Monument to hear Senator Henry S. Foote deliver the main address and witness
the deposit in the monument of some dust from the tomb of Thaddeus
Kosciusko. Rather than returning home after Foote's address, Taylor
stayed to listen to George Washington Parke Custis and other orators. He
apparently stood or sat in the sun for two hours and then walked along
the Potomac River. The president did not return to the White House until
nearly 4:00 P.M., well after his normal dining hour. He drank freely of
iced water and chilled milk, as well as eating cherries and possibly other
fruits and vegetables. All were foods or liquids that Washington's inhabitants had been warned to avoid because of the fear of a possible spread to
the nation's capital of the Asiatic cholera epidemic which was sweeping
parts of the country.[1]

1. Mangum to wife, July 10, 1850, in Henry Thomas Shanks (ed.), *The Papers of Willie
Person Mangum* (5 vols.; Raleigh, N.C., 1950–56), V, 181; Nathan Sargent, *Public Men
and Events* (2 vols.; Philadelphia, 1875), II, 369–70; W. T. Sherman to P. F. Smith, August
4, 1850, in Miscellaneous Papers, HSPa; Holman Hamilton, *Zachary Taylor* (2 vols.; Indianapolis, 1941, 1951), II, 387–88. Mangum claims that Taylor commonly drank as much
as two gallons of water before dinner.

The president spent an uncomfortable night but was well enough the next day to sign the ratification letter for the Clayton-Bulwer Treaty, to accept an invitation to attend the New York State Fair at Syracuse, and to send thanks to a Bostonian for the gift of a pair of iced salmon. Late in the day his discomfort worsened and he began to develop symptoms similar to those he had displayed in Pennsylvania. As yet, however, the ailment did not appear serious, but on Saturday, the sixth, the family began to have concerns. By late afternoon or evening someone at the White House called in Dr. Alexander S. Wotherspoon, an army surgeon. He diagnosed the illness as cholera morbus, a flexible mid–nineteenth-century term for intestinal ailments as diverse as diarrhea and dysentery but not related to Asiatic cholera. Wotherspoon prescribed calomel and opium, which appeared to produce an immediate improvement. He felt pleased enough with the progress of his patient to return home. The White House issued a bulletin announcing that the president was indisposed and rumors flew about Washington that the illness resulted from something he had eaten.

During Sunday, the seventh, the public heard reports that the president had rallied, but in reality he was slowly sinking. The patient displayed varied symptoms and intermittent fever. He was very thirsty and ate ice until his stomach began to reject fluids. Wotherspoon called in Assistant Surgeon Richard H. Coolidge of the army and Dr. James C. Hall, a popular Washington physician. Whether they first saw Taylor on Sunday or Monday is not certain. During Monday Dr. Wood arrived from Baltimore. He thought that the symptoms indicated a recurrence of the Pennsylvania attack and seems to have been concerned rather than worried.

By Monday the president was despondent and predicted that "in two days I shall be a dead man." That day dysentery appeared and vomiting increased. The bulletin sent to the newspapers that night reported the president seriously ill. Many in Washington by then apparently realized that Taylor was on his deathbed. The news reports that reached the public during Tuesday, July 9, were confusing. They reported, on what basis we do not know, improvement followed by a rapid decline. That morning Taylor told his doctors: "You have fought a good fight, but you cannot make a stand." He hung on to consciousness through the afternoon and into the evening.[2]

As the end drew near messengers departed from the White House to

2. ZT to E. P. Prentice, July 5, 1850, in ZT(LC), ser 2, r 1; Holman Hamilton, *Prologue to Conflict* (Lexington, 1964), 107; Hamilton, *Taylor*, II, 389–91; Hudson Strode, *Jefferson Davis, American Patriot* (New York, 1955), 227; Charles E. Rosenberg, *The Cholera Years* (Chicago, 1962), 74.

warn the two houses of Congress. In the House, then concluding its debate on the Galphin Claims, Representative Thomas H. Bayly of Virginia arose and informed his colleagues: "I understand that authentic information has reached the Capitol that the condition of the President of the United States is so critical [that] he will probably not survive one hour. I, therefore, move that this house adjourn." It did so by a vote of 176 to 16.

In the Senate Andrew P. Butler of South Carolina was about one hour into a dull proslavery speech when Daniel Webster rose and asked leave to interrupt. In an emotional voice he announced: "I have a sorrowful message to deliver. A great misfortune threatens the nation. The President of the United States, General Taylor, is dying, and may not survive the day." The Senate immediately adjourned without a vote.[3]

Jefferson Davis hastened directly to the White House, where he found the Woods, the Joseph Taylors, the Blisses, and Mrs. Taylor gathered. Betty Bliss was overcome with grief and her mother unable to stand unsupported. At about 10:00 P.M. the president called his wife to him, begged her not to grieve or weep and said: "I have always done my duty. I am ready to die. My only regret is for the friends I leave behind me." He shortly afterwards lost consciousness and died soon after 10:30 on July 9, 1850. Undertaker Samuel Kirby soon arrived to take charge of the body, which was not embalmed but kept packed in ice in accord with the wishes of Mrs. Taylor.[4]

The necessary official actions followed immediately. Fillmore, who had spent much of the day at the White House but who was resting at home, was called. The cabinet was notified and in turn it formally announced to the vice-president that the president had died. Fillmore, in turn, acknowledged the note and asked them to be present at noon the following day when he would take the oath of office in the House of Representatives. Fillmore made no speech following his swearing in by Chief Justice William Cranch of the district court. His written eulogy, included in his notification to the two houses of Taylor's death, was a more fitting tribute. "A great man has fallen," he wrote, "one whose life has been devoted to the public service, whose career in arms has not been surpassed in usefulness or brilliancy, who has been so recently raised by the unsolicited voice of the people to the highest civil authority in the Government, which he administered with so much honor and advantage to his country, and by whose sudden death so many hopes of future usefulness have been

3. *Congressional Globe*, 31st Cong., 1st Sess., 1360, 1363; Strode, *Davis*, 227–28.
4. James D. Richardson (ed.), *A Compilation of the Messages and Papers of the Presidents* (20 vols.; New York, 1897–1922), VI, 2590; Strode, *Davis*, 228; Brainerd Dyer, *Zachary Taylor* (Baton Rouge, 1946), 405–406; Hamilton, *Taylor*, II, 392–93.

blighted forever."[5] On the tenth Clayton officially notified American diplomats serving abroad and in a second note informed the foreign representatives in Washington and invited them to the funeral ceremonies. Fillmore closed all federal offices until the funeral and declared six months of official mourning.[6]

The two houses of Congress appointed a joint committee to make the funeral arrangements[7] and then indulged in a round of eulogies.[8] The general orders promulgated to the armed services by Secretaries Crawford and Preston spoke of Taylor as a man "solely engrossed in maintaining the honor and advancing the glory of his country[;] he rendered himself signal and illustrious. An unbroken current of success and victory . . . left nothing to be accomplished for his military fame. The simplicity of his character, the singleness of his purpose, the elevation and patriotism of his principles, his moral courage, his justice, magnanimity and benevolence, his wisdom, moderation, power of command, . . . add to the deep sense of the national calamity."[9] His death, in the words of Thomas Hart Benton, was "a public calamity." But even more impressive, coming from one of the senior members of Congress, was the observation that "his brief career showed no deficiency of political wisdom for want of previous political training."[10]

During the afternoon of Friday, July 12, public viewing of the body took place in the East Room of the White House. The black-draped casket had been placed on an elevated platform in the center of the room under a black canopy lined in silver. Taylor was shrouded in white satin with a cravat of the same color "gracefully thrown around the neck." The coffin was covered by a profusion of flowers which were constantly renewed as their numbers were reduced by light-fingered viewers.

The funeral took place the following day. At sunrise the military installations around Washington fired a national salute in honor of the late president. The weather was clear with a welcome breeze and the temperature moderate. An estimated 100,000 people thronged the city, especially along the funeral route. The funeral service was held at noon in the East Room. It was conducted by Dr. Smith Pyne, the rector of St. John's Epis-

5. Richardson (ed.), *Messages & Papers*, VI, 2600.

6. *Ibid.*, 2589–93; Robert J. Rayback, *Millard Fillmore* (Buffalo, 1959), 238. Since the Senate was in recess when the notification arrived, it was reprinted in the Journal for July 10.

7. Senators Daniel Webster, Lewis Cass, and W. R. King; Representatives C. M. Conrad, James McDowell, R. C. Winthrop, W. H. Bissell, William Duer, J. L. Orr, Daniel Beck, William Strong, S. F. Vinton, E. C. Cabell, J. B. Kerr, Edward Stanly, and N. S. Littlefield.

8. *Congressional Globe*, 31st Cong., 1st Sess., 1363–70; *Obituary Addresses Delivered on the Occasion of the Death of Zachary Taylor* (Washington, 1850), 7–67.

9. Richardson (ed.), *Messages & Papers*, VI, 2592–93.

10. Thomas Hart Benton, *Thirty Years View* (2 vols.; New York, 1854–56), II, 765.

copal Church, and Dr. C. B. Butler, the chaplain of the Senate. President Fillmore and his cabinet sat at the foot of the bier while the clergy took their posts at its head. To the left of the bier sat the pall bearers along with the male members of the family; Wood, Bliss, the grandsons, Joseph Taylor, and Jefferson Davis. Mrs. Taylor, prostrate in her room and attended by Varina Davis, did not attend. General Scott and the senior officers of the other services sat to the right of the bier in full uniform contending for splendor with the diplomatic corps. The members of Congress occupied seats on the western side of the room.

At 1:00 P.M. the funeral service concluded and a detachment of marines carried the casket to a splendid black catafalque or hearse festooned in white silk, above which thrust a deeply shrouded American eagle. The hearse was drawn by eight beautifully caparisoned white horses, each with its own groom dressed in white and wearing a white turban. The procession, organized by General Scott, stretched for nearly two miles when all the elements took their places. The military escort was composed of militia from Maryland, the District of Columbia, and Virginia, a battalion of marines, a battalion of artillerymen, and a mounted field artillery battery under Brevet Major John Sedgwick. They were followed by naval officers marching on foot, the militia commander (Major General Walter Jones of the District of Columbia), and General Scott, the latter resplendent in his dress uniform with a towering plume of yellow feathers decorating his helmet. Following the military units marched the Joint Congressional Committee and the twenty official pall bearers.[11] Behind them came the hearse and "Old Whitey," led by a groom. Taylor's famed horse carried the reversed spurs and stirrups which signified a funeral. Following the great white horse were three carriages carrying the family, the president and the cabinet, the two houses of Congress, the Washington City Council, Joseph Henry and the officers of the Smithsonian Institution, a group of firemen and Temperance Society members, a militia band, government clerks, the judiciary, and finally common citizens and strangers. Artillery detachments stationed near St. John's Church on Lafayette Square, at City Hall, and at the Capitol marked the progress of the procession by firing minute guns continually until three o'clock. At the Congressional Cemetery the troops formed a double line while the coffin, preceded by the clergy, passed on to the temporary vault in which it would be placed. There Dr. Payne read the solemn and moving Episcopal burial

11. Senators Henry Clay, Lewis Cass, J. M. Berrien, T. H. Benton, Daniel Webster, Truman Smith; Representatives R. C. Winthrop, James McDowell, Hugh White, Lynn Boyd, S. F. Vinton, I. E. Holmes, R. J. Walker; Chief Justice William Cranch; Generals T. S. Jesup and George Gibson of the army and Archibald Henderson of the marine corps; George Washington Parke Custis, Commodore H. E. Ballard, and Joseph Gales.

service. The body was not interred since it was Mrs. Taylor's desire that final burial take place in Kentucky.[12]

Although the City Council of Frankfort requested that Taylor be buried at the Kentucky capital, Mrs. Taylor chose the more fitting Taylor family cemetery outside of Louisville. Congress appropriated the money necessary to transport the president's remains there and on July 17 Webster secured unanimous approval in the Senate for the erection of a monument in his honor. In October Colonels Bliss and Joseph Taylor escorted the body by special train to Pittsburgh. On Monday, October 28, the casket was transferred to the packet steamer *Navigator*. She cast off and headed downstream, making stops at the principal cities along the way for local dignitaries to pay their last respects to the departed president. The waterborne cortege reached Louisville on November 1. Following a short ceremony the body was placed in an unpretentious limestone vault. The remainder of the family, escorted by Dr. Wood, left Washington on October 28 to travel overland to New Orleans, where the whole group was reunited in early November following Bliss's and Joseph Taylor's discharge of their sad duty. The site of the vault and the monument passed into federal hands as the Zachary Taylor National Cemetery where today he shares the grounds with the dead of America's subsequent conflicts.[13]

Although President Fillmore offered Mrs. Taylor continued residence in the White House, the widow departed immediately following the funeral for the home of Secretary of the Treasury Meredith. She remained there until July 18, when she left for Baltimore, never again to return to the nation's capital. Mrs. Taylor remained in Baltimore until departing for New Orleans in November. She soon moved into a modest cottage in East Pascagoula, Mississippi, where she died on August 14, 1852.[14]

The president's estate was settled during the summer and fall of 1850 by his lawyer in New Orleans, Judah P. Benjamin. Mrs. Taylor received the Kentucky property, the bank stock, household furniture, and some

---

12. *Obituary Addresses*, 75–104; Richardson (ed.), *Messages & Papers*, VI, 2594–97; Richard N. Current, *Daniel Webster and the Rise of National Conservatism* (Boston, 1955), 171; Dyer, *Taylor*, 407–408; Charles Winslow Elliott, *Winfield Scott, the Soldier and the Man* (New York, 1937), 602; Hamilton, *Taylor*, II, 396–98; Ishbel Ross, *First Lady of the South* (New York, 1958), 63.

13. Crittenden to J. P. Taylor, July 21, 1850, in ZT(LC), ser 2, r 1; Strode, *Davis*, 229; [T. B. Thorpe], "General Taylor's Residence at Baton Rouge," *Harper's New Monthly Magazine*, IX (1854), 765; W. C. Patterson to Bliss, October 10, 1850, in ZT(UKL); Hamilton, *Taylor*, II, 400; Frederick Way, Jr., *Way's Packet Directory, 1848–1983* (Athens, Ohio, 1983), 340. There were subsequently proposals in 1878 to move the body to Frankfort and in 1911 to shift it to Washington, D.C. A. Bedford to Richard Taylor, January 22, 1878, in ZT(LC), ser 3, r 2; unidentified clipping *ibid.*, ser 4, r 2.

14. Hamilton, *Taylor*, II, 399.

of the slaves. Each of the daughters received a legacy of $20,000 and Richard $21,000. Benjamin's final valuation of the estate was:

Cypress Grove Plantation	$20,000.00
131 slaves	56,650.00
Cash	18,601.77
95 shares of Bank of Louisville stock	9,500.00
30 shares of Northern Bank of Kentucky stock	3,000.00
100 shares of Western Bank of Baltimore stock	2,000.00
Cash held by Col. Bliss	7,018.25
TOTAL	$116,770.02

That total did not include the money which Taylor had advanced Richard to acquire Fashion Plantation. When it is added the total approaches $200,000. The family on December 9 agreed upon a division of the estate in a long, complicated twenty-three-page document and a separate agreement between the children on the handling of the Cypress Grove property, which Richard acquired.[15] Despite his constant complaints about his poor financial condition, Zachary Taylor had died a rich man, worth nearly $3,250,000 in 1983 dollars.

Taylor's papers, to the degree which he kept any, and his memorabilia remained in the possession of his son Richard at Fashion Plantation. Unfortunately, they became fair game when the plantation was sacked by Union troops in 1863. Only a few items have since appeared to be rescued by collectors and manuscript repositories, leading to the natural conclusion that most of what was there was destroyed by the boys in blue who looted "Dick Taylor's" plantation. Occasionally, items appeared. In July 1863, for instance, Major General Benjamin F. Butler, "the Beast of New Orleans," returned to Joseph Taylor the presentation sword from the State of Kentucky. It had been captured, Butler noted, from "disloyal hands."[16] The characterization is one which Zachary Taylor would have appreciated and with which he would have agreed.

Few presidents have proven in practice to be as different from their expected roles as Zachary Taylor. Except for a handful of very close

15. Benjamin to Richard Taylor, August 7, 1850, in ZT(LC), ser 6, r 2; Agreement Between Widow and Heirs, and Agreement Between Heirs, December 9, 1950, both *ibid.*, ser 3, r 1. Under the division between the children Ann Wood received twenty-three slaves, one hundred shares of Western Bank of Baltimore stock, forty-five shares of Bank of Louisville stock, cash held by Colonel Bliss, and half interest in Cypress Grove; Betty Bliss received twenty-five slaves, fifty shares of Bank of Louisville stock, Northern Bank stock, $8,310 in cash, and half interest in Cypress Grove. Richard's share was eighty-three slaves and $7,500 in cash.

16. Butler to J. P. Taylor, July 28, 1862, in ZT(LC), ser 3, r 2.

friends, it is doubtful that many Americans in 1848 would have predicted that the slaveholding planter from Louisiana would emerge as the champion of exclusion of slavery from the territories or that the victorious soldier of the Mexican War would have presided over the renunciation of Manifest Destiny and the curtailing of the Monroe Doctrine. Nor would many of his supporters in the South have rejoiced at voting for a candidate who would announce his embrace of protectionism. Was Taylor a turncoat? Or, was he a man of consistency who was misread by his contemporaries? That has been a question which has intrigued historians since his death. It is not easily or simply answered.

Like any man or woman, Zachary Taylor was a product of his time, place, and experience. Taylor was an aristocrat with a common touch. He was the product of frontier Kentucky, but the Kentucky of landowners and speculators not of the yeoman farmers like Thomas Lincoln. He grew to manhood in a family of stature whose estate and home fields stretched along the high ground drained by the Beargrass Creek, just outside of Louisville. During the years of his childhood and adolescence, Louisville was a settlement offering dynamic opportunity to the individual willing to gamble on the future as well as a sophisticated society which appreciated both success and manners.

As the younger son of an only moderately successful father,[17] his future lay beyond the family lands. Young Zachary chose one of the few professions that combined social acceptability with a reasonable income and no requirement for further education. For young men like Taylor who lacked the inclination or the talent for admission to one of the learned professions or the financial support necessary to become a banker, the army offered an attractive occupation. Moreover, it fitted in well with the frontier tradition of Kentucky and the concepts of service that Richard Taylor seems to have inculcated in his sons. Undoubtedly, military service, even in the miasmic swamplands of the lower Mississippi, had romanticism which appealed to a twenty-four year old.

The War of 1812 demonstrated some of the salient characteristics of the man. He was energetic yet conservative and cautious in his actions. His defense of Fort Harrison proved he could handle men under stress while retaining the flexibility which the military commander must possess if he is to respond successfully to the surprises of the battlefield. Even so, his slow promotion to major suggests that in the eyes of at least some of his contemporaries Taylor had weaknesses. This is less evident, however, when one looks at the promotions and appointments to the twenty-

17. The evidence is inconclusive but Richard Taylor's abandonment of land speculation after 1810 suggests earlier reverses.

one infantry regiments organized in 1812 and early 1813. Only nine of the majors had seen service as captains and only three of those were regulars. The remainder were appointed directly from civilian life. Nevertheless, it is characteristic of Taylor that he smarted under this fancied slight.

Often described as simple, kind, frank, and straightforward, he was also called "a man of strong and blind prejudices" and "very ambitious."[18] Taylor's temper was massive when it exploded. "I never knew a man of his years and character so easily and completely thrown off his balance by trifles," Major General John Pope reported. Taylor, on whose staff Pope had served, was "a very irascible man and flew into passion at the least provocation and for the most trifling causes."[19] Much of the time he either succeeded in restraining it or was slow to anger. His apparent ability to chafe under presumed slights for a long period before reacting may have been less a matter of personal control, which some of those who knew him well did not believe he had, as it was a delay in awakening to the violation of his rights or interests. This would explain his well-known ability to lose his temper over relatively petty incidents such as teamsters' inability to handle teams. At the same time, Taylor had a wry sense of humor which led him to enjoy putting on visitors by playing a country bumpkin. There are a raft of tales of young officers reporting to camp and mistaking Taylor for a laborer. That he played along with the joke in nearly all instances proves little beyond his adoption of the broad humor of the frontier.

Taylor possessed a store of common sense to complement his humor. His limited formal education and disinclination, despite Jefferson Davis' claims to the contrary, to broaden himself in later life led General Scott to comment that "General Taylor's mind had not been enlarged and refreshed by reading, or much converse with the world . . . he was quite ignorant, for his rank, and quite bigoted in his ignorance."[20] It is not surprising that throughout most of his life Taylor described himself as a Jeffersonian and consistently passed political judgments on the basis of measurement against a Jeffersonian yardstick. Although his father had been appointed collector of the port of Louisville by George Washington, the elder Taylor supported Jefferson when the break came. Jefferson Davis insisted that even in later life Taylor "always claimed to be a Jefferson

18. Lady Emmeline Stuart-Wortley, "American Nobilities," *Harper's New Monthly Magazine*, III (1851), 387; J. F. H. Claiborne, *Life and Correspondence of John A. Quitman* (2 vols.; New York, 1860), I, 240; Winfield Scott, *Memoirs of Lieut.-General Scott, LL.D.* (2 vols.; 1864; rpr. Freeport, N.Y., 1970), II, 383. The quotations are from Hitchcock, "Memoir," in W. A. Croffut Papers, IV, LC.
19. Undated clipping from *National Tribune* in Yale: WA, S641 T219.
20. Scott, *Memoirs*, II, 382.

Democrat."[21] Certainly, he joined the army under a Jeffersonian commission with the support of strong Jeffersonian political figures. To the degree that one can detect direction from Taylor's infrequent political statements before 1848 it is clear that he never strayed far from Jefferson's ideals of a very limited government drawing its powers from a narrowly interpreted constitution.

Taylor clearly felt an initial attraction to Andrew Jackson. That was scarcely surprising since they were both southerners, landowners, and nationalists. Precisely what caused Taylor to veer abruptly away from his attraction to the Tennessean is not known but it seems clear that Taylor viewed Jacksonian politics as too populist. Taylor, despite his common touch, was never a democrat. While he enjoyed the common man in isolation, he did not view him with great favor in groups. Presumably part of the basis was simply Taylor's long service in the army with its strictly hierarchical organization. But Taylor opposition goes deeper. It is tied to his concern about the Kentucky banking laws with their strong tilt toward the creditors. Some of his earliest and strongest complaints about politicians came in his attacks on the Kentucky legislature for passing laws that inhibited collection of debts. In Taylor's mind the politicians had merely surrendered to the pressure of the mob.

One aspect of his character which most contemporaries noted was Taylor's mulish refusal to be moved once he had settled upon an idea or action. It left him extremely short of flexibility either on the battlefield or in political office. It can be seen in his near refusal to change orders once he had begun a battle and his unwillingness to engage in any serious political negotiations once he entered the White House. If that was a serious drawback for the politician, it could be an advantage to the soldier, since Taylor did not confuse his subordinates by a stream of directives. His technique of command was to lay out for his juniors a general plan of action before commencing a battle and adhering to it thereafter unless prevented by events. Sometimes, as at Palo Alto, it was impossible to fight the battle as planned; Taylor did not attempt to carry out his original plan but neither did he issue new instructions. He merely kept his force on the defensive.

As a military commander Taylor was a conservative leader. He took no unnecessary chances. At Buena Vista, for instance, he jeopardized his forces on the field by keeping a substantial body of troops out of the battle until the last moment in order to protect his supply point at Saltillo. Yet, the garrison there was more than adequate to defend the depot against light Mexican horsemen and the temporary addition of Taylor's

21. Avery O. Craven, *The Coming of the Civil War* (New York, 1942), 235.

household troops gained very little. As a result of this maneuver the troops were not available to meet the initial Mexican attack on the morning of February 23.

Equally, we can see the same limitations in Taylor's investment policies. He invested in land and bought or sold property as directly dictated by the market and the state of his finances. None of his purchases were highly speculative, although that of Cypress Grove proved to be less successful, at least in his mind, than he expected. Had Taylor wished to gamble on his investment he could have acquired a sugar plantation which offered the possibility of a much greater return on his money. This is what his son Richard did when he purchased Fashion Plantation in 1850.

Despite his refusal to countenance disunion, which made him appear willing to take rash steps, Taylor's stewardship of the presidency was as conservative as his land speculation. When he entered the White Hosue he shared the prevailing Whig view that the president led in only limited areas of national political life like foreign affairs and military policy. He believed that a president should veto unconstitutional actions by Congress but otherwise acquiesce in the judgment of the legislature on matters of domestic concern. Like most others who have shared his office, he became increasingly disenchanted by the antics followed by the national legislature in arriving at its consensus on acceptable laws. This is a part, but only a part, of his continued resistance to the arrangements which came to make up the Compromise of 1850. Why, other than his antagonism toward Clay, he so adamantly opposed the legislative package is not easy for the historian to discern. In his own mind, Taylor had become convinced that the arrangement was bad law, probably because it did not go far enough in permanently settling the issue of slavery in the territories. That his solution was at least as flawed never occurred to him.

Taylor's conservatism, which verged on pragmatism, convinced him that support did not exist for the revamping of the banking system along Whig lines or the adoption of a stronger protective tariff. In this he was undoubtedly correct, considering the party divisions in the Thirty-first Congress. Indeed, that congressional split complicates any attempt to evaluate Taylor's domestic program since he was sufficiently nonpartisan or pragmatic to avoid showering Congress with proposed legislation that he knew could not pass. One result is that Taylor's domestic program, aside from his attempts to settle the territorial issue, had yet to develop before his death. We can postulate from his 1849 state of the union message and other hints that it would have been moderate but shaped to strengthen the administration's support in the industrialized Middle Atlantic states.

The administration's natural conservatism is clearly displayed in its foreign policy. The support which it was willing to extend to the revolutionary regimes in Germany and Hungary proved in practice to be very limited. Moreover, the administration conditioned its responses by adhering scrupulously to its treaty and international law obligations. Even in its disputes with France, Portugal, and Spain, the Whig administration never allowed its irritation to carry it beyond prudence. Taylor and Clayton blustered a great deal in their correspondence with the Europeans but at no time does the level of American rhetoric reach that of Andrew Jackson's excoriating of French motives during the spoilations claims crisis.

More representative of the administration's caution is its dealings with Britain. The dispute over Central America is fascinating in its explicit renunciation of the Monroe Doctrine by the United States and in the abandonment of Manifest Destiny as a policy. Indeed, few administrations have been as willing to countenance foreign involvement in Central America as did Taylor's. Apparently both Taylor and Clayton believed that the arrangement negotiated with Bulwer so limited the British presence that the recognition of the possession of Belize and the Moskito protectorate was a small price to pay. While it is true that the British withdrawal from Central America and their abandonment of any unilateral construction of a transisthmian canal date from the 1850 arrangement, it is less clear that the Clayton-Bulwer Treaty was the cause. Other British concerns combined with the lowering of tensions, brought about by the treaty, to bring the United States and Great Britain closer in their diplomatic aims. The administration can take credit for its role in creating the atmosphere which brought about the subsequent Anglo-American rapprochement.

If Taylor was a political conservative, can anything different be said of his military career? He was one of the army's more competent small-unit commanders, his commands having continually received high marks during their annual inspections. Jefferson Davis considered him to be underestimated as a military commander by those who knew him only slightly. He was also, said his son-in-law, "deeply read" in military history.[22] But Davis is the only contemporary who seems to have been aware of Taylor's historical knowledge. More common was Ethan Allen Hitchcock's accusation that "he was without the qualifications of a great general" or in employment of "combinations" and carried everything by a kind of blind force.[23]

As a field commander his record was mixed. During the War of 1812

22. Otto A. Rothbert, "Browsing in Our Archives," *Filson Club History Quarterly*, VIII (1934), 231.
23. Hitchcock, "Memoirs," 11, in Croffut Papers, IV.

he saw action only twice. His defense of Fort Harrison was well conducted but involved merely beating off a short Indian attack. At Credit Island his troops were ambushed and outgunned. Not until the Black Hawk War did Taylor see combat again. There he was present only for the concluding stages of the Battle of Bad Axe and played no significant role. In Florida, he fought the only battle of consequence but could do little more than any of his predecessors in bringing the Seminole conflict to a close. When he received command of the Army of Occupation in Texas in 1845 Taylor could not be considered one of the significant figures in the service, although he was certainly one of its more competent leaders.

The campaign waged by the Army of Occupation in Texas and northern Mexico was militarily very successful in the sense that it won all four of the major battles in which it participated. Just what credit Taylor deserves for the victories has long been debated by historians. Palo Alto was won by the artillery contrary to his expectations. He had assumed that it would take an infantry charge with fixed bayonets to drive the Mexicans from the field. But when faced for the first time by cavalry he withdrew to the defensive. At Resaca de la Palma his men carried the day in a series of uncoordinated small unit actions after he committed them piecemeal as they arrived on the battlefield. After his successes north of the Rio Grande he failed to organize a creditable pursuit and demonstrated his inability to plan ahead. Taylor had made no preparation for a crossing of the river despite the clear evidence that if hostilities came he would have to carry the fight to the Mexican shore.

Only after extensive preparations, largely initiated by officers and bureaucrats distant from his headquarters, did Taylor's army move against Monterrey. It was a well-conducted but very conventional advance culminating in a well-planned attack which probably was not the army commander's idea. During the fighting Taylor mishandled the troops under his personal command but once again his subordinates, especially General William J. Worth, proved equal to the challenge. Taylor's acceptance of a wide-ranging armistice on the heels of his troops' advance into the center of the city was in keeping with the instructions which had reached him, although in the specific instance it was less punishing to the Mexicans than the situation warranted.

Taylor's sulking at Monterrey and Saltillo following the spiriting away, as he saw it, of his troops for Scott's Mexico City campaign was perhaps an understandable reaction of a commander who believed himself unfairly treated by his superiors, but it was not one that commends him to history. Nor is his performance at Buena Vista especially notable, although he retained his composure under very difficult conditions and allowed his troops to fight their way out of a near defeat. Secretary of War

William L. Marcy wrote one of the best evaluations of Taylor as a general when he said:

I thought well of him as a General but never for a moment regarded him as a great one. His knowledge of military affairs beyond the details in which his life had been spent was very limited. Of the art of war, of strategy, of skillful arrangements, of a capacity to adapt his operations to meet emergencies as they arise and when they arise—all of the higher properties of a skillful commander in the field—I now and at all times regarded him as uncommonly deficient. But he was attentive to the duties of his command and brought a common sense judgement to bear on all subjects to the extent of his information. He was brave to a degree which commands admiration and remarkably firm in his purposes. His bravery and steadfastness of purpose are the summary of his high qualities as a commanding officer.[24]

One of the reasons that caused Taylor's contemporaries to question his mental agility was an unfortunate speech pattern which caused him to hesitate when speaking and amounted almost to a stammer. One contemporary described his delivery as a "terse, sententious style . . . never diffuse or demonstrative, and [he] wasted no words upon any body."[25] All of this appears to have been intensified when he was angry, when he is often described as sputtering with rage.

Zachary Taylor was a product of his background and of his age, a man who is hard for modern students to understand and even more difficult to explain. He was not a careful, logical thinker nor an emotional man whose actions could be foreseen by those who knew him. He was a man of limited emotional and intellectual capacity who appears to have developed a nearly impenetrable mask. Whether that was a result of his intellectual limitations, his military service, or his attachment to the soil was never discernible. He was and remains an enigma.

24. T. M. Marshall, "Diary and Memoranda of William L. Marcy, 1849–1851," *AHR*, XXIV (1919), 455.

25. [T. N. Parmalee], "Recollections of an Old Stager," *Harper's New Monthly Magazine*, XLVII (1873), 588.

ESSAY ON SOURCES

THIS STUDY is based primarily upon the surviving correspondence of Zachary Taylor. Since most of his personal papers were lost in the sacking of Fashion Plantation in 1862, the account relies heavily upon the official correspondence preserved in the National Archives and such private letters as survive in the collections of his correspondents. Although many repositories contain groups of Taylor papers, these in nearly every instance are letters to a single contemporary or duplicate copies of official correspondence. Most valuable are the Zachary Taylor Papers in the Library of Congress, which include most of the material retained by the family. They have been reproduced on microfilm with an index as part of the library's Presidential Papers series. The second most important group of Taylor papers are in the William K. Bixby Collection at the Huntington Library in San Marino, California, which contains the valuable letters written during the Mexican War to Dr. Robert C. Wood. They were edited by William H. Samson as *Letters of Zachary Taylor from the Battle-Fields of the Mexican War* (Rochester, 1908). Aside from copies of reports made during the Florida and Mexican Wars, Samson's volume is the only substantial collection of published Taylor correspondence.

Among the smaller holdings of Taylor materials are the Andre DeCoppet Collection at the Princeton University Library, the Minnesota Historical Society, the William K. Bixby Collection of the Missouri Historical Society, the Miscellaneous Collection of the Huntington Library, the Kentucky Historical Society, the University of Kentucky Library, the Louisiana State University Library, the Miscellaneous Papers of the New York Historical Society, and the Western Americana Collection at Yale University.

The collections of correspondence of Taylor's contemporaries which proved most useful for this study have been the Millard Fillmore Papers at the Buffalo and Erie County Historical Society; the Alice Elizabeth Trabue Collection, Orlando Brown, Presidential, and Miscellaneous Papers at the Filson Club in Louisville, Kentucky; the Orlando Brown, A. C. Bullitt, A. T. Burley, and Robert P. Letcher Papers at the Kentucky Historical Society; the John Jordan Crittenden Papers at the University of Kentucky Library; the John Ellis Wool Papers at the New York

State Library; the Dreer and Gratz Collections and the Meredith Family Papers at the Historical Society of Pennsylvania; the William H. Seward and Weed Papers at the University of Rochester; the Justin H. Smith Papers in the Latin American Collection at the University of Texas, Austin; and the James Watson Webb Papers at the Yale University Library. Among the massive holdings of the Library of Congress the most valuable have been the Henry Clay, John M. Clayton, John J. Crittenden, W. A. Croffut, Jefferson Davis, Thomas Sidney Jesup, William L. Marcy, and William C. Rives Papers.

The most fruitful official sources are the Letters Sent and Letters Received series of the Office of the Adjutant General preserved in Record Group (RG) 94 of the National Archives. They include most of the orders sent to Taylor as a general and reports from him throughout his career. Other files in RG 94 included the Returns of Posts and Regiments as well as the records of the Army of Occupation. Copies of orders to Taylor during his early career are frequently preserved in RG 393, Records of Army Continental Commands. Less valuable is the correspondence held in RG 107, Office of the Secretary of War, in RG 108, Headquarters of the Army, or in RG 75, Office of Indian Affairs. Very little correspondence between Taylor and his cabinet officers survives from the presidential years. Except for his wartime reports, almost none of his official correspondence is reprinted in the *American State Papers: Military Affairs* (7 vols.; Washington, 1832–61) or *Indian Affairs* (2 vols.; 1834), among the Congressional documents, or in B. Franklin Cooling (ed.), *The New American State Papers: Military Affairs* (19 vols.; Wilmington, Del., 1980).

The definitive study of Taylor is Holman Hamilton's majestic two-volume *Zachary Taylor* (Indianapolis, 1941, 1951). Published a decade apart, the two volumes are dissimilar in approach. The initial volume, subtitled *Soldier of the Republic*, presents a frontier army officer as understood by a young, uncritical newspaperman lacking extensive acquaintance with the military of the middle period. The second volume, subtitled *Soldier in the White House*, is a political study written by a mature academic historian who specialized in the period involved. Hamilton's view of Taylor is complex, as befits both his subject and the detail of his account, but tends to consider him primarily a nationalist and a natural politician. Unfortunately, Hamilton's documentation often leads those who follow in his footsteps through difficult terrain in search of his sources. Hamilton offered a later, but still favorable, evaluation in *The Three Kentucky Presidents: Lincoln, Taylor, Davis* (Lexington, 1978).

The three modern single-volume biographies of Taylor are markedly different in quality and thrust. Brainerd Dyer, *Zachary Taylor* (Baton Rouge, 1946), is a thoroughly researched, carefully argued study which devotes about half of its attention to the Mexican War. Silas Bent McKinley and Silas Bent, *Old Rough and Ready* (New York, 1946), is a life-and-times account of the frontier soldier and his presidency by a pair of professional writers. Edwin P. Hoyt, *Zachary Taylor* (Chicago, 1966), is a hastily written popular history which concentrates on the Mexican War. The only other serious biography is Oliver Otis Howard, *General Taylor* (New York, 1892), an uncritical, laudatory study by a Civil War general turned writer which concentrates on the pre–White House years.

The Mexican War, the 1848 campaign, and Taylor's unfortunate death produced a large number of biographical sketches, most of them short and worthless. The best are An Officer of the United States Army, *Life and Public Services of Gen. Z. Taylor* (New York, 1850); John Frost, *Life of Major General Zachary Taylor* (New York, 1847); J. Reese Fry, *A Life of Gen. Zachary Taylor* (Philadelphia, 1848); *General Taylor and His Staff* (Philadelphia, 1848); Henry Montgomery, *The Life of Major General Taylor* (Auburn, N.Y., 1851); *Pictorial Life of General Taylor* (Philadelphia, 1847); *Taylor and His Campaigns* (Philadelphia, 1848); *Taylor and His Generals* (Philadelphia, 1848); and *Obituary Addresses Delivered on the Occasion of the Death of Zachary Taylor* (Washington, 1850). Most drew upon Taylor's reports and stressed battlefield activities. References to Taylor appear frequently in Jefferson Davis' correspondence during 1846 to 1850 and in his biographies: Haskell M. Monroe, James T. McIntosh, and Lynda L. Crist (eds.), *The Papers of Jefferson Davis* (4 vols.; Baton Rouge, 1971–83, 13 vols. projected); Dunbar Rowland (ed.), *Jefferson Davis, Constitutionalist* (10 vols.; Jackson, Miss., 1923); Robert McElroy, *Jefferson Davis, the Unreal and the Real* (2 vols.; New York, 1937); Hudson Strode, *Jefferson Davis, American Patriot* (New York, 1955); and Clement Eaton, *Jefferson Davis* (New York, 1977).

Richard Taylor's career and property can be traced in John W. Gwathmey, *Historical Register of Virginians in the Revolution* (Baltimore, 1979); Francis B. Heitman, *Historical Register of Officers of the Continental Army During the War of the Revolution* (1914; rpr. Baltimore, 1967); Willard Rouse Jillson, *The Kentucky Land Grants* (Louisville, 1925); Katherine G. Healy, "Calendar of Early Jefferson County, Kentucky Wills," *Filson Club History Quarterly*, VI (1932), 1–37, 149–204, 294–340, and in the Jefferson County Tax Rolls preserved in the Kentucky Historical Society.

The best general histories of the army in which Taylor served are William Addleman Ganoe, *The History of the United States Army* (1942; rpr. Ashton, Md., 1964), and Russell F. Weigley, *History of the United States Army* (New York, 1967). Valuable special studies covering the entire period of Taylor's service include Francis B. Heitman, *Historical Register and Dictionary of the United States Army* (2 vols., 1903; rpr. Urbana, Ill, 1965); Thomas M. Exley, *A Compendium of the Pay of the Army from 1785 to 1888* (Washington, 1888); Raphael P. Thian, *Notes Illustrating the Military Geography of the United States, 1813–1880* (1881; rpr. Austin, 1979); Francis Paul Prucha, *A Guide to the Military Forts of the United States, 1789–1895*) (Madison, 1964); James A. Huston, *The Sinews of War* (Washington, 1966); and Erna Risch, *Quartermaster Support of the Army* (Washington, 1962).

Short biographies of most of the senior contemporaries of Taylor can be found in the *Dictionary of American Biography* (20 vols.; New York, 1928–36). Longer memoirs or biographies of officers with whom Taylor had extensive service include Roger L. Nichols, *General Henry Atkinson* (Norman, 1965); Rembert W. Patrick, *Aristocrat in Uniform: General Duncan L. Clinch* (Gainesville, 1963); James W. Silver, *Edmund Pendleton Gaines* (Baton Rouge, 1949); Chester L. Kieffer, *Maligned General: The Biography of Thomas Sidney Jesup* (San Rafael,

1979); Ethan Allen Hitchcock, *Fifty Years in Camp and Field*, ed. W. A. Croffut (New York, 1909); Winfield Scott, *Memoirs of Lieut.-General Scott, LL.D.* (2 vols., 1864; rpr., Freeport, N.Y., 1970); Charles Winslow Elliott, *Winfield Scott* (New York, 1837); James Ripley Jacobs, *Tarnished Warrior: Major General James Wilkinson* (New York, 1938); and Edward S. Wallace, *General William Jenkins Worth* (Dallas, 1953).

The activities of the army before the War of 1812 are detailed in James Ripley Jacobs, *The Beginnings of the U.S. Army* (Princeton, 1947); Reginald Horsman, *The Frontier in the Formative Years* (Albuquerque, 1975); and Mary C. Gillett, *The Army Medical Department, 1775–1818* (Washington, 1981). Western operations during the War of 1812 are described in H. M. Brackenridge, *History of the Late War Between the United States and Great Britain* (Philadelphia, 1844); John Brannan, *Official Letters of the Military and Naval Officers of the United States During the War with Great Britain in the Years 1812, 13, 14, & 15* (Washington, 1823); R. Carlyle Buley, *The Old Northwest* (2 vols.; Bloomington, 1962); Harry L. Coles, *The War of 1812* (Chicago, 1965); Logan Esarey (ed.), *Messages and Letters of William Henry Harrison* (2 vols.; Indianapolis, 1922); Alec R. Gilpin, *The War of 1812 in the Old Northwest* (Lansing, 1958); James Wallace Hammack, Jr., *Kentucky and the Second American Revolution* (Lexington, 1976); J. Mackay Hitsman, *The Increditable War of 1812* (New York, 1969), and "Wisconsin in the War of 1812," *Wisconsin Magazine of History*, XLVI (Autumn 1962), 3–15; Richard C. Knopf (ed.), *William Henry Harrison and the War of 1812* (Columbus, Ohio, 1951); Benson J. Lossing, *The Pictorial Field-Book of the War of 1812* (1869; rpr. Somersworth, N.H., 1976); Robert B. McAfee, *History of the Late War in the Western Country* (Lexington, 1816); John K. Mahon, *The War of 1812* (Gainesville, 1972); William Wood (ed.), *Select British Documents of the Canadian War of 1812* (4 vols.; Toronto 1920–26).

More specifically relating to Taylor's activities during 1812 to 1815 are A. C. Duddleston, "Fort Harrison in History," *Magazine of American History*, XXVIII (1892), 20–29; Robert Hamilton, "The Expeditions of Major-General Samuel Hopkins up the Wabash, 1812," *Indiana Magazine of History*, XLIII (1947), 393–403; William A. Meese, "Credit Island, 1814–1914," *Journal of the Illinois Historical Society*, VII (1914–15), 349–73; and Milo M. Quaife, "A Forgotten Hero of Rock Island," *ibid.*, XXIII (1930–31), 652–63. William E. Foley, *A History of Missouri* (3 vols.; Columbia, Mo., 1971), and Kate L. Gregg, "The War of 1812 on the Missouri Frontier," *Missouri Historical Review*, XXXIII (1938–39), 3–22, 184–202, 326–48, recount the little known operations beyond the Mississippi.

Post-1815 frontier military activities are described in Henry Putney Beers, *The Western Military Frontier, 1815–1846* (Philadelphia, 1935); Robert W. Frazer, *Forts of the West* (Norman, 1965); Francis Paul Prucha, *Sword of the Republic* (New York, 1969); and Edgar Bruce Wesley, *Guarding the Frontier* (1935; rpr. Westport, Conn., 1970). The Indian policy which governed that activity is discussed in Francis Paul Prucha, *American Indian Policy in the Formative Years* (Cambridge, 1962); Michael Paul Rogin, *Fathers and Children* (New York, 1975); and Grant Foreman, *Advancing the Frontier* (Norman, 1933). Taylor's posts are sketched in Louise Phelps Kellogg, "Old Fort Howard," *Wisconsin Magazine of History*, XVIII (1934–35), 125–40; Holman Hamilton, "Zachary Taylor and Minnesota," *Minnesota History*, XXX (1949), 97–110; Marcus L. Hansen, *Old Fort Snelling, 1818–1858* (Minneapolis, 1958); Evan Jones, *The Citadel in the Wilderness* (New York, 1966); "Zachary Taylor and Old Fort Snelling," *Minnesota History*, XXVIII (March 1947), 15–19; Edwin C. Bearss and Arrell M. Gibson, *Fort Smith* (Norman, 1979); and the extremely useful Bruce E. Mahan, *Old Fort Crawford and the Frontier* (Iowa City, 1926). John K. Mahon, "A Board of Officers Considers the Condition of the Militia in 1825," *Military Affairs*, XV (1951), 85–94, studies one of Taylor's infrequent Washington assignments. William B. Skelton discusses "Professionalization in the U.S. Army Officer Corps During the Age of Jackson," in *Armed Forces and Society*, I (1974–75), 443–71.

Taylor's part in the Black Hawk War can be traced in Robert Anderson, "Reminiscences of the Black Hawk War," *Collections of the State Historical Society of Wisconsin*, X (1888), 167–73; Reuben Gold Thwaites, "The Story of the Black Hawk War," *ibid.*, XII (1892), 217–65; Perry A. Armstrong, *The Sauks and the Black Hawk War* (Springfield, Ill., 1887); William T. Hagan, "General Henry Atkinson and the Militia," *Military Affairs*, XXIII (1959–60), 194–97, and *The Sac and Fox Indians* (Norman, 1958); Donald Jackson (ed.), *Ma-Ka-Tai-Me-She-Kiakiak—Black Hawk* (Urbana, 1955); Roger L. Nichols (ed.), "The Black Hawk War, Another View," *Annals of Iowa*, XXXVI (1961–63), 525–33; Milo M. Quaife (ed.), "Journals and Reports of the Black Hawk War," *Mississippi Valley Historical Review*, XII (1925), 393–409; and Frank E. Stevens, *The Black Hawk War Including a Review of Black Hawk's Life* (Chicago, 1903). His part in the Seminole War is explored in Edward C. McReynolds, *The Seminoles* (Norman, 1957); John K. Mahon, *History of the Second Seminole War* (Gainesville, 1967); Virginia Bergman Peters, *The Florida Wars* (Hamden, 1979); John T. Sprague, *The Origins, Progress, and Conclusion of the Florida War* (New York, 1848); and George Walton, *Fearless and Free* (Indianapolis, 1975).

The annexation of Texas and the operations of the Army of Occupation are discussed in Justin H. Smith, *The Annexation of Texas* (New York, 1911); Robert Seager II, *And Tyler Too* (New York, 1963); Nathan S. Jarvis, "An Army Surgeon's Notes of Frontier Service," *Journal of the Military Service Institution of the United States*, XXXIX (1906), 131–35, 275–85, 452–60, XL (1907), 269–77, 435–52, XLI (1908), 90–105; and Darwin Payne, "Camp Life in the Army of Occupation, Corpus Christi, July 1845," *Southwestern Historical Quarterly*, LXXIII (1969–70), 326–42; Gene M. Brack, *Mexico Views Manifest Destiny, 1821–1846* (Albuquerque, 1975), is the best study of the Mexican reaction.

The best recent bibliography of Mexican War writings is Norman E. Tutorow, *The Mexican-American War* (Westport, Conn., 1981), which has valuable annotation. The political direction of the war and Taylor's reaction to it is illuminated in Norman A. Graebner, "The Mexican War: A Study in Causation," *Pacific Historical Review*, XLIX (1980), 405–26; Eugene Irving McCormac, *James K. Polk* (1922; rpr. New York, 1965); James K. Polk, *Diary of James K. Polk During His Presidency, 1845 to 1849*, ed. Milo Milton Quaife (4 vols.; Chicago, 1910);

Charles Sellers, *James K. Polk, Continentalist* (Princeton, 1966); and Justin H. Smith, *The War with Mexico* (2 vols.; New York, 1919). Herbert Weaver, *et al.* (eds.), *Correspondence of James K. Polk* (4 vols.; Nashville, 1969–) has not yet reached the war period.

The military operations in northern Mexico are described in great detail in Smith's *War with Mexico*. Other general accounts include K. Jack Bauer, *The Mexican War, 1846–1848* (New York, 1974); Alfred Hoyt Bill, *Rehearsal for Conflict* (New York, 1947); Seymour V. Connor and Odie B. Faulk, *North America Divided* (New York, 1971); and Robert Selph Henry, *The Story of the Mexican War* (Indianapolis, 1950). David Lavender, *Climax at Buena Vista* (Philadelphia, 1966), and Edward J. Nichols, *Zach Taylor's Little Army* (Garden City, 1963), concentrate on the Army of Occupation. Among the most useful of the older books are Francis Baylies, *A Narrative of Major General Wool's Campaign in Mexico* (Albany, N.Y., 1851); Nathan Covington Brooks, *A Complete History of the Mexican War* (1849; rpr. Chicago, 1965); Henry B. Dawson, *Battles of the United States by Sea and Land* (2 vols.; New York, 1858); William S. Henry, *Campaign Sketches of the War with Mexico* (New York, 1847); John S. Jenkins, *History of the War Between the United States and Mexico* (Auburn, N.Y., 1851); Roswell Sabine Ripley, *War with Mexico* (2 vols.; New York, 1849); and Cadmus Marcellus Wilcox, *History of the Mexican War* (Washington, 1892). Taylor's more important reports are reprinted in *Senate Documents*, 29th Cong., 1st Sess., No. 388; 29th Cong., 2nd Sess., No. 1; 30th Cong., 1st Sess., Nos. 1, 14, 18, and 62; *House Executive Documents*, 30th Cong., 1st Sess., Nos. 17, 56, and 60.

The Mexican side is narrated in Ramon Alcaraz (ed.), *The Other Side*, trans. Albert C. Ramsey (New York, 1850); Manuel Balbontín, *La invasión americana, 1846 a 1848* (Mexico, 1883); José Bravo Ugarte, *Historia de México* (3 vols.; Mexico, 1959); Emilio del Castillo Negrete, *Invasión de los norteamericanos en México* (Mexico, 1890); Oficial de Infantría, *Compaña contra los americanos del norte* (Mexico, 1848); José María Roa Bárcena, *Recuerdos de la invasión norteamericana, 1846–1848* (3 vols.; Mexico, 1947); Alfonso Trueba, *Legítima gloria* (Mexico, 1959); and José C. Valades, *Breve historia de la guerra con los Estados Unidos* (Mexico, 1947).

Taylor's private letters to his son-in-law Surgeon Robert C. Wood are reprinted in William H. Samson (ed.), *Letters of Zachary Taylor from the Battlefields of the Mexican War* (Rochester, 1908). Among the numerous memoirs and letters of men who served under Taylor in Mexico the following were especially helpful for this study: Philip N. Barbour, *Journals of the Late Brevet Major Philip Norbourne Barbour*, ed. Rhoda Van Bibber Tanner (New York, 1936); James Henry Carleton, *The Battle of Buena Vista* (New York, 1848); Samuel E. Chamberlain, *My Confession* (New York, 1956); J. F. H. Claiborne, *Life and Correspondence of John A. Quitman* (2 vols.; New York, 1860); Luther Giddings, *Sketches of the Campaign in Northern Mexico* (New York, 1853); John R. Kenly, *Memoirs of a Maryland Volunteer* (Philadelphia, 1847); Benjamin F. Scribner, *Camp Life of a Volunteer* (Philadelphia, 1847); E. Kirby Smith, *To Mexico with Scott*, ed. Emma Jerome Blackwood (Cambridge, 1917); S. Compton Smith, *Chile con Carne*

(New York, 1857); and Isaac Ingalls Stevens, *Campaigns of the Rio Grande and of Mexico* (New York, 1851). Grady McWhiney and Sue McWhiney (eds.), *To Mexico with Taylor and Scott* (Waltham, 1969), and George Winston Smith and Charles Judah (eds.), *Chronicles of the Gringos* (Albuquerque, 1968) reprint short accounts.

R. C. Buley, "Indiana in the Mexican War," *Indiana Magazine of History*, XV (1919), 260–326, XVI (1920), 46–68; Owen Perry, *Indiana in the Mexican War* (Indianapolis, 1908); and Herman J. Viola, "Zachary Taylor and the Indiana Volunteers," *Southwestern Historical Quarterly*, LXXII (1968–69), 335–46, discuss Taylor's report of the breaking of the 2nd Indiana at the Battle of Buena Vista. Other controversial aspects of that battle are covered in K. Jack Bauer (ed.), "General John E. Wool's Memoranda of the Battle of Buena Vista," *ibid.*, LXXVII (1972–73), 111–23; and Ellen Hardin Walworth, "The Battle of Buena Vista," *Magazine of American History*, III (1879), 705–38.

The political and cultural conditions in the United States which made Taylor a viable presidential candidate are discussed from various points of view in William J. Cooper, Jr., *The South and the Politics of Slavery* (Baton Rouge, 1978); Avery O. Craven, *Civil War in the Making* (Baton Rouge, 1968), and *Growth of Southern Nationalism* (Baton Rouge, 1953); Clement Eaton, *The Growth of Southern Civilization, 1790–1860* (New York, 1961), and *The Mind of the Old South* (Baton Rouge, 1967); Stephen E. Maizlish and John J. Kushma (eds.), *Essays on American Politics, 1840–1860* (College Station, Tex., 1983); Allan Nevins, *Ordeal of the Union: Fruits of Manifest Destiny* (New York, 1947); David M. Potter, *The Impending Crisis* (New York, 1976); and Glendon G. Van Deusen, *The Jacksonian Era* (New York, 1959).

The development of Taylor's presidential candidacy and the election of 1848 are discussed in William H. Adams, *The Whig Party of Louisiana* (Lafayette, La., 1973); Frederick J. Blue, *The Free Soilers* (Urbana, 1973); Kinley J. Brauer, *Cotton Versus Conscience* (Lexington, 1967); Randolph Campbell, "The Whig Party of Texas in the Elections of 1848 and 1852," *Southwestern Historical Quarterly*, LXXIII (1969–70), 17–34; Arthur C. Cole, *The Whig Party in the South* (Washington, 1913; Betty Carolyn Congleton, "Contenders for the Whig Nomination in 1848 and the Editorial Policy of George D. Prentice," *The Register of the Kentucky Historical Society*, LXVII (1969), 119–33; Norman A. Graebner, "Thomas Corwin and the Election of 1848," *Journal of Southern History*, XVII (1955), 162–79; Edgar Allan Holt, "Party Politics in Ohio, 1840–1850," *Ohio Archaeological and Historical Publications*, XXXVIII (1929), 360–402; Ernest McPherson Lander, *Reluctant Imperialists: Calhoun, the South Carolinians, and the Mexican War* (Baton Rouge, 1980); Malcolm C. McMillan (ed.), "Joseph Glover Baldwin Reports on the Whig Convention of 1848," *Journal of Southern History*, XXV (1959), 366–82, and "Taylor's Presidential Campaign in Alabama," *Alabama Review*, XIII (1960), 83–108; Chaplain W. Morrison, *Democratic Politics and Sectionalism* (Chapel Hill, 1967); Henry H. Mueller, *The Whig Party in Pennsylvania* (New York, 1922); George Rawlings Poage, *Henry Clay and the Whig Party* (Gloucester, 1965); Edwin H. Price, "Election of 1848 in Ohio," *Ohio Archaeological and Historical Publications*, XXXVI (1927), 188–

301; Joseph G. Rayback, *Free Soil* (Lexington, 1970), "The Presidential Ambitions of John C. Calhoun, 1844–1848," *Journal of Southern History*, XIV (1948), 331–56, and "Who Wrote the Allison Letters," *Mississippi Valley Historical Review*, XXXVI (1949–50), 51–72; and Brian G. Walton, "The Elections for the Thirtieth Congress and the Presidential Candidacy of Zachary Taylor," *Journal of Southern History*, XXXV (1969), 186–202.

   Memoirs and biographies of political figures which were valuable for this book include: Myrta Lockett Avary (ed.), *Recollections of Alexander H. Stephens* (New York, 1910); Frederick Bancroft, *The Life of William H. Seward* (2 vols.; New York, 1900); Thurlow Weed Barnes, *Memoir of Thurlow Weed* (Boston, 1884); Irving H. Bartlett, *Daniel Webster* (New York, 1978); Thomas Hart Benton, *Thirty Years View* (2 vols.; New York, 1854–56); Mrs. Chapman Coleman (ed.), *The Life of John J. Crittenden* (2 vols.; Philadelphia, 1871); Calvin Colton (ed.), *The Private Correspondence of Henry Clay* (New York, 1856); Joseph P. Comegys, *Memoirs of John M. Clayton* (Wilmington, 1882); James L. Crouthamel, *James Watson Webb* (Middletown, Conn. 1969); Richard N. Current, *Daniel Webster and the Rise of National Conservatism* (Boston, 1955); Robert F. Dalzell, Jr., *Daniel Webster and the Trial of American Nationalism* (Boston, 1973); Claude Moore Fuess, *Daniel Webster* (2 vols.; Boston, 1930); Horace Greeley, *Recollections of a Busy Life* (New York, 1868); Hamilton Andrews Hill, *Memoir of Abbot Lawrence* (Boston, 1884); H. Draper Hunt, *Hannibal Hamlin of Maine* (Syracuse, 1969); J. Franklin Jameson (ed.), "Correspondence of John C. Calhoun," *Annual Report of the American Historical Association, 1899* (Washington, 1900), Vol. II; Robert W. Johannsen, *Stephen A. Douglas* (New York, 1973); Albert D. Kirwan, *John J. Crittenden* (Lexington, 1962); Thornton Kirkland Lathrop, *William Henry Seward* (Boston, 1896); Andrew C. McLaughlin, *Lewis Cass* (New York, 1980); Robert L. Meriwether et al., (eds). *The Papers of John C. Calhoun* (14 vols.; Columbia, 1959–   ); Joseph Howard Parks, *John Bell of Tennessee* (Baton Rouge, 1950); Ulrich B. Phillips (ed.), "The Correspondence of Robert Toombs, Alexander H. Stephens, and Howell Cobb," *Annual Report of the American Historical Association, 1911* (Washington, 1913), and *The Life of Robert Toombs* (New York, 1913); Robert J. Rayback, *Millard Fillmore* (Buffalo, 1959); Carl Schurz, *Henry Clay* (2 vols.; New York, 1968); Frank H. Severance (ed.), *Millard Fillmore Papers* (2 vols.; Buffalo, 1907); Frederick W. Seward, *Seward at Washington as Senator and Secretary of State* (New York, 1891); Henry Thomas Shanks (ed.), *The Papers of Willie Person Mangum* (5 vols.; Raleigh, 1950–56); Elbert B. Smith, *Magnificent Missourian: The Life of Thomas Hart Benton* (Philadelphia, 1957); W. G. L. Smith, *The Life and Times of Lewis Cass* (New York, 1856); Edward M. Steel, Jr., *T. Butler King of Georgia* (Athens, Ga., 1964); William Y. Thompson, *Robert Toombs of Georgia* (Baton Rouge, 1966); Glendon G. Van Deusen, *Horace Greeley* (Philadelphia, 1953), *The Life of Henry Clay* (Boston, 1937), *William Henry Seward* (New York, 1967), and *Thurlow Weed* (Boston, 1947); Fletcher Webster (ed.), *The Private Correspondence of Daniel Webster* (2 vols.; Boston, 1857); Harriet A. Weed (ed.), *Autobiography of Thurlow Weed* (Boston, 1884); Charles M. Wiltse, *John C. Calhoun*

Sectionalist (Indianapolis, 1951); and Frank B. Woodford, *Lewis Cass* (New Brunswick, 1950).

Taylor's official presidential papers are reprinted in James D. Richardson (ed.), *A Compilation of the Messages and Papers of the Presidents* (20 vols.; New York, 1897–1922). His messages to Congress, with their accompanying documents, are included in the House and Senate Executive Documents of the 31st Cong., 1st Sess. The debates in Congress are summarized in the *Congressional Globe*. The Taylor administration is outlined in William O. Lynch, "Zachary Taylor as President," *Journal of Southern History*, IV (1938), 279–94, and its great scandal in William P. Brandon, "The Galphin Claim," *Georgia Historical Quarterly*, XV (1931), 113–41. Charles W. Ramsdell discusses "The Natural Limits of Slavery Expansion" in *Mississippi Valley Historical Review*, XVI (1929), 151–71. The administration's activities in California are described in Theodore Grivas, *Military Governments in California* (Glendale, 1963), and Neal Harlow, *California Conquered* (Berkeley, 1982). Those in New Mexico are covered in William Campbell Binkley, *The Expansionist Movement in Texas* (Berkeley, 1925), and "The Question of Texas Jurisdiction in New Mexico Under the United States, 1848–1850," *Southwestern Historical Quarterly*, XXVII (1920–21), 1–38; Loomis Morton Ganaway, *New Mexico and the Sectional Controversy, 1846–1861* (Philadelphia, 1976); William A. Keleher, *Turmoil in New Mexico, 1846–1868* (Santa Fe, 1952); Kenneth F. Neighbors, "The Taylor-Neighbors Struggle Over the Upper Rio Grande Region of Texas in 1850," *Southwestern Historical Quarterly*, LXI (1957–58), 431–63. The sectional crisis of 1850 is described in: Henry J. Carman and Reinhard Luthin, "The Seward-Fillmore Feud and the Crisis of 1850," *New York History*, XXIV (1943), 163–84; Herbert Darling Foster, "Webster's Seventh of March Speech and the Secession Movement, 1850," *American Historical Review*, XXVII (1922), 245–70; Philip May Hamer, *The Secession Movement in South Carolina, 1847–1852* (Allentown, Pa., 1918); Holman Hamilton, "Democratic Senate Leadership and the Compromise of 1850," *Mississippi Valley Historical Review*, XLI (1954), 403–18, and *Prologue to Conflict* (Lexington, 1964); George D. Harmon, "Douglas and the Compromise of 1850," *Journal of the Illinois State Historical Society*, XXI (1928–29), 453–99; F. H. Hodder, "The Authorship of the Compromise of 1850," *Mississippi Historical Review*, XXII (1936), 525–36; John T. Hubbell, "Three Georgia Unionists and the Crisis of 1850," *Georgia Historical Quarterly*, LI (1967), 307–23; Thelma Jennings, *The Nashville Convention* (Memphis, 1980); George Fort Milton, *The Eve of Conflict* (Boston, 1934); Joseph H. Parks, "John Bell and the Compromise of 1850," *Journal of Southern History*, IX (1943), 328–56; Robert R. Russel, "What Was the Compromise of 1850?" *Journal of Southern History*, XXII (1956), 292–309; St. George L. Sioussat, "Tennessee, the Compromise of 1850, and the Nashville Convention," *Mississippi Valley Historical Review*, II (1915), 313–47.

General accounts of the diplomatic activities of the Taylor administration appear in Mary Wilhelmine Williams, "John M. Clayton," Samuel Flagg Bemis and Robert H. Ferrell (eds.), *American Secretaries of State and Their Diplomacy*

(18 vols.; New York, 1927–72), VI, and Paul A. Varg, *United States Foreign Relations, 1820–1860* (Lansing, 1979). Detailed discussions of the Clayton-Bulwer negotiation occur in H. C. Allen, *Great Britain and the United States* (New York, 1955); Richard W. Van Alstyne, "British Diplomacy and the Clayton-Bulwer Treaty, 1850–60," *Journal of Modern History*, XI (1939), 149–83; and Mary Wilhelmine Williams, *Anglo-American Isthmian Diplomacy, 1815–1915* (Washington, 1916). The related diplomatic messages are reprinted in William R. Manning (ed.), *Diplomatic Correspondence of the United States, Inter-American Affairs, 1831–1860* (12 vols.; Washington, 1932–39). The López filibustering expeditions are discussed in Charles H. Brown, *Agents of Manifest Destiny* (Chapel Hill, 1980); Robert Granville Caldwell, *The López Expeditions to Cuba* (Princeton, 1915); and Louis N. Feipel, "The Navy and Filibustering in the Fifties," *United States Naval Institute Proceedings*, XLIV (1918), 767–80, 1009–29, 1219–30, 1527–45, 1830–48.

INDEX